MODERNIST WAR POETRY

Edinburgh Critical Studies in Modernist Culture
Series Editors: Tim Armstrong and Rebecca Beasley

Available

Modernism and Magic: Experiments with Spiritualism, Theosophy and the Occult
Leigh Wilson

Sonic Modernity: Representing Sound in Literature, Culture and the Arts
Sam Halliday

Modernism and the Frankfurt School
Tyrus Miller

Lesbian Modernism: Censorship, Sexuality and Genre Fiction
Elizabeth English

Modern Print Artefacts: Textual Materiality and Literary Value in British Print Culture, 1890–1930s
Patrick Collier

Cheap Modernism: Expanding Markets, Publishers' Series and the Avant-Garde
Lise Jaillant

Portable Modernisms: The Art of Travelling Light
Emily Ridge

Hieroglyphic Modernisms: Writing and New Media in the Twentieth Century
Jesse Schotter

Modernism, Fiction and Mathematics
Nina Engelhardt

Modernist Life Histories: Biological Theory and the Experimental Bildungsroman
Daniel Aureliano Newman

Modernism, Space and the City: Outsiders and Affect in Paris, Vienna, Berlin, and London
Andrew Thacker

Modernism Edited: Marianne Moore and the Dial Magazine
Victoria Bazin

Modernism and Time Machines
Charles Tung

Primordial Modernism: Animals, Ideas, transition (1927–1938)
Cathryn Setz

Modernism and Still Life: Artists, Writers, Dancers
Claudia Tobin

The Modernist Exoskeleton: Insects, War, Literary Form
Rachel Murray

Novel Sensations: Modernist Fiction and the Problem of Qualia
Jon Day

Hotel Modernity: Corporate Space in Literature and Film
Robbie Moore

The Modernist Anthropocene: Nonhuman Life and Planetary Change in James Joyce, Virginia Woolf and Djuna Barnes
Peter Adkins

Asbestos – The Last Modernist Object
Arthur Rose

Visionary Company: Hart Crane and Modernist Periodicals
Francesca Bratton

Modernist War Poetry: Combat Gnosticism and the Sympathetic Imagination, 1914–19
Jamie Wood

Forthcoming

Modernism and the Idea of Everyday Life
Leena Kore-Schröder

Modernism and Religion: Poetry and the Rise of Mysticism
Jamie Callison

Abstraction in Modernism and Modernity: Human and Inhuman
Jeff Wallace

Sexological Modernism: Queer Feminism and Sexual Science
Jana Funke

Modernism, Material Culture and the First World War
Cedric Van Dijck

www.edinburghuniversitypress.com/series/ecsmc

MODERNIST WAR POETRY

Combat Gnosticism and the Sympathetic Imagination, 1914–19

Jamie Wood

EDINBURGH
University Press

Edinburgh University Press is one of the leading university presses in the UK. We publish academic books and journals in our selected subject areas across the humanities and social sciences, combining cutting-edge scholarship with high editorial and production values to produce academic works of lasting importance. For more information visit our website: edinburghuniversitypress.com

Edinburgh University Press Ltd
The Tun – Holyrood Road
12(2f) Jackson's Entry
Edinburgh EH8 8PJ

Typeset in 10/12.5 Adobe Sabon by
IDSUK (DataConnection) Ltd, and
printed and bound in Great Britain

A CIP record for this book is available from the British Library

ISBN 978 1 4744 9774 9 (hardback)
ISBN 978 1 4744 9776 3 (webready PDF)
ISBN 978 1 4744 9777 0 (epub)

CONTENTS

Timelines   vi
Acknowledgements   vii
Series Editors' Preface   x

Introduction   1
1   Early Modernist Responses to Combatant Poetry:
   1914–Spring 1915   24
2   Reassessing Disaster: 1915   53
3   The Three Lives of Gnosticism: 1916–Summer 1917   90
4   An Emergent Critique of War Experience: Autumn 1917–Spring
   1919   135
5   The Form and Practice of Modernist Distaste: Summer–Autumn
   1919   174
Conclusion   214

Bibliography   221
Index   255

TIMELINES

1.1	September 1914–February 1915	31
2.1	Spring 1915	57
2.2	June–December 1915	77
3.1	1916	93
3.2	January–August 1917	124
4.1	September 1917–May 1918	145
4.2	June 1918–April 1919	161
5.1	May–December 1919	178

ACKNOWLEDGEMENTS

This book originates in doctoral study at Birkbeck, University of London. I am grateful to my supervisors Professor Rebecca Beasley, Professor Kate McLoughlin, Professor Laura Salisbury and Professor Jo Winning. The conditions faced by independent literary scholars in the United Kingdom are increasingly perilous, but I was exceptionally fortunate to have had an incredible array of scholars to read and guide my work, and to have had the backing and financial support of the Arts and Humanities Research Council throughout the doctorate. My gratitude too to Professor Tim Armstrong and Professor Patricia Waugh for their support and advice as this project transitioned from thesis to book. The anonymous readers at Edinburgh University Press gave very valuable feedback and the Press's editorial team have significantly advanced the final work. Thank you to the staff at both the Hull History Centre and Keele University Library for time spent in the T. E. Hulme archives. This book owes a very great deal to Professor Lynne Pearce's guiding influence at the beginning of my academic career and to that of Professor Beasley at its end. Thank you to my grandparents and to my parents. Their influence is on every page. I share this book entirely with Amee, Rufus and Sejal with love.

The author and publisher would like to thank the following for permission to reproduce copyrighted material in relation to the following highlighted authors: **Mary Borden:** permission of Patrick Aylmer; **Vera Brittain:** the quotation from 'To My Brother' from *Because You Died: Poetry and Prose of the First World War and After* by Vera Brittain, edited and introduced by Mark Bostridge (2008), is included by permission of Mark Bostridge and T. J. Brittain-Catlin, Literary Executors for the Estate of Vera Brittain 1970; **Margaret Postgate Cole**: reprinted by permission of David Higham Associates Limited; **H.D. [Hilda Doolittle]**: extracts from critical essays and *Bid Me to Live* © 1916, 1960 by Hilda Doolittle, reprinted by permission of New Directions Publishing Corp; extracts from *Collected Poems 1912–1944* copyright © 1982 by the Estate of Hilda Doolittle, reprinted by permission of New Directions Publishing Corp and by kind permission of Carcanet Press, Manchester, UK; extracts from archive material and letters from New Directions Pub. acting as agent, copyright © 2022 by the Schaffner Family Foundation, reprinted by permission of New Directions Publishing Corp; extracts from 'Notes on Thought and Vision' copyright © 1982 by the Estate of Hilda Doolittle, reprinted with the permission of The Permissions Company, LLC on behalf of City Lights Books, citylights.com; **Euripides**: volume VI, edited and translated by David Kovacs, Loeb Classical Library Volume 495, Cambridge, MA: Harvard University Press, copyright © 2002 by the President and Fellows of Harvard College. Loeb Classical Library ® is a registered trademark of the President and Fellows of Harvard College. Used by permission. All rights reserved; **F. S. Flint**: extracts from poetry permission of Linda Flint; **Wilfrid Wilson Gibson**: permission of the Trustees of the Wilfrid Gibson Estate; **T. E. Hulme**: Special Collections and Archives, Keele University Library; **William Inge**: extracts from notebooks permission of Christopher Inge; **D. H. Lawrence**: extracts from *Kangaroo*, *The Letters of D. H. Lawrence* and *The Poems* © Cambridge University Press, 2013, permission of Paper Lion Ltd, the Estate of Frieda Lawrence Ravagli and Cambridge University Press; **Wyndham Lewis**: extracts from *Pound/Lewis: The Letters of Ezra Pound and Wyndham Lewis*, edited by Timothy Materer, permission of the Wyndham Lewis Memorial Trust (a registered charity); **Mina Loy**: extracts from 'Songs to Joannes' courtesy of Roger Conover, editor of *The Lost Lunar Baedeker*; **Edgar Lee Masters**: permission of John D. C. Masters; **Thomas Sturge Moore**: kind permission of Charmian O'Neil and Leonie Sturge-Moore; **John Middleton Murry**: extracts from *The Evolution of an Intellectual* permission of The Society of Authors as the Literary Representative of the Estate of John Middleton Murry; **Wilfred Owen**: extracts from *The Complete Poems and Fragments* permission of Dr Jane E. Potter as Senior Trustee for the Wilfred Owen Royalties Trust; **Ezra Pound**: unpublished and archival material ©2022 by Mary de Rachewiltz and the Estate of Omar S. Pound, reprinted by permission of New Directions Publishing Corp; published and subsequently uncollected material ©1915, 1917, 1918, 1919, 1920, 1921, 1932 by Ezra Pound, reprinted by permission of New Directions Publishing Corp; material from the following volumes reprinted by permission of New Directions Publishing Corp: 'An Anachronism at Chinon' from *Pavannes and Divisions* (©1918 by Ezra Pound); *Literary Essays* (©1918 by Ezra Pound); 'A List of Books' from *Instigations* (©1920 by Ezra Pound); *Cathay*, 'Homage to Sextus Propertius',

Hugh Selwyn Mauberley, 'Near Perigord', 'Provincia Deserta', notes, 'The Coming of War' from *Personae* (©1926 by Ezra Pound); *Pound/Lewis* (©1985 by The Trustees of the Ezra Pound Literary Property Trust); *Profile* (©1932 by Ezra Pound); *The Cantos* (©1934, 1948 by Ezra Pound); *The Letters of Ezra Pound* (©1950 by Ezra Pound); *The Spirit of Romance* (©1968 by Ezra Pound); *Selected Prose* (incl. 'Affirmations IV') (©1973 by the Estate of Ezra Pound); 'Poem'/'Trenches: St Eloi' from *Collected Early Poems* (©1976 by the Ezra Pound Literary Property Trust); 'Affirmations–I' from *Ezra Pound and Music* (©1977 by The Trustees of the Ezra Pound Literary Property Trust); *Ezra Pound and the Visual Arts* (incl. 'Wyndham Lewis') (©1980 by The Trustees of the Ezra Pound Literary Property Trust); *A Walking Tour in Southern France* (©1992 by The Trustees of the Ezra Pound Literary Property Trust); **André Salmon**: permission of Jacqueline Gojard; **Siegfried Sassoon**: extracts from *Counter-Attack and Other Poems* copyright Siegfried Sassoon, reprinted by kind permission of the Estate of George Sassoon; **Gertrude Stein**: extracts from 'Lifting Belly' in *The Unpublished Writings of Gertrude Stein* permission of David Higham Associates Limited; **James Stephens**: reprinted by permission of The Society of Authors as the Literary Representative of the Estate of James Stephens; **Wallace Stevens**: 'Phases III', 'Phases VI' and 'Lettres d'un Soldat (1914–1915)' from *Opus Posthumous* by Wallace Stevens, copyright © 1957 by Elsie Stevens and Holly Stevens, used by permission of Alfred A. Knopf, an imprint of the Knopf Doubleday Publishing Group, a division of Penguin Random House LLC. All rights reserved; extracts published in A. Walton Litz, *Introspective Voyager: The Poetic Development of Wallace Stevens* reproduced with permission of the Licensor through PLSclear; **Virginia Woolf**: extracts from *The Diary of Virginia Woolf* permission of The Society of Authors as the Literary Representative of the Estate of Virginia Woolf; **W. B. Yeats**: extracts from 'A Meditation in Time of War' permission of United Artists; **Francis Brett Young**: permission of David Higham Associates Limited.

Although I have tried to trace and contact all copyright holders before publication, this has not been possible in every case. If notified, the publisher will be pleased to make any necessary arrangements at the earliest opportunity.

Parts of Chapters 4 and 5 represent a modified version of an article that first appeared in the 41.1 (Winter 2018) issue of *Biography* published by the University of Hawai'i Press. The cover image – 'Knee-deep in slimy mud in the communications trench in an exposed front line area. Near La Brasse Ville, 21st Battalion. 25.11.18', © IWM E(AUS) 1497 – is reprinted by permission and licence of the Imperial War Museum.

SERIES EDITORS' PREFACE

This series of monographs on selected topics in modernism is designed to reflect and extend the range of new work in modernist studies. The studies in the series aim for a breadth of scope and for an expanded sense of the canon of modernism, rather than focusing on individual authors. Literary texts will be considered in terms of contexts including recent cultural histories (modernism and magic; sonic modernity; media studies) and topics of theoretical interest (the everyday; postmodernism; the Frankfurt School); but the series will also reconsider more familiar routes into modernism (modernism and gender; sexuality; politics). The works published will be attentive to the various cultural, intellectual and historical contexts of British, American and European modernisms, and to inter-disciplinary possibilities within modernism, including performance and the visual and plastic arts.

Tim Armstrong and Rebecca Beasley

INTRODUCTION

THE PROBLEM WITH COMBAT GNOSTICISM

A recurrent claim in combatant narratives of the First World War is that direct experience of battle, the mud and blood of it all, separated participants from civilians. At its core, the claim is that the phenomenology of trench combat was so profoundly alien that it occupied a realm beyond the abilities of the ordinary imagination. 'I would that war were what men dream,' wrote Francis Brett Young in 'The Pavement' (1919), 'A crackling fire, a cleansing flame, / That it might leap the space between / And lap up London and its shame.'[1] According to this combatant, a discharged medical officer who served in East Africa, the gap between the fronts of battle was so large that only a combatant could walk in another combatant's shoes. Young graphically illustrates the point in a poem which contrasts the act of pounding London's pavements with marching into the hell of Passchendaele. One cannot it seems be knee-deep in a traumatising horror such as this: knowledge of the most grotesque aspects of human existence, the intimate and violent realms of the real, would appear to require that we be up to the neck in it all.

As literary scholars, we naturally recoil from these claims. We recognise the specificity of the suffering they document, but we recoil from the suggestion that the projective abilities of the sympathetic apparatus might face a limit. In

---

[1] Francis Brett Young, 'The Pavement', in Francis Brett Young, *Poems, 1916–1918* (London: W. Collins, 1919), pp. 56–7 (p. 57).

recent years epistemologies of combat and veterancy such as those of Young have become especially contentious. The notion of a space between fronts, and its consequent valorisation of one side of that space, runs counter to the expansionist impulses within modernist studies. James Campbell has provided us with the most complete rebuttal of such claims. Analysing the war's principal poetic genre, the trench lyric developed by Wilfred Owen and Siegfried Sassoon amongst others, Campbell gave the combatant's claims the label 'combat gnosticism':

> This is what I mean by combat gnosticism: a construction that gives us war experience as a kind of gnosis, a secret knowledge which only an initiated elite knows. Only men (there is, of course, a tacit gender exclusion operating here) who have actively engaged in combat have access to certain experiences that are productive of, perhaps even constitutive of, an arcane knowledge.[2]

Campbell argued that the trench lyricists widely deployed this reactionary combat gnosticism and that it had also taken root in the canonising scholarship of the genre over the next century. This was a powerful deconstruction of a deeply embedded ideology. It has rightly led us away from what we had termed War Poetry, that monolithic, masculine and soldierly form which spoke from the centre of empire, and which dominated all other poetries of the First World War throughout twentieth-century criticism and culture. We now have a much more comprehensive understanding of war writing, a critical concept whose origins lie in the feminist recovery of a widespread series of war literatures and the call for a more thorough understanding of home front cultures.[3]

However, *Modernist War Poetry* argues that this shift has left in its wake a failure to account for combat gnosticism as a widespread historical structure with a life outside the narrow confines of the trench lyric's ideology. It aims to chart the oscillation of the concept in the public and intellectual cultures of Anglo-American modernity between 1914 and 1919, seeking to understand how, following Fredric Jameson's model, it became manifest within the stylistic features of the various modernisms.[4] We will find that combat gnosticism was in wide

---

[2] James Campbell, 'Combat Gnosticism: The Ideology of First World War Poetry Criticism', *New Literary History*, 30.1 (1999), 203–15 (p. 204).

[3] The principal example of such a shift is *The Cambridge Companion to War Writing*, ed. by Kate McLoughlin (Cambridge: Cambridge University Press, 2009). On the feminist origins of this work, see Sandra M. Gilbert and Susan Gubar, *No Man's Land: The Place of the Woman Writer in the Twentieth Century*, 3 vols (New Haven: Yale University Press, 1988–94), III: *Letters from the Front* (1994), p. xi.

[4] This follows Fredric Jameson's idea of a political or artistic unconscious taking shape within style. See Fredric Jameson, *The Political Unconscious: Narrative as a Socially Symbolic Act* (London: Methuen, 1981; repr. Abingdon: Routledge Classics, 2002).

---

circulation in this period, alongside *both* a fully formed critique of it, remarkably similar in nature to the one deployed by Campbell, *and* a more ambivalent or conflicted poetic which did not quite know what to do with it. *Modernist War Poetry* develops the argument that the critique of combat gnosticism was central to the evolving poetic of T. S. Eliot, Ezra Pound and Wallace Stevens. All three poets demanded an aesthetic that insisted on non-participation in war, on not having fought, as a constitutive requirement for poetry. This is termed 'non-combat gnosticism'. In contrast, we can find the more anxious response in poets such as H.D., Gertrude Stein and Edward Thomas. This 'combat agnosticism' openly worried about the interplay of experience with imagination and the war's impact on the limits of poetry.[5]

That there should be a pre-history of Campbell's concept of combat gnosticism and of his critique of it follows from the difficulties enfolded in these ideas. The problem of other minds and what goes on within them is really a particularly challenging problem.[6] Whilst we can accept Campbell's thesis as a description of literary history, it is another matter to accept it philosophically. Is there, despite the uncomfortable ideological implications, a gnosis associated with combat, an actual space between reality and the imagination? In the spring of 1915 in 'Thoughts for the Times on War and Death' (1915), Sigmund Freud believed so. He drew the distinction between 'those who themselves risk their lives in battle, and those who have stayed at home and have only to wait for the loss of one of their dear ones by wounds, disease or infection'. Freud reached that conclusion by considering other extreme acts of imagination: 'it is indeed impossible to imagine our own death; and whenever we attempt to do so we can perceive that we are in fact still present as spectators.'[7] In 'The Storyteller' (1936), Walter Benjamin described war as a unique technological force field. It eventuated in a human becoming with the might of the shell concentrated

---

[5] These terms are adaptations of those developed in Kate McLoughlin, *Authoring War: The Literary Representations of War from the 'Iliad' to Iraq* (Cambridge: Cambridge University Press, 2011). McLoughlin speaks of both a 'combat *agnosticism*' (pp. 43–4 n. 114) and a 'non-combatant agnosticism' (p. 160), the latter exemplified by the Kantian position, an unscathed spectator seeing the sublime. In relation to the latter term, as will become clear, *Modernist War Poetry* sees this as a form of gnosticism rather than agnosticism.

[6] For the genealogy of the problem within the analytic tradition see Anita Avramides, *Other Minds* (London: Routledge, 2001). For the phenomenological tradition see Dan Zahavi, 'Empathy, Embodiment and Interpersonal Understanding: From Lipps to Schutz', *Inquiry*, 53.3 (2010), 285–306.

[7] Sigmund Freud, 'Thoughts for the Times on War and Death', in *The Standard Edition of the Complete Psychological Works of Sigmund Freud*, ed. and trans. by James Strachey, 24 vols (London: Hogarth Press, 1957–74; repr. London: Vintage, 2001), XIV: *1914–1916: 'On the History of the Psycho-Analytic Movement', 'Papers on Metapsychology', and Other Works* (1957; repr. 2001), pp. 273–302 (pp. 291–2, 289).

at the site of 'the tiny, fragile human body'.[8] This traumatic encounter with evisceration, with the body in pieces to use Trudi Tate's memorable phrase from *Modernism, History and the First World War* (1998), might be considered a glimpse into the violent kernel of the technological real of modernity.[9] This finds support in Elaine Scarry's *The Body in Pain* (1985) where war is understood as ultimately the state-sponsored rearrangement of enemy body tissue.[10] Or as Simone Weil defined it in reflections on *The Iliad*, the force of war is 'that x that turns anybody who is subjected to it into a thing'.[11]

There may be then something about war, its relationship to the body and to the mind, to the mechanisms of endocrinology, which makes it a profoundly alien experience. By setting aside these difficult issues, we might even consider whether the only fundamentally addressable issue is the idea that there is something about war that causes us to repeatedly believe, in fear or hope, that it is alien. Such a belief would have its own history. Our understanding of the First World War as an unparalleled affective experience, especially in Sarah Cole's *Modernism, Male Friendship, and the First World War* (2003) and Santanu Das's *Touch and Intimacy in First World War Literature* (2005), supports this approach.[12] So too does the recent work of Anders Engberg-Pedersen, Yuval

---

[8] Walter Benjamin, 'The Storyteller: Reflections on the Works of Nikolai Leskov', in Walter Benjamin, *Illuminations*, ed. by Hannah Arendt, trans. by Harry Zorn (New York: Harcourt, Brace & World, 1968; repr. London: Pimlico, 1999), pp. 83–107 (p. 84).

[9] Trudi Tate, *Modernism, History and the First World War* (Manchester: Manchester University Press, 1998), p. 49. Similarly, see Patricia Rau, ed., *Conflict, Nationhood and Corporeality in Modern Literature: Bodies-at-War* (Basingstoke: Palgrave Macmillan, 2010). The statistical record supports the argument that evisceration was one of the major unique features of the First World War, even though the military never recovered or accounted for thousands of bodies. The British government pensioned 65,000 for nervous complaints. There were a further 41,000 amputees, 272,000 injured in a single limb, 60,500 with head or eye injuries and 89,000 with other bodily injuries. Fiona Reid, *Shell Shock, Treatment and Recovery in Britain 1914–30* (London: Bloomsbury, 2010), p. 10; Joanna Bourke, *Dismembering the Male: Men's Bodies, Britain and the Great War* (London: Reaktion, 1996), p. 33. Throughout, the word 'traumatic' refers to Ruth Leys's definition of 'trauma', the affective response to terror that leads to the mind's dissociation. It does not refer to the more general concept that the encounter with that which is not itself foundationally wounds consciousness. Ruth Leys, *Trauma: A Genealogy* (Chicago: University of Chicago Press, 2000), p. 2.

[10] Elaine Scarry, *The Body in Pain: The Making and Unmaking of the World* (New York: Oxford University Press, 1985), pp. 63–81.

[11] Simone Weil, '*The Iliad*, or the Poem of Force', *Chicago Review*, 18.2 (1965), 5–30 (p. 6). First published in *Cahiers du Sud* (December 1940–January 1941). Similarly, see Allyson Booth, *Postcards from the Trenches: Negotiating the Space between Modernism and the First World War* (Oxford: Oxford University Press, 1996).

[12] Sarah Cole, *Modernism, Male Friendship, and the First World War* (Cambridge: Cambridge University Press, 2003); Santanu Das, *Touch and Intimacy in First World War Literature* (Cambridge: Cambridge University Press, 2005).

Noah Harari and Kate McLoughlin, who highlight the highly probabilistic nature of pain in modern warfare, the fleshwitness's increasing need to testify to its suffering, and the memory's refusal to let go of horrors that the mind has failed to fully integrate.[13] The First World War, it might then be argued, was not only an extraordinary manifestation of what is more generally an extraordinary human experience, it was also understood by those who lived it as such.

There are several ways in which one could live within a society which valorises gnosticism and look to oppose it. Contrasting *Erlebnis* (that is the beingness or feeling of being human in the present moment) to that 'which one presumes to know but which is unattested by one's own experience', Hans-Georg Gadamer's *Truth and Method* (1975) cites five distinct ways that knowledge might arise. Gadamer says we might take over the experience from others, garner it through hearsay, simply infer or surmise it from our own experience, or imagine it.[14] Campbell, writing at a time when the deeper ideologies of the trench lyric had thoroughly permeated literary studies, was firmly on the side of the imagination. 'Mere imagination is insufficient' is how his essay somewhat scornfully describes the suggestion that we should be unable to walk in the combatant's shoes.[15] Instead of an aesthetic based, Campbell said, 'merely on experience', we ought to have faith in the power of imaginative acts to bridge gaps in experience.[16] If combat gnosticism has an ideology then its critique clearly has one too. It is an ideology of the aesthetic in its purest form, a version of the literary imagination which can reach across minds and then inside wounds. It is suggestive of the faith in acts of sympathy and empathy that originate in late-nineteenth-century *Lebensphilosophie* detailed by Martin Jay in *Songs of Experience* (2005).[17] And if the

---

[13] Anders Engberg-Pedersen, *Empire of Chance: The Napoleonic Wars and the Disorder of Things* (Cambridge, MA: Harvard University Press, 2015); Yuval Noah Harari, 'Scholars, Eyewitnesses, and Flesh-Witnesses of War: A Tense Relationship', *Partial Answers: Journal of Literature and Ideas*, 7.2 (June 2009), 213–28; Kate McLoughlin, *Veteran Poetics: British Literature in the Age of Mass Warfare, 1790–2015* (Cambridge: Cambridge University Press, 2018).

[14] Hans-Georg Gadamer, *Truth and Method* (1975), trans. by Joel Weinsheimer and Donald G. Marshall (London: Bloomsbury, 2013), p. 56. From around 1870 the German language differentiated between *Erlebnis* (lived immediacy, the common feeling of being alive, the sum of will, feeling and memory in conjunction with sensation) and *Erfahrung* (experience taken as an object, reflected upon, given meaningful conceptualisation). See Rex Ferguson, *Criminal Law and the Modernist Novel* (Cambridge: Cambridge University Press, 2013), pp. 32–4.

[15] Campbell, p. 213. See similar terms and views in Ian Clark, *Waging War: A Philosophical Introduction*, reissued edn (Oxford: Clarendon Press, 1990), pp. 2–3.

[16] Campbell, p. 209.

[17] Martin Jay, *Songs of Experience: Modern American and European Variations on a Universal Theme* (Berkeley: University of California Press, 2005), pp. 225–30; Jim Fodor, 'Hermeneutics', in *The Oxford Handbook of Theology and Modern European Thought*, ed. by Nicholas Adams and others (Oxford: Oxford University Press, 2013), pp. 499–521 (p. 507). The specific imaginative act under consideration here is an act of projective imagining from the inside, a state we

ideology of combat gnosticism stealthily exports its inherent gender and racial biases, then the ideology of its critique imports a form of epistemic violence. Following Gayatri Chakravorty Spivak in 'Can the Subaltern Speak?' (1985), by valorising imagination we risk setting aside that our knowledge of the Other is never fully innocent, that it might always be prey to the interests of its producer.[18]

If there is a pre-history of Campbell's critique of combat gnosticism it arises then because his terms of engagement are really part of a much bigger problem. Combat gnosticism is ultimately part of the long history of those representational claims made on the one hand by experience in its embodied and fleshy form, and on the other by imagination in its most ebullient and projective mood. The latter is the mood inextricably bound to the eighteenth-century emphasis on the act of expression, the lamp-like presence that emerged from Kantian transcendental idealism as the creative power of the world.[19] It would seem reasonable then, even as a conditional statement at this stage, that these issues engaged and divided the modernists.

The contemporary debate on the philosophy of other minds is lively and divisive.[20] *Modernist War Poetry* is however interested in combat gnosticism

---

achieve by placing our minds into a conscious awareness that we believe resembles that which is the object of imagination. For contemporary definitions and determinations see Karsten R. Stueber, 'Empathy and the Imagination', in *The Routledge Handbook of Philosophy of Imagination*, ed. by Amy Kind (London: Routledge, 2016), pp. 368–79; Eva T. H. Brann, *The World of the Imagination: Sum and Substance* (Lanham, MD: Rowman & Littlefield, 1991), pp. 17–26. I. A. Richards describes it as the third form of imagination, a sympathetic reproduction of an other's mind state. I. A. Richards, *Principles of Literary Criticism* (1924), rev. edn (London: Kegan Paul, Trench, Trübner, 1934), p. 241.

[18] Gayatri Chakravorty Spivak, 'Can the Subaltern Speak?', in *Marxism and the Interpretation of Culture*, ed. by C. Nelson and L. Grossberg (Basingstoke: Macmillan, 1988), pp. 271–313.

[19] Andrew Bennett, 'Expressivity: The Romantic Theory of Authorship', in *Literary Theory and Criticism*, ed. by Patricia Waugh (Oxford: Oxford University Press, 2006), pp. 48–57 (pp. 48–9).

[20] For recent and very accessible discussions see Paul Bloom, *Against Empathy: The Case for Rational Compassion* (New York: Ecco, 2016); J. M. Coetzee, *Disgrace* (New York: Penguin, 2000); J. M. Coetzee, *Elizabeth Costello: Eight Lessons* (London: Vintage, 2004). The *locus classicus* is Thomas Nagel, 'What Is It Like to Be a Bat?', *Philosophical Review*, 83.4 (October 1974), 435–50. Nagel's stated interest is in the conceptual rather than the epistemological problem of other minds. The epistemological problem arises from the asymmetry between what we know about ourselves and what we know about others. In other words, if we define knowledge as a justified true belief, the question is how might we justify our beliefs about other people's mental states? For Nagel, the hard realist, this is a genuine but unalterable problem: other minds exist but our lack of knowledge necessarily limits our comprehension. In contrast, the conceptual problem arises from the question, how does one understand the concept of mind in such a way that it can apply to oneself and to others? That is, how might we garner the concepts of mental states belonging to others? It is debatable if the two problems are indeed separate. For similar investigations of the same theme see R. D. Laing, *'The Politics of Experience' and 'The Bird of Paradise'* (Harmondsworth: Penguin, 1967), p. 16; Frank Jackson, 'Epiphenomenal Qualia', *Philosophical Quarterly*, 32.127 (April 1982), 127–36 (p. 132); David J. Chalmers, 'Facing up to the Problem of Consciousness',

solely as a problem *qua* problem, a recurring, awkward and unwelcome historical problem. More specifically, it is interested in the problem's impact on intra-war poetics. The problem for poetry is this: how can poetry find an aesthetic position both sufficiently proximate to an atypical experience to know it and, at the same time, sufficiently distant that it can be represented and then received? How can poetry overcome its essential privacies for the public good during wartime? To borrow an idiom, the rubber meets the road here.[21] War is a live test of poetry's ability to express difficult experience, of the use of one emotional landscape to sympathise with the Other at a moment of extreme. In this sense, war threatens poetry with a foundational rupturing. This is keenly so with the advent of a technological modernity that bifurcates the commonality of experience, redefining what we mean by 'universal' and 'quotidian' as normality becomes increasingly abnormal. War threatens to restrict poetry to what James Longenbach aptly termed in *The Plain Sense of Things* (1991) an art of 'diminished particulars'.[22]

This tack back towards the battle front leaves *Modernist War Poetry* open to an obvious criticism. Does the idea of rethinking modern literary history through gnosticism serve to redraw the lines of battle so painstakingly unpicked? Does it not take Vera Brittain's words and pain from the poem 'To My Brother' (1918) and re-prioritise 'battle-wounds' over the 'scars upon my heart'?[23] There is clearly that risk. The argument does place significant emphasis on the phenomenological encounter with the morcellated body as

---

Journal of Consciousness Studies, 2.3 (1995), 200–19 (p. 200). Nagel's most persuasive critic is Daniel C. Dennett, *From Bacteria to Bach and Back: The Evolution of Minds* (New York: W. W. Norton, 2017). It might be hard to imagine, Dennett suggests, but all our inferences tell us that we should be able to know. We should try harder rather than give up on the problem. Daniel C. Dennett, *Consciousness Explained* (Boston: Little, Brown, 1991), p. 439. In literary studies see Elaine Scarry, 'The Difficulty of Imagining Other Persons', in *The Handbook of Interethnic Coexistence*, ed. by Eugene Weiner (New York: Abraham Fund, 1998), pp. 40–62; McLoughlin, *Authoring War*, pp. 42–4; David A. Buchanan, *Going Scapegoat: Post-9/11 War Literature, Language and Culture* (Jefferson, NC: McFarland, 2016), pp. 15–46.

[21] Simon Bainbridge argues that this is a problem particularly bound to the conditions of war, traceable to the emergence of the English Romantic imagination and its thirst to know something of the first major European wars. Simon Bainbridge, *British Poetry and the Revolutionary and Napoleonic Wars: Visions of Conflict* (Oxford: Oxford University Press, 2003), pp. 17–18. Notably, Jonathan Culler chooses to set aside the relation of lyric to combat in *Theory of the Lyric* (Cambridge, MA: Harvard University Press, 2015) on the grounds of its complexity.

[22] James Longenbach, *Wallace Stevens: The Plain Sense of Things* (New York: Oxford University Press, 1991), pp. 42–3.

[23] Vera Brittain, 'To My Brother', in *Scars upon my Heart: Women's Poetry and Verse of the First World War*, ed. by Catherine W. Reilly (London: Virago, 1981; repr. 2006), p. 15. See also Vera Brittain, 'To My Brother', in Vera Brittain, *Because You Died: Poetry and Prose of the First World War and After*, ed. and intro. by Mark Bostridge (London: Hachette Digital, 2010), ebook.

the unique experience of the First World War. It ought to be possible for us to define such an encounter encompassing soldiers, conscripts, nurses, ambulance and supply drivers, photographers and journalists, and official war artists, those within the traditional battle front, alongside those witnesses to Zeppelin attack and munition injury on the home front. Take as examples of the latter the horrific morcellations in Helen Zenna Smith's *Not So Quiet. . .* (1930) and in Irene Rathbone's *We That Were Young* (1932).[24] Drawing the distinction between people along somatic rather than spatial lines follows from the work of Benjamin, Scarry and Weil. It also follows Cole in *At the Violet Hour* (2012) by seeing the war as a somatic catastrophe, the culmination of a set of industrial and technological processes ranged against the human body.[25]

This is however ancillary to the main argument. *Modernist War Poetry* is interested in the history rather than the ethics. It argues that poets who were active during the war, irrespective of school or tradition, irrespective of front, the form of their combat or service, even irrespective of wound, actively worried about the question of whether there was a gnostic element to the horrifying encounter with the body in pieces. Or they worried that others thought there was a gnostic element such that this ideology would take hold within the cultures of modernity and thereby exclude them from it.

Take as illustration of this point Mina Loy's desire to experience war: '"What wonderful poems I could have written—round about a battle field!"' Loy wrote in letters to Carl Van Vechten documenting her service with the Italian Red Cross. It was, she said, an experience '"entirely devoid of sentiment—*entirely* on the chance of getting near a battlefield & hearing a lovely noise!"', one characterised by the excitement of being amidst '"the blood & mess for a change"'.[26] Categorising these reflections according to a front or a role, even by gender, is highly problematical. They do not fit easily. Loy believed that war held something unique for the poet and we will see in later chapters that the modernists all at various points yearned for something of its secrets. To rethink intra-war poetry through combat gnosticism would be then to think about a uniform and entirely understandable anxiety driving the otherwise disparate narratives of the trench lyric, home front elegy and modernist long poem, something that we might loosely call modern again without returning to Modernism.

---

[24] Helen Zenna Smith [Evadne Price], *Not So Quiet . . .* (London: Albert E. Marriott, 1930; repr. London: Virago, 1988), p. 95; Irene Rathbone, *We That Were Young* (London: Chatto & Windus, 1932; repr. London: Virago, 1989), p. 267.

[25] Sarah Cole, *At the Violet Hour: Modernism and Violence in England and Ireland* (Oxford: Oxford University Press, 2012), pp. 22–4.

[26] Mina Loy, letters to Carl Van Vechten ([undated]), qtd in Carolyn Burke, *Becoming Modern: The Life of Mina Loy* (New York: Farrar, Straus and Giroux, 1996), p. 187.

Modernisms and the War

To suggest a certain aesthetic intimacy between these different forms of poetry clearly cuts against the critical grain. Whilst both the trench lyric and the modernist long poem have seen significant revision since Campbell's essay, the antagonistic relationship of the one to the other is unchanged. According to the three canonical accounts of the war and literature – Paul Fussell's *The Great War and Modern Memory* (1975), Samuel Hynes's *A War Imagined* (1990) and Jay Winter's *Sites of Memory, Sites of Mourning* (1995) – these two poetic forms are fundamentally and irreconcilably opposed.[27] The argument can be seen in more recent reappraisals of the period, for example Ana Carden-Coyne's *Reconstructing the Body* (2009) and Randall Stevenson's *Literature and the Great War 1914–1918* (2013).[28] To be clear, we are speaking here of the relationship between the genres and not their individual treatments. Within modernist studies, for example, a notion that appeared in the 1980s and 1990s alongside the bedrock of the modernist genealogy in Hugh Kenner's *The Pound Era* (1971), Sanford Schwartz's *The Matrix of Modernism* (1985) and Malcom Bradbury's *Modernism* (1991) has not dated quite as quickly as it ought. Their view followed the lead of the New Critics: the war, whilst important socially, was a mostly inactive genealogical agent within aesthetics; it was an intellectual void in poetic development. This was especially the case in that extremely specific genealogy of what we once termed high modernist form, the narrative leading from the Image's emergence around 1910 through the Eliot-Pound axis to *The Waste Land* (1922).[29] Again we have not displaced these precepts to

---

[27] Paul Fussell, *The Great War and Modern Memory*, 25th anniversary edn (Oxford: Oxford University Press, 2000), pp. 313–14; Samuel Hynes, *A War Imagined: The First World War and English Culture* (London: Bodley Head, 1990; repr. London: Pimlico, 1992), p. 348; Jay Winter, *Sites of Memory, Sites of Mourning: The Great War in European Cultural History* (Cambridge: Cambridge University Press, 1995), pp. 2–5.

[28] Ana Carden-Coyne, *Reconstructing the Body: Classicism, Modernism, and the First World War* (Oxford: Oxford University Press, 2009), pp. 17–21; Randall Stevenson, *Literature and the Great War 1914–1918* (Oxford: Oxford University Press, 2013), p. 230.

[29] Hugh Kenner, *The Pound Era* (Berkeley: University of California Press, 1971), p. 261 describes the war period under the title 'Interregnum'. Sanford Schwartz, *The Matrix of Modernism: Pound, Eliot, and Early Twentieth-Century Thought* (Princeton: Princeton University Press, 1985) does not mention the war at all except in passing. Malcolm Bradbury, 'London 1890–1920', in *Modernism: A Guide to European Literature 1890–1930*, ed. by Malcolm Bradbury and James McFarlane, rev. edn (London: Penguin, 1991), pp. 172–90 (p. 188) sees the war as mostly a generalised crisis in production. Similarly, see Ronald L. Bush, *The Genesis of Ezra Pound's Cantos* (Princeton: Princeton University Press, 1976); Christine Froula, *To Write Paradise: Style and Error in Pound's 'Cantos'* (New Haven: Yale University Press, 1984); James Longenbach, *Modernist Poetics of History: Pound, Eliot, and the Sense of the Past* (Princeton: Princeton University Press, 1987). For the clearest summary of the content and context of this work see Rebecca Beasley, *Theorists of Modern Poetry: T. S. Eliot, T. E. Hulme, Ezra Pound* (Abingdon: Routledge, 2007).

quite the same extent as other material in these admirable studies. In *Modernisms* (1995) Peter Nicholls treats the war as mostly a signpost to what came before and after.[30] Christine Froula in *The Cambridge Companion to the Poetry of the First World War* (2013) sums up the mood with the argument that 'the Great War did not make modernist poetics, but it did make modernist poems whose voices echo down history's corridors'.[31]

This general mood has taken sustenance from two broader propositions within modernist studies. Marjorie Perloff's concept of the '*Avant Guerre*' vested pre-war aesthetics with a dynamism and gravity prior to hostilities that it could nourish itself throughout the hostilities. It could even resist the brief strain of Nietzschean bravado that threatened to infect and divert it with Futurist militarism.[32] Similarly, Michael Levenson's description of Eliot as a '*deus ex machina*' in *A Genealogy of Modernism* (1984) proposed a poet who had completely modernised himself by 1914 and who arrived in London to save the literary arts from its Georgian fate.[33] Both propositions suggest the die was cast before hostilities broke out. In Michael North's *Reading 1922* (1999), Jean-Michel Rabaté's *1913: The Cradle of Modernism* (2007) and Trevor Dodman's *Shell Shock, Memory, and the Novel in the Wake of World War I* (2015) we are taken outside the intra-war years in line with Nicholls's proposal.[34] Lawrence Rainey's groundbreaking study *Institutions of Modernism* (1998) begins with the pre-war avant-gardes before moving to the 1920s.[35] In Paul Sheehan's *Modernism and the Aesthetics of Violence* (2013) we have turned to excavating the deeper historical origins of the modernist fascination with violence.[36]

---

[30] Peter Nicholls, *Modernisms: A Literary Guide* (Berkeley: University of California Press, 1995), p. 252.

[31] Christine Froula, 'War, Empire and Modernist Poetry, 1914–1922', in *The Cambridge Companion to the Poetry of the First World War*, ed. by Santanu Das (Cambridge: Cambridge University Press, 2013), pp. 210–26 (p. 223).

[32] Marjorie Perloff, *The Futurist Moment: Avant-Garde, Avant Guerre, and the Language of Rupture*, rev. edn (Chicago: University of Chicago Press, 2003). Similarly, see Paul Peppis, *Literature, Politics, and the English Avant-Garde: Nation and Empire, 1901–1918* (Cambridge: Cambridge University Press, 2000).

[33] Michael H. Levenson, *A Genealogy of Modernism: A Study of English Literary Doctrine 1908–1922* (Cambridge: Cambridge University Press, 1984), p. 148.

[34] Michael North, *Reading 1922: A Return to the Scene of the Modern* (New York: Oxford University Press, 1999); Jean-Michel Rabaté, *1913: The Cradle of Modernism* (Malden, MA: Blackwell, 2007); Trevor Dodman, *Shell Shock, Memory, and the Novel in the Wake of World War I* (Cambridge: Cambridge University Press, 2015).

[35] Lawrence Rainey, *Institutions of Modernism: Literary Elites and Public Culture* (New Haven: Yale University Press, 1998).

[36] Paul Sheehan, *Modernism and the Aesthetics of Violence* (Cambridge: Cambridge University Press, 2013). Sheehan persuasively argues that the modernist desire for innovation was coterminous with its desire for violation, resulting in a transgressive artistic desire that stood outside culture to better violate and subvert.

In Oliver Tearle's work we have turned our attention to the recovery of lost post-war voices such as those of Nancy Cunard and Hope Mirrlees.[37] There is the suggestion that the intra-war period itself, at least its direction, is something of a closed story.[38]

Modernist War Poetry also cuts against work that deals more directly with the war. Two revisionary accounts have proved durable here, both of which took aim at one or other of the canonical accounts referred to above. In an important essay of 1999, Sandra Gilbert developed Winter's argument in *Sites of Memory, Sites of Mourning* that the universality of mourning during the war years repropagated the vocabulary of romanticism, classicism and religiosity. While Winter took this as evidence that there had been no intra-war stylistic rupture, Gilbert used it to reread *The Waste Land* as a form of pastoral elegy broken asunder by the *unheimlich* nature of combat experience. For Gilbert, the war was a singularity so powerful that it tore 'a gaping hole in history', contaminating genre for everyone in the process.[39] This allowed us to read Owen's 'Strange Meeting' (published in *Wheels*: November 1919; written *March 1918*; see note for references of this form hereafter) and *The Waste Land* as the two sides of the same affective coin. Both functioned, in their own peculiar ways, as testimonials to the elegiac and haunting effects of unburied bodies on their respective fronts.[40]

In *The Great War and the Language of Modernism* (2003) Vincent Sherry, in contrast, chose to challenge Fussell's *The Great War and Modern Memory*. Sherry was concerned about Fussell's totalising claim that the jarring juxtaposition between grotesque combat experience and the traditional expectations of Georgian society brought the ironic imagination into modern aesthetics. Sherry disagreed; despite their shock and outrage the combatant poets simply could not carry such theoretical weight; theirs was a narrow aesthetic which could only collapse under the enormity of the irony Fussell wanted them to carry into modern consciousness. Instead, Sherry proposed broader shoulders, claiming that it was not in the private world of pain and pathos but 'in the public, civilian culture of the English war [. . .] that the cause and the meaning of the war

---

[37] See for example Oliver Tearle, *The Great War, 'The Waste Land' and the Modernist Long Poem* (London: Bloomsbury, 2019).

[38] The one prominent exception to this is the early work of James Longenbach. Longenbach argued for the influence of war in the cases of Pound (seeing soldiers drilling on the heath outside Stone Cottage) and Stevens (seeing a military parade on a business trip). James Longenbach, *Stone Cottage: Pound, Yeats, and Modernism* (Oxford: Oxford University Press, 1988), pp. 117–19; Longenbach, *Wallace Stevens*, p. 82.

[39] Sandra M. Gilbert, '"Rats' Alley": The Great War, Modernism, and the (Anti) Pastoral Elegy', *New Literary History*, 30.1 (Winter 1999), 179–201 (p. 184).

[40] Parenthesised publication dates occurring between 1914 and 1919 take the format (*journal of first publication*: date of first publication; *estimated date composition begun/finished*).

were first projected'. The invention of modern irony belonged then to the formalists, reflecting according to Sherry the English Liberal Party's illogical and contorted support for a war it ought rightly to have opposed.[41]

Despite their obvious differences, the similarity of these positions is intriguing. Both are, in effect, critiques of combat gnosticism. Both openly side with the imagination. For Gilbert, the pervasiveness of violence in the early decades of the twentieth century meant that the phenomenological gap between soldier and civilian did not exist. For Sherry, the civilian modernists were no passive witnesses but instead were possessed of 'a vanguard awareness' that penetrated the real meaning and value of the war.[42] Whereas Gilbert's essay opened the confines of shellshock through a more widespread social trauma, Sherry vested a different set of initiates with an alternative form of esoteric knowledge, if not of the body in pieces then of language itself.[43]

We can find the tenor of this work in recent scholarship. Increasingly we have replaced Allyson Booth's sensitive approach in *Postcards from the Trenches* (1996), a book aptly subtitled *Negotiating the Space between Modernism and the First World War*, with the psychological tropes introduced by Gilbert in favour of those broad-shouldered writers in Sherry's study. Tate's study refers to a 'war neurotics'; in *Shell Shock and the Modernist Imagination* (2013) Wyatt Bonikowski develops the idea of a 'traumatic wartime'. These are images that bind battle front shock to home front symptomologies.[44] These accounts are exemplary of the generalised traumatic turn in the understanding of modernist form. Both Karen DeMeester (1998) and Margaret R. Higonnet (2002), for example, propose this form is naturally suited to trauma narrative.[45] Its tendency towards montage and ellipsis seems to make it the perfect companion for Mark Seltzer's 'wound culture'.[46] Peter Howarth argues for modernist form as the means to

---

[41] Vincent Sherry, *The Great War and the Language of Modernism* (New York: Oxford University Press, 2003), p. 8.

[42] Ibid. p. 19. See similarly Pericles Lewis, 'Inventing Literary Modernism at the Outbreak of the Great War', in *London, Modernism, and 1914*, ed. by Michael J. K. Walsh (Cambridge: Cambridge University Press, 2010), pp. 148–64 (p. 148).

[43] For one article that sensitively deals with the arguments raised by both Gilbert and Sherry, see Jewel Spears Brooker, 'The Great War at Home and Abroad: Violence and Sexuality in Eliot's "Sweeney Erect"', *Modernism/modernity*, 9.3 (September 2002), 423–38.

[44] Tate, pp. 10–40; Wyatt Bonikowski, *Shell Shock and the Modernist Imagination: The Death Drive in Post-World War I British Fiction* (Farnham: Ashgate, 2013), p. 7. For similar images see Tim Armstrong, *Modernism: A Cultural History* (Cambridge: Polity Press, 2005), pp. 15–22; Carl Krockel, *War Trauma and English Modernism: T. S. Eliot and D. H. Lawrence* (Basingstoke: Palgrave Macmillan, 2011), pp. 8–9.

[45] Karen DeMeester, 'Trauma and Recovery in Virginia Woolf's *Mrs Dalloway*', *Modern Fiction Studies*, 44.3 (1998), 649–73; Margaret R. Higonnet, 'Authenticity and Art in Trauma Narratives of World War I', *Modernism/modernity*, 9.1 (2002), 91–107.

[46] Mark Seltzer, 'Wound Culture: Trauma in the Pathological Public Sphere', *October*, 80 (Spring 1997), 3–26.

'really convey the derangements of the war on the psyche'.[47] Tearle describes *The Waste Land* as 'at once a war poem and a post-war poem', the diagnosis and treatment of Eliot's aboulia mirroring the effects of post-traumatic stress disorder.[48] In *The Edinburgh Dictionary of Modernism* (2018) Adam Piette suggests modernist short stories can mime shellshock, a condition Sheehan likens in *Modernism and the Aesthetics of Violence* to 'a psychopathological précis of a modernist novel'.[49] Roger Luckhurst, one of the central cultural theorists of contemporary trauma narrative, has gone further and identified a pervasive 'trauma aesthetic' with 'a broadly modernist-identified aesthetic allergic to realism', one 'suspicious of familiar representational and narrative conventions'.[50]

There are two distinct risks here. The first need not detain us in this study although this is not to denigrate its importance. It relates to the simplification of historical accounts of trauma and the blurring of distinct types of shock.[51] The second is at stake here. Have we not begun to give too much power to the literary imagination, particularly in its most innovative and allegedly radical forms? Is this faith in the modernist imagination then subject to a form of the same criticism Campbell levelled at Fussell? Is it recursively adopting its own subject, adopting specifically the modernist faith in *écriture*? Is this not a sign that something especially important was and is at stake, that a discipline found and finds itself again threatened?

COMBAT GNOSTICISM AS THREAT

To approach these questions, *Modernist War Poetry* intends to pivot from this body of work. It sets up the idea that the trench lyric served as a threatening point of crystallisation in the long history of the competing claims of experience and imagination of which combat gnosticism is but one part. The study

---

[47] Peter Howarth, 'Poetic Form and the First World War', in Das, ed., pp. 51–65 (p. 53).

[48] Tearle, *The Great War*, pp. 4, 38. Notably, this shift in scholarship tends to see the war as a temporal disruption in line with established notions of post-traumatic stress disorder as 'a disease of time'. Allan Young, *The Harmony of Illusions: Inventing Post-Traumatic Stress Disorder* (Princeton: Princeton University Press, 1995), p. 7.

[49] Adam Piette, 'War', in *The Edinburgh Dictionary of Modernism*, ed. by Vassiliki Kolocotroni and Olga Taxidou (Edinburgh: Edinburgh University Press, 2018), pp. 392–6 (p. 394); Sheehan, p. 171.

[50] Roger Luckhurst, 'Beyond Trauma: Torturous Times', *European Journal of English Studies*, 14.1 (2010), 11–21 (p. 12); Roger Luckhurst, *The Trauma Question* (Abingdon: Routledge, 2008), p. 81.

[51] Tracey Loughran, 'Shell-Shock and Psychological Medicine in First World War Britain', *Social History of Medicine*, 22.1 (2009), 79–95 (p. 88); Tim Armstrong, 'Two Types of Shock in Modernity', *Critical Quarterly*, 42.1 (2000), 60–73; Marinella Rodi-Risberg, 'Problems in Representing Trauma', in *Trauma and Literature*, ed. by J. Roger Kurtz (Cambridge: Cambridge University Press, 2018), pp. 110–23 (pp. 114–15). Luckhurst has recently speculated whether there could even be a singular aesthetic of trauma. Luckhurst, 'Beyond Trauma', p. 12.

treats the trench lyric – the principal but as we will see not the only form of combat gnosticism – as a form of pure poetic taboo that threatened to swamp modernist cultures. There can be no doubt that modernist hostility was open. In an infamous letter to Dorothy Wellesley in 1936 W. B. Yeats described Owen as 'all blood, dirt & sucked sugar stick'.[52] Eliot suggested in 'A Preface to Modern Literature' (1923) that '"War Poetry"' was really 'a distasteful topic', and he hoped (in vain, as it turned out) never to return to it.[53]

Why such hostility? We might isolate several distinct factors. At its core, as Campbell rightly saw, the trench lyric manifested its combat gnosticism through what we would now term a metaphysics of presence following Jacques Derrida in *Of Grammatology* (1967). Its subject is always the suffering ego or the inside of experience. It seeks coherence by denying the imagination of those outside. Such coherence is always of course tenuous: the speaking voice suggests it owns a primordial form of language which can somehow escape any attendant signifying effects.[54] Take as example Owen's scorn for textuality in his heavily redrafted preface published posthumously in *Poems* (1920). 'Above all ~~Its This The book~~ I am is ~~certainly~~ not concerned with Poetry,' Owen wrote, trying to efface the written. 'All a poet can do today is ~~to~~ warn,' he said.[55] That final shift, from the to-infinitive to the zero-infinitive around the warning, brings the tense into a continuous present. It functions as an etymological regression too. It shifts meaning closer to a much older form of the verb 'to warn'. The Old English *warnian* was a notice of impending danger, an evolutionary and inbuilt anti-predation alarm signal. It is beyond language or believes itself to be beyond language. If it ever manages to exit the body at the mouth it does so at such a high frequency that it somehow avoids signification.

The difference here is between what we experience and then speak and what we imagine and then write; it is the difference between *parole* and *écriture* in Derrida's terms. Take the most concrete example in the multiple rhetorical ifs Owen directed at his reader in 'Dulce et Decorum Est' (1920): 'If in some smothering dreams', 'If you could hear', if you could only see those 'eyes writhing in his face'. The idea is illogical: the poem's existence depends on a mute

---

[52] W. B. Yeats, letter to Dorothy Wellesley (21 December [1936]), in *Letters on Poetry from W. B. Yeats to Dorothy Wellesley* (Oxford: Oxford University Press, 1940), pp. 123–5 (p. 124).

[53] T. S. Eliot, 'A Preface to Modern Literature', in *The Complete Prose of T. S. Eliot*, ed. by Ronald Schuchard and others, The Critical Edition, 8 vols (Baltimore and London: Johns Hopkins University Press and Faber and Faber, 2014–19), II: *The Perfect Critic, 1919–1926*, ed. by Anthony Cuda and Ronald Schuchard (2014), pp. 482–8 (p. 484).

[54] Jacques Derrida, *Of Grammatology*, trans. by Gayatri Chakravorty Spivak, corrected edn (Baltimore: Johns Hopkins University Press, 1997), p. 12.

[55] Wilfred Owen, 'Appendix A: Owen's Preface', in Wilfred Owen, *The Complete Poems and Fragments*, ed. by Jon Stallworthy, 2 vols (London: Chatto & Windus, 2013), II: *The Manuscripts and Fragments*, pp. 535–6 (p. 535).

'You' who is necessarily situated outside the experience. Instead, Owen grants himself the right to speak about a known event. It is the right to use simile rather than metaphor. He allows himself the ability to connect one absurd reality with another rather than resorting to mere fantasy: 'His hanging face, like a devil's sick of sin', 'froth-corrupted lungs, / Obscene as cancer, bitter as the cud'.[56] Campbell was understandably suspicious of the terms of trade within this discourse. Instead, we might read it more generously, as Peter Sacks does in *The English Elegy* (1985), as an act orientated towards self-comforting, an attempt to affirm and then hold the self compassionately as it suffers.[57]

Either way, we can see the trench lyricist as a manifestation of a wider burgeoning culture of sensibility. He comes from Eliot's sentimental age, from the period when sensibility dissociated giving birth to an emphasis on reflection and rumination over ratiocination.[58] To redeploy Harari's terms, Owen claimed to be a fleshwitness. His testimony relied on his physical and emotional investment in a lived experience, one felt on the skin rather than glimpsed through the eyes.[59] Winter (2007) suggests this makes the trench lyricist the twentieth century's first 'moral witness', Avishai Margalit's term in *The Ethics of Memory* (2002) for one who gives voice to mass murder by having risked the skin through 'knowledge-by-acquaintance of suffering'.[60] Whilst Yeats railed against such an ethics of passive humanism in *The Oxford Book of Modern Verse* (1936), Margalit constructed it as a form of ethical knowledge obtained at great personal risk. It was a facing down of evil for the public's benefit.[61] Understood this way, we might see the trench lyricist as a signpost towards

---

[56] Wilfred Owen, 'Dulce et Decorum Est', in Owen, *The Complete Poems and Fragments*, I: *The Poems*, pp. 140–1 (p. 140).

[57] Campbell, p. 209; Peter Sacks, *The English Elegy: Studies in the Genre from Spender to Yeats* (Baltimore: Johns Hopkins University Press, 1985), pp. 1–2.

[58] Most famously in T. S. Eliot, 'The Metaphysical Poets' (1921), in *The Perfect Critic*, pp. 375–85 (pp. 380–1).

[59] Harari, p. 218.

[60] Jay Winter, 'The "Moral Witness" and the Two World Wars', *Ethnologie française*, 37.3 (March 2007), 467–74; Avishai Margalit, *The Ethics of Memory* (Cambridge, MA: Harvard University Press, 2002), pp. 147, 149. For a similar connection see Sarah Cole, 'Siegfried Sassoon', in Das, ed., pp. 94–104 (p. 97).

[61] See also Campbell, p. 211. For analysis of the Yeatsian concept of passivity see Jonathan Allison, 'War, Passive Suffering, and the Poet', *Sewanee Review*, 114.2 (Spring 2006), 207–19. Margalit's language notably returns to the split of *kennen* (to know, *noscere*, *connaître*, familiarity with phenomena) and *Wissen* (knowledge, *scire*, *savoir*, communicable phenomena). In William James, the opposition is between '*knowledge of acquaintance* and *knowledge-about*'. William James, *The Principles of Psychology*, 2 vols (New York: Henry Holt, 1890; repr. New York: Dover, 1950), I, p. 221. In Bertrand Russell, it is 'knowledge by *acquaintance*' and 'knowledge of things by *description*'. Bertrand Russell, *The Problems of Philosophy* (1912), 2nd edn (Oxford: Oxford University Press, 1998; repr. 2001), p. 25.

twentieth-century post-genocide testimony.[62] That form of testimony has held an important place in our literature for over a century, and, especially in the work of Elie Wiesel, has done so by placing significant limits on the imagination of those outside the horrifying experience.[63] In other words, the trench lyricist as moral witness might be seen as a powerful threat to poetries outside the greatest spectacles of modernity. He threatened to reduce poetry to 'diminished particulars' on the sidelines of wound culture.

Ross Chambers's thesis in *Untimely Interventions: AIDS Writing, Testimonial, and the Rhetoric of Haunting* (2004) helps us theorise this argument. Chambers argues that wounding personal events and experiences tend to become the object of witnessing practices, which, in circulation, the public interpret as highly threatening. He proposes that such practices are often stylistically elusive and haunting, and argues further for the grotesque, that generic boundary phenomenon caught betwixt and between laughter and horror, as one of the principal representational tools deployed within such witnessing practices.[64] It is the emphasis on the grotesque that results in texts that are at once easily recognisable yet oddly distorted, texts that are neither entirely beyond a culture nor fully integrated within it, such as the trench form of the lyric.[65] These texts sit on the boundaries of good taste inciting a distaste because they are ruptures of the accepted law or convention, disturbances within an established set of social rules. They are social infractions – 'a generic anomaly' to use Chambers's term – upending the established genre arrays that act to prohibit the obscene as subject matter in the first place.[66] Understood as one of these witnessing practices, the trench lyric can be historicised as a powerful threat to an emergent modernist aesthetic of trauma, a threat so immediate that it naturally elicited disgust.

Despite the power we have vested in the modernist imagination it is not clear that its sympathetic apparatus was well prepared for this challenge. The history

---

[62] Carolyn J. Dean, *The Moral Witness: Trials and Testimony after Genocide* (Ithaca, NY: Cornell University Press, 2019), pp. 4–7.

[63] Elie Wiesel, 'Art and the Holocaust: Trivializing Memory', *New York Times*, 11 June 1989, section 2, p. 1; Elie Wiesel, 'TV View: The Trivializing of the Holocaust: Semi-Fact and Semi-Fiction', *New York Times*, 16 April 1978, section 2, p. 29. See also Samuel Hynes, *The Soldier's Tale: Bearing Witness to Modern War* (New York: Penguin, 1997), pp. 1–2.

[64] Lyn Marven argues, albeit in a different context, that the grotesque works to explode our notion of presence in a way that mirrors the traumatic alienation of consciousness from the body. Lyn Marven, *Body and Narrative in Contemporary Literatures in German: Herta Müller, Libuše Moníková, and Kerstin Hensel* (Oxford: Clarendon Press, 2005), p. 49.

[65] Ross Chambers, *Untimely Interventions: AIDS Writing, Testimonial, and the Rhetoric of Haunting* (Ann Arbor: University of Michigan Press, 2004), pp. 33–4. Luckhurst, using Chambers's analysis, has recently suggested that it might be through genre, particularly the blurring of established genre categories, that we might best approach the ineffable aspects of trauma. Luckhurst, 'Beyond Trauma', p. 17.

[66] Chambers, p. 25.

suggests it was instead profoundly unstable. The most widely held model of sympathy, John Stuart Mill's empiricist analogical model, was already under attack by 1914. Mill had postulated in 1865 that one can draw conclusions about one's own feelings because one's own bodily experience contains a narrative about the contiguity of feelings and acts.[67] The problem with inference, despite and because of its simplicity, was that Mill predicated it on a remarkably close similarity between the subject and the object. In any case, the theory held no information about what it is like for the Other to have a feeling. The war could only accentuate the concept's steady decline. How could analogy hold in the presence of such atypical bodily experience, of shellshock, neurotic gaits and tics, terrifying recurrent dreams, dismemberment, gas poisoning and head-to-toe burns?[68]

The modernists understood the problems inherent in analogy. Henri Bergson structured intuition as a 'kind of *intellectual sympathy*' in *An Introduction to Metaphysics* (1903). He described it as the self's imaginative insertion into an object or thing.[69] Whilst Bergson saw this as a form of self-sympathy that moved within duration from self to others, it was simultaneously revealed in *Time and Free Will* (1910) as 'a need for self-abasement, an aspiration downwards', a searching out of pain.[70] Repeatedly we find in Bergson's work mediatory warnings against the risk of mechanisation that might result from intuition and illustrations of its essentially violent character.[71] In both *Prolegomena to the Study of Greek Religion* (1908) and *Themis* (1912) we find Jane Harrison's historical imagination punctuated by pleas for 'a severe effort of the imagination' to 'think ourselves back into'.[72] As Adam Smith had recognised, these types of imaginative act can result in simulacrum or an illusory sympathy: we risk feeling a state of mind as an imitation of the Other, but one that is in fact merely a copy with no original.[73] Even Wilhelm Dilthey, the father of *Lebensphilosophie*, considered some forms of mental life to represent a limit to human knowledge.[74]

---

[67] Avramides, pp. 4–7, 164–72; John Stuart Mill, *An Examination of Sir William Hamilton's Philosophy*, 2nd edn (London: Longmans, Green, 1865), p. 208.

[68] Michael Roper, *The Secret Battle: Emotional Survival in the Great War* (Manchester: Manchester University Press, 2009), p. 243.

[69] Henri Bergson, *An Introduction to Metaphysics* (1903), trans. by T. E. Hulme, rev. edn (New York: G. P. Putnam, 1912; repr. Indianapolis: Hackett Publishing, 1999), p. 23.

[70] Henri Bergson, *Time and Free Will: An Essay on the Immediate Data of Consciousness*, trans. by F. L. Pogson (London: George Allen & Unwin, 1910; repr. Abingdon: Routledge, 2013), p. 19.

[71] Bergson, *Time and Free Will*, p. 237; Bergson, *An Introduction to Metaphysics*, p. 45.

[72] Jane Ellen Harrison, *Prolegomena to the Study of Greek Religion*, 2nd edn (Cambridge: Cambridge University Press, 1908), p. 212. See also Jane Ellen Harrison, *Themis: A Study of the Social Origins of Greek Religion* (Cambridge: Cambridge University Press, 1912), p. 478.

[73] Robert Mitchell, *Sympathy and the State in the Romantic Era: Systems, State Finance, and the Shadows of Futurity* (New York: Routledge, 2007), pp. 78–9.

[74] Wilhelm Dilthey, 'Ideas Concerning a Descriptive and Analytical Psychology', in Wilhelm Dilthey, *Descriptive Psychology and Historical Understanding* (1894), trans. by Richard M. Zaner and Kenneth L. Heiges (The Hague: Martinus Nijhoff, 1977), pp. 21–120 (p. 80).

The scholarly record accurately reflects the sense of confusion. The intra-war imagination was caught between past and future, between that is the critique of sympathy (an ethical feeling for the Other) and the unfulfilled promise of phenomenological empathy (a feeling with the Other).[75] Johanna Winant (2018) graphically describes the mind of the Other within modernist literature repeatedly opening to investigation and then snapping firmly closed again, a process, it might be added, entirely consistent with the yo-yoing of modernist attitudes towards feeling, authenticity and sentimentality.[76] In *Empathy and the Psychology of Literary Modernism* (2014) Meghan Marie Hammond persuasively argues for a modernism caught in the stand-off between its fear of solipsism and the promise of intersubjectivity.[77] In *Modernist Empathy* (2019) Eve C. Sorum suggests a modernist imagination that destabilised the notion of coherent selfhood in the act of taking up the Other's perspective, painfully revealing the isolation of the self and exposing the ephemeral and contextual notion of subjectivity.[78]

We can briefly illustrate here, as a prelude to the detailed examination in the following chapters, something of the range of possibilities and a sense of confusion by comparing the views of Eliot and Pound on the imagination, the two poets most closely allied in the intra-war period. Pound seems to have rarely doubted the mind's abilities. His faith in hermeneutics, inherited from Friedrich Schleiermacher's '*divinatory* method', gave licence to what Pound termed in *The Spirit of Romance* (1910) the idea of a 'permanent basis in humanity' that allowed imagination free transit from self to Other.[79] In contrast, Eliot

---

[75] For the history of these concepts see Amy Coplan and Peter Goldie, 'Introduction', in *Empathy: Philosophical and Psychological Perspectives*, ed. by Amy Coplan and Peter Goldie (Oxford: Oxford University Press, 2011), pp. ix–xlvii (p. xi). For further background see Judith Ryan, *The Vanishing Subject: Early Psychology and Literary Modernism* (Chicago: University of Chicago Press, 1991); Suzanne Keen, *Empathy and the Novel* (Oxford: Oxford University Press, 2007); Timothy C. Vincent, 'From Sympathy to Empathy: Baudelaire, Vischer, and Early Modernism', *Mosaic: A Journal for the Interdisciplinary Study of Literature*, 45.1 (2012), 1–15.

[76] Johanna Winant, 'Empathy and Other Minds in *Ulysses*', *James Joyce Quarterly*, 55.3–4 (2018), 371–89. On sentimentality see Michael Bell, *Sentimentalism, Ethics and the Culture of Feeling* (Basingstoke: Palgrave, 2000), p. 2; Karsten R. Stueber, *Rediscovering Empathy: Agency, Folk Psychology, and the Human Sciences* (Cambridge, MA: MIT Press, 2006), pp. 5–6; Suzanne Clark, 'Sentimental Modernism', in *Gender in Modernism: New Geographies, Complex Intersections*, ed. by Bonnie Kime Scott (Urbana: University of Chicago Press, 2007), pp. 125–36 (p. 129).

[77] Meghan Marie Hammond, *Empathy and the Psychology of Literary Modernism* (Edinburgh: Edinburgh University Press, 2014), pp. 1–18.

[78] Eve C. Sorum, *Modernist Empathy: Geography, Elegy, and the Uncanny* (Cambridge: Cambridge University Press, 2019), pp. 3–5.

[79] Friedrich Schleiermacher, 'Hermeneutics and Criticism' (1838), in Friedrich Schleiermacher, '*Hermeneutics and Criticism' and Other Writings*, ed. and trans. by Andrew Bowie (Cambridge: Cambridge University Press, 1998), pp. 1–224 (p. 92); Ezra Pound, 'Psychology and Troubadours' (1912), in Ezra Pound, *The Spirit of Romance*, new edn (New York: New

inherited from F. H. Bradley's *The Presuppositions of Critical History* (1874) a more ambivalent imagination. Eliot recognised that idiosyncrasies marked the imagination and that this required the creation of a counter critical intelligence. This took shape in the idea of a much-refined mind that could apply knowledge rather than one passively receiving the minutiae of experience. Even within camps the modernist imagination was highly mobile.

The unresolved nature of this sympathy-empathy complex between 1914 and 1919 leads to use of the term 'sympathetic imagination' in *Modernist War Poetry*. First, this allows us to preserve the historical meanings of sympathy and empathy, especially since these terms have since shifted a great deal. 'Sympathetic imagination' also better reflects modern usage, defining the capacity to feel the Other's pain as a multilevel and interlinked mind and body complex.[80] Second, the term 'empathy' is especially problematic. Although there has been a rich turn to phenomenological empathy within modernist studies, and there is a clear pre-history of the subject in German aesthetics, there is little direct support for this in the work of the poets under analysis here prior to 1920 without needing to resort to a model of a more generalised intellectual contagion bringing the work of Edmund Husserl and others into English circulation.[81]

Directions, 1952; repr. 2005), pp. 87–100 (p. 92). See also Ezra Pound, 'I Gather the Limbs of Osiris' (1911–12), in Ezra Pound, *Selected Prose 1909–1965*, ed. by William Cookson (New York: New Directions, 1973), pp. 21–43 (p. 23).

[80] For recent theorisations see Stueber, 'Empathy and the Imagination', p. 372. Four distinct faculties within the apparatus of the sympathetic imagination are now commonly identified: two non-resonance processes – personal distress (an aversive state non-congruent with the Other, self-oriented and egoistic) and sympathy (a *sui generis* emotion involving feelings of sorrow for the Other, that is Other-oriented, altruistic and often the consequence of empathy) – and two resonance/replication processes – empathy (an emotional response that stems from another's state and is congruent with it, not a separate emotion but an inductive process of sharing, one which distinguishes more or less between self and Other and is similar to nineteenth-century sympathy) and contagion (mimicry or synchronisation of facial expressions, vocalisations, posture and movement of the Other). The term 'empathy' continues to divide theorists, particularly in relation to the distinction between self and Other and the question of what is shared. Some theorists argue the need for empathiser and empathised to be in the same affective state, whilst others, especially those in the phenomenological tradition aiming to make empathy *sui generis*, argue the empathiser can see the affective state of the Other as an intentional object without feeling that state.

[81] Edmund Husserl's first British lecture was in June 1922. Eliot read *Logische Untersuchungen* (1900–1) in Marburg and Oxford (July–October 1914), Hulme during 1915. Hulme also read 'Philosophie als strenge Wissenschaft' (1910–11) where Husserl discusses intersubjectivity through the concept of intimation (the insight into a speaker's experience via speech). We can date Husserl's principal interest in empathy to the Göttingen lectures (1910–11) and the concept of the lived body. After *Ideen I* (1913), read by neither Eliot nor Hulme it appears, Husserl published little until 1929. Edith Stein wrote *Zum Problem der Einfülung* (1917) under Husserl by building on both *Ideen I* and what Husserl published in *Ideen II* (1952). As a critique of Max Scheler's work, it argued for empathy as intentionality directed at alien experience. Husserl's

The term 'sympathetic imagination' is designed then to designate something of the sense of uncertainty and risk explicit in modernist imaginative acts, of the challenges these writers faced when they responded to the combatant's sense of certainty.

ARGUMENT, STRUCTURE, SCOPE

In summary, *Modernist War Poetry* aims to read the trench lyricist as a moral witness, in turn as a lightning rod for three latent crises within modernity: a crisis in witnessing practices marked by the increasingly dominant public position of the fleshwitness, a crisis of experience symbolised by the shifting grounds of *Erlebnis*, and a crisis of the imagination itself, caught betwixt a discredited concept of sympathy and a partially formed one of empathy. The study proposes that we can best examine this collision of crises through the intra-war history of the concept of combat gnosticism, and the debate that it set up about the relationship between experience and imagination.

How would we then fit such a thesis within our understanding of modernist cultures? How should we locate it theoretically? Jameson's *A Singular Modernity* (2002) describes the history of the hegemony of capital within the imperialist stages of the European nation states. In *The Modernist Papers* (2007) Jameson links this history to a catastrophic compartmentalisation of mind which resulted in a foundational 'gap between individual and phenomenological experience and structural intelligibility'.[82] This builds on Jameson's proposal (1988), republished in *Nationalism, Colonialism, and Literature* (2001), that we see colonialism in this way. That is, we see colonialism as the supreme echo of the mechanisms of reification that resulted from the Taylorising emphasis on

---

views were not however formalised until around 1929 and in *Méditations cartésiennes* (1931). There is no evidence that Eliot, Pound or Hulme read Stein's work before 1920. Hulme did read Scheler's *Über Ressentiment und moralisches Werturteil* (1912) and *Der Genius des Krieges und der deutsche Krieg* (1915) and, around November 1915, *Zur Phänomenologie und Theorie der Sympathiegefüle und von Liebe und Hass* (1913) which develops Scheler's intermediary theory of sympathy. However, Hulme's documented interest was in Scheler's nationalism not his ideas on empathy. See Herbert Spiegelberg, *The Phenomenological Movement: A Historical Introduction*, 3rd edn (Dordrecht: Kluwer Academic, 1994), p. 662; J. N. Mohanty, 'The Development of Husserl's Thought', in *The Cambridge Companion to Husserl*, ed. by Barry Smith and David Woodruff Smith (Cambridge: Cambridge University Press, 1995), pp. 45–77 (pp. 70–3); Christos Hadjiyiannis, *Conservative Modernists: Literature and Tory Politics in Britain, 1900–1920* (Cambridge: Cambridge University Press, 2018), pp. 156–61. For work suggesting stronger links to phenomenology see Ariane Mildenberg, *Modernism and Phenomenology: Literature, Philosophy, Art* (London: Springer Nature, 2017), pp. 2–3.

[82] Fredric Jameson, *A Singular Modernity: Essay on the Ontology of the Present* (London: Verso, 2002); Fredric Jameson, 'Rimbaud and the Spatial Text' (1984), in Fredric Jameson, *The Modernist Papers* (London: Verso, 2007), pp. 238–54 (p. 240).

efficiency.[83] By relocating the economic system to the outside, an unimaginable spatial zone beyond daily life and the metropolis, colonialism left in its wake a certain lack, one defined by the inability to know the system as a whole, a dangerous space beyond *Verstehen*. For Jameson, what makes a work modernist is precisely the self-reflexive acknowledgement of this dilemma: it is the awkward recognition that experience cannot be grasped immanently and must reach out beyond itself or else forever live in some form of privation.[84] We might then use the problem of combat gnosticism, the tension between experience and imagination, to highlight the self-reflexive nature of intra-war poetics, its need to negotiate with this lack, its refusal to accept privation.

Modernist War Poetry sets out these claims in a chronological format. Its narrative moves from the start of the war in 1914 to the doctrine of impersonality in 1919. Chapter 1 examines the underlying fault lines in the aesthetics of both the literary impression and the Image on the eve of war. It moves through the critical and satiric responses to patriotic war verse in the autumn of 1914 and ends with the emergence of what we might term the first modernist war poetries. The ability of the modernists to stand apart from war dissolves in Chapter 2 with the growing sense of calamity in England. This is coexistent with the return of the first combatants (most notably Rupert Brooke, T. E. Hulme and May Sinclair) to modernist cultures. Here we find the first signs of a crude model of the shocked mind, and, in contrast in the work of H.D., the first doubts about imaginative flight into battle. By 1916 in Chapter 3 we find the three basic gnostic responses to the war taking fuller shape: the combat gnosticism of Mary Borden, Wyndham Lewis and Isaac Rosenberg, the combat agnosticism of H.D., D. H. Lawrence and Edward Thomas, and the tentative non-combat gnosticism of Wallace Stevens. The chapter contrasts this with a brief but noticeable sense of doubt appearing in Pound's work, and with Stein's poetry as a radical and highly nuanced intervention. Chapters 4 and 5 finally turn to the work of Eliot. The first of the two considers the influence of John Middleton Murry's critique of Sassoon's poetry. The second turns to new readings of both 'Tradition and the Individual Talent' (part I: *The Egoist*: September 1919; *July 1919*; part II: *The Egoist*: December 1919; *late 1919*) and 'Gerontion' (1920; *May–September 1919*). The conclusion returns to several unresolved themes set up in this Introduction, especially the nature of Eliot's stated distaste for poetries of war and his attempt to negatively valence that genre.

---

[83] I am referring here to Jameson's inflected use of the concept of reification in *The Political Unconscious*, pp. 215–18. That is the split between the worker and the product of their own labour.

[84] Fredric Jameson, 'Modernism and Imperialism' (1988), in Terry Eagleton, Fredric Jameson and Edward W. Said, *Nationalism, Colonialism, and Literature* (Minneapolis: University of Minnesota Press, 2001), pp. 41–66 (p. 51).

Five choices require preliminary defence. First, several textual choices may appear regressive. This is deliberate. The study is a revisionary history of an extremely specific genealogy, and that focus causes a return to the narrative that eventuated in *The Sacred Wood* (1920). Throughout, recently recovered narratives face the old canon. The emphasis on texts and meta-texts which grapple with or expose the emergence of the problem of combat gnosticism as a problem also limits the scope of the study.

Second, where to begin and end the narrative is moot. The 'intra-war period' here ranges from the anticipation of war in *Blast* (July 1914) to the demobilisation of combatants in the summer and autumn of 1919. This period is usefully bookended by the completion of 'Gerontion' and by the publication of *The Fourth Canto* (October 1919; *April 1919*), the first of the intra-war drafts Pound preserved for *A Draft of XVI Cantos* (1925). It was in November 1919 that Eliot appears to have first seriously considered drafting a long poem having read a draft of 'The Seventh Canto' (*Dial*: August 1921; *September–December 1919*). Although the narrative addresses early drafts, this means it does not consider *The Waste Land* in detail, nor *Hugh Selwyn Mauberley* (1920; *April 1920*).

Third, there are significant terminological and chronological difficulties in speaking about literatures of the First World War. Should we speak of war poets, soldier-poets, war poetry or a War Poetry? The overlap between the term 'War Poetry' and the modernist's own favourite term, 'war verse', only complicates matters. As does the attempt to differentiate between combat theatres. Most modernists believed the work of soldier-poets was the only poetry of war and that the work of non-combatants, meaning those who did not fight, was a different class of literature altogether. Some did not however share this view and their story is especially important here. To avoid confusion, the unfolding narrative avoids these terms so that when they do appear we can assume they are modernists' own words. In contrast, the study's critical framework and apparatus uses the terms 'war poetries' and 'war writing' to suggest the range of approaches in the intra-war period. It is worth repeating here that *Modernist War Poetry* tends to emphasise the trench lyric as the exemplary form of combat gnosticism because it was the form which manifested that ideology most clearly and which functioned as the principal target of modernist antipathy. It was not however the exclusive form in which combat gnosticism appeared as the narrative explains.

Fourth, readers might take the genealogical approach, the classification of typologies of gnosis, the detailed timelines and the stylistic emphasis placed on a story as an unwelcome imposition of order on to what the moderns experienced as chaos. The decision to move some contextual material to the accompanying footnotes in order not to detract from the flow of the narrative might accentuate this feeling. These are all intended as structural devices that present a large array of material in an analytical fashion.

And finally, fifth, the restricted focus on poetry raises the question of the chosen genre. This is partly a matter of target. Revision of the foundational genealogies of modernist aesthetics has tended in recent years to centre on the modernist novel and the short story, especially in studies of the war.[85] It is also a conscious choice. In general, the relationship between the sympathetic imagination and fiction has already proved fertile ground.[86] Dorrit Cohn's aptly titled *Transparent Minds* (1978) clearly demonstrates how modernist fiction inherited from Henry James a complete narratology of *qualia*.[87] In terms of imagining the Other, the poet faces a quite different challenge. Readers of fiction tend to accept that narrative fiction is set apart from reality, that it presents itself to us as an attempt at semblance. As Käte Hamburger explains most cogently in *The Logic of Literature* (1973), this serves to grant it a special relationship in the struggle between realism and the mimesis of consciousness.[88] Poetry tends to struggle with this dynamic. The expectations brought to a poem contaminate both the objective element of a poem's story and the attempt to tell that story from a point of view. As Chapter 5 shows this is particularly acute in a poem like 'Gerontion'. It is the extreme '*self*-consciousness of consciousness' in modern poetry, to borrow Hugh Underhill's phrase from *The Problem of Consciousness in Modern Poetry* (1992), that serves to set up the poetic self's separation from the Other.[89] Whilst there are obvious ways to explore combat gnosticism in intra-war modernist prose – for example in Lawrence's 'The Blind Man' (1920; *December 1918*) and Rebecca West's *The Return of the Soldier* (*Century Magazine*: serialised beginning February 1918) – the focus here is on poetry.

---

[85] For example, Tate and Bonikowski.

[86] For example, Lisa Zunshine, *Why We Read Fiction: Theory of Mind and the Novel* (Columbus: Ohio State University Press, 2006).

[87] Dorrit Cohn, *Transparent Minds: Narrative Minds for Presenting Consciousness in Fiction* (Princeton: Princeton University Press, 1978), pp. 11–14. In *Modernist War Poetry* the term '*qualia*' means a series of qualitative mental states. John R. Searle, *The Mystery of Consciousness* (New York: New York Review of Books, 1997), pp. 8–9.

[88] Käte Hamburger, *The Logic of Literature*, trans. by Marilynn J. Rose (Bloomington: Indiana University Press, 1973).

[89] Hugh Underhill, *The Problem of Consciousness in Modern Poetry* (Cambridge: Cambridge University Press, 1992), p. 300.

I

EARLY MODERNIST RESPONSES TO COMBATANT POETRY: 1914–SPRING 1915

MODERNIST POETICS ON THE EVE OF WAR

In *The Problems of Philosophy* (1912) Bertrand Russell suggested an ethical imperative to his examination of the basic principles of matter. If we are unable to verify the existence of a material object, Russell proposed, then all other material objects, including other people's bodies and minds, necessarily collapse into a void, leaving us alone in a desert.[1] Russell's call for a cogent philosophy of matter in support of an ethics of otherness serves as a graphic reminder that the inevitably inward pilgrimage of early-twentieth-century aesthetics harboured a deeper strategy. Fredric Jameson has termed this work a 'literature of inwardness and introspection'.[2] However, in *The Problems of Philosophy* we can take note of the desperate need to break the legacies of what Walter Pater described in *The Renaissance* (1888) as 'that thick wall of personality through which no real voice has ever pierced'.[3] Russell's modernism is a modernism negotiating with, to take Toril Moi's apt phrase, 'the death of idealism'.[4] In David Perkins's

---

[1] Russell, *The Problems of Philosophy*, p. 7. See also here the work of G. F. Stout, Russell's tutor. Stout made clear that no one can know what passes in the mind of the Other. G. F. Stout, *A Manual of Psychology* (London: University Correspondence College, 1899), p. 20.

[2] Jameson, 'Rimbaud and the Spatial Text', p. 241.

[3] Walter Pater, *The Renaissance: Studies in Art and Poetry*, rev. edn (London: Macmillan, 1888), p. 248.

[4] Toril Moi, *Henrik Ibsen and the Birth of Modernism: Art, Theater, Philosophy* (Oxford: Oxford University Press, 2006), p. 13.

A History of Modern Poetry (1976) and Leon Surette's *The Birth of Modernism* (1993) we discover a modernism grappling with the legacies of scepticism rather than a modernism inventing scepticism.[5] As James Longenbach argues in *Modernist Poetics of History* (1987), it was Pater's *Plato and Platonism* (1893) with its search for a form of permanent common sense independent of each personality which greatly influenced the early work of W. B. Yeats.[6] As Russell intuited, to doubt the Other's mind, to doubt our ability to conceptualise it in the same terms as we understand our own mind, is to believe certain things about the world with potentially horrifying consequences.[7]

The established pre-war genealogy of modernist aesthetics has made the divisive and unstable impact of this encounter with epistemological scepticism abundantly clear. Take the broadly established genealogy of Ford Madox Ford's literary impressionism for example. In the work of Joseph Conrad and Henry James this very distinctive fictional style turned to the investigation of subjectivity as the means to more accurately express how an individual truly experiences real events. In *A Genealogy of Modernism* Michael Levenson describes how, in the months leading up to the war, Ford's early demand – most memorably in 'Impressionism – Some Speculations' (1913) – to register a public history in personal terms had eventually begun to give way under the weight of egoism.[8] In Levenson's account this left behind a mode which emphasised the writer and representation rather than external truth value, a process that inevitably pushed further away from shared reality into the idiosyncrasies of a very private vision.[9] Ford's subsequent shift towards much stricter or rigidly enforced impressionism, a literary mode that retreated further inwards and away from the real, took the aesthetic inside those momentary perceptions, emotions and sensations that precede ego formation.[10] The ends of that retreat are evident in *The Good Soldier* (March 1915). As both Damon Marcel DeCoste (2007) and Paul Armstrong (2015) illustrate, this is an unfathomable text which in seeking to problematise the relationship between knowledge and representation ends

---

[5] David Perkins, *A History of Modern Poetry: From the 1890s to the High Modernist Mode* (Cambridge, MA: Belknap Press, 1976); Leon Surette, *The Birth of Modernism: Ezra Pound, T. S. Eliot, W. B. Yeats, and the Occult* (Montreal: McGill-Queen's University Press, 1993).

[6] Longenbach, *Modernist Poetics of History*, p. 33; Walter Pater, *Plato and Platonism: A Series of Lectures* (London: Macmillan, 1893), p. 137.

[7] For work charting other minds as one obvious goal of empiricist psychology see Ann Banfield, *The Phantom Table: Woolf, Fry, Russell and the Epistemology of Modernism* (Cambridge: Cambridge University Press, 2000); Manju Jain, *T. S. Eliot and American Philosophy: The Harvard Years* (Cambridge: Cambridge University Press, 1992); Ryan, *The Vanishing Subject*.

[8] Ford Madox Ford, 'Impressionism – Some Speculations', in *Critical Writings of Ford Madox Ford*, ed. by Frank MacShane (Lincoln: University of Nebraska Press, 1964), pp. 139–52 (p. 141).

[9] On Ford's pre-war transformations see Levenson, pp. 115–17.

[10] Levenson, p. 118.

by foregrounding its own narratorial processes.[11] By August 1914, the development of the literary impression in Ford's hands epitomised the crisis of the imagination within modernity set out in the Introduction. Jesse Matz's *Literary Impressionism and Modernist Aesthetics* (2001) describes the impression as a caught aesthetic, one stranded between its empiricist legacy and the promise of a phenomenological future. In other words, the impression became a materialism unable to reach the safety of intentionality.[12]

We can make similar claims about the development of the Image in the early 1910s. As an affective and intellectual complex plucked from duration and then captured figuratively it shared the impression's overall goal. The volatile trajectory of Ezra Pound's pre-war career – the influence of Yeats, and then of Ford and then finally Wyndham Lewis – suggests Pound had long harboured suspicions about the Image. Vincent Sherry's *Modernism and the Reinvention of Decadence* (2015) describes the problem here as the Image's creation of a 'private readerly space' which called into question its ability to hold on to objective reality, especially in the face of the rise of mass violence.[13] Like the literary impression, the Image harboured the risk that contact with the real might be lost in its multiple folds of representation. Hence the Image's natural but surely unintended inclination towards deathliness, its 'cryptaesthetic' to use Daniel Tiffany's phrase from *Radio Corpse* (1995). It showed a repeated willingness to dally with non-being despite its obvious emphasis on instantaneity.[14] As a strategy designed to avoid both the epic and the prosaic, the Image often lapsed only into elegy.[15]

Might we find a potential counter aesthetic to these problems in T. E. Hulme's idiosyncratic theories on modern art? In his January 1914 lecture to the Quest Society, 'Modern Art and its Philosophy', Hulme turned explicitly towards the concept of empathy. The lecture has become the *locus classicus* of modernist antipathy to art forms based in an empathetic or imitative relationship to nature. Building from his reading of Wilhelm Worringer's *Abstraktion und Einfühlung* [*Abstraction and Empathy*] (1908), Hulme valorised primitive art, especially its

---

[11] Paul Armstrong, 'What Is It Like to Be Conscious? Impressionism and the Problem of Qualia', in *A History of the Modernist Novel*, ed. by Gregory Castle (Cambridge: Cambridge University Press, 2015), pp. 66–83 (p. 67); Damon Marcel DeCoste, '"A Frank Expression of Personality"? Sentimentality, Silence and Early Modernist Aesthetics in *The Good Soldier*', *Journal of Modern Literature*, 31.1 (Fall 2007), 101–23.

[12] Jesse Matz, *Literary Impressionism and Modernist Aesthetics* (Cambridge: Cambridge University Press, 2001), p. 29.

[13] Vincent Sherry, *Modernism and the Reinvention of Decadence* (New York: Cambridge University Press, 2015), p. 171.

[14] Daniel Tiffany, *Radio Corpse: Imagism and the Cryptaesthetic of Ezra Pound* (Cambridge, MA: Harvard University Press, 1995), pp. 26–7, 148–58.

[15] Levenson, p. 46; Nicholls, pp. 170–1.

sculptural abstract qualities. It expressed, both he and Worringer proposed, a horror at the human's isolated position within the universe. They contrasted it with the mode of empathy, a style arising from a sense of self-assuredness about the relation of self and world. Whereas primitive art expressed the bewilderment of being, empathetic art was a manifestation of the self's safety and confidence in the world.

At face value this would appear to set the anti-humanistic strain within early modernism that eventually reached through Hulme to Eliot and Pound in the 1920s firmly against any art that called upon the sympathetic apparatus. Surely Hulme destroyed empathy as a meaningful concept before the war had even begun? There could be then no meaningful intra-war history, especially in relation to Eliot and Pound?[16] The applicability of Hulme's account to *Modernist War Poetry* is however highly questionable. This pivots on the unstable notion of pre-war empathy and Hulme's unstable interpretation of it.

Einfühlung itself was hardly a stable concept in 1914.[17] Edmund Husserl referred to it at the start of the war as a phoney term: do we project our self into the Other or is it our encounter with the Other?[18] And what of the prejudicial demands latent within aesthetic *Einfühlung*? It demanded a bourgeois viewer as a precondition for the gendered, leisure and moneyed collapse into the work of art. Only after the war do we find a full account of empathy as a *sui generis* form of intentionality, one that shed the mechanisms of imitation and transportation to become the direct experience of the Other's mind as minded. Pre-war empathy was an empathy bouncing between analogy, inference and perceptual theories of other minds.[19]

Hulme nonetheless chose one of the most idiosyncratic sources for *Einfühlung*. We might argue that Worringer's trademark bifurcation of artistic styles was, at least in its original form, closer to the concept of self-estrangement than *Einfühlung*. Worringer actually argued the point clearly, suggesting that the self

---

[16] Hulme's influence on Eliot appears certain. See Ronald Schuchard, 'Did Eliot Know Hulme? Final Answer', *Journal of Modern Literature*, 27.1/2 (Autumn 2003), 63–9.

[17] According to Robert Vischer (1873), empathy was the viewer's active perceptual engagement in a work of art. It destabilised the identity of the viewer and animated the artwork. In Theodor Lipps's 'Das Wissen von fremden Ichen' (1907) empathy was a *sui generis* concept, although he still linked it to instinctual imitation, resonance and simulation phenomena. He treated it as the perception of a gesture, or an expression, reproduced in such a way that it evoked the feeling known from the viewer's own experience. The viewer could then attribute it to the Other through projection. Juliet Koss, 'On the Limits of Empathy', *Art Bulletin*, 88.1 (March 2006), 139–57.

[18] Zahavi, pp. 289–90.

[19] Ibid. pp. 288–91; Stueber, *Rediscovering Empathy*, pp. 5–19. The perceptual argument was still in circulation at the war's end. See for example Nathalie A. Duddington, 'Our Knowledge of Other Minds', *Proceedings of the Aristotelian Society*, 19 (1918–19), 147–78.

that became lost within *Einfühlung* ought to meet itself in abstraction's universal processes of discomfort.[20] Rather than Hulme's binary opposition we have in Worringer the following view: 'these two poles [empathy and abstraction] are only gradations of a common need, which is revealed to us as the deepest and ultimate essence of all aesthetic experience: this is the need for self-alienation.'[21] Worringer described this as the locking of an eternal knot. He illustrated and exaggerated the point with the image of the serpent eating its own tail, strategically placed on the cover of his book. What Worringer initially proposed then was abstraction as a cognitively superior version of empathy, one that he wanted to distinguish from the mirroring aspects of empathy suggested by Theodor Lipps. It achieved its effects by arresting the flow of time, seizing the object, conveniently for Hulme at this time in his intellectual development, from duration.[22]

We might argue then that Worringer's concept of abstraction was primarily an anti-naturalistic strategy. It served as a synonym for personal style. Only much later did Worringer recognise that modern artists had begun the reappropriation of the primitive from non-western modes of art. There is some confusion here. Helen Carr (2006), for example, has linked Georg Simmel's support for Worringer's ideas about primitive art to Worringer's preface in the third edition of *Abstraktion und Einfühlung*.[23] Worringer dates that preface November 1910. Simmel's backing here is particularly important given the emphasis he placed in 'Die Großstädte und das Geistesleben' [The Metropolis and Mental Life] (1903) on the links between urban life and primitive battles with nature. However, Worringer did not introduce Simmel's sponsorship of his project until he revised the preface in an edition of May 1948. Worringer explained the delay in documenting this as the indulgence of old age, but it certainly also created a coherent and consistent narrative for modernist primitivism.[24] Simmel's support may have come at any point up to his death in September 1918. Which Worringer did Hulme hear then in 1913?

Hulme's account of Worringer in the Quest lecture only creates further problems. It performed a complete separation of Worringer's snake. By shifting to a

---

[20] David Morgan, 'The Enchantment of Art: Abstraction and Empathy from German Romanticism to Expressionism', *Journal of the History of Ideas*, 57.2 (April 1996), 317–41.

[21] Wilhelm Worringer, *Abstraction and Empathy: A Contribution to the Psychology of Style* (1908), trans. by Michael Bullock (London: Routledge & Kegan Paul, 1953; repr. Chicago: Elephant Paperbacks, 1997), p. 23.

[22] Koss, p. 149.

[23] Helen Carr, 'T. E. Hulme and the "Spiritual Dread of Space"', in *T. E. Hulme and the Question of Modernism*, ed. by Edward P. Comentale and Andrzej Gasiorek (Farnham: Ashgate Publishing, 2006; repr. Abingdon: Routledge, 2016), pp. 93–112 (pp. 103–5).

[24] Mary Gluck, 'Interpreting Primitivism, Mass Culture and Modernism: The Making of Wilhelm Worringer's *Abstraction and Empathy*', *New German Critique*, 80 (Spring–Summer 2000), 149–69.

binary geometrical and vital impulse in art, Hulme argued for a further version of *Einfühlung*. It returned to the pre-history of empathy in German Romanticism, a pantheistic account long discredited by Wilhelm Dilthey and Robert Vischer, the latter the chief architect of *Einfühlung*. As Hulme described it to the Quest Society, in vital art 'there is always a feeling of liking for, and pleasure in, the forms and movements to be found in nature'.[25] This sounds more like a rebuttal of an emergent *élan vital* than an intervention in the debate on empathy. This is not to rule out the idea that Hulme was deeply suspicious of a certain concept of empathy. It does mean though that we need to be extremely cautious with Hulme and the alleged certainties in his account. Whilst his work might appear to warn us against any account of the intra-war modernisms that looked to place value on the sympathetic imagination, Hulme's obvious ideological intent, coupled to his conservatism, suggests his true target was the latent Romanticism within Bergsonism.[26]

On the eve of war, the seeds of the challenge that would appear from combat gnosticism were already growing within modernist aesthetics. Whilst laying claim to the inner mysteries of soma and psyche neither the literary impression nor the Image, nor the geometric art sketched out by Hulme, created a truly stable notion as to how the very precise mechanics of subjective representation might become an account of the Other's mind. While such ambivalence might go untested within the safe and leisured space of *Einfühlung*, a space which created a common substrate of experience through deliberate exclusion of that which is other, what then of the space of war? To use Ford's words from 'On Impressionism' (1914), how should an artist whose main task is to give the 'reader the impression that he was witnessing something real, that he was passing through an experience', deal with a technological modernity marked by the increasing bifurcation of human experience?[27] How should an artist, again to use Ford's phraseology, this time from an essay of 1920 on W. H. Hudson, fulfil the public's demand for vicarious experience in a society marked by patterns of ordinary life that broke apart the common substrate demanded by analogy and logical inference?[28] Ford's gendering was an obvious symptom of the very problem.

[25] T. E. Hulme, 'Modern Art and its Philosophy' (1924), in *The Collected Writings of T. E. Hulme*, ed. by Karen Csengeri (Oxford: Clarendon Press, 1994), pp. 268–85 (p. 273).

[26] Michael H. Whitworth, 'Introduction', in *Modernism*, ed. by Michael H. Whitworth (Malden, MA: Blackwell, 2007), pp. 3–60 (pp. 28–9); Oliver Tearle, *T. E. Hulme and Modernism* (London: Bloomsbury, 2013), p. 105.

[27] Ford Madox Hueffer [Ford Madox Ford], 'On Impressionism' (1914), in *Critical Writings of Ford Madox Ford*, pp. 33–55 (p. 42).

[28] Ford Madox Ford, 'W. H. Hudson: Some Reminiscences', *Little Review*, 7.1 (May–June 1920), 3–12 (p. 12).

RIDICULE AND THE NEW PATRIOTIC VERSE

There was little time for these modernisms to catch breath once the war broke. The poetic outpouring was so swift following the declaration of war on 4 August 1914 that Chatto & Windus had an anthology ready by the end of October. *Poems of the Great War* (1914), published on behalf of the Prince of Wales's National Relief Fund, included poems by Laurence Binyon, Robert Bridges, G. K. Chesterton, John Drinkwater, Rudyard Kipling, Henry Newbolt and Alfred Noyes. Several had already appeared in publications ranging from the *Daily Chronicle* to *Punch*. John Lane's *Songs and Sonnets for England in War Time* (1914) soon followed for the same cause. It added Gilbert Cannan, Thomas Hardy, Evelyn Underhill and even the Bishop of Lincoln to the mix. Methuen, with *Remember Louvain! A Little Book of Liberty and War* (1914), and Cope and Fenwick, with *Lord God of Battles: A War Anthology* (1914), added new voices to the literary greats.

We now tend to think of this body of poetry through the singular frame of an early patriotic verse. This verse often shows jingoism, naive enthusiasm and an ignorance of combat. It is a mood that we contrast to the later emphasis in the trench lyric on the *unheimlich* nature of battle. This is however a simplistic narrative of a diverse body of work as Elizabeth Vandiver (2013) best explains.[29] These early anthologies are certainly distinct, for example, from the combatant poems of Rupert Brooke, especially his '1914' (*New Numbers*: January 1915; *October 1914*), and from Julian Grenfell's 'Into Battle' (*The Times*: May 1915; *April 1915*). We can read these poems as sentimental more than jingoistic. Nonetheless, it is clear from *The Egoist*, the *Little Review*, the *New Age* and the *TLS* that the modernists made no distinctions within the broad genre of war writing. They treated any poetry of war as a single and ugly generic instance.

Pound was the first of those dissenting voices. He demanded that the 'twopenny poets' in 'War Verse (1914)' (1988; *September 1914*) put down their 'pop-guns'.[30] A few weeks later, Edward Shanks said he had already had enough of the outpouring of war poetry:

> We have had lyrical outrages from railway porters, dairymen, postmen, road scavengers, and what not, with their names and professions duly appended, in the delectable fashion set some time ago by *The English Review*. Meanwhile, in France, young poets are killing one another.[31]

---

[29] Elizabeth Vandiver, 'Early Poets of the First World War', in Das, ed., pp. 69–80 (pp. 69–70).

[30] Ezra Pound, 'War Verse (1914)', in Ezra Pound, *Poems and Translations*, ed. by Richard Sieburth (New York: Library of America, 2003), p. 1176. Given there is no widely available scholarly edition of Pound's poetry, references to his poetry include the details of both volume/journal of first publication (where available) and *Poems and Translations*, the most complete single volume.

[31] E. Buxton Shanks, 'London Letter', *Little Review*, 1.9 (December 1914), 55–7 (p. 55).

Timeline 1.1 September 1914–February 1915

	Composition	*Publication, Exhibition, Event*
1914		
September	Eliot, 'Morning at the Window' Lawrence, 'Study of Thomas Hardy' (1936) Monro, 'Youth in Arms' Pound, 'War Verse'	Binyon, 'For the Fallen' (*Times*) Pound and Eliot first meeting
October	Brooke, '1914' Ford, *Antwerp* Pound, 'Provincia Deserta' Stevens, 'Phases'	Eliot at Oxford Gibson, 'Breakfast', 'Messages' (*Nation*) *Poems of the Great War*
November	Gaudier-Brzeska, 'Vortex' Lawrence, 'Ecce Homo', redrafts *Rainbow* Sinclair, 'Field Ambulance in Retreat' Yeats, 'Meditation in Time of War'	Lawrence, *The Prussian Officer* Marinetti, 'War, the Only Hygiene' (*Little Review*) (1911) 'Poems of War' (*Poetry*) Sandburg, 'Among the Red Guns' (*Poetry*) Sinclair, serialisation of 'Journal of Impressions' (*English Review*) Stevens, 'Phases' (*Poetry*)
December	Brooke, '1914' Hulme, 'Diary from the Trenches' (1955) Pound, *Cathay* Thomas, 'March', 'Old Man', 'The Combe'	Lawrence, 'Service of all the Dead' (*Poetry*) (*New Statesman*: November 1913) Monro, *Children of Love* Pound, 'Dead Iönè' (*Poetry*)
1915		
January	Freud, 'Mourning and Melancholia' (1917) Thomas, 'A Private', 'Adlestrop', 'Tears'	Ford, *Antwerp* *King Albert's Book* including Sinclair 'Field Ambulance in Retreat' Pound and Yeats at Stone Cottage Pound, 'Webster Ford' (*Egoist*) Zeppelin raids on England
February	Eliot poems incl. 'Afternoon', 'In the Department Store', 'Paysage Triste', 'Suppressed Complex' (1988) Pound, 'The Coming of War', '1915: February' Thomas, 'The Owl' Yeats, 'A Reason for Keeping Silent'	Aldington list of dead/wounded (*Egoist*) Battles: Dardanelles Campaign begins Brooke, '1914' (*New Numbers*) Myers, 'Study of Shell Shock' (*Lancet*) Sandburg, 'Buttons' (*Masses*)

Guide to Timelines

Works arranged in alphabetical order within each month.

Publication dates given in parenthesis, except if given in the main text, endnotes or elsewhere in timelines.

Titles shortened for brevity.

Shanks's outrage typified a widespread sense of violation at the piercing of bourgeois salon culture, that space ordinarily reserved for *Einfühlung*, by the labouring classes. Meanwhile, we could add, young railway porters and their like were killing each other in France too.

Most critics agreed with him. Separating out sentiment from patriotism, John Middleton Murry wrote in the *TLS* that 'it is odious not to love one's country, but it is ridiculous to express that love in certain fashions'.[32] Parody was John Gould Fletcher's weapon too in *The Egoist*. He scornfully recommended that everyone should go out and buy a copy of Chatto's anthology and send it to the Kaiser. 'The German Army will explode with laughter,' he said, 'and everyone will see that "poetry, or at any rate verse," is of some use after all.'[33] Two weeks later, Fletcher was even more scathing when he took apart competing anthologies. He found them full of the insincerity and sentimentalism *The Egoist* had long claimed to lie at the heart of modern poetry.[34] This was a foretaste of T. S. Eliot's critique of sentimentality and of what Pound would classify in 1918 as 'sob-stuff'.[35] It also anticipated Yeats's infamous assertion that his 'distaste' for the trench lyric reflected the view that 'passive suffering is not a theme for poetry'.[36] *The Egoist* was quick to advertise Fletcher's articles as a series that had 'amusingly exposed the stupidity of these "fake" productions'.[37]

Astutely recognising the change in public demand, *Poetry* in contrast offered '$100 for a War Poem' in September. There were over 700 entries. Eliot drafted a poem for the contest entitled 'Up Boys and at 'em!' and he sent it as a private joke to Conrad Aiken on 30 September. It is ugly homophobic doggerel.[38] In 'Phases' (1989; *October 1914*), Wallace Stevens took on the jingoists and sentimentalists with their 'crisp, sonorous epics / Mongered after every scene'.[39]

---

[32] [John Middleton Murry], 'The French Poetry of the Franco-German War', *TLS*, 660 (10 September 1914), 416.

[33] John Gould Fletcher, 'War Poetry', *The Egoist*, 1.21 (2 November 1914), 410–11 (p. 411).

[34] John Gould Fletcher, 'More War Poetry', *The Egoist*, 1.22 (16 November 1914), 424–6 (p. 426). Similarly, see A. E. Watts, 'Pastiche: Echoes of Croce', *New Age*, 18.2 (11 November 1915), 45.

[35] Ezra Pound, 'Breviora', *Little Review*, 5.6 (October 1918), 23–4 (p. 23).

[36] W. B. Yeats, 'Introduction to *The Oxford Book of Modern Verse*' (1936), in *The Collected Works of W. B. Yeats*, ed. by Richard J. Finneran and George Mills Harper, 14 vols (New York: Scribner and others, 1989–2015), V: *Later Essays*, ed. by William H. O'Donnell (New York: Charles Scribner's Sons, 1994), pp. 181–203 (p. 199).

[37] [Advertisement], '*The Egoist*: An Individualist Review', *Poetry*, 5.5 (February 1915), [258].

[38] T. S. Eliot, letter to Conrad Aiken (30 September 1914), in *The Letters of T. S. Eliot*, ed. by Valerie Eliot, John Haffenden and Hugh Haughton, 9 vols to date (London: Faber and Faber, 1988–), I: *1898–1922*, ed. by Valerie Eliot and Hugh Haughton, rev. edn (2009), pp. 62–4 (p. 64).

[39] Wallace Stevens, 'Phases', in Wallace Stevens, *Collected Poetry and Prose*, ed. by Frank Kermode and Joan Richardson (New York: Library of America, 1997), pp. 525–9 (p. 527). As late contributions to Monroe's competition (which Stevens sent under a pseudonym), Monroe had space to publish only four sections (II–V) of the eleven-poem sequence in November. Wallace Stevens, 'Phases', *Poetry*, 5.2 (November 1914), 70–1; Robert Buttel, *Wallace Stevens: The Making of 'Harmonium'* (Princeton: Princeton University Press, 1967), p. 231 n. 2.

'Mongered' evokes the tropes used by Pound and Shanks. These soldier-poets traded in commodity goods; they were not the architects of something valuable or patentable.[40] Pound, who was appalled at the whole fiasco, labelled the competition 'the war-poem scandal' in an incredulous letter to Harriet Monroe.[41] *Poetry's* 'War Poems Prize Awards' edition appeared nonetheless in November with Louise Driscoll's prizewinning poem alongside submissions by Richard Aldington, Maxwell Bodenheim, Joseph Campbell, Carl Sandburg and Stevens.[42]

D. H. Lawrence was outraged too. Upon receipt of *Poetry*, he drafted a quick response. Initially entitled 'Ecce Homo', it was published by *The Egoist* as 'Eloi, Eloi, Lama Sabachthani?' in the Imagist edition of May 1915. In a characteristic outburst Lawrence told Monroe that *Poetry's* war poets had extraordinarily little tolerance for emotional pressure. 'Their safety valve goes off at the high scream when the pressure is still so low,' he said.[43] This was to be a consistent theme in the modernist opposition to the poetries of war. To Lawrence and others, the genre was the mere spilling out of emotion; it was a failure of language to containerise affect. Or as Harold Monro noted in *Poetry and Drama* in less dramatic terms during September 1914, 'the effects of war are [. . .] apt to stimulate poetry, but they do not necessarily produce it'.[44] This may well be good criticism, especially at this stage of the war. It did serve to expose a strain of the crass commercialism that Douglas Goldring later exposed in the pages of *Art and Letters*.[45] Goldring went even further in the *Chapbook* by suggesting that the promotion of war verse was an example of the many frauds the media and popular culture used to hoodwink readers.[46]

'Good criticism' does not however fully explain either the speed or the force of these angry responses to this generic incursion. It does not account for a recurrent willingness to figure this genre as a foreign object within the (organic) system. Shanks described war verse as 'merely a sloughing of the old skin, a last

---

[40] In *Minaret* (February 1916), Shaemas O'Sheel vociferously argued against Stevens's poem. Shaemas O'Sheel, 'from "Chicago Poets and Poetry"', in *Wallace Stevens: The Critical Heritage*, ed. by Charles Doyle (London: Routledge, 1985), pp. 25–6 (p. 26).

[41] Ezra Pound, letter to Harriet Monroe (2 October 1915), in *The Letters of Ezra Pound 1907–1941*, ed. by D. D. Paige (London: Faber and Faber, 1951), p. 109.

[42] [Anonymous], *Poetry*, 5.2 (November 1914), [cover].

[43] D. H. Lawrence, letter to Harriet Monroe (17 November 1914), in *The Letters of D. H. Lawrence*, ed. by James T. Boulton and others, The Cambridge Edition, 8 vols (Cambridge: Cambridge University Press, 1979–2000), II: *June 1913–October 1916*, ed. by George J. Zytaruk and James T. Boulton (1981), pp. 232–3 (p. 232).

[44] [Harold Monro], 'Varia Notes News: War Poetry', *Poetry and Drama*, 2.3 (September 1914), 250.

[45] Douglas Goldring, 'An Appreciation of D. H. Lawrence', *Art and Letters*, 2.2 (Spring 1919), 89–99 (p. 90).

[46] Douglas Goldring, 'Modern Critical Prose', *Chapbook*, 2.8 (February 1920), 7–14 (p. 7). Similarly, C.F., 'Montmartre at War', *The Athenæum*, 4704 (25 June 1920), 844.

discharge of the old disease'.[47] In *Blast* Lewis described 'a certain sort of black-guard', one 'who uses the blood of the Soldier for his own everyday domestic uses'.[48] For F. S. Flint, 'war verse which is mere foaming at the mouth, or worse, expectoration, or tedious rhetoric and eloquence, or simply silly declamation, I do not touch.'[49] These modernists conceived war verse as uncontrolled affect. It was a form of pure *parole*, a verse that eventually evaporated as soon as it touched the lips.

Pound consistently linked the genre to the digestive system. 'Most of the war verse has been such slop,' he told Monroe in February 1915.[50] And then again two years later that 'undigested war is no better than undigested anything else'. He proposed there was no real aesthetic difference or historical distinction between the work of Binyon, Brooke and Charles Sorley. 'Now no one has time to digest,' Pound went on.[51] This resulted in a bolus that eventually and inevitably found its way down the alimentary canal:

> 'Il est la guerre!' I wish I could recapture the accent of that phrase as used by a fine and permanent writer, as used, to be frank, by De Bosschère himself, to analyse, summarize, and finally excrete a popular figment of transient imprint and publication. De Bosschère is not 'la guerre', he is 'a man who has come back from that country'.[52]

Tropes like this would survive well into 1919 when the influenza epidemic replaced sputum and excreta. Murry's line in *The Athenæum* was to define the boom in intra-war poetry as a form of actual harm to the body of cultural consciousness.[53] *Coterie* chose to deploy the *Daily Herald*'s description of war verse as something '"like an everlasting Spanish influenza epidemic"'.[54] Aldous Huxley continued the *Chapbook*'s line. He feared the tidal wave of poetry had 'threatened, during the last two years of the war, to swamp our literature completely'.[55] For Pound it was a 'flood of "war" poetry'.[56] In 'A Brief Treatise on

---

[47] Shanks, p. 57.

[48] Wyndham Lewis, 'The Exploitation of Blood', *Blast*, 2 (July 1915), 24.

[49] F. S. Flint, 'Some Modern French Poets (A Commentary with Specimens)', *Monthly Chapbook*, 4.1 (October 1919), 2.

[50] Ezra Pound, letter to Harriet Monroe (20 February 1915), qtd in Longenbach, *Stone Cottage*, p. 119.

[51] Ezra Pound, letter to Harriet Monroe (26 August 1917), in *The Letters of Ezra Pound*, pp. 175–7 (p. 176).

[52] Ezra Pound, 'Durability and De Bosschère's Presentation', *Art and Letters*, 2.3 (Summer 1919), 125–6 (p. 126).

[53] M. [John Middleton Murry], 'Intimations of Mortality', *The Athenæum*, 4683 (30 January 1920), 133–4 (p. 134).

[54] Qtd in [Anonymous] [Russell Green?], 'Editorial', *Coterie*, 6–7 (Winter 1920–21), 3–5 (p. 3).

[55] Aldous Huxley, 'The Subject-Matter of Poetry', *Chapbook*, 2.9 (March 1920), 11–16 (p. 15).

[56] Pound, 'Durability and De Bosschère's Presentation', p. 126.

the Criticism of Poetry' (1920), Eliot identified the emergence of 'an enormous mass of verse' accompanied by 'an enormous mass of appreciations of this verse'.[57] Amateurism threatened to engulf and to suffocate.

THEORISING AFTERWARDNESS

Why protest so loudly about something so allegedly appalling? We can reserve psychological explanations for the Conclusion. Monro supplied a more obvious explanatory clue in his article in *Poetry and Drama*. He concluded that 'in a civilised age they [the effects of war] will more probably be revealed after than during the event'.[58] This sets up a clear distinction between experience and art. It is like Lawrence's rage. The white heat of immediate affective experience was not the natural space of artistic reflection. The gilded salon of *Einfühlung* was anathema to event; poetry as opposed to verse arose after and not during action. It took its source from repose and reflection, the soothing balm of serotonin rather than the motivating kick of cortisol.

This was Edward Thomas's theme in the first extended meditation on the new genre in the December edition of *Poetry and Drama*. War poetry, Thomas claimed, must always be ephemeral because no other class of poetry disappears so quickly. 'The public, crammed with mighty facts and ideas it will never digest, must look coldly on poetry where already those mighty things have sunk away far into "The still sad music of humanity"', he concluded.[59] Digestion again. Here Thomas's emphasis is on poetry's durability and its contrast to the momentary joys and fears that arise from an event. A poetry attuned to event, Thomas suggested, must always collapse by necessity into epithalamium, panegyric, philippic and encomium, making war poetry one extreme moment of flourishing in the long but chequered history of occasional verse. Not then a poetry at all.

Thomas's hostility repurposed a long tradition of animosity to poetic occasionality. Based on a perceived entangled relationship to life and a consequent dependence on it, the position was obviously ideological although Thomas presented it as an accepted law.[60] Others have looked on the genre differently. Stéphane Mallarmé saw *vers d'occasion* [occasional verse] as a *vers de circonstances* [verse of circumstances], a poetics of the ordinary or of everyday life. The Hegelian concept of *pièces d'occasion* [occasional pieces] suggests the genre

---

[57] T. S. Eliot, 'A Brief Treatise on the Criticism of Poetry', in *The Perfect Critic, 1919–1926*, pp. 202–11 (p. 202).

[58] [Monro], 'Varia Notes News', p. 250. See as a later example of the same points Marianne Moore, 'Reinforcements', *The Egoist*, 5.6 (June–July 1918), 83.

[59] Thomas's subject was patriotic war poetry. Edward Thomas, 'War Poetry', in *A Language Not to Be Betrayed: Selected Prose of Edward Thomas*, ed. by Edna Longley (Manchester: Carcanet, 1981), pp. 131–5 (pp. 131, 132).

[60] Marian Zwerling Sugano, *The Poetics of the Occasion: Mallarmé and the Poetry of Circumstance* (Stanford: Stanford University Press, 1992), p. 4.

as one means to break poetic isolationism and reconnect the naturally reclusive tendencies of poetry to a living world.[61] It is entirely plausible to read the earliest poetic products of war as both occasional and as sympathetic expressions of collective emotion, as a communal product poets produced to assuage a social (rather than a purely egoistic) sense of shock.[62] That was not however the line taken by Thomas. His 'war poetry', at this stage of his critical career, was 'the hour of the writer who picks up popular views or phrases, or coins them, and has the power to turn them into downright stanzas'.[63] Following the established critical theme, the war poet was a linguistic central banker. He monetised public opinion by churning out ever more instruments of exchange.

Thomas's article avoided any clear statement on its theoretical basis. We can easily detect the antecedents though. 'I need hardly say that by becoming ripe for poetry the poet's thoughts may recede far from their original resemblance to all the world's, and may seem to have little to do with daily events,' Thomas proposed, offering experience, reality and truth as the alternative pathways to sentiment.[64] The interplay between receding, resembling and seeming suggests an Aristotelian ground. It reminds us of the poet's necessary subjunctive mood, in Aristotle's words taken from *On the Art of Poetry*, 'to describe, not the thing that has happened, but a kind of thing that might happen'.[65] By experience Thomas did not mean the fleshiness of lived experience but the experience that Aristotle describes in *Nicomachean Ethics*, *Metaphysics* and *Posterior Analytics*. That is, the experience that is part of a system resting on a hierarchy of values, one that begins with perception, moves from memory to experience, before it arrives at universals.[66] In that system, those with raw perceptual experience might recognise their case as similar to another but they lacked the ability to identify a common element that might mark off the class. They achieve only a ghostly foreshadowing of the universal unable to select what is relevant. To paraphrase Eliot's later terminology, in turn taken from F. H. Bradley, only the genuine artist can explain what it is that they know and what they do, while those trapped at the level of empirical experience cannot.[67]

---

[61] Ibid. pp. 1–2.

[62] For readings of a similar nature see Stephen Wilson, 'Poetry and its Occasions: "Undoing the Folded Lie"', in *A Companion to Poetic Genre*, ed. by Erik Martiny (Chichester: John Wiley, 2012), pp. 490–504.

[63] Thomas, 'War Poetry', p. 133.

[64] Ibid. pp. 132, 133.

[65] Aristotle, *On the Art of Poetry*, trans. by Ingram Bywater (Oxford: Clarendon Press, 1920; repr. 1988), p. 43.

[66] These are the same texts Eliot claimed played a crucial role in his own education at Oxford between October 1914 and June 1915. Robert Crawford, *Young Eliot: From St Louis to 'The Waste Land'* (London: Vintage, 2015), p. 215.

[67] Richard D. McKirahan Jr, *Principles and Proofs: Aristotle's Theory of Demonstrative Science* (Princeton: Princeton University Press, 1992), pp. 240–9.

Alongside these classical precepts we should also note an obvious strain of Romanticism in Thomas's harking back to '"the still sad music of humanity"'. It is an appeal to that seminal act of poetic witnessing at Tintern Abbey, to William Wordsworth's concept in *Lyrical Ballads* (1800) of 'emotion recollected in tranquillity' and its panoptic role in the discipline and control of 'the spontaneous overflow of powerful feelings'.[68] 'Tranquillity' would prove to be a ready-made concept in the intra-war period that allowed critics to summarily dismiss war verse. Aldington asked rhetorically in *The Egoist* of December 1914, for example, 'how can one be interested in poems about a war when the war is going on?' He said, 'the proper time to write about a war is afterwards—as [Walt] Whitman did. "Emotion remembered in tranquillity"—we shall get no war poem till peace is declared.'[69] Aldington was wrong about the compositional history of Whitman's *Drum-Taps* (1865), but this did not get in the way of his appeal to a poetical common sense.[70] Pound described Ford's injury on the Somme in August 1916 to John Quinn as 'shell shock, or nerve shock or something due to shell bursting too close for detached and placid literary contemplation of the precise "impression and the mot just required to render it"'.[71] Virginia Woolf suggested in 'Before Midnight' (*TLS*: March 1917) that 'the vast events now shaping across the Channel are towering over us too closely and too tremendously to be worked into fiction without a painful jolt in the perspective'.[72] Following combat Aldington would later claim that poetry was made through exposure to immediate experience rather than through style. Rebutting that conclusion in the *Little Review* William Carlos Williams argued that this could not be the case; there was simply some barrier between poetry and combat

---

[68] William Wordsworth, 'Preface: *Lyrical Ballads*, 1800 Edition', in Samuel Taylor Coleridge and William Wordsworth, *Lyrical Ballads 1798 and 1800*, ed. by Michael Gamer and Dahlia Porter (Peterborough, Ontario: Broadview Editions, 2008), pp. 171–87 (p. 183).

[69] Richard Aldington, 'War Poems and Others', *The Egoist*, 1.24 (15 December 1914), 458–9 (p. 459). Similarly, but much later, see Nelson Antrim Crawford, 'New War Poets', *Poetry*, 16.6 (September 1920), pp. 336–40 (p. 336).

[70] As Whitman described to Horace Traubel, he wrote them in a piecemeal fashion on the battlefield and in field hospitals. Roy Morris Jr, *The Better Angel: Walt Whitman in the Civil War* (New York: Oxford University Press, 2000), p. 144; Cody Marrs, *Nineteenth-Century American Literature and the Long Civil War* (Cambridge: Cambridge University Press, 2015), p. 27.

[71] Qtd in Max Saunders, *Ford Madox Ford: A Dual Life*, 2 vols (Oxford: Oxford University Press, 1996–2012), II: *The After-War World*, rev. edn (2012), p. 14.

[72] Virginia Woolf, 'Before Midnight', in *The Essays of Virginia Woolf*, ed. by Andrew McNeillie and Stuart N. Clarke, 6 vols (London: Hogarth Press, 1986–2011), II: *1912–1918*, ed. by Andrew McNeillie (London: Hogarth Press, 1987; repr. Orlando: Harcourt Brace Jovanovich, 1990), pp. 87–8 (p. 87).

---

since 'no poet was able to exist during and in the war'.[73] In 'The Daughter of Necessity' (*Voices*: April 1919), Murry defined the artist as 'he, who stood apart'.[74] Thomas Moult was still looking forward in January 1920 to the 'great poem of the war (when it comes, for it did not come from Flanders, nor will it come necessarily from one who has been a soldier)'.[75] We can summarise this attitude using Samuel Weinstein's review of the exhibition *The Nation's War Paintings* of December 1919. 'Are we not too near to War', Weinstein asked, 'to expect of it so quickly any real art-expression? We can record the shriek of pain, the languor, the comic relief. It is recorded a thousand times in these paintings. The dread experience has only just bitten into our blood and senses. It will be expressed in some later day.'[76] The very thing that combatant poetry claimed to be uniquely its own – its proximity to the event – became the very force that militated against it. What counted was the distance and reflection of the bystander.

These modernist responses argued that the wounding encounters of war were a permanent barrier to art. Ford's later prose would repeatedly confront this problem from the inside. We can trace its earliest expression though to an article by Remy de Gourmont translated by Aldington for *Poetry* in January 1915. It gave aesthetic afterwardness a scientific basis:

> During a battle the imagination has no time to work. A man is suddenly borne into surroundings which absorb and inspire him, while he blanches before a peril which he has had time to consider coldly. The best and happiest soldiers are the men without imagination. It is the same in ordinary life, which is also dangerous sometimes: imagination destroys the power for action.

Romantic tranquillity appears rooted in physiology here. Not a theory then but a fact hard-wired into human evolution. Absorption in an event severs the endocrinological response; it prevents the feedback loop between emotion and motor response. By literally stopping the imagination, it makes *écriture* impossible. Not only was this true at the emotional extremes, according to de

---

[73] William Carlos Williams, 'Four Foreigners', *Little Review*, 6.5 (September 1919), 36–9 (p. 36). For Aldington's claim see Richard Aldington, 'The Poetry of the Future', *Poetry*, 14.5 (August 1919), 266–9 (p. 267). For Aldington's response to Williams's essay see Richard Aldington, letter to Harriet Monroe (14 October 1919), qtd in Charles Doyle, *Richard Aldington: A Biography* (Basingstoke: Macmillan, 1989), p. 72.

[74] John Middleton Murry, 'The Daughter of Necessity', in John Middleton Murry, *The Evolution of an Intellectual* (New York: Alfred A. Knopf), pp. 50–8 (p. 57).

[75] Thomas Moult, 'The Poetic Futility of Flanders', *English Review*, 30 (January 1920), 68–71 (p. 71).

[76] S. Winsten [Samuel Weinstein], 'Notes on Present-Day Art: Painting', *Voices*, 3.2 (March 1920), 81–2 (p. 82).

Gourmont, but it was also true in daily life more generally and in such a way that poetry must always be anathema to event:

> It is for this reason that at this time I think above all of the poets, of the men of imagination, of the dreamers. They also make good soldiers, soldiers for the sake of duty, but they are more deserving of praise than the common people with their coarser brains, who only perceive evil at the moment they feel it themselves.

The class biases of *Einfühlung* are on display here again. There is also a strange inversion of the wounding experience. De Gourmont does not link the closing down of brain function to a repressive mechanism. It is the lack of proportion in the brain that means the common soldier (a phrase that will reappear in Chapter 4 in the work of Stevens) can simply ignore the evidence of the senses. The common soldier's immersion in battle allows him to set aside that 'there were so many killed' at Charleroi 'that the bed of the [River] Meuse was choked'.[77] It is the dreamers who shall inherit this earth. It is those who are so shocked by their ability to look beyond the present moment that they live in a state of suffering. De Gourmont vests them with an imagination that can see the permanent presence of evil in the world and the wound at the heart of self-consciousness.

This is slightly disingenuous: very few poets have written war during the most intense moments of battle, pen in one hand and gun in the other. The question is surely related to temporal distance. De Gourmont moves too far and does not untangle, perhaps intentionally, the moments within an event from the overall experience of that event. His argument was not however dissimilar to Sigmund Freud's contemporaneous 'Thoughts for the Times on War and Death', written around March–April 1915. For Freud, 'our intellect [. . .] can function reliably only when it is removed from the influences of strong emotional impulses; otherwise it behaves merely as an instrument of the will and delivers the inference which the will requires.'[78] Freud merges the imagination and the intellect here, but his point is the same. At some level of affective overload, the body becomes a logic machine. It does what the will tells it to do: move there, do that. Again, it is a pre-programmed survival instinct. Not only does this preference the logical world over the emotional world, a reality experienced through coldness, objectivity and reason rather than one explored through feelings, but the imagination dies in the heat of any battle. An emergent poetics of afterwardness it seemed had the support of the emergent sciences of physiology and psychology.

---

[77] Remy de Gourmont, 'French Poets and the War, translated by Richard Aldington', *Poetry*, 5.4 (January 1915), 184–8 (pp. 187–8).
[78] Freud, p. 287.

THE FIRST MODERNIST WAR POETRIES: D. H. LAWRENCE, FORD MADOX FORD, WALLACE STEVENS, W. B. YEATS

Despite their opposition, all the major Anglo-American modernist poets none-theless tried their hand at variants of the war poem. Pound's call for poetic silence in 'War Verse (1914)' was particularly illustrative. He ignored both his own advice that poets be silent and all the rules of Monroe's competition. He sent her his poem without the use of a pseudonym, and he asked that Monroe then print it anonymously.[79] Pound was offering commentary on the competi-tion, not an entry. '"These things are not written because somebody offers two months board,"' Pound lectured Monroe; '"no one is going to grind out a mas-terpiece on two weeks notice."'[80] Behind the ostensible call to silence there lay a counter strategy then, one that aimed to evict the amateur from the poetical stage to allow the professional's quiet return.

Yeats's poems of 1914–15 also tell us to look away from the combat theatre. In 'A Meditation in Time of War' (1920; *November 1914*), the narrator looks from the physical and aggressive qualities of humankind towards the consola-tion of a mystical unitary otherness: 'I knew that One is animate, / Mankind inanimate phantasy.'[81] That seems to be the position Yeats tried to adopt in 'A Reason for Keeping Silent' (January 1916; *February 1915*), a poem written for Edith Wharton's *The Book of the Homeless* (1916). Yeats told Henry James that this would be his last poem about war, although it certainly was not. He planned to spend the war instead consorting with 'the seven sleepers of Ephesus [. . .] till bloody frivolity is over', a disinterestedness that would later earn Yeats censure.[82] Yeats nonetheless repeatedly tinkered with the poem. He renamed it 'On being asked for a War Poem' (1917) when the Cuala Press published *The Wild Swans at Coole* (1917) and changed the opening lines. What was 'I think it better that at times like these / We poets keep our mouths shut' became 'I think it better that in times like these / A poet keep his mouth shut'.[83] Not

---

[79] Monroe wanted each entry to be subject to blind review. [Harriet Monroe], '$100 for a War Poem', *Poetry*, 4.6 (September 1914), 251; [Harriet Monroe], 'Notes', *Poetry*, 5.2 (November 1914), 96–7.

[80] Ezra Pound, letter to Harriet Monroe (15 September 1914), qtd in Longenbach, *Stone Cottage*, p. 114.

[81] W. B. Yeats, 'A Meditation in Time of War', in *The Collected Works of W. B. Yeats*, I: *The Poems*, ed. by Richard J. Finneran, 2nd edn (New York: Scribner, 1997), p. 192. On the problematic dating of this poem see Peter McDonald, *Serious Poetry: Form and Authority from Yeats to Hill* (Oxford: Clarendon Press, 2002), p. 20 n. 11. Composition may date as late as April 1917.

[82] W. B. Yeats, letter to Henry James (20 August 1915), qtd in McDonald, p. 19.

[83] W. B. Yeats, 'A Reason for Keeping Silent', in *The Book of the Homeless (Le livre des Sans-Foyer)*, ed. by Edith Wharton (New York: Charles Scribner, 1916), p. 45; W. B. Yeats, 'On being asked for a War Poem', in W. B. Yeats, *The Wild Swans at Coole, Other Verses and a Play in Verse* (Dundrum: Cuala Press, 1917), p. 16.

satisfied, the second line would be altered again in *The Collected Poems of W. B. Yeats* (1933) to 'A poet's mouth be silent'.[84] The change of pronouns and the gendering alters the poet's relationship to peers. The change distinguishes between amateur versifiers and the genuine poetic article. The final shift from the colloquialism of keeping one's mouth shut also holds out the possibility that *écriture* might survive *parole*.

These changes served to make more explicit what was implicit in the poem of 1915. The poem originally argued for silence through the claim that 'We have no gift to set a statesman right; / He's had enough of meddling who can please / A young girl in the indolence of her youth'.[85] Who is it though who has had 'enough'? The 'he' implicates the 'statesman'. What is 'he' doing in the poet's business though? Could the 'he' be just one of the 'we'? Is it the poet calling time on the 'meddling' in the business of the 'statesman', or is the 'statesman' the one concerned at the 'meddling'? The confusion is surely Yeats's point: the statesman and the poet should both stick to their own lanes. Except of course for the brute fact of the poem. Yeats's instruction to keep silent was, like that of Pound before him, the very means by which he vested the poet with the right to speak. This was whispering not silence.

Also take Lawrence's confused attitude to 'Ecce Homo'. Lawrence wrote it hastily. He was frustrated by the heartbreaking consequences of war and the ineptitude of *Poetry*'s contributors. 'I don't care what you do with my war poem,' Lawrence told Monroe. 'I don't particularly care if I don't hear of it any more.' There was nonetheless a good deal of care. Lawrence sent the 'war poem' to close friends such as S. S. Koteliansky and to J. C. Squire at the *New Statesman*. The letter to Monroe ends with the request that the editor 'take care how you regard my war poem – it is good'.[86] Lawrence flung out the poem in disgust on the one hand and yet wanted Monroe to tend it with absolute care. Such abjection surely signals both a fear of the real and an entangled desire to meet it. Lawrence was resistant to any further criticism. When Aldington asked for Lawrence to shorten it, it nevertheless appeared in *The Egoist* in full.[87]

Ford's *Antwerp* (January 1915; *October 1914*), composed amidst the drama surrounding Monroe's prize, is especially illustrative of this interplay between disgust and voyeurism. The poem focuses on the poet-narrator's inability to understand the decision by the Belgians not to allow Germany passage through its territory in 1914. It was a decision that compromised the German offer of

---

[84] W. B. Yeats, 'On being asked for a War Poem', in *The Poems*, p. 156. Published as 'On being asked for a War Poem' (1933) in *The Collected Poems of W. B. Yeats*.

[85] Yeats, 'A Reason for Keeping Silent', p. 45.

[86] Lawrence, letter to Monroe (17 November 1914), pp. 232–3.

[87] Richard Aldington, letter to Amy Lowell (5 April 1915), in *Richard Aldington: An Autobiography in Letters*, ed. by Norman T. Gates (University Park: Pennsylvania State University Press, 1992), pp. 12–16 (p. 12).

neutrality and brought Belgium into a battle it could never hope to win. The poem's opening sections have a self-conscious and doggerel quality. It opens with the bathos of the word 'GLOOM!'. It takes its momentum from there as it forces and exaggerates its rhymes: it hooks 'dived' to 'hived', 'anthem' to 'them' and 'Allah's' to 'Valhallas'. Given the poem's message, in keeping with the didacticism of Pound and Yeats, that 'it is not for us [poets] to make them [the Belgians] an anthem', it is hard not to see it as again partly parodic.[88] In 'The Vigil', for example, famously published on the front page of *The Times* on 5 August 1914, Newbolt created rhymes from a whole series of unlikely pairings, most notably from the words ruth (an archaic term, even in 1914, for grief) and truth.

Ford, we might suggest, was asking poets to reconsider the ease with which a rhyme might appear to mind and yet carry very real consequences in the world. In the Belgian case, abstract concepts such as glory, freedom and honour had led to brutal consequences. Ford's use of eye rhyme – 'For you cannot praise it with words / Compounded of lyres and swords' – makes concrete the link between language and blood.[89] We are faced then with a lonely and stranded Belgian soldier at the instant of his death, when the 'grey mud / Is turned to a brown purple drain'. The mimicry stops abruptly. The appalling reality of the situation, its pointlessness and the sense of loss, arrests the parody. The soldier 'lies, an unsightly lump on the sodden grass . . . / An image that shall take long to pass!'[90] Whilst entirely in keeping with Fletcher's exposé of war verse in *The Egoist*, the poem's subtlety, the links it makes between language and violence, helps go some way to explicating Eliot's observation in 'Reflections on Contemporary Poetry [III]' (*The Egoist*: November 1917) that *Antwerp* was 'the only good poem' on the war.[91]

This raises the question of Ford's own act of poetry making. Despite the instruction not to poeticise, here was a poem, one published as a standalone volume illustrated by Lewis. Ford's poem finds itself uncannily drawn to the image of the dead Belgian soldier. The image engraves itself on the poet's mind the poem tells us. The ultimate problem with this image is that there is and was no original version of it. Ford imagined it. It drags him compulsively into a war when he wants to stand at a distance: 'the thought of the gloom and the rain / And the ugly coated figure, standing beside a drain, / Shall eat itself into your brain'.[92] This landscape, the 'clutter of sodden corses / On the sodden Belgian grass', was for Ford 'a strange new beauty'.[93] As one of the first recognitions of a new form of mass violence this

---

[88] Ford Madox Hueffer [Ford Madox Ford], *Antwerp* (London: Poetry Bookshop, [1915]), p. [1].

[89] Ibid. p. [4].

[90] Ibid. p. [2].

[91] T. S. Eliot, 'Reflections on Contemporary Poetry [III]', in *The Complete Prose of T. S. Eliot*, I: *Apprentice Years, 1905–1918*, ed. by Jewel Spears Brooker and Ronald Schuchard (2014), pp. 608–12 (p. 610).

[92] [Ford], *Antwerp*, p. [4].

[93] Ibid. p. [3].

was surely the earliest instantiation of what Yeats would more famously describe as 'A terrible beauty' in 'Easter, 1916' (1916; *September 1916*).[94] Ford's poem seems then very much aware of its own complicity in the crime. It wants to look and wants at the same time not to look. It holds within itself the violent ability to make an aesthetic object of the real and in turn to influence action.

We can read Stevens's 'Phases' in the same way. This poem speaks of another imagined combatant's journey into battle. It also moves from parody to a position, less self-consciously than in Ford, which exposes its own desire to know something of this new felt experience of combat. In the third section we can find the poem searching for the right phrase to describe the catastrophe of battle:

> This was the salty taste of glory,
> That it was not
> Like Agamemnon's story.
> Only, an eyeball in the mud,
> And Hopkins
> Flat and pale and gory![95]

It highlights the modernists' need to turn to mythology to frame contemporary events. It is also an arresting image. It tries to transform the transparent Emersonian eyeball which absorbs nature as divine inspiration into the mud-caked opacity of a slaughter, the force of which rips the eye from its socket. It raises again the question though of what is the 'this' and 'that' with which the poem begins. Is it not an empty space? The battle itself is simply not there, and knowingly not there. The full sequence of poem glosses over the actual scene of battle in pursuit of this prefabricated image, a glimpse of the body in pieces except in an overly stylised manner. Unlike Ford's poem the bathos does not work in the final line. The exclamation mark is the point at which the epic frame collapses into the mundane. There is even the sense that the poem seeks refuge in comedy rather than allowing the horror of the grotesque to take hold. It seems aware of its own failure.

In 'Ecce Homo' Lawrence also insisted on imagining experience at the front line. Here the link between sexual desire and violence is the guiding motif:

> And when I ran across to the trenches
> And saw his face with blue eyes, startled, frightened, agonised,
> And I knew he wanted it, he wanted it
> Like a fierce magnet he drew my bayonet
> Like a spent shaft it sank to its rest[.]

[94] W. B. Yeats, 'Easter, 1916', in *The Poems*, pp. 182–4 (p. 183).
[95] Stevens, 'Phases', p. 526.

'I felt it crunch in his chest,' Lawrence wrote as he thought himself into the *qualia* of a murder scene.[96] This homoeroticism was unprecedented in 1914 and 1915 but the imagery lacks subtlety. Stevens at least recognised the emergence of a new type of military arsenal capable of somatic morcellation. In contrast, Lawrence's chosen weapon exemplified his remoteness from battle. As the title of the poem suggests – taken from Pilate's mocking description of degraded mankind following the flagellation and crowning of Christ with thorns – Lawrence's purpose was to see the war as a recurrence of the violence perpetuated by women against man's instinct of brotherhood.[97]

Ezra Pound's *Cathay*: The Poem in Nature

Irrespective of their success these poems defied the modernist instruction to avoid the war. Pound, despite his protestations, also felt the need to write war more fully in *Cathay* (April 1915; *December 1914*).[98] Unlike Ford's poem which subtly complicates the act of sympathetic imagination, there is something monolithic about Pound's imagination in this collection. It accords with the spirit of *Lebensphilosophie* taken over from his graduate work in philology. He was far from alone in these beliefs. The idea of a common and unchanging set of human emotions, of a humanity distinguished only by certain distinctive creative personalities, was widespread in pre-war cultures. In Jane Ellen Harrison's work, for example, intellectual divination was a form of sympathy. 'The first necessity', Harrison argued in her defence of historical analysis, 'is that by an effort of the sympathetic imagination we should think back the "many" we have so sharply and strenuously divided, into the haze of the primitive "one".'[99] This 'think[ing] back' was a re-inhabitation of the primitive mentality to recover true feeling.[100] As Shanyn Fiske (2013) describes it, this was an alternate way of knowing.[101] For Allen Upward in *The Divine Mystery* (1915), 'to the thoughtful mind all history is sacred' because 'there is a universe within him [man] as without; the network of his frame is a battleground wherein unseen and uncalculated forces meet and struggle for the mastery; his very thoughts are not his own, but the reincarnations of ancestral spirits, or else the angels

---

[96] D. H. Lawrence, '[Ecce Homo]', in D. H. Lawrence, *The Poems*, ed. by Christopher Pollnitz, The Cambridge Edition, 3 vols (Cambridge: Cambridge University Press, 2013–18), III: *Uncollected Poems and Early Versions* (2018), pp. 1515–16 (p. 1515).

[97] Several pages of this manuscript are unlocated and may hold a much fuller description of the front line. Lawrence, '[Ecce Homo]', p. 1515.

[98] Both Kenner, p. 202 and Longenbach, *Stone Cottage*, p. 116 argue for *Cathay* as a war poetry.

[99] Harrison, *Prolegomena*, p. 164.

[100] Harrison, *Themis*, p. 178.

[101] Shanyn Fiske, 'From Ritual to the Archaic in Modernism: Frazer, Harrison, Freud, and the Persistence of Myth', in *A Handbook of Modernism Studies*, ed. by Jean-Michel Rabaté (Chichester: John Wiley, 2013), pp. 173–91 (pp. 180–5).

of heavenly and hellish powers'.[102] This model of the unique within the general was contiguous with Pound's model of *virtù* in 'I Gather the Limbs of Osiris' (*New Age*: November 1911–February 1912). In Robert T. Kern's words from *Orientalism, Modernism, and the American Poem* (1996), it was that essential element within a universal or transcendental soul which distinguished and held back the individual from those around him, and which, in certain hands, became art.[103] We see it as early as Pound's poem 'Histrion' (1908) and again in the essay 'Religio or, The Child's Guide to Knowledge' (1913) where the gods function as metaphors of an eternal mood or state of mind.[104] Such theories underpinned the entire shape of *The Cantos* (1954–87), especially Pound's deployment of what he termed 'the "repeat in history"', that is of history as a series of echoes which eventually touch the sacred.[105] Pound did doubt, as Chapter 3 illustrates, but on the whole he would repeatedly manage to banish historical relativism by replacing it with the idea of history as an unchangeable system of values.[106] It would not be until 1939, ahead of another world war, that Pound admitted modernity might be hampered by its lack of a common spiritual and moral system. 'I haven't an Aquinas-map, Aquinas *not* valid now,' he told Hubert Creekmore.[107] It was a belatedness with vicious consequences.

Unlike the imagined war poems that precede it, *Cathay* used this theoretical grounding to offer a solution to afterwardness. That is, it aimed to solve the problem of how a poet might gain the necessary distance from the chaos of affect and yet still be able to imagine the experience of another immediate historical being. Chapter 2 will describe how this position shifted and Chapter 5 how Eliot entirely recalibrated it, but at this stage Pound's solution did not depend on other fleshwitness accounts of war. Pound knew full well from his primary sourcebook for *Cathay*, Herbert Giles's *A History of Chinese Literature* (1901), that one of the poets he was translating, Li Po, was no combatant. On the contrary, as Giles explained, the poet lived a 'wild Bohemian life', a 'gay and dissipated career at Court', and died by drowning 'in a drunken effort to

---

[102] Allen Upward, *The Divine Mystery: A Reading of the History of Christianity Down to the Time of Christ* (Boston: Houghton Mifflin, 1915), p. xiv.

[103] Robert T. Kern, *Orientalism, Modernism, and the American Poem* (Cambridge: Cambridge University Press, 1996), pp. 202–5.

[104] Ezra Pound, 'Religio or, The Child's Guide to Knowledge' (1913), in Pound, *Selected Prose*, pp. 47–8 (p. 47). See also Longenbach, *Modernist Poetics of History*, pp. 30–1.

[105] Ezra Pound, letter to Homer L. Pound (11 April 1927), in *The Letters of Ezra Pound*, pp. 284–6 (p. 285).

[106] Michael North, *The Political Aesthetic of Yeats, Eliot, and Pound* (Cambridge: Cambridge University Press, 1991), pp. 142–4.

[107] Ezra Pound, letter to Hubert Creekmore (February 1939), in *The Letters of Ezra Pound*, pp. 417–18 (p. 418).

embrace the reflection of the moon'.[108] For Pound the problem of combat gnosticism simply did not exist as a problem within a theory of emotion divorced from cultural and historical specificity. If all emotion is the same throughout time, there are no limits to the sympathetic imagination. There is only the question of skill.

Several scholars, most clearly Zhaoming Qian in *Orientalism and Modernism* (1995), describe how Pound freely altered his source material to emphasise the point.[109] *Cathay* pares back the affective life of all its combatants to the most basic human emotions. In 'Song of the Bowmen of Shu' they are tired, 'hungry and thirsty', homesick and uncomfortable.[110] The 'Lament of the Frontier Guard', the sense of exclusion from a society tearing itself apart, is a simple repetition: 'And sorrow, sorrow like rain. / Sorrow to go, and sorrow, sorrow returning, / Desolate, desolate fields'.[111] Lice pester the narrator of 'South-Folk in Cold Country'.[112] These are hard-wired and universal somatic responses, unchanging it seems throughout time and place, akin to the physiological models of de Gourmont.

Pound structured these poems as an answer to whether individual experience might be narrativised for posterity. The bowman asks, 'who will know of our grief?'[113] The frontier guard wonders ironically 'how shall you know the dreary sorrow at the North Gate' once the poet and soldiers are dead.[114] And the narrator in 'South-Folk in Cold Country' asks, 'Who will be sorry for General Rishogu?'[115] In other words, how can the immediate experience endure, how can the reader continue to know these feelings? To which the poems give their own answer: emotions are constant and enduring, war is always like this, Li Po is the proof of that, and the skilful poet need only create the proper tone or a mood which captures, according to the lessons of the 'Cold Country', the idea that all 'Emotion is born out of habit'.[116]

It is a position very much consistent with the source material, what we can term the *materia poetica*, Pound received from the front line. Gaudier-Brzeska

---

[108] Herbert A. Giles, *A History of Chinese Literature* (New York: D. Appleton, 1901; repr. 1927), pp. 151, 153.

[109] Zhaoming Qian, *Orientalism and Modernism: The Legacy of China in Pound and Williams* (Durham, NC: Duke University Press, 1995), pp. 73–6.

[110] Ezra Pound, 'Song of the Bowmen of Shu', in *Cathay: For the Most Part from the Chinese of Rihaku, from the Notes of the Late Ernest Fenollosa, and the Decipherings of the Professors Mori and Ariga* (London: Elkin Mathews, 1915), pp. 5–6 (p. 5) (*Poems and Translations*, p. 249).

[111] Ezra Pound, 'Lament of the Frontier Guard', in *Cathay*, pp. 16–17 (p. 16) (*Poems and Translations*, p. 254).

[112] Ezra Pound, 'South-Folk in Cold Country', in *Cathay*, p. 31 (*Poems and Translations*, p. 259).

[113] Pound, 'Song of the Bowmen of Shu', p. 6 (*Poems and Translations*, p. 249).

[114] Pound, 'Lament of the Frontier Guard', p. 17 (*Poems and Translations*, p. 254).

[115] Pound, 'South-Folk in Cold Country', p. 31 (*Poems and Translations*, p. 259).

[116] Ibid.

left London on 5 September for the French army and kept in sporadic contact with Pound thereafter. Although letters to others revealed fears and a certain sentimentalism absent in the correspondence with Pound, Gaudier-Brzeska's aesthetic response to combat was markedly stoical. In 'Vortex' (*Blast*: July 1915), an essay written at the front line and which Pound received amidst the final stages of the drafting of *Cathay*, Gaudier-Brzeska concluded that despite the unnerving experience of trench warfare 'NOTHING IS CHANGED, EVEN SUPERFICIALLY'.[117] That was to be the overarching message in the war edition of *Blast* where the essay first appeared. As Lewis proposed in the essay 'A Super-Krupp—or War's End', the avant-garde was already post-war since 'all art that matters is already so far ahead that it is beyond the sphere of these disturbances'.[118]

Pound evaluated his approach by sending Gaudier-Brzeska three of the *Cathay* poems.[119] The recruit was to be the living and breathing test case against which to ground the manufactured emotion, a combatant who had already received the authenticating mark of direct experience, a battle wound. Gaudier-Brzeska replied to Pound on 18 December 1914 that 'the poems depict our situation in a wonderful way'.[120] Having read them to fellow soldiers, Gaudier-Brzeska told Olivia Shakespear on 11 April 1915 that 'I like them very much. I keep the book in my pocket, indeed I use them to put courage in my fellows.'[121] This was a two-way imaginative process, with Gaudier-Brzeska writing to Pound on 18 December 1914, 'doubtless you see the swamps as well as I.'[122] Through their shared capacity for feeling they had become imaginatively telepathic. It may well be that this positive feedback loop led Pound to change the shape of *Cathay*. Although Pound appears to have made all the translations at roughly the same time, both 'Lament of the Frontier Guard' and 'South-Folk in Cold Country' were only added to the manuscript shortly

---

[117] Henri Gaudier-Brzeska, 'Vortex', *Blast*, 2 (July 1915), 33–4 (p. 33). Written between 9 and 17 November as Gaudier-Brzeska recovered from a bullet wound and received by Pound on 1 December. Henri Gaudier-Brzeska, letters to Ezra Pound (9 November 1914, 1 December 1914), qtd in Ezra Pound, *A Memoir of Gaudier-Brzeska*, rev. edn (New York: New Directions, 1970), p. 58.

[118] Wyndham Lewis, 'A Super-Krupp—or War's End', *Blast*, 2 (July 1915), 13–14 (p. 13).

[119] According to Pound 'a couple of translations from the Chinese of Rihaku, and another by Bunno [. . .] wrongly ascribed to Kutsugen'. Gaudier-Brzeska's reference to 'old fern shoots' suggests one of the poems was 'Song of the Bowmen of Shu'. The other two were 'Lament of the Frontier Guard' and, most probably, 'South-Folk in Cold Country'. Henri Gaudier-Brzeska, letter to Ezra Pound (18 December 2014), qtd in Pound, *A Memoir of Gaudier-Brzeska*, p. 58. Longenbach, *Stone Cottage*, p. 116 argues Pound sent *Cathay* to Gaudier-Brzeska in its entirety, but this does not seem to have been the case until later in the spring.

[120] Pound, *A Memoir of Gaudier-Brzeska*, p. 58.

[121] Ibid. p. 68.

[122] Ibid. p. 58.

before it went to press.[123] And notably, as Ronald Bush (1985) first observed, Pound set these poems along with the 'Bowmen of Shu' such that they open, close and mark the approximate centre of the collection.[124] What might have been a series with a war poem became a book focused on war.

We can see that Pound saw *Cathay* as a landmark from one essay published in *The Egoist* during January 1915 following completion of the draft collection. If imagining death must (as Freud suggested) inevitably leave behind a trace of the subjectivity that is doing the looking, then the poet, according to Pound, might achieve authenticity instead by assuming idiosyncratic experience is but a manifestation of a permanent and common human substrate:

> Good poetry is always the same; the changes are superficial. We have the real poem in nature. The real poet thinking the real poem absorbs the *decor* almost unconsciously. In the fourth century B.C. he writes:— 'quivers ornamented with fish-skin'; in the twentieth of our era, he writes:— 'khaki, with a leather strap for his map-case.' But the real poem is the same.[125]

This is Pound as scientific reductionist. The 'real poem in nature' is the common substrate, the one substance. The 'real poet thinking the real poem' is then primally bound to this well of knowledge. The imagination simply absorbs what is universally true. As Giles said of Li Po, the Chinese poets held suggestion to be the essence of real poetry.[126] Accordingly, poetry, within the confines of a totalising concept that binds the real, can function purely figuratively. Using implication, suggestion and association, this oblique way of looking (but not seeming to look), the poet might use an abstract object to conjure an emotional chain in the reader's mind.

So oblique is the First World War in *Cathay* that many of its first reviewers completely failed to note any connection between the ancient and the modern.[127] Ford did not miss the point. He grasped at once that Pound had reappropriated an established poetical method for 'so rendering concrete objects that the emotions produced by the objects shall arise in the reader', a prototype affective correlative.[128] The emphasis had shifted from an emotion arising as a

---

[123] Zhaoming Qian, 'Cathay', in *The Ezra Pound Encyclopedia*, ed. by Demetres P. Tryphonopoulos and Stephen J. Adams (Westport, CT: Greenwood Press, 2005), pp. 53–4 (p. 53).

[124] Ronald Bush, 'Pound and Li Po: What Becomes a Man', in *Ezra Pound among the Poets*, ed. by George Bornstein (Chicago: University of Chicago Press, 1985), pp. 35–62 (pp. 59–60 n. 5).

[125] Ezra Pound, 'Webster Ford', *The Egoist*, 2.1 (1 January 1915), 11–12 (p. 11).

[126] Giles, p. 155.

[127] For example, R.H.C. [A. R. Orage], 'Readers and Writers', *New Age*, 17.14 (5 August 1915), 332–3.

[128] Ford Madox Hueffer [Ford Madox Ford], 'From China to Peru', *Outlook*, 35 (19 June 1915), 800–1 (p. 800).

simulacrum to the use of a surrogate object to help the process of transmission. Ford's description was sufficiently exact as a summary of Pound's method that Eliot reused it to describe the radicalism of *Cathay* in a seminal essay on intra-war poetics, *Ezra Pound: His Metric and Poetry* (January 1918).[129] For his part, Pound worked hard to make this a consistent story by including *Cathay* as one of the '*Major Personae*' in *Umbra: The Early Poems of Ezra Pound* (1920).[130]

It is also worth considering what Pound left out of *Cathay*. Pound's raw material was the 150 Chinese poems translated by Ernest Fenollosa, forty-eight of which were in two notebooks. Pound marked out seventeen of these for translation. One of the forty-eight, 'The Nefarious War', not included in *Cathay* nor alongside the four Fenollosa poems added to the American edition of *Lustra* (October 1917), takes as its subject the combatant's graphic encounter with the body in pieces. It describes scavenging birds feeding from human corpses littering the surrounding dead trees.[131] Would the poem not have suited the anti-war tone typically found in *Cathay*'s response to the unfolding conflict in Belgium and France? It describes a long war far from home; but so do the others in the series. What we have here is a version of the real that Pound, unlike Ford, Stevens and Lawrence, either did not want to confront or was unable to confront in poetry. Only when the poet was able to quarantine the body in pieces, distil it through a satiric edge, would it enter Pound's *Mauberley*.[132] The problem this Chinese poem posed for *Cathay* was that it dealt with atypical human experience, the firmly non-quotidian experience of parting flesh, the ineffability of pain.

'Is, in heaven's name, IS a war poem, as a work of art in any way different or more meritorious than any other poem?' Pound had demanded of Monroe.[133] Despite this, and like his peers, Pound felt the need to write about this new realm of experience. He pushed deeper into that question in the spring of 1915 when he completed '1915: February' (first published 1988) during a winter retreat with Yeats at Stone Cottage. As the pair watched an artillery battery practising manoeuvres on the neighbouring heath, Pound listened as Yeats

---

[129] T. S. Eliot, *Ezra Pound: His Metric and Poetry*, in *Apprentice Years, 1905–1918*, pp. 616–47 (p. 643).

[130] By including 'The Seafarer' (1911) in the *Cathay* grouping Pound could further strengthen the impression of contiguity. Ezra Pound, 'Notes', in *Umbra: The Early Poems of Ezra Pound* (London: Elkin Mathews, 1920), pp. 127–8 (p. 128).

[131] Li-Po, '97. The Nefarious War', in *The Works of Li-Po: The Chinese Poet*, ed. and trans. by Shigeyoshi Obata (New York: E. P. Dutton, 1922), p. 141. On the background to these translations see especially Bush, 'Pound and Li Po', pp. 59–60 n. 5.

[132] E. P. [Ezra Pound], *Hugh Selwyn Mauberley* (London: Ovid Press, 1920), p. 12 (*Poems and Translations*, pp. 547–63 (p. 552)).

[133] Pound to Monroe (15 September 1914), qtd in Longenbach, *Stone Cottage* p. 114.

read aloud Thomas Sturge Moore's 'Tocsin to Men at Arms' from *The Times* of 18 February.[134] Aldington's extensive list of the dead and the missing in the February edition of *The Egoist* graphically showed the depth of the war's cost.[135] 'Mentions in Dispatches', the list of gallantry in conflict, had grown so large by this date that it was taking up more than two entire pages of *The Times*.[136] The 'Roll of Honour' alone extended to three columns, and that was just for those dead, missing and wounded since Christmas.[137] The headlines in *The Times* gave Pound a clearer illustration of the gravity of the situation: '"Frightfulness" in Belgium. Massacre in Namur Province',[138] '"Blockade." Burning of a Zeppelin. Russians in Retreat', 'German Supplies Cut Off', 'Fighting in the Marshes. A German Claim to 50,000 Prisoners'. *The Times* dubbed it '"PIRATE DAY"' to mark the beginning of the German submarine blockade of Great Britain.[139] The policy was popularly seen as an extension of '"Schreck-lichkeit"', of state-sponsored terrorism against civilians that had begun with the first atrocity reports arriving from Flanders.[140] Before it was even in print, the landscapes of *Cathay* appeared outpaced by events.

It is the paucity of combat experience that is particularly evident in '1915: February'.[141] The poem's source was Pound's earlier poem 'The Coming of War: Actaeon' (*Poetry*: March 1915), probably completed over the winter of 1914–15.[142] The earlier poem begins with 'An image of Lethe', and moves into a highly stylised reflection on death and grief before ending with a divine revelation.[143] So cold is this image of mass mourning that it winnows the

---

[134] Longenbach, *Stone Cottage*, pp. 117–18. Units of the British Army have trained in Ashdown Forest, next to the village of Coleman's Hatch and Stone Cottage, since the eighteenth century.

[135] Richard Aldington, 'French Authors and the War', *The Egoist*, 2.2 (February 1915), 28.

[136] [Anonymous], *The Times*, 18 February 1915, pp. 4–6.

[137] [Anonymous], *The Times*, 18 February 1915, p. 8.

[138] [Anonymous], *The Times*, 18 February 1915, p. 9.

[139] [Anonymous], *The Times*, 18 February 1915, p. 10.

[140] [Anonymous], 'The Day', *The Times*, 18 February 1915, p. 11.

[141] Longenbach claims too much by suggesting that Pound's encounter with the artillery squad at Coleman's Hatch was 'immediate experience of the battlefield'. Longenbach, *Stone Cottage*, pp. 117–18.

[142] The dating is unclear. Pound sent several poems to Monroe on 23 May 1914 which she published in August's *Poetry*. 'Dead Iönè' appeared in *Poetry and Drama* (December 1914). Pound was, he said, '"cleaned out" of verse' by *Poetry* and *Blast* in early February 1915. Ezra Pound, letter to H. L. Mencken (18 February 1915), in *The Letters of Ezra Pound*, pp. 93–4 (p. 93). The Imagist form of 'The Coming of War: Actaeon' suggests it might precede 'Provincia Deserta' (1915), a poem written around October 1914. Longenbach, *Stone Cottage*, pp. 123–4. In *Profile* (1932), an anthology of modern poetry collected by Pound fifteen years later, but one, as discussed in Chapter 2, suspect in its compositional history, Pound dated the poem to 1913, possibly to exaggerate its visionary qualities.

[143] Ezra Pound, 'The Coming of War: Actaeon', *Poetry*, 5.6 (March 1915), 255–6 (p. 255) (*Poems and Translations*, p. 285).

emotions of the assembled mourners out of the poem entirely in pursuit of its point. Actaeon would later become, initially in *The Fourth Canto*, a distinct figure for Pound's anxieties about poetic voyeurism. He became a symbol of both the capacity to witness beauty and the self-destructive risk of such seeing. In 'The Coming of War: Actaeon', however, Actaeon is oddly martial, wearing greaves as if he is Achilles. It is unclear why he is here at all. The poem serves to emphasise only the Image's tendency to deathliness rather than concern for the dead.

In '1915: February' Pound tried to overcome these flaws. He transformed the Elysian-bound Actaeon into a modern 'smeared, leather-coated, leather-greaved engineer' in response to the artillery soldiers marching behind their war machines outside Coleman's Hatch.[144] Pound could not however look at reality without lapsing into metaphors. He knew it, writing on the manuscript '"presentation marred by 2 inescapable comparisons"'. The poem's multiple similes give the game away: there was no first-hand experience here. It was merely a series of forced and borrowed comparisons. Pound went on to label the rest of the poem '"damn'd talk"', revealing his frustration.[145] As the title of the poem suggests, he intended to draft an occasional poem. He wanted to mark the event set out in *The Times*. The poem however finds itself, like its earlier version, magnetically drawn back into the apparent safety of the Image in its final lines: 'We have about us only the unseen country road, / The unseen twigs, breaking their tips with blossom.'[146] These are the only lines Pound did not subject to self-critique. We can imagine Pound publishing them at an earlier time in the decade on their own without the preamble. Pivoting on the repetition of the word 'unseen' – on the 'unseen' understood as both things absent from immediate perception and things that are nonetheless foreseeable – the poet says he has 'only' what is before him. However, he can still imagine and then dramatise the somewhere in which spring is blossoming to life. This is the real poem in nature. By reversing the position of 'unseen' in the second of these lines Pound actualised the process of bringing things unseen to mind. It allows us to see that road and those trees blossoming.

As with Lawrence's earlier war poem, rejected and tended, Pound's relationship to this poem was highly ambivalent. Pound admitted to H. L. Mencken in February that he had written it 'blinded' by his 'fury' and that he had confused 'the cause with the result'.[147] He went further in a letter to Monroe in May as he turned his attention to drafting a long poem:

---

[144] Ezra Pound, '1915: February', in *Poems and Translations*, pp. 1176–7 (p. 1176).
[145] Qtd in Longenbach, *Stone Cottage*, p. 120.
[146] Pound, '1915: February', p. 1177.
[147] Pound, letter to H. L. Mencken (18 February 1915), p. 93.

'I do not like my damn poem, it is too rhetorical, it contains too much that is not presentation. Please send it back, I don't know whether I've another copy. It may make part of a sequence. I want to put down real war emotion, not the froth, the conventional "what-is-to be-expected-of-all-patriotic-poets-in-war-time," horrors of blood, etc.'[148]

What was this 'real war emotion'? Pound tells us it is neither sentiment nor jingoism. It was not an account of the body in pieces. What then was the real? Yeats's oration had spiked something in Pound's soul. Moore's alarm bell was very much 'patriotic', but it also pressed the need to win with a moral victory, to '"Fight to conquer, not to revenge"', to '"Hold good! Hold good!— / Clear honour has more patience than bad faith!"'[149] There was then something at stake in poetries of war. As a mark of this recognition, Pound clipped Moore's poem and sent it to Monroe two days after *The Times* published it. Pound's confusion only grew as his opinion of '1915: February' changed repeatedly over the coming months. It was barely acceptable at all to him by the autumn of 1915. Then he said Monroe ought to publish it anyway, before finally retracting it entirely.[150] Nothing had changed in the autumn of 1914: poetry should not write the war. By the spring of 1915 everything had changed.

---

[148] Ezra Pound, letter to Harriet Monroe (May 1915), qtd in Longenbach, *Stone Cottage*, p. 120.

[149] T. [Thomas] Sturge Moore, 'Tocsin to Men at Arms', *The Times*, 18 February 1915, p. 11.

[150] Ezra Pound, letters to Harriet Monroe (autumn 1915, 24 December 1915, 1916), qtd in Longenbach, *Stone Cottage*, p. 123.

2

REASSESSING DISASTER: 1915

Rupert Brooke, Modernist Piñata

The war's vicious turn in the months leading up to Easter 1915 left an indelible imprint on modernist cultures. The deaths of Rupert Brooke, Julian Grenfell, Jean Verdenal and then Henri Gaudier-Brzeska occurred within the space of six weeks in that spring. Those months also marked the first use of chlorine gas, the sinking of the *Lusitania* and an escalation of atrocity stories. Public confidence in the war effort waned and the military finally broke ranks from government policy. Sir John French, the British Expeditionary Force's Commander-in-Chief, collaborated with the editorial team at *The Times* on 14 May to describe how British casualties at Aubers Ridge resulted from a series of shell shortages.[1] The question of institutional culpability accelerated a week later with the Quintinshill rail disaster. Following a signalling problem, five trains collided and became engulfed by a gas fire in what is still the worst rail accident in British history. Over 200 victims, including troops, were trapped alive or splintered by shrapnel.[2] Charlotte Mew's 'May, 1915' (first published 1929), composed the day after Quintinshill, the day also of Ezra Pound's first concrete reference to the evolution of his long poem, captured this historical

[1] Alan Moorehead, *Gallipoli*, new edn (London: Hamish Hamilton, 1967), pp. 157–8.
[2] Jack Richards and Adrian Searle, *The Quintinshill Conspiracy: The Shocking True Story behind Britain's Worst Rail Disaster* (Barnsley: Pen and Sword Transport, 2013).

moment.[3] The poem implores readers to hold on to the hope that the natural world, marked by the arrival of spring, will provide some rearrangement to the order of things. Despite this, its opening confidence progressively leaks away into melancholia. We can see the idea that the war might be quick or civilised leeching out of English society in 'May, 1915', especially when the unavoidable reality of the body in pieces stood in the way of poetry.[4]

It was within this mood of mounting anxiety and anger that Brooke rose to public fame and poetic ignominy. There was an element of fortuity in this. Although Brooke drafted his series of famous war sonnets, '1914', in the autumn and finished them in early 1915, the January edition of *New Numbers* in which they first appeared was not in circulation until February 1915 at the earliest.[5] The *TLS* published several sonnets under Walter de la Mare's patronage although not until 11 March. This set the stage for Dean Inge's famous canonisation of Brooke's (alleged) religiosity in his Easter Day sermon at St Paul's Cathedral. *The Times* duly recorded Inge's sermon and established Brooke's fame in the popular imagination. On 15 April *The Times* printed 'The Soldier', the fifth of the sonnets, with its image of the combatant's corpse having become 'a richer dust' and making an England 'of a foreign field' on its front page.[6] Setting aside the unglamorous nature of Brooke's death from an insect bite as he awaited deployment at sea, Winston Churchill leaped on the propaganda value of Brooke's heroism in an obituary for *The Times* on 26 April. The previous day, the British government had announced the Gallipoli campaign. Although most often associated from the perspective of literary production with the early mood of nostalgic optimism, Brooke's sonnets were from the perspective of reception coterminous with the very moment the war changed to a more deadly course.

The growth of what *Masses* termed 'the Rupert Brooke Myth' was a widely noted phenomenon at the time of its public dominance, and Aaron Jaffe's *Modernism and the Culture of Celebrity* (2005) admirably charts its course.[7] The abuses inflicted on Brooke's corpse and corpus deserve further attention though. This abuse cut both ways. Virginia Woolf's diary records the disgrace

---

[3] Tim Kendall, 'Notes: Charlotte Mew', in *Poetry of the First World War: An Anthology*, ed. by Tim Kendall (Oxford: Oxford University Press, 2013), pp. 244–5 (p. 244 n. 46); E. P. [Ezra Pound], letter to Isabel Pound (23 May 1915), in *Ezra Pound to his Parents–Letters 1895–1929*, ed. by Mary de Rachewiltz, A. David Moody and Joanna Moody (Oxford: Oxford University Press, 2011), pp. 347–8 (p. 347).

[4] Charlotte Mew, 'May, 1915', in Kendall, ed., *Poetry of the First World War*, p. 46.

[5] Alisa Miller, *Rupert Brooke in the First World War* (Clemson, SC: Clemson University Press, 2017), p. 80.

[6] Rupert Brooke, '1914: V. The Soldier', in Rupert Brooke, *The Poetical Works*, ed. by Geoffrey Keynes (London: Faber and Faber, 1970), pp. 19–23 (p. 23).

[7] F.D. [Floyd Dell?], 'English Youth', *Masses*, 8.11 (September 1916), 34–5 (p. 35); Aaron Jaffe, *Modernism and the Culture of Celebrity* (Cambridge: Cambridge University Press, 2005), pp. 146–8.

of the sentimental rhapsodies that celebrated Brooke's ugly death from septi-caemia.[8] Equally many used his death to pillory him. 'Dead he is as bad a poet as he was alive,' wrote A. R. Orage in the *New Age*.[9] T. S. Eliot never forgave the letters Henry James sent to Edward Marsh, first as praise of Brooke's poetry and then as eulogy. Eliot drily described them as evidence of James's snobbish-ness.[10] According to confidants, T. E. Hulme disliked Brooke from their first meeting in Germany. He was, in Hulme's view, a faux intellectual.[11]

Brooke's reputation seems undeserved in both directions. Prior to the January edition of *New Numbers*, modernist cultures regarded him as a divisive figure. He was widely known as a Fabian, 'a youth of evil taste', wrote one reviewer in the *New Age* in 1912.[12] Critics found Brooke's early work hard to situate. J. C. Squire, again in the *New Age*, wondered if Brooke was 'the unflinching realist, ironist, or the solemn and sentimental enthusiast'?[13] Brooke's tone was always mobile. Babette Deutsch later singled out in *Poetry* the coexistence of both the 'lovely things' and 'sensitive satire' in Brooke's work.[14] There was an experimen-tal edge to this, a self-conscious romanticism but also a mixing-up of genres, a peculiar and historically unprecedented '"mélange"', said George Woodberry in the introduction to Brooke's collected poems.[15] Within other modernist cultures this might have been seen as tentatively collagist. Henry James, for example, highlighted that Brooke was often at the one moment 'whimsical and personal' and at others 'hauntingly (or hauntedly) English'.[16] 'A Channel Passage' (1911; *1909*), for example, a poem Eliot particularly despised for its analogy of love and seasickness, demonstrates the point. It is both comic and cruel, remarkably

---

[8] Virginia Woolf, diary entry (Tuesday, 23 July 1918), in *The Diary of Virginia Woolf*, ed. by Anne Olivier Bell and Andrew McNeillie, 5 vols (Orlando: Harcourt Brace, 1977–84), I: *1915–1919*, ed. by Anne Olivier Bell (1977), pp. 170–1 (p. 171).

[9] R.H.C. [A. R. Orage], 'Readers and Writers', *New Age*, 19.24 (12 October 1916), 565.

[10] Christopher Ricks, *Reviewery* (New York: Handsel Books, 2002), p. 20. On James's letters see, for example, Henry James, letter to Edward Marsh (28 March 1915), in *The Letters of Henry James*, ed. by Percy Lubbock, 2 vols (London: Macmillan, 1920), II, pp. 479–81 (p. 480).

[11] Ethel Kibblewhite, letter to Michael Roberts (12 November 1937), in T. E. Hulme Papers (GB 172 HUL), Special Collections and Archives, Keele University Library, reference number 34 (hereafter, this archive cited as KHUL followed by reference number); 'Talk, Ashley Dukes and Samuel Hynes, Mercury Theatre London, 19 January 1954', in T. E. Hulme Ferguson Papers (GB 172 HULF), Special Collections and Archives, Keele University Library, file number 8 (hereafter, this archive cited as KHULF followed by file number).

[12] [Anonymous], 'Present-Day Criticism', *New Age*, 12.5 (5 December 1912), 109–10 (p. 109).

[13] Jack Collings [J. C.] Squire, 'Recent Verse', *New Age*, 10.12 (18 January 1912), 281–2 (p. 281).

[14] Babette Deutsch, 'Out of the Den', *Poetry*, 16.3 (June 1920), 159–62 (p. 161).

[15] George Edward Woodberry, 'Introduction', in *The Collected Poems of Rupert Brooke* (London: John Lane, 1915), pp. v–xiv (p. xiii).

[16] Henry James, letter to Edward Marsh (6 June 1915), in *The Letters of Henry James*, II, pp. 489–91 (p. 491).

modern in its sense for self-consciousness. It suggests a penchant for the macabre which ran throughout Brooke's early verse, one that also reminds us his career began, to Eliot's chagrin, as a scholar of Jacobean drama.[17] This is all quite different from the poet Pound privately rechristened in a much later letter to Eliot as 'Rabbit Brooke'.[18] It is more in keeping with the Brooke that Woolf remembered. In an essay for the August 1918 edition of the *TLS*, Woolf described Brooke as a man 'exorcising the devils of the literary and the cultured', a man conducting 'an experiment in living'. He owned a sensibility marked by 'a profound and true sympathy'.[19]

This makes the accusations of naivety aimed at Brooke's war sonnets far better suited to Inge's reading of 'The Soldier'. Given its timing and importance in the creation of the Brooke hagiography, it amounted to a seminal misreading. It gives us crucial insight into the rising institutional value of combat gnosticism. Gnosis was Inge's lifelong subject. He had lectured and written extensively on the varieties of religious experience in *Christian Mysticism* (1899) and *Studies of English Mystics* (1906). Isaiah, the prophet who had most clearly perceived the mysteries of the Trinity, was for Inge the most important of the mystics.[20] Inge read Brooke in relation to the twenty-fifth and twenty-sixth chapters of Isaiah, sections Inge described as 'perhaps the clearest anticipation of Christian hope that are to be found in the Old Testament'. What Inge admired above all was the 'spontaneous flash of inspired insight' appearing from the prophet's incoherence.[21]

Inge's purpose in appropriating Brooke's poetry was highly ethical. He wanted to help the British public reconcile the unfolding disaster with the idea of God. It is Inge's reading of the poem where the problem arises. He read 'The Soldier' as a form of esoteric knowledge rescued from the chaos of modernity, ignoring entirely that this was the work of a poet prone to irony and satire. Although falling short in its fleshy fallen humanness, the sonnet was, Inge proposed, a denuded Christian vision clutched from the heat of battle. It was important because it was emotion without tranquillity. We can see from Inge's draft manuscripts how this idea changed to fit his purpose. Brooke's vision, Inge maintained, was remarkable because its 'enthusiasm of pure and elevated patriotism' was 'free from hate, bitterness, and ~~despair~~ fear'.[22] Perhaps a trifle

---

[17] John Lane published Brooke's dissertation of 1911–12 as *John Webster and Elizabethan Drama* in 1916.

[18] Ezra Pound, letter to T. S. Eliot (25 April 1936), in *The Letters of Ezra Pound*, p. 370.

[19] Virginia Woolf, 'Rupert Brooke', in *The Essays of Virginia Woolf*, II, pp. 277–84 (p. 279).

[20] William Ralph Inge, *Christian Mysticism: Considered in Eight Lectures Delivered before the University of Oxford* (New York: Charles Scribner's Sons, 1899), p. 18.

[21] Dean [William Ralph] Inge, 'Notebook containing sermon, St Paul's, Easter 1915', in The Papers of Rupert Chawner Brooke (RCB/Xb/2/2), King's College Cambridge, pp. 1–5 (p. 1).

[22] Ibid. p. 3.

Timeline 2.1 Spring 1915

	Composition	Publication, Exhibition, Event

March	Eliot, 'Hysteria'
	Kipling, 'Mary Postgate'
		H.D., poems including 'The Pool',
		    'Moonrise' (*Poetry*) later sequenced
		    as 'The God' (1925)
		Ford, *When Blood is their Argument*
		Pound, 'Coming of War: Actaeon', 'Exile's
		    Letter', 'Provincia Deserta', 'Dogmatic
		    Statement Concerning the Game of
		    Chess' (*Poetry*)

8	Sinclair, 'Dedication (*To a Field Ambulance in Flanders*)'	
11		De la Mare review of Brooke's sonnets, with IV and V published in full (*TLS*)
17		Ford, *The Good Soldier*
18	Mansfield, *Aloe* (1930)	
26		Woolf, *Voyage Out*

April	Eliot, 'To Helen', 'Do I know how I feel?'
	    (1996), 'Death of St Narcissus'
	Freud, 'Thoughts for the Times on War
	    and Death'
	Lawrence, redrafts 'Ecce Homo' as 'Eloi,
	    Eloi, Lama Sabachthani?'
		Brooke, 'Nineteen-fourteen' (*Poetry*)
		Hardy, 'The Pity of It' (*Fortnightly Review*)
		Masters, *The Spoon River Anthology*
		Pound, *Cathay*
		Some Imagist Poets

4	Stevens, 'Sunday Morning' Thomas, 'Digging ("Today I think")'	Dean Inge Easter Day sermon
6	Thomas, 'In Memoriam (Easter, 1915)'	
8	Stein and Toklas arrive in Mallorca	
14		Hulme wounded at St. Eloi
15		Brooke, 'The Soldier' (*Times*)
18	Pound, 'L'Homme Moyen Sensuel'	
22		First use of chlorine gas
23		War dead: Brooke
29	Grenfell, 'Into Battle'	
May	Eliot, '"Boston Evening Transcript"' T.E.H., 'Trenches: St Eloi' Thomas, 'The Glory'	Brooke, *1914 and Other Poems* Sandburg, 'Murmurings in a Field Hospital' (*Masses*)
1		Lawrence, 'Eloi, Eloi, Lama Sabachthani?' (*Egoist*) Sinclair, 'After the Retreat' (*Egoist*)
2		War dead: Verdenal

	Composition	Publication, Exhibition, Event
7		War dead: sinking of *Lusitania*
9		Aubers Ridge
10		Crucified Canadian atrocity story (*Times*)
21		Death of H.D.'s daughter
22		War dead: Quintinshill rail disaster
23	Pound's first reference to a long poem Mew, 'May, 1915'	
26		War dead: Grenfell
28		Grenfell, 'Into Battle' (*Times*)
31		First Zeppelin attacks on London

Guide to Timelines
Works arranged in alphabetical order within each month.
Publication dates given in parenthesis, except if given in the main text, endnotes or elsewhere in timelines.
Titles shortened for brevity.

materialistic, Inge added, but 'a worthy thought, that the dust out of which ~~a~~ the ~~dead soldi~~ happy warrior's body was once compacted is consecrated for ever by the cause for which he died'.[23] All signs of the body in pieces, any suggestion that Brooke's eventual death might be a tawdry psychological affair, a sepsis well away from Troy's plains, were written out in order to see Brooke as one in a long line of Christian gnostics.

This is a difficult reading to support. Brooke had seen only one confused retreat from Antwerp in October 1914 prior to the composition of the sequence. Vincent Sherry, in *The Cambridge History of Twentieth-Century Literature* (2004), uses Brooke's image of 'swimmers into cleanness leaping' as an example of the way the early war poets idealised war experience within the context of Georgian nationalism.[24] There were however no mud-caked trenches in Antwerp. The 'monstrous distended belly' of mud which slowly consumes combatants in Mary Borden's poem 'The Song of the Mud', the second part of 'At the Somme' (*English Review*: August 1917; *October 1916*), and Wilfred Owen's memorable vision of the front as 'an octopus of sucking clay' both lay in a future Brooke did not live to see.[25] Brooke's letters also suggest he too was far from

---

[23] Ibid. p. 4.

[24] Brooke, '1914: I. Peace', p. 19; Vincent Sherry, 'Literature and World War I', in *The Cambridge History of Twentieth-Century Literature*, ed. by Laura Marcus and Peter Nicholls (Cambridge: Cambridge University Press, 2004), pp. 152–72 (pp. 152–3).

[25] Mary Borden, 'At the Somme', in Kendall, ed., *Poetry of the First World War*, pp. 76–81 (p. 79); Wilfred Owen, letter to Harriett Susan Shaw ([undated]), qtd in Jon Stallworthy, *Wilfred Owen*, rev. edn (London: Pimlico, 2013), p. 156.

satisfied with the sonnets. He recognised the need for the serenity of distance from the stresses of military life in the compositional process. To Sybil Pye he specifically highlighted the failure of the first three sonnets.[26]

The religiosity of Inge's reading, its transference of the poem from page to pulpit, stripped the poetry of any irony. It suggested the poem was entirely sincere, leaving it open to the accusation of sentimentality. This is not the only way to read it. It is notable that during 1915 newspapers, journals and Dean Inge tended to publish or cite the sequence in a piecemeal fashion. This was the case in the *TLS* and *The Times*, and in the sermon. In this form it is impossible to note the jarring change of perspective that occurs in the final of the five sonnets. On its own we can certainly read 'The Soldier' as sincere and bend it to any propagandist perspective. Placed back in sequence, though, it is a distortion. The lofty collective rhetoric of the preceding sonnets ('Blow, bugles, blow!') gives way to a reflective ego, one that has moved away from the public mood of patriotic fanfare to one calmly contemplating its own extinction: 'If I should die, think only this of me'.[27] How should we think about this process of 'think[ing] only'? Is the 'thinking' laced with Brooke's penchant for the macabre? Are we to imagine that the corpse becoming dust is how the poet would wish others remember him, nothing more and nothing less? This would be to understand 'only' as 'solely'? Or could it mean how Brooke imagined the public might inevitably remember him? Does it dramatise the oscillation of a young soldier's self-conscious awareness of both these possibilities? It seems far from clear.

I do not want to suggest Brooke's sonnets are devoid of sentiment and jingoism. The argument is that we often read Brooke's sonnets in a way that strips them of their historical context and any sense of irony. We do this with few other poets. Reading Brooke this way also agrees with the way the modernists read Brooke, how the modernists wanted the public to read Brooke, and how, following Inge, the public read Brooke. In contrast, Brooke described to Violet Asquith that the genesis of these poems resembled something like the developing of a photograph.[28] It is suggestive of both a literal desire to capture a vivid and realistic historical moment and a certain self-conscious meta-poesis, not a taking of but a distillation, the chemical treatment of a visible image. Brooke described the series as roughs, mere 'camp-children'.[29] This is true: compositionally they were the product

---

[26] Rupert Brooke, letter to Sybil Pye ([undated]), qtd in E.M. [Edward Marsh], 'Memoir', in *The Collected Poems of Rupert Brooke: With a Memoir* (London: Sidgwick & Jackson, 1918), pp. xi–clix (pp. cxxxvi–cxxxvii n. 2).

[27] Brooke, '1914: III. The Dead', p. 22; Brooke, '1914: V. The Soldier', p. 23.

[28] Rupert Brooke, letter to Violet Asquith ([26 December 1914]), in the *Letters of Rupert Brooke*, ed. by Geoffrey Keynes (London: Faber and Faber, 1968), p. 643.

[29] Rupert Brooke, letter to [?] (24 January 1915), qtd in [Marsh], 'Memoir', pp. cxxxvi–cxxxvii.

of being in camp, the progeny of mobilisation, of being amidst the 'swimmers'. They chart the enthusiastic rapture of a camp that had had no taste of trench mud. They are a variant on that 'strange new beauty' imagined by Ford Madox Ford at the same site, Antwerp. We might also suggest that they display a formal campness. They are highly dramatised and theatricalised, extravagantly effeminate in the historical gender terms of the day and within the context of a military retreat. This ambivalence is self-evident in the poem's closing feminine rhyme:

> And think, this heart, all evil shed away,
> A pulse in the eternal mind, no less
> Gives somewhere back the thoughts by England given;
> Her sights and sounds; dreams happy as her day;
> And laughter, learnt of friends; and gentleness,
> In hearts at peace, under an English heaven.

The 'this' that we are asked to think of this combatant is that 'this' life can be sacrificial because it is but 'A pulse in the eternal mind'. Such sentiment would certainly have pleased Inge. The yoking together of 'by England given' with 'an English heaven' is hardly final though as Brooke's notably decapitalised abode of the deities becomes a nationalistic paradise. All is not then as it seems. Does Brooke's combatant want to casually cast away life for this camp ideology or want the body to be 'Washed by the rivers, blest by suns of home'?[30] Read this way, as a developing photograph rather than as a definitive autograph, granted the irony we grant to Ford's *Antwerp* for example, the poem voices a pincer movement. Personal desire and the state simultaneously capture the self. Public opinion buffets it. The poem was indeed then a vision. Not of Isaiah, but of the eventual fate of Brooke's corpse, pulled to pieces by the institutions of modernity.

MAY SINCLAIR'S COMBATANT IMPRESSION

'Rabbit Brooke', the straw version of Brooke, is an image that will repeatedly recur throughout this narrative as a workable piñata for modernist cultures. Its emergence as a trope in the spring of 1915 requires a firm stake in the ground. Almost simultaneous with it, Pound turned to assembling a new collection of poetry for Elkin Mathews, what would become the *Catholic Anthology 1914–1915* (November 1915).[31] It is an important anthology and Pound used it to show the multiplicity of approaches available to those outside the Imagist

---

[30] Brooke, '1914: V. The Soldier', p. 23.
[31] Elkin Mathews has agreed to publication in principle by March 1915. Ezra Pound, letter to Harriet Monroe ([? March] 1915), in *The Letters of Ezra Pound*, pp. 98–9 (p. 98).

group. According to Pound, the Image had by this time become Amy Lowell's. This was to be a highly didactic anthology and Pound designed it as a response to the contemporary poetic scene. Notably, Pound chose to include a handful of his older poems – 'The Garret', 'The Garden' and 'In a Station of the Metro' (*Poetry*: April 1913), along with 'Albâtre' (*Poetry and Drama*: March 1914) – even though these fell outside the anthology's stated period of focus. These are poems Richard Aldington parodied in 'Penultimate Poetry: Xenophilometropolitania' (*The Egoist*: January 1914), an essay that made obvious the rupture between a poetics of the Vortex and an increasingly Hellenised Image. Pound also opted to reprint several widely published meta-poems whose titles expose their intent: 'Further Instructions' (*Poetry*: November 1913), 'The Study in Aesthetics' (*Poetry*: August 1914) and 'Dogmatic Statement Concerning the Game of Chess: Theme for a Series of Pictures' (*Poetry*: March 1915 and *Blast* 2). The anthology's opening poem, an italicised version of W. B. Yeats's 'The Scholars' (1915), supported the didactic intent. Its disdain for the '*BALD heads*' of the '*Old, learned*' who '*Edit and annotate the lines*' of the young served as a preface to an anthology that then took its lead on the next page with 'The Love Song of J. Alfred Prufrock' (*Poetry*: June 1915).[32] Pound's own contributions, positioned towards the end of the anthology, sat omnisciently reflecting on the processes of poetry and on the nature of literary tradition.

The anthology also clearly displays its need for a war poem. The public very much demanded an image of its grimace here. It was a lack within Pound's rival camp of poets accentuated by the decision of the remaining members of the Imagist group to connect their poetic with the war in May 1915 with a '*Special Imagist Number*' of *The Egoist*. In a letter to Lowell of 5 April 1915, discussing the structure of this edition, Aldington made clear the need to deal with the changed public mood. The 1 April edition of the *Mercure de France* was, Aldington told Lowell, dominated by war almost entirely; he added that he could now finally understand why Remy de Gourmont had insisted that '"il faut rattacher votre Imagism à la guerre"' [you must link your Imagism to the war].[33] Engagement with the war was now a necessity (*falloir*) not an option. In *The Egoist* F. S. Flint notably credited Edward Storer and Hulme – the latter notably 'now in the trenches of Ypres', said Flint – as the founders of the Imagist movement. It served to write Pound out of the movement's genesis.[34] *The Egoist* also published D. H. Lawrence's war poem 'Eloi, Eloi, Lama Sabachthani?', the latest version of 'Ecce Homo', alongside May Sinclair's 'After the Retreat'. According to Helen Carr in *The Verse Revolutionaries* (2009), the latter was a coup for

---

[32] W. B. Yeats, 'The Scholars', in *Catholic Anthology 1914–1915*, ed. by [Ezra Pound] (London: Elkin Mathews, 1915), p. [1]. See also W. B. Yeats, 'The Scholars', in *The Poems*, p. 141.

[33] Aldington, letter to Lowell (5 April 1915), pp. 13–14.

[34] F. S. Flint, 'The History of Imagism', *The Egoist*, 2.5 (1 May 1915), 70–1 (p. 70).

the Imagists because Sinclair had chosen to support their splinter group.[35] When asked for poems to publish in the May 1915 edition, Pound did not, according to Aldington, unusually for an inveterate letter writer, respond at all.[36]

We have underplayed Sinclair's role here. Harbouring, as she would later tell Mew, doubts about the Imagist ability to deal with extreme moments of passion, Sinclair's alignment with *The Egoist* reflected her desire to support and to develop the aesthetic.[37] Sinclair was one of the first literary combatants in the battle zone and the first to bring that experience back to London's literary circuit. Pound knew Sinclair had a sliver of that increasingly precious *materia poetica* of 'real war emotion'. He told Harriet Monroe that Sinclair had 'been pulling wounded off the field' in Belgium with the Red Cross.[38] The material collected by Sinclair in the daybook that documented her experience was also quickly in circulation as the *English Review* serialised extracts from *A Journal of Impressions in Belgium* (September 1915). The titles of these essays give a sense of Sinclair's assuagement of the public demand for gnosticism: 'From behind the Front' (*English Review*: November 1914), 'From the French Front' (*English Review*: March 1915), 'Relief in Belgium: A Report' (*English Review*: May 1915) and 'The War of Liberation: From a Journal' (*English Review*: May–July 1915).

Sinclair's time in the combat zone was brief. It came to an abrupt halt after seventeen days. Theophilus E. M. Boll, Sinclair's biographer, speculates that her desire to experience the front was a little too keen for her colleagues. This death wish led to her enforced return to England soon after arrival in Ghent.[39] In the poem used as an epigraph to *A Journal*, 'Dedication (*To a Field Ambulance in Flanders*)' (September 1915; *March 1915*), we keenly sense Sinclair's bitterness at the exclusion from battle. The poem laments the lost opportunity to meet the danger zone head on. It wants more of what it has only briefly glimpsed, leaving Sinclair's dedication to colleagues partly choked with envy, by the desire to see the wounded and the dead, the artillery, the destruction, the mud and blood of it all.[40] It is a poem that believes in combat gnosticism.

The representational method Sinclair developed for *A Journal of Impressions in Belgium* highlights the careful consideration of how the artist might

[35] Helen Carr, *The Verse Revolutionaries: Ezra Pound, H.D. and the Imagists* (London: Jonathan Cape, 2009), p. 741; May Sinclair, 'After the Retreat', *The Egoist*, 2.5 (1 May 1915), 77.

[36] Aldington, letter to Lowell (5 April 1915), p. 13.

[37] May Sinclair, letter to Charlotte Mew (9 June 1915), qtd in Theophilus E. M. Boll, *Miss May Sinclair: Novelist, A Biographical and Critical Introduction* (Cranbury, NJ: Associated University Presses, 1973), p. 109.

[38] Ezra Pound, letter to Harriet Monroe (9 November 1914), in *The Letters of Ezra Pound*, pp. 85–8 (p. 87).

[39] Boll, p. 107.

[40] May Sinclair, 'Dedication (*To a Field Ambulance in Flanders*)', in May Sinclair, *A Journal of Impressions in Belgium* (New York: Macmillan, 1915), pp. [i–ii].

bring the white heat of extreme experience to the page. Its introduction, written on 15 July 1915, begins conventionally enough. It describes the impossibility of immediate artistic production within battle and the requirement that the artist scribble down instead a series of notes:

> When you had made fast each day with its note, your impressions were safe, far safer, than if you had tried to record them in the flux as they came. However far behind I might be with my Journal, it was *kept*. It is not written 'up,' or round and about the original notes in my Day-Book, it is simply written *out*. Each day of the seventeen had its own quality and was soaked in its own atmosphere; each had its own unique and incorruptible memory, and the slight lapse of time, so far from dulling or blurring that memory, crystallized it and made it sharp and clean. And in writing *out* I have been careful never to go behind or beyond the day, never to add anything, but to leave each moment as it was.[41]

This is a definitive attempt to ready the literary impression for the conditions of war. It echoes but goes much further than de Gourmont. It tries to find a point of balance between chaos and tranquillity whereby the artist makes safe the impression, grabbing it from the past and the future in order that it can then organically expand into a fuller more objective form.

The chain of events here – the movement from experience/impression to daybook to *A Journal of Impressions in Belgium* – is particularly notable. It moves from raw physiology through a primitive form of the sign to a fully fledged aesthetic object. Sinclair places great emphasis on the passing of time. Time elapses between both the 'flux' and the note, and between the note and the journal. This delay functions as a much-shortened form of afterwardness. It crystallises the literary impression from the fleshy and endocrinal chaos of experience. Sinclair describes her own method as 'behindhand'.[42] There is though no degradation in the original impression. When the note becomes aesthetic it does so through a writing '*out*' and not a writing '"up"' or 'round'. The process is expansive and organic. The writer protects the aura of the original impression through the refusal to go behind or beyond the note. In aggregate, it is a process that tentatively rewrites the poetics of tranquillity for the age of ballistics, for an age of abnormal or extreme emotion, for the encounter between the self and the *unheimlich*.

There is clearly a profound issue here. It tries extremely hard to avoid *écriture* at the cost of making the written especially obvious. In the opening pages of Sinclair's introduction to *A Journal of Impressions in Belgium* the impression is

---

[41] Sinclair, *A Journal of Impressions*, p. [iv].
[42] Ibid. pp. [iii].

not actually in the note at all. It only exists, as Sinclair admits, when the writer is 'cold-blooded enough' to write it out. How then does the impression nonetheless find itself within the note? Which is it? Is the impression affective or aesthetic? There is a risk that Sinclair was not simply writing '*out*' affect but really writing it '"up"'. Sinclair's claim that *A Journal of Impressions in Belgium* had only a certain claim on psychological accuracy, partly because some impressions were not substantial or else not captured on the spot, throws the issue in the air, emphasising just how stylised this text is.[43]

Nonetheless, *A Journal of Impressions in Belgium* marks the spot in a crucial moment in this genealogy. It was the first comprehensive sourcebook of combat emotion to enter wide circulation within modernist cultures. It argued firmly for combat gnosticism. It testified to the competing demands of experience and imagination using the poetic laws of recollection and tranquillity as a guide. It might be straining things to suggest this was the first account of combat trauma. It certainly does though try to understand how an emotion might function in surviving the journey from body into word. The historicity is also key. By yoking her position to *The Egoist* amidst the growing popularisation of Brooke's poetry of war, Pound needed to reattach the Vorticist breakaway poetic to the war. Aldington thrashed Pound in the May edition of *The Egoist* precisely because of his lack of contact with the new real. Pound was no more than a Romantic, Aldington said, a poet (now rubbing salt) with a gift for what Edward Thomas had termed the occasional: 'the moment he began to try to make poetry out of the realities of existence, instead of from vague impulses and romantic emotions and bookish enthusiasms, his poetry became arid.'[44] Sinclair in contrast had touched the soil.

Imagining Trenches at St Eloi: T. E. Hulme/Ezra Pound

Pound's answer to this challenge was a poem in the *Catholic Anthology*, one initially attributed to 'T.E.H.'. The anthology gave it the title 'Poem: Abbreviated from the Conversation of Mr. T.E.H.' and subtitled it 'Trenches: St Eloi' (November 1915; *May 1915*).[45] Most notably, the poem was written – a deliberately passive clause as we will see – most probably towards the end of May

---

[43] Ibid. p. [iii].

[44] Richard Aldington, 'The Poetry of Ezra Pound', *The Egoist*, 2.5 (1 May 1915), 71–2 (p. 71).

[45] The version of the poem in *Poems and Translations* (Ezra Pound, 'Poem: Abbreviated from the Conversation of Mr. T.E.H.', in *Poems and Translations*, p. 568), excepting title and author, is textually the same as T.E.H. [T. E. Hulme?], 'Poem: Abbreviated from the Conversation of Mr. T.E.H.', in *Catholic Anthology 1914–1915*, p. 22 and T. E. Hulme, 'Poem', in *Umbra*, p. 125. There are two manuscripts of the poem in Kate Lechmere's hand. The first has one minor textual variant (high [?] versus wide) in line 2. The Papers of Thomas Ernest Hulme 1907–1974 (U DHU), Hull History Centre, box 9 (hereafter this archive cited as HDHU followed by box number). The second does not include the textual variant. KHUL 8.

in the weeks following the '*Special Imagist Number*' of *The Egoist*. How can we be so precise? Pound began to collect the poems published in the *Catholic Anthology* in early 1915. He agreed to its publication in March and Elkin Mathews published it in November. The 'T.E.H.' of the poem, Hulme, returned to England from the Ypres Front following injury on 19 April. The anecdotal story of the poem's composition has Hulme and Pound conversing during the former's hospitalisation.[46] We should also note that there is absolutely no melancholy in the poem, little sense for the dead, suggesting composition pre-dated news of Gaudier-Brzeska's death. This reached London in early June. Most decisively, the poem refers directly to shortages of ammunition similar to those discussed at the head of this chapter. This links it to the public anger in the wake of the tragedy at Aubers Ridge on 9 May. Mid to late May would seem then the likely date of composition.

In keeping with the didactic and meta-poetic theme in the *Catholic Anthology*, the poem's core subject is how to write about war emotion when one does not have it directly. It does so through a process that looks incredibly like Sinclair's three-stage process. The poet signals this via the poem's elaborate title. The first stage, 'conversation', involves the passing on of emotion. It is Hans-Georg Gadamer's hearsay, Walter Benjamin's *Wissen*. It is an affective experience handed over from the Other. The second stage is an intermediate quasi-aesthetic/quasi-administrative act of 'abbreviation'. Akin to Sinclair's notation, this act shortens and orders the chaos of direct experience but does so without ever fully giving itself up to *écriture*. The 'abbreviation' clips, orders and sharpens the source material, a crude bolus which needs pitching and roughing out. The third stage is the act of producing the 'Poem' itself. This is the perfected object that appears from the poet's chiselling away at the bolus. It is an act of writing out that lies on the other side of a colon. The colon acts as a kind of sieve that results in the pure aesthetic object:

> Over the flat slope of St Eloi
> A wide wall of sandbags.
> Night,
> In the silence desultory men
> Pottering over small fires, cleaning their mess-tins:
> To and fro, from the lines,
> Men walk as on Piccadilly,
> Making paths in the dark,
> Through scattered dead horses,
> Over a dead Belgian's belly.

[46] Robert Ferguson, *The Short Sharp Life of T. E. Hulme* (London: Allen Lane, 2002; repr. London: Faber and Faber, 2012), pp. 211–12. Hulme's date of injury was 14 April, at St Eloi.

> The Germans have rockets. The English have no rockets.
> Behind the lines, cannon, hidden, lying back miles.
> Before the line, chaos:
>
> My mind is a corridor. The minds about me are corridors.
> Nothing suggests itself. There is nothing to do but keep on.[47]

It is a highly stylised and geometric creation. The poem constructs its images from horizontals, organises them by degrees of flatness and by the slope of angle cuts it all through with the crisscrossing of paths and lines. It might easily be a description of a pre-war canvas by Wyndham Lewis, one that conforms to Hulme's glorification in the Quest Society lecture of angularity, rigidity and the non-vital means of conveying emotional intensity.[48] Photographs in the Imperial War Museum's collection show it to be in many respects a very accurate description of the scene at St Eloi.[49] The poet has clearly still taken rhetorical licence. The German positions at St Eloi sat on an infamous mound of death rather than a mere slope. 'Piccadilly' was a commonly used moniker for a number of trench systems in the Ypres Salient, but at St Eloi they were Hyde Park Corner and Queen Victoria Street.[50] Moreover, when Allied troops took over the trenches at St Eloi in January 1915 what they noted was a soft sucking world below sea-level. They found themselves '"ankle, knee and even waist deep in liquid mud"', Peter Chasseaud records in *Rats Alley* (2017), not amidst the hard geometricity of the Vorticist landscape in 'Trenches: St Eloi'.[51] St Eloi was far less known for its trenches than for the underground passageways that were dug in the shallow loam and slurry of the Belgian lowlands during the spring of 1915 to undermine the enemy positions. The journey from experience to poem via conversation was then neither simple nor straightforward.

I read this poem as an attempt to account for the experience of shock. The poem deploys its resources – the arrested pace, the accumulation of monosyllables, the simplicity of tone, the absence of any music or relieving rhyme, the participles arresting time – as a metonym of trench-life. These features signal the banality, the monotony and the numbing incomprehensibility of being stuck in the middle of the chaos. They eventuate in the closing motif of the corridor, that

---

[47] T.E.H., 'Poem: Abbreviated from the Conversation of Mr. T.E.H.', in *Catholic Anthology*, p. 22.

[48] Hulme, 'Modern Art and its Philosophy', pp. 271–2.

[49] See, for example, [Unknown], 'British wire defences in front of sandbags at St. Eloi, May 1915', Imperial War Museum, Q 52028 Mrs Morris Alfred Collection, <https://www.iwm.org.uk/collections/item/object/205285665> [accessed 24 March 2022].

[50] Peter Chasseaud, *Rats Alley: Trench Names of the Western Front, 1914–1918*, 2nd edn (Stroud: History Press, 2017), para. 21.127–21.128, British Library ebook. Trench maps show a Piccadilly Farm close to St Eloi and Wytschaete (para. 47.1048).

[51] Ibid. para. 20.15.

notoriously interstitial space. Steven Connor (2004) has described the betwixt and between nature of the corridor, the way it retards progress, forces us to wait, stops time, suspends action, as an incubatory space spawning fantasies of horror and violence.[52] In 'Trenches: St Eloi', the corridor and mind become one in line with de Gourmont's assessment of battle. This mind-at-combat cannot understand what is in front of it because it is dealing with the brutal facts of survival. Soldiers reduced to domesticity use cadavers for bridges. By conflating the labyrinthine structure of the trench system with that of the shocked mind, two running spaces to use the etymological roots (*currere*) of the word 'corridor', combat experience becomes not a source for poetry but a blockage. Combat results only in the dumb blank impermanence of minds to each other.

Only the genuine 'Poem' can resolve this. This act of transformation comes in the penultimate sentence where the poet complicates meaning. Where is the stress in the line 'Nothing suggests itself'? If these are the combatant's words equally unstressed then they give evidence of a shocked and overloaded mind and its metaphorical relationship to the physical structure of the trench system. They reinforce the blankness of combatants unable to understand and communicate their experience, unable to transform anything beyond the mere data related to supply lines. The stress might however be on 'suggests' as an active verb. As in the closing *haiku* of '1915: February', for this poet that 'nothing', the nothing of the combatant's shock, becomes a definite something. In other words, out of nothingness this poet dramatises the act of poetic creation. It is an act that selects the important material from the minutiae of data to universalise it. For this poet, war experience is no more problematical than any other type of experience, it is merely more grist to the imaginative mill.

This of course raises the obvious question as to who this poet is. The contents page of the *Catholic Anthology* names 'T.E.H.', accepted modernist shorthand for Hulme. It is clearly an unstable position, not least because it conflates the alleged poet with the original orator. The *Catholic Anthology* took care to mark each of its poems with its poet's capitalised name. Each poet signs each section in italics. Pound however inserted 'Trenches: St Eloi' into the collection in a way that would appear to deliberately confuse our concepts of authorship and attribution, confuse how we think about the relationship between authenticity of emotion and the poem as a historical document. Whose consciousness is where in this poem of processes? And how does this impinge on meaning?

By 1915 Hulme and Pound were a well-known poetical double act, regularly publishing side by side and creating a space for the other to interject into each other's texts. It was principally for friendship and posterity, Pound

---

[52] Steven Connor, 'A love letter to an unloved place', *Nightwaves*, BBC Radio 3, 22 June 2004, <http://www.stevenconnor.com/corridors/> [accessed 24 March 2022].

claimed, that he published Hulme's poetry in *Ripostes* (1912).[53] Whether Hulme had really given up on poetry or whether Pound was repaying intellectual theft will remain unknown.[54] Pound's intention to form an intellectual alliance seems credible enough though. Appearing in *Ripostes* and *Canzoni and Ripostes of Ezra Pound* (1913), Hulme's poems were an important part of Pound's response to aesthetic insult. As Flint sensed when trying to pull the two poets apart in the history of Imagism, Pound wanted readers to see his project moving in tandem with Hulme's. Hulme's poems first appeared in the *New Age* on 25 January 1912, a matter of weeks after serialisation of Pound's 'I Gather the Limbs of Osiris', contemporaneous with the publication of Hulme's most important essays on Bergson and the composition of the essay that became 'Romanticism and Classicism' (1924).

The emergence of a poem that blended the two consciousnesses into one at the meta-poetic level would be entirely consistent with that narrative. In *Umbra*, Pound clarified the situation, explaining that following Hulme's death the only poem that he could add to those published in *Ripostes* was his abbreviation of Hulme's hospital talk. Pound gave Hulme a half share of the credit.[55] Although Pound still printed the poem as Hulme's, the contents page of the volume separated it from the earlier poems with a short line. In the contents of the volume the title became simply 'Poem', the previous titles relegated to a subtitle and set out to match the typography of Hulme's other poems.[56] Since *Umbra* appeared in the midst of the memorialisation of Hulme's legacy by Orage in the *New Age* and at a time when opposition to Pound was both vociferous and the vogue, perhaps the playful brotherhood of the *Catholic Anthology* was no longer apposite.[57] Perhaps, Pound simply felt the need to be clear.

In 1915 however Pound appears to have wanted the poem to appear as if it was Hulme's poem. That is, he wanted it to appear as a poem by a wounded combatant back from the front, a poem with 'real war emotion' to rival Sinclair in *The Egoist*. Hulme's wound was a sign of the *Catholic Anthology*'s authenticity and modernity. In contrast, by 1920, Pound wanted readers to see him as the guiding author and to see that the emphasis was on 'Poem' (the retained title) and not the genesis story that began with a 'conversation' (an act now relegated

---

[53] E.P. [Ezra Pound], 'The Complete Poetical Works of T. E. Hulme, Prefatory Note', in *Ripostes of Ezra Pound* (London: Stephen Swift, 1912), pp. 58–9 (p. 58).

[54] Richard Aldington, letter to Samuel Hynes (30 April 1954) (KHULF 8). Similarly, 15 May 1952. On the allegation of theft and the competition between Hulme and Pound see John Gould Fletcher, *Life Is My Song* (New York: Farrar & Rinehart, 1937), pp. 75–6.

[55] [Ezra Pound], 'Headnote: The Complete Poetical Works of T. E. Hulme', in Pound, *Umbra*, p. 123.

[56] Pound, *Umbra*, p. 10.

[57] On Hulme's legacy see R.H.C. [A. R. Orage], 'Readers and Writers', *New Age*, 27.17 (26 August 1920), 259–60. This article was followed later by T. E. Hulme, 'Fragments', *New Age*, 29.23 (6 October 1921), 275–6. On the opposition to Pound see especially Ben Hecht, 'Pounding Ezra (*A Conversation* . . . .)', *Little Review*, 5.7 (November 1918), 37–41.

to the subtitle). Pound's much later retreat from the position in *Umbra* makes these issues even more problematical. In conversation with Samuel Hynes at St Elizabeth's Hospital, Pound said the poem was in fact Hulme's all along, that he had recited it when he returned from battle but had refused to set it down in writing.[58] Where then does Hulme end and Pound begin? Is that very confusion the poem's attempted response to the problem of combat gnosticism?

The poem's history in the canon illustrates precisely what is at stake here. The major architects of Hulme's reputation – Herbert Read (1924), Michael Roberts (1938) and Karen Csengeri (1994) – give little or no credit to Hulme for the poem.[59] Alun R. Jones (1960) did partly reclaim it for Hulme although Hynes (1955) hedged the bets.[60] Prior to St Elizabeth's Pound did his best to shun the poem too. He excluded it from all six impressions of *Personæ* between 1926 and 1944.[61] And he excluded it from *Profile* (1932) too, an anthology of poems which Pound said had stuck in his 'memory and which may possibly define their epoch'. Instead he chose to mark the war with 'The Coming of War: Actaeon' and two poems by Donald Evans, the American poet typically associated with the Greenwich aesthetes, entitled 'The Hero' and 'Invalided Home' (both 1916).[62] Not only did Pound misdate these poems, the former to 1913 and the latter to 1919, in order to form a bracket around the intra-war period, their overly aesthetic frames evaporate the reality of war into mythologies.[63] In 1949,

---

[58] Copy made by Robert Ferguson of Samuel Hynes, 'Conversation with Ezra Pound, 31 August 1953, St Elizabeth's Hospital, Washington, D.C.'. KHULF 8. Original held at Harry Ransom Center, Texas. Pound could not recall if Hulme had seen the final poem.

[59] Csengeri does not mention the poem. Read did not include the poem in T. E. Hulme, *Speculations: Essays on Humanism and the Philosophy of Art* (1924), ed. by Herbert Read (London: Routledge & Kegan Paul, 1960). Nor did Roberts in Michael Roberts, *T. E. Hulme* (London: Faber and Faber, 1938).

[60] Jones reprinted and attributed it to Hulme in Alun R. Jones, *The Life and Opinions of T. E. Hulme* (London: Victor Gollancz, 1960), pp. 36–7. Hynes argued it was Pound's poem, although added that it 'sounds like authentic Hulme'. Samuel Hynes, 'Introduction', in *Further Speculations by T. E. Hulme*, ed. by Samuel Hynes (Minneapolis: University of Minnesota Press, 1955), pp. vii–xxxi (p. xxviii).

[61] Pound consulted both Aldington and Eliot when collating the volume in 1925 and threw out what he called the '"soft" stuff' and other experimental or metrical exercises. Ezra Pound, letter to Homer Pound (28 November 1925), qtd in A. David Moody, *Ezra Pound: Poet, A Portrait of the Man and his Work*, 3 vols (Oxford: Oxford University Press, 2007–15), II: *The Epic Years 1921–1939* (2014), p. 67. Reviewing *Umbra* in 1920, Edwin Muir found it the volume's least successful poem, a mere copy of Aldington's work, although it obviously pre-dates that work. E.M. [Edwin Muir], 'Recent Verse', *New Age*, 27.12 (22 July 1920), 186–7 (p. 187).

[62] Ezra Pound, *Profile: An Anthology Collected in MCMXXXI* (Milan: John Scheiwiller, 1932), p. 13.

[63] Evans published both poems in *Nine Poems from a Valetudinarium* (1916) before his enlistment. Pound's wayward dating in *Profile* is clear throughout. He dated Eliot's 'The Hippopotamus' (1917; *June 1917*) and 'Burbank with a Baedeker: Bleistein with a Cigar' (1919; *August 1918*) to 1915–16 for example.

Pound and New Directions added a number of early poems from the *New English Weekly* to *Personæ* to make up *The Collected Poems of Ezra Pound*. These included Hulme's early poetry but not 'Trenches: St Eloi'. Editors also excluded the poem from both English editions of 1952 and 1968. It only reappeared in *Collected Early Poems* (1976) as an uncollected text.

More recently, however, in the lead up to the centenary of the First World War, this reluctance has given way to a reciprocal desire to lay claim to the poem. Patrick McGuinness includes it in *Selected Writings* (1998), the most complete collection of Hulme's poetry.[64] Although the introduction avoids the issue of authorship directly, more recently McGuinness (2014) has suggested that it is unusual Hulme is excluded from First World War poetry anthologies and links the poem's language to Hulme's trench diaries.[65] Pound's most recent biographer, A. David Moody (2007), claims it in Pound's name. 'It is a strong poem,' Moody argues, 'partly because it articulates the experience of someone who had been in the front line, and partly because Pound knew how to condense the detail into a timeless image of men at war.'[66] Robert Ferguson (2002), Hulme's biographer, claims it for his subject too though.[67] *The Penguin Book of First World War Poetry* (2006) has it as Pound's poem.[68] *The Wordsworth Book of First World War Poetry* (1995) and *The Winter of the World: Poems of the Great War* (2007) give it to Hulme, although Pound is often credited with some of the composition.[69] Carol Rumens (2011) says Hulme was certainly the author, and embellishes the genesis story by explaining that either Pound or Kate Lechmere – since the surviving manuscripts of the poem are in her hand – transcribed the poem whilst Hulme lay injured in hospital. If Pound

[64] McGuinness's version includes several minor textual variants. T. E. Hulme, 'Trenches: St Eloi. TEH Poem: Abbreviated from the Conversation of Mr. T.E.H.', in T. E. Hulme, *Selected Writings*, ed. by Patrick McGuinness (Manchester: Carcanet, 1998), p. 12.

[65] Patrick McGuinness, 'From Mud and Cinders: T. E. Hulme, "A Certain Kind of Tory at War"', *TLS*, 19 November 2014, 14–15.

[66] A. David Moody, *Ezra Pound: Poet, A Portrait of the Man and his Work*, I: *The Young Genius 1885–1920* (2007), p. 261.

[67] Ferguson, *Short Sharp Life*, p. 212.

[68] Ezra Pound, 'Poem: Abbreviated from the Conversation of Mr. T.E.H.', in *The Penguin Book of First World War Poetry*, ed. by George Walter, rev. edn (London: Penguin, 2006), p. 58. See also Sheehan, pp. 144–5.

[69] T. E. Hulme, 'Trenches: St Eloi', in *The Wordsworth Book of First World War Poetry*, ed. by Marcus Clapham (Ware: Wordsworth Editions, 1995), p. 41; T. E. Hulme, 'Trenches: St Eloi', in *The Winter of the World: Poems of the Great War*, ed. by Dominic Hibberd and John Onions (London: Constable & Robinson, 2007), p. 58. See also Stevenson, p. 175; Henry Mead, *T. E. Hulme and the Ideological Politics of Early Modernism* (London: Bloomsbury, 2015), pp. 183–4; Patrick McGinness [Patrick McGuinness], 'Hulme, Thomas Ernest (1883–1917)', in Tryphonopoulos and Adams, eds, pp. 152–3 (p. 153); Christos Hadjiyiannis, 'Logic of the Heart: Affective Ethical Valuing in T. E. Hulme and Max Scheler', in *Modernism and Affect*, ed. by Julie Taylor (Edinburgh: Edinburgh University Press, 2015), pp. 66–74 (para. 11.7), British Library ebook.

did make revisions or abbreviations Hulme approved them says Rumens.[70] The memorial to the tunnellers at St Eloi, although dedicated to the Actions of St Eloi Craters in the following year, cites the poem as an epitaph with Hulme as the author. The cemetery records at Coxyde Military Cemetery state that Hulme was amongst the 'war poets'.[71]

GNOSIS AND A MODEL OF SHOCK

It is especially notable how these positions have arisen in the wake of James Campbell's critique of combat gnosticism. For, if the poem was Hulme's poem, then it is a valuable historical document of the gnostic quality of combat. It is the raw experience of shock brought back from the front and presented unmediated to the reader. It becomes, to use Rumens's words, 'arguably the most radical of any of the English first world war poems'.[72] In contrast, if the poem was Pound's, then it is a perfect illustration of the alleged powers of expressivity, of the poet's imaginative skill in manipulating basic materials. As C. D. Blanton (2006) elegantly puts it, the poem is 'either the most remarkably experimental lyric penned by a combatant or the most remarkable bit of poetic ventriloquism undertaken by a civilian'.[73] One road leads us back to the haunted voices of the trench lyricists, the other to the haunting voices of *The Waste Land*. Which is it?

The poem's original title is likely to be the evidence here. Pound crafted a poem using the raw material of Hulme's experience to specifically illustrate a method, one to rival that in *The Egoist*, one to prove the poet's capacities in relation to contemporary history, one designed as a rug for pulling from under the public's growing obsession with direct experience. We can go further than speculation. The Lechmere manuscripts are a red herring.[74] There are arguments

---

[70] Carol Rumens, 'Poem of the Week: Trenches: St Eloi by TE [T. E.] Hulme', *The Guardian*, 10 October 2011, <https://www.theguardian.com/books/2011/oct/10/poem-of-the-week-t-e-hulme> [accessed 24 March 2022], para. 2 of 10.

[71] Commonwealth War Graves Commission, 'Lieutenant Hulme, Thomas Ernest', <https://www.cwgc.org/find-war-dead/casualty/89831/hulme,-thomas-ernest/> [accessed 24 March 2022].

[72] Rumens, para. 3.

[73] C. D. Blanton, 'The Politics of Epochality: Antimonies of Original Sin', in Comentale and Gasiorek, eds, pp. 187–208 (p. 188).

[74] The Keele manuscript's headed notepaper reads: 'TELEGRAMS:– Adlington, Cheshire. STATION:–Adlington, L. and N.W.R. STARKIE HOUSE, ADLINGTON, MACCLESFIELD'. T. E. Hulme, 'Trenches: St Eloi' manuscript, KHUL 8. From at least 1914 to 1922, the Mather family occupied Starkie House. They controlled the Mather and Platt group of industrial businesses. Loris-Emerson Mather attended Harrow and Trinity College Cambridge. This offers up the prospect that he and Hulme were friends. Hulme's undergraduate college, St Johns, is next to Trinity. Emerson did not, however, matriculate until 1905, well after Hulme's first stay in Cambridge between October 1902 and March 1904. Although Hulme attended a series of philosophy lectures at Trinity in 1907, there is no further evidence to corroborate Hulme knowing

which date them to the post-war world.[75] The likely explanation is that Lechmere wrote down the poem after Hulme's death.[76] The Hulme archive at Hull holds examples of Lechmere copying out Hulme's work and letters to him for various scholars. Most importantly, there is nothing at all, other than reminiscence, to corroborate the idea that these manuscripts originated from the hospital scene of the Hulme-Pound conversation.

There is much more compelling textual evidence that points to Pound's authorship accounting for more than half of the poem. Take the two major poems he wrote before and after 'Trenches: St Eloi', *Cathay* and 'Near Perigord' (*Poetry*: December 1915; *June 1915*). The sorrowful existence of the combat group in 'Song of the Bowmen of Shu' finds itself repeated in the dead and flat lines of 'Trenches: St Eloi'.[77] The latter's 'The Germans have rockets. The English have no rockets' is but a form of the bowman's reflection on the troop's horses: 'The generals are on them, the soldiers are by them'.[78] The conclusion in 'South-Folk in Cold Country', that 'Emotion is born out of habit', predicts the senselessness of the later poem's ending. Pound's point was that all wars are the same; Hulme's reflections only corroborated Li Po and Gaudier-Brzeska. As Pound noted in his January 1915 essay for *The Egoist*, the tools or technologies of the trade change but flawed equipment invariably betrays the combatant. Combatants always become bored, hungry and dirty. There is only one type of shock. If there is no change in combat, then Pound could grant himself the freedom to conjure Richard Lionheart at Chalus in 'Near Perigord':

Mather. Ferguson, *Short Sharp Life*, p. 35. Hulme's family did originate from this area; Hulme's aunt and benefactor Alice Pattinson (visited often by Hulme) lived close by. There is no evidence linking Hulme to Starkie House. It is possible the notepaper belonged to Lechmere. According to Hulme's biographer, Lechmere nursed near Macclesfield during the war and Hulme visited there. Ferguson, *Short Sharp Life*, pp. 218–19, 243. The extant records leave the matter unresolved. Lechmere was a volunteer nurse between 1 May and 30 November 1916 with J.W.V.A.D. in London 128 as part of Brighton 2nd Eastern General. 'Miss Kate Elizabeth Lechmere', *First World War Volunteers*, <https://vad.redcross.org.uk/Card?fname=Kate&sname=Lechmere&id=131644&first=true&last=true> [accessed 24 March 2022]. There was a nursing station at Hurdsfield House in Macclesfield. Pattinson served there from March 1915 to March 1919. 'Miss Alice M. Pattinson', *First World War Volunteers*, <https://vad.redcross.org.uk/Card?fname=alice&sname=pattinson&id=168248&first=true&last=true> [accessed 24 March 2022].

[75] Lechmere was a frequent visitor to the region after the war. Kate Lechmere, letter to A. R. Jones (7 February 1961). HDHU 5.

[76] Before 1923 seems likely, the date when the London and North Western Railway (the 'N.W.R.' of the notepaper) became part of the London, Midland and Scottish Railway. The manuscript notably follows the *Catholic Anthology* rather than *Umbra*, including the subtitle and preserving the arrangement of the final line.

[77] Pound, 'Song of the Bowmen of Shu', p. 249.

[78] Ibid. p. 249.

The crackling of small fires, the bannerets,
The lazy leopards on the largest banner,
Stray gleams on hanging mail, an armorer's torch-flare
Melting on steel.[79]

Compare this to 'Trenches: St Eloi'. In the twelfth century war metal becomes armour. In the First World War we have 'mess-tins'. The heraldic waving of the lion *passant* Pound replaces with bags of sand. The war camp it appears is, as Gaudier-Brzeska testified from the front, just the same. 'Trenches: St Eloi' is almost certainly Pound's poem. It served to prove – and Pound constructed it to prove – that the poet could transmute the base metals of experience into the gold standard of poetic utterance.

We can then impute Pound's conclusion: there was and is no problem of combat gnosticism because the Other's mind is accessible to the poet possessed of *virtù*. In contrast, it is combat shock that estranges experience from representation. It estranges the self from the self. It makes necessary an aesthetic intervention. Or as Pound put it better in the *New Age*'s 'Affirmations' series in January 1915, when 'a man walked sheer into "nonsense"' it was the poet's job, and had always been the poet's job, to make sense of individual confusions. It was the poet's job to transform confusion into mythology and allegory to enable humans to better understand their unknowable traumas. Knowledge not then through 'conversation' but through its symbolic other, the 'Poem', which Pound defined in the *New Age* as 'an impersonal or objective story', one woven out of the poet's 'own emotion, as the nearest equation that he was capable of putting into words'.[80]

Pound made 'Trenches: St Eloi' by piecing together found objects in an act of sympathetic ventriloquism. It would be more precise to say this is a poem that oscillates somewhere between the assemblage (a text made exclusively from found material), a form of found poetry (one that relies on found language) and an outright found poem (the poem being that which is found and redistributed in a modified form). It may even be that Pound found its method in Sinclair's combat impression. This oscillation between the found and the imagined sets up a stylistic ambivalence that complicates the authentication of the underlying affective experience and raises it to the aesthetics of the problem.[81] The colon in the poem's title becomes especially decisive then. It is the final call to order, a demand for close attention, a demand that we focus on

---

[79] Ezra Pound, 'Near Perigord', *Poetry*, 7.3 (December 1915), 111–19 (p. 117) (*Poems and Translations*, pp. 302–8 (p. 306)).

[80] Ezra Pound, 'Affirmations—I. Arnold Dolmetsch', *New Age*, 16.10 (7 January 1915), 246–7 (p. 246).

[81] Lacy Rumsey, 'Modes of Found Poetry', in Martiny, ed., pp. 361–76 (pp. 361–4).

language, that we ought to expect ambiguity. It is what Jonathan Culler refers to in *Structuralist Poetics* (2002) as the mark of a poem's unity and the poet's request to claim significance.[82]

Whilst we can debate the success of the poem and the nature of its borrowings, the chutzpah of Pound's poem is remarkable. Pound wrote it very soon after the Cubists began incorporating the residua of modernity into art. Marcel Duchamp's *Bicycle Wheel* (1913) and *In Advance of the Broken Arm* (November 1915) both bracket it, but the theoretical basis of the readymade was not clear until the second edition of *The Blind Man* in May 1917. We typically trace the origin of the found poem to Blaise Cendrars's collection *Dix-neuf poèmes élastiques* (1919), even if we can note earlier instances in 'Mee Too Buggi' (*July 1914*) and 'Dernière Heure' (*January 1914*). 'Trenches: St Eloi' may then be one of the first examples of the use of collage for poetry in the English language.

Equally however there is a profoundly conservative aspect to the poem's formalism. The collage inhabits a fragile space as its objects transition from one context to another. There is always the risk of kitsch. Not the knowing or self-reflexive quality of kitsch. 'Trenches: St Eloi' is in earnest. The kitsch here is the kitsch that falls prey to obtrusiveness, to that which betrays the transition, exaggerates its status as either manufactured or ill-equipped for its new surroundings. In Pound's case the problem arises because Pound was in fact dealing with an abbreviated copy of a spoken copy of an original emotion. Once on the other side of the colon, Pound was dangerously close to the Baudrillardian concept of the simulacrum as a copy without any original. That danger was always implicit in Pound's lack of real interest in the squalor and *unheimlich* quality of the battlefield. He ignored Li Po's body-strewn war poems and reduced the brutish Provençal theatre of war to a display of regnal ceremony. In 'Trenches: St Eloi' he concentrated energy on the mute externality of shellshock rather than its grotesque internal psychodrama. Pound betrays his conservatism by the interest he takes in the overall scheme, the broad idea rather than the individual details.

Unlike Sinclair's intimation of the effects of memory, this conservatism results in a highly conventional representation of the shocked mind. It is dazed, blank, vacant and uncomprehending. This has distinctly Georgian origins. In the poems collected as *Battle* (September 1915), for example, Wilfrid Wilson Gibson, after failing to enlist on multiple occasions, attempted instead to imagine being 'beside the brazier's glow' of a camp, eating breakfast with fellow soldiers, hearing the shells 'screeching overhead'.[83] In poems written during September and October 1914 we find Gibson at one moment taking on the

---

[82] Jonathan Culler, *Structuralist Poetics: Structuralism, Linguistics and the Study of Literature*, rev. edn (London: Routledge, 2002), p. 204.

[83] Wilfrid Wilson Gibson, 'Before Action', in Wilfrid Wilson Gibson, *Battle* (New York: Macmillan, 1915), p. 9; Wilfrid Wilson Gibson, 'Breakfast', in *Battle*, p. 10.

guise of a murderous combatant and at the next a grieving widow. Gibson's personae lie in trenches, face the fear of death, meet amputees, watch blood ooze from wounds. In 'Hit' (*Poetry*: August 1915), a lazy body lies on the sun-drenched beach of Falmouth Bay becoming a soldierly 'I' who feels 'A trickle of warm blood— / And found that I was sprawling in the mud / Among the dead men in the trench'.[84] There is an emptiness to the immediate psychological transformation here, an emptiness often filled in *Battle* by a voyeuristic and hyper-aesthetic fascination with 'screeching' ballistics, the 'dying squeal', the 'oozing quietly / Out of the gaping gash'.[85] We are left with combatants who can 'never know' their own experience, 'Half-puzzled'.[86] Civilians wander around 'Bewildered'.[87] And dismembered combatants express their psychological wounds through fragmentary 'muttering', snatched pieces of a past life.[88] In 'The Messages', a combatant, 'Stone-deaf and dazed, and with a broken knee', lapses into a dirge, recalling deaths witnessed, becoming a medium for the dying messages of colleagues.[89] Are these, as Dominic Hibberd (2006) first suggested, an early attempt at representing shellshock?[90] To support that conclusion we would need to vest Gibson's figurative language with an astonishing level of intuition, a vision that was certainly lacking within military and medical communities and their purely physical aetiology of shellshock.[91] We might instead read *Battle* as a dramatisation of a distinct lack of experience, of Gibson's emptiness in the face of a desired encounter, an emptiness which might look a little like the shock of the Other but which more obviously dramatises Gibson's masochistic yearning for limit experience.

We can read Harold Monro's 'Youth in Arms' (December 1914; *September 1914*) in the same way. Like Stevens's contemporaneous 'Phases', Monro follows a fictional combatant, modelled on Basil Watt, a close friend who would die at Loos, from the early stirrings of patriotism to enlistment and through the first recorded encounter with battle to his eventual death. In the third section, 'Retreat', the poem shifts to an interior monologue to describe the shock of battle. It is a brain that the poem tells us is 'scragged and banged'.[92] Scrag's

---

[84] Wilfrid Wilson Gibson, 'Hit', in *Battle*, pp. 30–1.

[85] Gibson, 'Breakfast', p. 10; Wilfrid Wilson Gibson, 'The Bayonet', in *Battle*, p. 11; Wilfrid Wilson Gibson, 'Victory', in *Battle*, p. 37.

[86] Wilfrid Wilson Gibson, 'The Question', in *Battle*, p. 12; Wilfrid Wilson Gibson, 'The Quiet', in *Battle*, p. 40.

[87] Wilfrid Wilson Gibson, 'Salvage', in *Battle*, p. 14.

[88] Wilfrid Wilson Gibson, 'In the Ambulance', in *Battle*, pp. 20–1 (p. 20).

[89] Wilfrid Wilson Gibson, 'The Messages', in *Battle*, pp. 38–9 (p. 38).

[90] Dominic Hibberd, *Harold Monro and Wilfrid Gibson: The Pioneers* (London: Cecil Woolf, 2006), p. 15.

[91] Loughran, 'Shell-Shock and Psychological Medicine', p. 88.

[92] Harold Monro, 'Youth in Arms', in Harold Monro, *Children of Love* (London: Poetry Bookshop, 1914), pp. 23–8 (p. 27).

etymological roots in English stretch back to violent origins and invasion. War has roughed up the brain. Whereas in Gibson's imagined war poems repetition functioned as the means to figure a disjointed, aporetic and circular mind, here we see instead a soldier broken apart by a cacophony of voices. This is more like Lear's breakdown than shellshock. Monro's soldier collapses into mono-syllables. Monro gives him access to only basic masculine rhymes and snatches of song. The soldier's speech oscillates between the first and third person as he strays into memories that disrupt time's flow. The narrative breaks down into repeated punctuation marks, the shifting of typeface and variable line length. This is a species of madness, but it nonetheless leads Monro to the frankly per-verse image of 'the lovely curve' of Watt's wasting body 'Against a ridge of the ploughed land's watery swerve'.[93] The closing image of the dead soldier picked apart and returned to the earth as fuel for spring seems either a clear precedent or source for Brooke's more famous image of the mixing of the English soldier's dust with earth.[94]

In these three unlikely poetic allies – Gibson, Monro and Pound – we find a model of the shocked mind that depends on the self's internal experience func-tioning in the same way that the self presents itself externally. In other words, these poems depend on the idea that the shocked mind is a broken mind, that its broken relationship to the world manifests itself in a broken relationship with itself. Hence the recurrence of images associated with the edge and the abyss, of fracture and ruin. Fragmentariness is a trope that runs deep in the modernist lexicon. It is especially crucial to Christine Froula's genetic account of the evolution of the fourth of Pound's *Cantos* in *To Write Paradise* (1984) for example. Froula argued for a 'poetics of the fragment' as the stylistic mainstay of the entire *Cantos* project. *To Write Paradise* goes further by suggesting that this concept predicted aspects of both Fussell's account of soldierly experience and Benjamin's idea that the war ruptured experience and communicability. Froula took part of the evidence for this claim from Pound's 'MS Ur1' (1984; *November 1915*), an early version of *The Fourth Canto*, most probably drafted around the time Pound penned 'Trenches: St Eloi'. This shard of verse describes the scattered experiences and fragmentary conversation of an Englishman who makes his way back through Europe at the start of the war to enlist. Pound's combatant, like the one at St Eloi, cannot understand the war. His confused and broken dialogue portrays the war as an incursion of senseless hostility into life. National boundaries do not define him. For Froula, the poem's formal con-fusion, its riff on absurdity, the abandonment of the convention of narrative closure and the overlapping but inconclusiveness of different mythic traditions serve as a prototype of modernist form. This poetics is the stylistic correlative

---

[93] Ibid. p. 28.
[94] Brooke, '1914: V. The Soldier', p. 23.

for the confusion of the combatant's actual experience. It is how Pound first glimpsed a way towards reuniting the epic with the ordinary. Froula positions 'MS Ur1' then as a radical moment in the genealogy. It allowed Pound to resolve his fear that any shift from immediate experience would leave him, as it had left Robert Browning in *Sordello* (1840), fictionalising history.[95]

Timeline 2.2 June–December 1915

	Composition	*Publication, Exhibition, Event*
June	Joyce writes early draft of 'Telemachus' Lawrence, 'England, My England' Mew, 'June 1915' (1929) Pound, 'Near Perigord'	Eliot, 'Prufrock' (*Poetry*); marries Vivien Haigh-Wood Jones (Ernest), 'War and Individual Psychology' (*Sociological Review*) War dead: Gaudier-Brzeska
July	Eliot, 'Mr. Apollinax', 'The Engine' Lawrence, *Twilight in Italy* (1916) Shaw Stewart, 'I saw a man this morning' (1920)	*Blast* 2 (cover: Lewis, *Before Antwerp*) Gaudier-Brzeska, 'Vortex' (*Blast*, 2) Loy, 'Love Songs' (*Others*) Saunders, 'Vision of Mud' (*Blast*, 2)
August	Eliot, 'Cousin Nancy', 'Introspection' Loy, draft of 'Songs to Joannes' Stein, *Lifting Belly*	Gibson, poems from *Battle* (*Poetry*)
September		Eliot, 'Portrait of a Lady' (*Others*) Gibson, *Battle* Joyce, serialisation ends of *Portrait of the Artist* (*Egoist*) Kipling, 'Mary Postgate' (*Nash's* and *Century*) Lawrence, *The Rainbow* Richardson, *Pointed Roofs* Sinclair, *Journal of Impressions in Belgium* War dead: Kipling's son
October	Lawrence, 'The Thimble', 'Resurrection' Sorley, 'When you see millions of the mouthless dead'	Eliot, '"Boston Evening Transcript"', 'Aunt Helen', 'Cousin Nancy' (*Poetry*) Hulme, 'Preface to Sorel's *Reflections on Violence*' (*New Age*) Lawrence, 'England, My England' (*English Review*) Sandburg, 'Killers' (*Poetry*) War dead: Sorley, Mansfield's brother Leslie Beauchamp

---

[95] Froula, *To Write Paradise*, pp. 14–16. Froula notes Pound's foresight in the fragment's emphasis on the incomprehensibility of the soldier's patriotism. Pound was probably only picking up that theme from Ford's *Antwerp*.

	Composition	*Publication, Exhibition, Event*

November	Freud, 'On Transience' (1916)
	 Pound, 'MS Ur1', draft fragment of
	     The Fourth Canto
	 Sassoon, 'The Redeemer' (1917)
		Aldington, 'Zeppelins Over London'
		     (*Little Review*)
		 Catholic Anthology, including Eliot's
		     'Hysteria' and T.E.H.'s 'Trenches:
		     St. Eloi'
		 Georgian Poetry, 1913–1915
		 H.D., 'Choruses from *Iphigeneia in
		     Aulis*' (*Egoist*)
		 Hulme, serialisation of 'War Notes'
		     (*New Age*)
		 Stevens, 'Sunday Morning' (*Poetry*)

December	Pound, early drafts of the first five
	     cantos
	 Rosenberg, 'Marching'
	 Thomas, 'This is no case of petty right
	     or wrong' (March 1916)
	 West, *The Return of the Soldier*
		Fry, *Men of Europe*, translation of
		     Jouve's *Vous êtes des hommes*
		     (1915)
		 Hulme, serialisation of 'A Notebook'
		     (*New Age*)
		 McCrae, 'In Flanders Field' (*Punch*)
		 Pound, 'Near Perigord' (*Poetry*)

Guide to Timelines

Works arranged in alphabetical order within each month.

Publication dates given in parenthesis, except if given in the main text, endnotes or elsewhere in timelines.

Titles shortened for brevity.

'Trenches: St Eloi' is then a much-neglected waypoint in the genealogy. It is a poem steeped in the historicity of the problem of gnosis within modernist cultures. The poem shows, in support of Ronald Bush's argument in *The Genesis of Ezra Pound's Cantos* (1976), the speed with which Pound had chosen to adapt the Jamesian model of narration for poetry.[96] He had shifted *Cathay*'s description of common or basic ahistorical mental events to a dramatic *in medias res* rendering of mental life caught in the lights of unknowable events. If we can already see the germ of *The Waste Land* here and the later poem's status as the pre-eminent poetic account of wartime shock, we have to note that it is also a poem that relies very heavily on a crude model which reduces the mental life of the trauma victim to mute incomprehensibility. It speaks nothing of the grotesque nature of the wounding event, of the multiplicities of emotion, of traumas in their plurality. There is more than a little sense of projection here. Pound's account is the unshocked account of the shocked, the intact mind's

[96] Bush, *The Genesis of Ezra Pound's Cantos*, pp. 225–6.

account of the broken mind. It is an early staging post in a method that would come to rely on the constant juxtaposition of fragments or points of view. It evokes Peter Howarth's analysis of Friedrich Schlegel in *British Poetry in the Age of Modernism* (2005). The poetics of the fragment was the means to resist any external attempt to encompass whilst setting up the prospect of perpetual possibility.[97] In 'Trenches: St Eloi' fragmentation became a tool which could describe a modernity best understood through the psychological tropes of repetition and compulsion.[98]

DISSENTING MODERNISMS: MINA LOY, H.D.

If Pound had begun to sense the eventual destination of the modernist long poem in 1915, there were also anxious voices concerned about his imaginative brinkmanship. Most provocatively there was Helen Saunders's poem 'A Vision of Mud' published in the second edition of *Blast*.[99] As Paul Peppis (1997) first noted, this begins with the suggestion that the poem will transport us to the battle front. There is a mud that chokes. Bodies strangely intertwine. Hands grope amidst pain. A band plays somewhere as strange ghostly shapes hover in the air.[100] There is even the suggestion of a streak of blood. This recalls Ford's Belgian combatant bleeding out in *Antwerp*, but this dislocating experience is not the battle front at all, but a communal mud, the mud of David Bomberg's *The Mud Bath* (1914). Gaudier-Brzeska had written to Pound on 14 March 1915, at much the same time that Saunders completed this poem, describing his own mud bath and explaining its benefit for rheumatism, arthritis and lumbago.[101] Saunders however transforms the site of the bath to a crude health resort. It is a stark reversal. Our gendered expectations that this is a poem focused on the mud of Flanders collapse into the reality of this commercial vulgarity.

The careless editorial misspelling of Saunders's name on the contents page of *Blast* only adds to the effect here. As does the absence of the details of the poem's authorship. *Blast* allowed such detail to the contributions by Eliot, Ford and Pound but denied it to Saunders. It is a stark reminder of the position of women within Vorticism and, in turn, an illustration of what was at stake in Saunders's pivot of our expectations in the poem. All of Lewis's short fiction from *Blast* through to the end of the war turns to stereotypes of men and women and of their respective roles in society. In the most historically immediate example, 'A Young Soldier' (*The Egoist*: March 1916), we find 'a born warrior, meant to

---

[97] Peter Howarth, *British Poetry in the Age of Modernism* (Cambridge: Cambridge University Press, 2005), pp. 51–9.

[98] Karolyn Steffens, 'Modernity as the Cultural Crucible of Trauma', in Kurtz, ed., pp. 36–50 (p. 39).

[99] H. Sanders [Helen Saunders], 'A Vision of Mud', *Blast*, 2 (July 1915), 73–4.

[100] Paul Peppis, '"Surrounded by a Multitude of Other Blasts": Vorticism and the Great War', *Modernism/modernity*, 4.2 (1997), 39–66 (pp. 57–8).

[101] Pound, *A Memoir of Gaudier-Brzeska*, p. 61.

kill other men as much as a woman is meant to bear children'.[102] It was around the time of *Blast*'s publication that Pound suggested Vorticist dinners 'would maintain an higher intellectual altitude if there were a complete & uncontaminated absence of women'.[103] Saunders's poem entered *Blast* then as a startling accusation: what after all did you expect? Not the warrior's sucking mud but a cosmetic pampering. Its pointed critique takes aim at Lewis in the poem's closing image of two alienated lovers facing the war in different directions.

The incursion of war into private sexual space is central to Mina Loy's 'Songs to Joannes' (*Others*: April 1917). *Others* published the first four sections of the sequence, albeit in a slightly emended form, as 'Love Songs' during July 1915. In *Profile*, Pound would label Loy's stylistic innovations in work such as this a form of Gongorism. He intended it pejoratively, but the description holds some critical value. The Baroque forms of *gongorismo* sacrificed the classicist rules of meaning and plot. They aimed to replace the orthodoxies of Aristotelianism with imaginative metaphor and syntactical difficulty. Pound's point was that Loy's work marked the intra-war emergence of an attention to detail which disregarded the main point of a poem.[104] As elsewhere in *Profile*, Pound wrongly dated this change to 1918. He probably had in mind the April 1917 edition of *Others* devoted entirely to Loy's sequence, and the publication of *Others: An Anthology of New Verse* (1917). According to John Rodker in the *Little Review*, the latter volume allowed access to enough of Loy's poems that readers could assess her significance properly.[105]

In 'Songs to Joannes' we can see *gongorismo*'s fondness for catachresis at work. The sequence's metaphors seem odd and illogical. Loy pushes metaphysical conceits to the point of breaking, notably in contrast to Pound's creation of oblique imaginative correlatives for subjective experience. One image is especially illustrative:

> Voices break on the confines of passion
> Desire   Suspicion   Man   Woman
> Solve in the humid carnage
>
> Flesh from flesh
> Draws the inseparable delight
> Kissing at gasps   to catch it[.][106]

---

[102] Wyndham Lewis, 'A Young Soldier', *The Egoist*, 3.3 (March 1916), 46.

[103] Ezra Pound, letter to Wyndham Lewis ([before July 1915], in *Pound/Lewis: The Letters of Ezra Pound and Wyndham Lewis*, ed. by Timothy Materer, The Correspondence of Ezra Pound (New York: New Directions, 1985), p. 12.

[104] Pound, *Profile*, p. 127.

[105] John Rodker, 'List of Books', *Little Review*, 5.7 (November 1918), 31–3 (p. 31).

[106] Mina Loy, 'Songs to Joannes', in *The Lost Lunar Baedeker: Poems of Mina Loy*, ed. by Roger L. Conover (Manchester: Carcanet, 1996), pp. 53–68 (p. 57).

The third line here, sitting between the lines demarcating gendered oppositions and a parting of flesh, ought sensibly to be 'human carnage'. Instead, we get both a deliberate use of 'humid' to suggest the passion and aggression of sexual relationship, and its conscious misappropriation. Loy uses 'humid' as an adjective of human, a variant on 'human' and '-oid'. The heat of sex, the sweat of copulation and the commingling of mistrust and arousal become inextricably enmeshed with the weaponised parting of flesh. Rather than allowing Loy's gnostic yearning for the chaos of war to direct the content of the poem towards the battle front, these strangely distended metaphors wrap the war's violence into the privacy of sexual space. Or as Loy says it better, 'We might have given birth to a butterfly / With the daily news / Printed in blood on its wings'.[107]

In the groundbreaking study of H.D.'s poetry *Penelope's Web* (1990), Susan Stanford Friedman made similar claims for H.D.'s *Sea Garden*. Scholars now generally accept that this volume, to use Friedman's own words, is 'never directly about *it*, [. . .] [but] nonetheless *of* the Great War'.[108] Interpreted this way, we could take *Sea Garden* and its recurrent turn to tropes of violence as useful evidence for the developing argument in *Modernist War Poetry*. Diana Collecott's *H.D. and Sapphic Modernism* (1999) clearly establishes the origins of H.D.'s modernism as an explicit counter modernism. This modernism, with its emphasis on beauty and the possibilities of sentimentality and non-heteronormative cultures, naturally sets itself up against the hard Poundian poetics of impersonality, Vorticism and Futurism.[109]

I have concerns about making this move though. In particular, there is questionable support for Friedman's well-made argument that we can date the poems in *Sea Garden* to the period after August 1914.[110] Admittedly, the compositional history here is difficult to pin down. There is evidence in Carr's *The Verse Revolutionaries* taken from the poem's geographies, flora and fauna which may suggest H.D. began drafting as far back as a trip to Capri in 1912.[111] And whilst Constable published *Sea Garden* in October 1916, it was much delayed by paper shortages. They had actually accepted the manuscript for publication in February 1916. Several poems were certainly complete by the spring of 1915 when they appeared in *Poetry*, *Some Imagist Poets*, the *Little Review* and *The Egoist*. Publication and distribution are no dependable guide to composition either. H.D. published 'Mid-day', for example, in *Some Imagist*

---

[107] Ibid. p. 54.
[108] Susan Stanford Friedman, *Penelope's Web: Gender, Modernity, H.D.'s Fiction* (Cambridge: Cambridge University Press, 1990), pp. 60–1.
[109] Diana Collecott, *H.D. and Sapphic Modernism* (Cambridge: Cambridge University Press, 1999).
[110] Friedman, p. 60.
[111] Carr, *The Verse Revolutionaries*, p. 556.

Poets of May 1916 alongside previously unpublished work even though *The Egoist* had already published it in May 1915. H.D. did not send it to Lowell until October 1915.[112] We also know that during the summer and autumn of 1915 H.D. turned to work for the *Poets' Translation Series. Sea Garden* might then belong substantially to the earliest months of the war, if at all.

This is of more than bibliographic interest. The compositional uncertainty raises to attention two distinct problems. First, it becomes difficult to align the handling of violence in *Sea Garden* with the anti-masculinist and anti-militarist statements that H.D. set out in her essays for *The Egoist* during the autumn of 1916 and in a later unpublished essay on Yeats's *Responsibilities*.[113] Again we could take this as support of an emergent counter modernism, one somewhat similar to the position taken by Saunders in relation to Vorticist logic, if it were not the case that these essays post-date *Sea Garden* by at least twelve to eighteen months. We also have misdated the later essay to 1914.[114]

Second, this compositional uncertainty calls into question close reading. The ecosystem of violence is obvious in *Sea Garden* with its sea battles, spear heads and arrows, slashing and tearing, the clashing of sea, wind and sun. This might well be a very oblique metaphor or figuration. Equally however we can find a world structured by the natural currents of aggression in H.D.'s work prior to the war. It is particularly obvious in 'Orion Dead' and 'Oread' (both *The Egoist*: February 1914) for example. Is the violence in *Sea Garden* the echo of history or the playing out of a recurrent pattern? War was after all a permanent feature of the Hellenic world. H.D., as Lawrence recorded, critiqued *Look! We Have Come Through!* (November 1917) on the grounds that its poems were not sufficiently eternal, too much soaked in the emotions.[115] From the reader's perspective what stands out in *Sea Garden* is its mutated synaesthesia, the 'rigid myrrh-bud, / camphor-flower' of 'Sea Iris' (*Little Review*: May 1915) for example.[116] It is an aestheticism that challenges Miranda B. Hickman's (2012) reading of the volume's frequent references

[112] H.D., letter to Amy Lowell (7 October 1915), qtd in Louis Silverstein, 'H.D. Chronology, Part Two (1915–March 1919)', <https://www.imagists.org/hd/hdchron2.html> [accessed 25 March 2022].

[113] H.D., 'Marianne Moore', *The Egoist*, 3.8 (August 1916), 118–19 (p. 118); H.D., 'Typescript corrected by H.D. of unpublished review of *Responsibilities and Other Poems* by William Butler Yeats', undated, in H.D. Papers (YCAL MSS 24), Beinecke Library, box 35, folder 915, <https://brbl-dl.library.yale.edu/vufind/Record/3472735> [accessed 30 March 2022], pp. [66–9].

[114] H.D.'s review was of *Responsibilities and Other Poems* (November 1916) and not *Responsibilities: Poems and a Play* (1914). Claire Buck, '"This Other Eden": Homoeroticism and the Great War in the Early Poetry of H.D. and Radclyffe Hall', in *Women's Experience of Modernity, 1875–1945*, ed. by Ann L. Ardis and Leslie W. Lewis (Baltimore: Johns Hopkins University Press, 2003), pp. 63–80 (p. 72).

[115] D. H. Lawrence, letter to Catherine Carswell ([9 March 1917]), in *The Letters of D. H. Lawrence*, III: *October 1916–June 1921*, ed. by James T. Boulton and Andrew Robertson (1984), p. 102.

[116] H.D., 'Sea Iris', in H.D., *Collected Poems 1912–1944*, ed. by Louis L. Martz (New York: New Directions, 1983), pp. 36–7 (p. 36).

to shells as indirect war metaphors.[117] H.D.'s 'broken shells' first appeared in 'The Wind Sleepers' (*Poetry*: March 1915) but Monroe often held back poems before publication.[118] The compositional dating of *Sea Garden* might remain one of its secrets and certainly deserves more attention.

There is compelling evidence from those poems that we can date to 1915 that H.D.'s intra-war poetry can be read as a response to the structure of feeling in *Sea Garden*. In other words, we can see them as a direct intra-war response to *Sea Garden*'s pre-war ecstatic seeking out of violence, the need best expressed in 'Sheltered Garden' (1916) in 'to find a new beauty / in some terrible / wind-tortured place'.[119] Indeed, the question raised by the aestheticism in *Sea Garden* is how we ought to read its overt valorisation and veneration of violence. Is its 'poetics of sublime violence', to borrow Hickman's (2010) useful term and analysis, resolved through tropes of survival, renewal and transformation and by its images of flowers strengthened, ennobled and finally emancipated by their struggle with natural salt, wind and sun? Or is the collection's repeated turn to the combative encounter between self and Other an eroticisation brutally out of step with history, a taking of refuge in the sublime?[120]

Hickman's essays argue for a unifying force running from *Sea Garden* into H.D.'s later poetry centred on the interplay of violence, the necessary shattering of self and of recovery. However, seeing *Sea Garden* as a product of the pre-war world allows us to suggest a significant change in H.D.'s work of 1915. A change that is in relation to the valorisation of violence. This is most concrete in H.D.'s translation of choruses from Euripides' *Iphigeneia in Aulis*. H.D. first published these neglected pieces in part in *The Egoist* of November 1915 (numbers I:1–9 and II). The full set followed in the Aldington-Doolittle-organised *Poets' Translation Series* published by *The Egoist* and privately by Clerk's Private Press in late 1915 (or early 1916; it is unclear which). H.D. published the series again alongside translations taken from *Hippolytus* in 1919 as part of a second set of the *Series*. These translations seem to self-consciously engage with the ambivalent possibilities left behind by *Sea Garden*. It is an engagement which supports Claire Buck's (2003) critique of the earlier volume's erotics of violence, its upending of straight norms that simultaneously threaten its own critique of masculinity and militarism.[121]

---

[117] Miranda B. Hickman, '"Uncanonically Seated": H.D. and Literary Canons', in *The Cambridge Companion to H.D.*, ed. by Nephie J. Christodoulides and Polina Mackay (Cambridge: Cambridge University Press, 2012), pp. 9–22 (p. 15).

[118] H.D., 'The Wind Sleepers', in *Collected Poems*, p. 15.

[119] H.D., 'Sheltered Garden' (1916), in *Collected Poems*, pp. 19–21 (p. 21).

[120] Miranda Hickman, 'Modernist Women Poets and the Problem of Form', in *The Cambridge Companion to Modernist Women Writers*, ed. by Maren Tova Linett (Cambridge: Cambridge University Press, 2010), pp. 33–46 (p. 39); Carr, *The Verse Revolutionaries*, pp. 830–1.

[121] Buck, p. 76.

The 'Choruses from *Iphigeneia*' pitch the reader straight into the landscape of *Sea Garden*. The 'split conch-shells' of 'Sea Poppies' (*Little Review*: April 1917), 'the salt track of the marsh' in 'The Helmsman' (*The Egoist*: April 1916) and the 'sea-hawks and gulls' of 'The Wind Sleepers' give way to the choruses' 'sand-hills' and 'sea-drift', 'the surf' and 'cut pine-trees', the 'clumps of marsh-reed / And spear-grass'.[122] The figurative violence of the earlier volume becomes a real scene as civilians gather from Chalcis on the island of Euboea to see the Athenian fleet depart for Troy. The effect is of stepping from one volume to the next, moving from one war-like patriarchal society bound by oaths of brother-hood to one gathering and arming itself for war. H.D.'s deliberation here is important. Advertisements for the *Poets' Translation Series* in *The Egoist* suggest that, even as late as September 1915, H.D. planned to produce 'Choruses from the "Rhesos" of Euripides' for the *Series*. That play breaks a pivotal scene out of the *Iliad*'s battlefields in order to focus on the relationship between a grieving mother and a dead son.[123] The January 1916 *Egoist* suggests H.D. also considered *Ion*, a play that deals with rape and conception.[124] In opting for the 'Choruses from *Iphigeneia*' H.D. moved the reader out of both the heat of battle and the effects of its aftermath to its very beginnings, its front edge, a space betwixt and between home front and battle front where civilians and combat-ants might mix. It moves us from *Sea Garden*'s beaches bathed in hues of amber and violet, to another beach, physically unchanged in appearance but now pre-paring for the slaughter of a woman in the name of a masculine code of honour.

These were radical choices. In *H.D. and Hellenism: Classic Lines* (1997) Eileen Gregory took note of the unique flavour of H.D.'s classicism. In particu-lar Gregory isolated H.D.'s decision to eschew Aeschylus, Homer and Sopho-cles for the unfashionable, decadent and enlightened rationalism of a tragedian noted for his reworking of traditional mythologies and especially of those asso-ciated with women's histories.[125] H.D.'s translation is also especially unusual. J. H. Kim On Chong-Gossard (2008) explains how in Euripides' play the chorus is no more than a pack of nosy bystanders who have come to gawk at unfold-ing military events.[126] In contrast H.D.'s version exaggerates the chorus's desire

---

[122] H.D., 'Sea Poppies', in *Collected Poems*, p. 21; 'The Helmsman', in *Collected Poems*, pp. 5–7 (p. 5); 'The Wind Sleepers', p. 15; H.D., 'From the *Iphigeneia in Aulis* of Euripides', in *Collected Poems*, pp. 71–84 (p. 71).

[123] [Advertisement], 'The Poets' Translation Series', *The Egoist*, 2.9 (September 1915), 148. *The Egoist* advertised the change to the *Iphigeneia* in October.

[124] [Advertisement], 'The Poets' Translation Series (Second Prospectus)', *The Egoist*, 3.1 (January 1916), 15.

[125] Eileen Gregory, *H.D. and Hellenism: Classic Lines* (Cambridge: Cambridge University Press, 1997), p. 25.

[126] J. H. Kim On Chong-Gossard, *Gender and Communication in Euripides' Plays: Between Song and Silence* (Leiden: Brill, 2008), pp. 12–13.

to see the spectacle of war, a desire that in turn makes them deeply conflicted bystanders to conflict. They express a deep-seated need to be at the site of war, to be there as a necessary ground for or as a prelude to witnessing. 'I have heard all this. I have looked too,' the chorus insists repeatedly.[127] It results in a kind of ecstatic worship of the combatants, one that touches on the voyeuristic links between witnessing, sexual desire and violence. The point is illustrated by placing H.D.'s translations next to Edward P. Coleridge's prose translation of the play from 1891:

H.D.	*Coleridge*
I crept through the woods	Through the grove of Artemis,
Between the altars:	rich with sacrifice, I sped my
Artemis haunts the place.	course, the red blush mantling
Shame, scarlet, fresh-opened – a flower,	on my cheeks from maiden
Strikes across my face.	modesty, in my eagerness to
And sudden—light upon shields,	see the soldiers' camp, the tents
Low huts—the armed Greeks,	of the mail-clad Danai, and
Circles of horses.	their gathered steeds. [Two
	chieftains there I saw met
I have longed for this.	together in council; one was
I have seen Ajax.	Aias, son of Oileus; the other
I have known Protesilaos	Aias, son of Telamon, crown
And that other Ajax—Salamis' light	of glory to the men of Salamis;
They counted ivory-discs.[128]	and I saw Protesilaus[.][129]

In H.D.'s account of the preliminary scenes that eventuate in Iphigeneia's slaughter, bashfulness becomes guilt. The longing to be inside the theatre of battle, to see, to hear, to feel it, even at its edges, eventuates in a form of knowledge that becomes carnal. Coleridge's chorus simply sees Protesilaos. David Kovacs's 2002 translation of the same passage for the Loeb Classical Library supports that reading.[130] In H.D. however the chorus comes to

---

[127] H.D., 'From the *Iphigeneia in Aulis* of Euripides', p. 76.

[128] Ibid. p. 72.

[129] Euripides, *Iphigenia at Aulis*, in *The Plays of Euripides, Translated into English Prose from the Text of Paley*, trans. by Edward P. Coleridge, 2 vols (London: George Bell, 1891), II, pp. 389–444 (p. 396).

[130] Euripides, *Iphigenia at Aulis*, in Euripides, *Bacchae, Iphigenia at Aulis, Rhesus* [*Euripides, volume VI*], ed. and trans. by David Kovacs, Loeb Classical Library, 495 (Cambridge, MA: Harvard University Press, 2002), pp. 155–344 (p. 185).

'know' this hero, the first of the Greek combatants ashore at Troy and the first to die there. The suggestion is that they have got so close they have sexually consummated their desires.

In H.D.'s version of martial society a madness is loose. It results from the literal and figurative pursuit of combatants into the battle theatre, a recursiveness in which violence in the public's name feeds back into private acts of violence. It anticipates by almost four years Yeats's 'blood-dimmed tide' in 'The Second Coming' (1920; *January 1919*) and Eliot's 'fractured atoms' in 'Gerontion'.[131] It is also the first definitive glimpse of an agnosticism in relation to combat, a counter to the trench lyricist's gnosticism, a reluctance, if not yet an outright refusal, to imagine combat. The imagination was no longer a transparent and uncomplicated tool. This is a vastly different response to the violence in *Sea Garden*; it casts the personae of that collection, their absorption in and by violence, as guilty perpetrators. Here the chorus is aware of its culpability:

H.D.	*Coleridge*
If a god could stand here	Next I sought the countless fleet, a
He could not speak	wonder to behold, that I might fill
At the sight of ships	my girlish eyes with gazing, a
Circled with ships.	sweet delight.[133]
This beauty is too much	
For any woman.	
It is burnt across my eyes.[132]	

Coleridge's Victorian propriety might partly account for the difference here. H.D.'s account however differs from Kovacs's Loeb version too. He has 'I came to reckon and to behold / their wonderous ships, / to fill with pleasure / the greedy vision of my female eyes'.[134] Whereas Kovacs's chorus is a pack of busybodies, H.D.'s is on the edge of orgasm at the beauty of this society of spectacle. That this process is traumatically burnt into memory becomes clear in H.D.'s closing image when we compare all three versions:

---

[131] W. B. Yeats, 'The Second Coming', in *The Poems*, pp. 189–90 (p. 189); T. S. Eliot, 'Gerontion', in *The Poems of T. S. Eliot*, ed. by Christopher Ricks and Jim McCue, 2 vols (London: Faber and Faber, 2015), I: *Collected and Uncollected Poems*, pp. 31–3 (p. 33).

[132] H.D., 'From the *Iphigeneia in Aulis* of Euripides', pp. 73–4.

[133] Euripides, *Iphigenia at Aulis*, trans. by Coleridge, p. 397.

[134] Euripides, *Iphigenia at Aulis*, ed. and trans. by Kovacs, p. 187.

H.D.

I have heard all this.
I have looked too
Upon this people of ships.
You could never count the Greek
    sails
Nor the flat keels of the foreign
    boats.

I have heard—
I myself have seen the floating
    ships
And nothing will ever be the
    same—
The shouts,
The harrowing voices within the
    house.
I stand apart with an army:
My mind is graven with ships.[135]

Coleridge

There I saw the naval armament, but
some things I heard at home about
the gathered host, whereof I still
have a recollection.[136]

Loeb

such is the armada
I saw here and what I remember,
from what I heard at home,
of the assembled army.[137]

It is not only that H.D. changed the emphasis to direct aural experience as the means of authenticating the act of testimony. It is that H.D. made the chorus into combatants. They are set apart from those who have not heard or seen. The chorus is the war. It is both implicated as perpetrator and its victim. Blood lust has changed everything. H.D. transformed what was in Euripides no more than a troubling memory into a genuinely traumatic social experience, one chiselled on the mind. The desire to see or to partake in the gnosis of combat, to live it and feel it, inevitably drags these civilians into war.

Unusually Eliot noticed the modernity of H.D.'s translations twice, once in print and once in draft. Only Lewis and Pound received that sort of intra-war attention. Whilst Eliot singled H.D.'s work out from the other five in the *Poets' Translation Series* in his essay 'Classics in English' (*Poetry*: November 1916) he was unimpressed by the deviations from the Greek original. Ignoring the obvious innovation in H.D.'s choruses – the way they freely adapted classical content to reflect on contemporary history – Eliot argued the translations searched too hard for the right image. Rather than a mind 'graven' by its foretaste of death, Eliot offered instead '"I keep the memory of the assembled army"', proposing H.D.'s version offered no improvement and only a loss of dignity.[138] Had

---

[135] H.D., 'From the *Iphigeneia in Aulis* of Euripides', p. 76.
[136] Euripides, *Iphigenia at Aulis*, trans. by Coleridge, p. 398.
[137] Euripides, *Iphigenia at Aulis*, ed. and trans. by Kovacs, p. 193.
[138] T. S. Eliot, 'Classics in English', in *Apprentice Years, 1905–1918*, pp. 493–6 (p. 494).

Eliot missed the point, or was he avoiding it?[139] Either way, Eliot would return to Euripides' play as a central principle in 'Gerontion', especially to the play's opening motif which contrasts Agamemnon, the warrior readying for Troy, with an indolent old man passing through life without the risk of danger.[140]

Pound appears to have entirely ignored the translations until he opted to republish them in a smaller selection (choruses I:1–4, I:[9] and II) in the November 1918 issue of the *Little Review*. That republication is easy to miss: H.D.'s name is missing from the journal's opening page and the translations are instead subsumed into an article by Pound prefaced with an apology for not having praised the choruses previously:

> I can not tell how much interest they will stir, or have stirred, of them-
> selves as poems isolated, but certainly the first, second, third, fourth and
> ninth strophes of the first chorus, and the brief second chorus, as H.D.
> has given them, are enough to make anyone with an interest in Greek
> drama in English wish that more of it were available in this form.[141]

The neglect and eventual rediscovery of the choruses bracket a crucial period in Pound's conception of *The Cantos*. In May 1915, Pound had begun that journey using the rudimentary skeleton provided by 'Provincia Deserta' (*Poetry*: March 1915; *October 1914*) and 'Near Perigord'. By the winter of 1918 he would finish 'Homage to Sextus Propertius' (October 1919). He would also finish the first version of *The Fourth Canto* which begins with a scene of destruction taken from Euripides' *The Trojan Women*. Like *Iphigeneia*, *The Trojan Women* is a play that speaks directly about the suffering and eventual fate of women in martial societies. It was a particularly important cultural reference point during the war. Harley Granville-Barker produced and directed Gilbert Murray's translation of the play in the United States during the summer of 1915. Under Jane Addams, the Woman's Peace Party sponsored a fifteen-week American tour of the play around the same time.[142]

---

[139] The second review, an unpublished and undated manuscript ('Autour d'une traduction d'Euripide'), was more generous. It considers the way translation can develop the historical mind and reveal the relationships between the dead, the living and those to come. Notably, a further anonymous review in the *New Age* took the negative line, following Eliot's earlier essay by objecting to H.D.'s errors of translation and assuming it must be the work of a man. [Anonymous], '"*The Poems of Anyte of Tegea*". Translated by Richard Aldington. *Choruses from Iphigeneia in Aulis*. Translated by H.D.', *New Age*, 18.1229 (30 March 1916), 524.

[140] Euripides, *Iphigenia at Aulis*, ed. and trans. by Kovacs, p. 169.

[141] E.P. [Ezra Pound], 'H.D[.]'s Choruses from Euripides', *Little Review*, 5.7 (November 1918), 16–20 (p. 16).

[142] Marilyn Fischer, 'Trojan Women and the Devil Baby Tales: Addams on Domestic Violence', in *Feminist Interpretations of Jane Addams*, ed. by Maurice Hamington (University Park: Pennsylvania University Press, 2010), pp. 81–106 (p. 84).

Pound's rediscovery of the choruses in 1918, then, particularly the way they appeared in the *Little Review* as a rediscovery by Pound of another found poem, suggests again an appropriation of method. It was precisely where Eliot found such fault – in H.D.'s willingness to transmogrify the source, to break away from stock phrases without losing full contact with the historical context, to break a shape without destroying it – that the innovation lay.[143] H.D. had found a way to speak about war without needing to rest on the gambit of imagining the soldier's experience and shock. Poetry could document the insidious impacts of martial society instead; it could be war writing. Lawrence appears to have been the first to understand the important direction this work was taking, that its central conceit, the making over of the chorus into a poem in its own right – what Eliot saw as a perversion – was a breakthrough for modernist culture against war verse.[144] In tribute, the earliest titles Lawrence considered for the collection that would become *New Poems* (1918) were 'Chorus of Women' and 'Choir of Women'.[145] It suggests that volume with its series of broken spirits was in direct dialogue with H.D.'s congregation of civilian combatants devastated by the effects of total war.

---

[143] Eliot, 'Classics in English', p. 493.

[144] Ibid.

[145] D. H. Lawrence, letter to J. B. Pinker (18 June 1918), in *The Letters of D. H. Lawrence*, III, pp. 254–5 (p. 255 n. 2).

3

THE THREE LIVES OF GNOSTICISM: 1916–SUMMER 1917

In *Kangaroo* (1923) D. H. Lawrence perfectly captured the changing mood
as the appalling events of 1915 gave way to the widespread recognition of an
unfolding disaster:

> It was in 1915 the old world ended. In the winter of 1915–1916 the spirit
> of the old London collapsed, the city, in some way, perished, perished
> from being a heart of the world, and became a vortex of broken passions,
> lusts, hopes, fears, and horrors. The integrity of London collapsed, and
> the genuine debasement began, the unspeakable baseness of the press and
> the public voice[.][1]

Lawrence had in mind quite specific personal circumstances in these lines: the
ongoing suppression of his work, his eventual retreat to Cornwall and fear
of conscription. The image still suggests a more generalised emptiness, a cultural vacuum at the eye of the storm. T. S. Eliot and Ezra Pound would fill the
space created by war. Eliot finished his delayed postgraduate dissertation in

---

[1] D. H. Lawrence, *Kangaroo* (1923), ed. by Bruce Steele, The Cambridge Edition (Cambridge:
Cambridge University Press, 1994; repr. 2002), p. 216.

April 1916 and, after the publication of work on Gottfried Leibniz in October, his focus turned to literature with the first in a series of lectureships. Henri Gaudier-Brzeska was dead. Henry James died in February 1916. Ford Madox Ford was on the Somme by the summer of that year, Richard Aldington with the Expeditionary Force by December. Both T. E. Hulme and Wyndham Lewis either returned from or began military training in March 1916 and they both embarked for France in May. By the summer of 1917, the stage was clear for Eliot and Pound to work through what was common and different in their approaches. In a much later essay of 1932, Pound termed the resulting period a '"movement to which no name has ever been given"'.[2] Pound soon became Foreign Editor at the *Little Review* and Eliot the Assistant Editor at *The Egoist*. Together they held the means to write the blank agenda left by the vortex. Unlike their conscripted European peers, until well into 1918 they sat beyond the coercive reach of their own governments.

The English public first heard the distraught voice of the moral witness in the summer of 1916. We need to be precise in the dating of this event.[3] As the first evidence take Henri Barbusse's *Le Feu*, the novel Jay Winter identifies as the seminal account of moral witnessing in modernity.[4] It was a literary sensation on first publication. Initially serialised in *L'Œuvre* in August 1916 and then published in full in December, it was followed by W. Fitzwater Wray's English translation in July of the following year. By September 1917, *Le Feu* had become the fastest-selling book in French literary history and won the Goncourt Prize.[5] Both *The Englishwoman* in March and the *English Review* in September reviewed it favourably. John Middleton Murry reviewed it for the *TLS* in April, praising its honesty in making the war's 'monstrous inhumanity human'.[6] Muriel Ciolkowska was a strong proponent in *The Egoist* although concerned with its focus on the suffering of a single proletarian class.[7] Ciolkowska's reviews repeatedly turned to *Le Feu*'s 'meticulously faithful rendering', the 'excessive care for truthfulness', the reproduction of '*argot*' and the

---

[2] Ezra Pound, 'Harold Monro', qtd in Levenson, p. 153.

[3] Vandiver (pp. 77–8) argues for the writing and publication of Charles Sorley's 'When you see millions of the mouthless dead' (January 1916; *October 1915*).

[4] Jay Winter, 'Introduction: Henri Barbusse and the Birth of the Moral Witness', in Henri Barbusse, *Under Fire*, trans. by Robin Buss (London: Penguin, 2003), pp. vii–xix (p. ix).

[5] Jerry Palmer, *Memories from the Frontline: Memoirs and Meanings of the Great War from Britain, France and Germany* (London: Palgrave Macmillan, 2018), p. 153.

[6] [John Middleton Murry], 'Le Feu', *TLS*, 794 (5 April 1917), 164. Similarly, [John Middleton Murry], 'La Troisième France', *TLS*, 801 (24 May 1917), 246.

[7] Muriel Ciolkowska, 'The French Word in Modern Prose. II. – Henry Barbusse, *L'Enfer*', *The Egoist*, 3.2 (1 February 1916), 27–8; Muriel Ciolkowska, 'Passing Paris', *The Egoist*, 4.7 (August 1917), 105–6; Muriel Ciolkowska, 'Passing Paris', *The Egoist*, 4.11 (December 1917), 168–9; Muriel Ciolkowska, 'Passing Paris', *The Egoist*, 5.2 (February 1918), 23–4.

'minutely recorded' horror of battle.[8] The novel's popularity owed a good deal, as Margaret C. Anderson observed in the *Little Review* during July 1917, to a series of graphic descriptions of the body in pieces, most of which avoided the censor and allowed it to function as a realism without any apparent limits.[9] In August 1917, Paul Rosenfeld, writing in the *Seven Arts*, ranked it alongside Euripides' *The Trojan Women* because of Barbusse's willingness to sacrifice formalism for stark honesty. It was as if, Rosenfeld said, 'the man had felt that literary taste should conform to his matter, and not his matter to literary taste'.[10] The following month, the *New Age* ranked it as the one book most likely to convey the real experience of combat to the civilian.[11] In *Poetry* during 1919, Aldington crowned Barbusse's novel as the greatest popular success of the war years.[12]

Based on Barbusse's time with the French army, the novel made combat gnosticism explicit. In one key closing scene, one soldier tries 'to describe his feeling that war is unimaginable and immeasurable in time and space':

> 'When you talk about the war,' he said, meditating aloud, 'it's as though you didn't say anything. It stifles words. We are here, looking at this, like blind men.'
> A bass voice rumbled a little way off:
> 'No, you can't imagine it.'
> A sudden outburst of laughter greeted this remark.
> 'To begin with, how could anyone imagine this, without having been here?'
> 'You'd have to be mad!' said the *chasseur*.[13]

Barbusse notably brackets the limits on imagination with two muted forms of speech neither of which results in knowledge. Whose is the bass voice? It might be a senior officer's instruction or as metaphor a distant shell impact. Whose is the laughter? These two indistinct utterances seem to come from a deep logic that exists within a personified version of the war. They serve as a macabre confirmation of its insanity. It was on these terms that Barbusse's novel circulated

---

[8] Muriel Ciolkowska, '"Le Feu". Goncourt Prize for 1916', *The Egoist*, 4.4 (May 1917), 55–7 (pp. 55, 56).

[9] M.C.A. [Margaret C. Anderson], '"The World's Immense Wound"', *Little Review*, 4.3 (July 1917), 27–8 (p. 27).

[10] P.R. [Paul Rosenfeld], 'The Seven Arts Chronicle for August. "Le Feu"', *Seven Arts*, 1.8 (August 1917), 518–20 (p. 519).

[11] [Anonymous], 'Reviews: Under Fire', *New Age*, 21.21 (20 September 1917), 453.

[12] Richard Aldington, 'Reviews: Recent French Poetry', *Poetry*, 15.1 (October 1919), 42–8 (pp. 42–3).

[13] Barbusse, *Under Fire*, trans. by Robin Buss, p. 303.

Timeline 3.1 1916

	Composition	*Publication, Exhibition, Event*
January	Thomas, 'Rain', 'Roads'	Enlisters: Lewis H.D., *Choruses from Iphigeneia in Aulis* (English edn) Sorely, *Marlborough and Other Poems* Wharton, *The Book of the Homeless*
February	Thomas, 'February Afternoon' (December 1918)	Battles: Verdun begins Flint, 'War-time' (*Poetry*) H.D. moves with Aldington to Devon Mott, article on explosives/nervous system (*Lancet*)
March	Thomas, '"Home"' (October 1917) Sassoon, 'A Working Party' (1917)	Masters, 'All Life in a Life' (*Poetry*) Lewis, 'The French Poodle' (*Egoist*) Military Service Act comes into force Nevinson, *La Mitrailleuse* (1915) Strachey conscientious objection to war Thomas, *Six Poems* including 'A Private' War dead: David Thomas
April	Lawrence, redrafts 'The Sisters' / *The First 'Women in Love'* (1998) Sassoon, 'The Kiss' (1917)	*Éirí Amach na Cásca* Lewis, serialisation of 'Tarr' (*Egoist*) Pound, *Gaudier-Brzeska* War dead: Faversham munitions explosion
May	Thomas, 'Cherry Trees' (October 1917), 'The sun used to shine', 'No one cares less than I' (December 1918), 'As the team's head-brass'	Enlisters: Aldington Graves, *Over the Brazier* Pound, serialisation of 'Dialogues of Fontenelle' (*Egoist*) *Some Imagist Poets* Leonard Woolf exempted from service
June	Rosenberg, 'Break of Day in the Trenches'	H.D. becomes assistant Editor at *Egoist* Lawrence, *Twilight in Italy* Russell tried under Defence of Realm Act Stein returns to Paris
July	H.D., *The Islands* series (including 'The Islands', 'Amaranth', 'Eros', 'Envy') and poems in 'The God' sequence ('The God', 'The Tribute', 'Circe', 'Adonis', 'Pygmalion')	Battles: Somme Offensive begins Enlisters: Thomas H.D. at Corfe Castle War dead: Seeger Wounded: David Jones, Graves
August		Barbusse, serialisation of *Le Feu* (*L'Œuvre*) H.D., *Choruses from Iphigeneia in Aulis* (American edn); 'Marianne Moore' (*Egoist*) Woolf 'Heard on the Downs' (*Times*)

	Composition	Publication, Exhibition, Event

September	Blunden, 'Thiepval Wood' (1930)
	Ford, 'Arms and the Mind'
	Thomas, 'Gone, gone again',
	    'Trumpet' (both October 1917)
	Yeats, 'Easter, 1916'
		Battles: Tanks used at Flers
		H.D., review of Mew's poetry (*Egoist*)
		Eliot, 'Conversation Galante', 'La
		    Figlia Che Piange', 'Mr. Apollinax',
		    'Morning at the Window' (*Poetry*)
		Flint, 'Soldiers' (*Egoist*)
		Pound, *Lustra* (English ed.); *Noble Plays
		    of Japan*
		Nevinson exhibition (Leicester Galleries)

October	Borden, 'At the Somme'
	Stein, war poems published in *Useful
	    Knowledge* (1928)
		H.D., *Sea Garden*
		Eliot begins *Modern French Literature*
		    lectures in Ilkley for Oxford
		    University Extension Delegacy
		    (to December 1916) and *Modern
		    English Literature* lectures in
		    Southall for University of London
		    Extension Board
		Richardson, *Backwater*

November	Lawrence, 'All of Us', 'Samson &
	    Delilah'
	Thomas, 'Lights Out', 'The long
	    small room' (both October 1917)
		Eliot 'Classics in English' (*Poetry*)
		H.D., 'The Tribute' (*Egoist*)
		Woolf and Mansfield first meeting

December	Frost, 'On Talk of Peace at this Time' Yeats, 'Sixteen Dead Men' (1920)	Aldington leaves for France H.D., 'Circe' (*Egoist*) Barbusse, *Le Feu* Romains, *Europe* Rosenberg, 'Trench Poems' (*Poetry*) *Wheels* 1

Guide to Timelines

Works arranged in alphabetical order within each month.

Publication dates given in parenthesis, except if given in the main text, endnotes or elsewhere in timelines.

Titles shortened for brevity.

within modernist cultures. In *From Bapaume to Passchendaele 1917* (1918) the journalist Philip Gibbs found it difficult to describe the soldiers to his readers, particularly what goes on in their minds. They belong to another world, Gibbs proposed, 'and there is no code which can decipher their secret, nor any means of self-expression on their lips'.[14] Both the English and the American edition (December 1918) of Siegfried Sassoon's *Counter-Attack*, along with *The War Poems of Siegfried Sassoon* (October 1919), included a French quotation from *Le Feu* singling out the combatant's rite of passage which we can translate as 'these men whom fatigue had tormented, whom rain had scourged, whom

---

[14] Philip Gibbs, *From Bapaume to Passchendaele, 1917* (Toronto: William Briggs, 1918), p. 20.

night-long lightning had convulsed, these survivors of volcanoes and flood'.[15] The warrior sees and suffers evil, the double burden of Avishai Margalit's moral witness.

Running contemporaneously with the serialisation of *Le Feu*, C. R. W. Nevinson's exhibition of war paintings at the Leicester Galleries in September 1916 offers a further example. Nevinson was already known as a war artist. He exhibited three canvases, *La Mitrailleuse* (1915), *Night: Light: Crowd* (1916) and *Violence* ([1916]), completed during time in Dunkirk with the Friends' Ambulance Unit alongside the Allied Artists in March 1916. He called the three canvases an illustration, an interpretation and an abstraction. In *Modern War Paintings* (1917), the catalogue accompanying the exhibition at the Leicester Galleries, P. G. Konody highlighted this subtitling as a specific process. It was designed, he said, by Nevinson 'to demonstrate the manner in which pictorial art gradually emerges from its bondage to the representation of facts'.[16] Nevinson's tripartite meta-aesthetic, uncannily similar to that of May Sinclair in prose and Pound in poetry, served as a guide to how the artist translates the privacy of immediate experience into a public good, the means by which an artist salvages *Wissen* from the chaos of a purely personal shock.

Konody, the art critic at *The Observer* and one of *Blast*'s blessed, was Nevinson's strongest supporter. Konody's introduction to Nevinson's work singled out the focus on a new type of warfare that required profound representational change to a new synthetic method.[17] The chemical analogy will recur later in this narrative in Eliot's work but here Konody used it to point to Nevinson's key innovation, specifically the willingness to draw explicit attention to direct involvement in the battle zone. Whilst this experience, first as an ambulance driver and then as a medical orderly, had caused personal breakdown, Nevinson had according to Konody become the fleshwitness: he had gained a form of 'compensation in the collecting of rich experience'. 'Compensation': the fleshwitness's investment in chaos brings its own profit, something to weigh against the wound, the ability to feel more in both quantity and quality because of this encounter with the kernel of the real.

According to Konody, however, it was not the battlefield per se that was key but rather the encounter with the body in pieces: 'If he missed the excitement of bayonet charges, bombing, and sniping, of attack and of defence, he had his fill of the horrors of war at first-aid stations and base hospitals.'[18]

---

[15] The translation is from Henri Barbusse, *Under Fire: The Story of a Squad (Le Feu)*, trans. by Fitzwater Wray (New York: E. P. Dutton, 1917), pp. 343–4. For Sassoon's citation see Siegfried Sassoon, *Counter-Attack and Other Poems* (New York: E. P. Dutton, 1918), p. [vi].

[16] *Modern War Paintings by C. R. W. Nevinson with an Essay by P. G. Konody* (London: Grant Richards, 1917), p. 22.

[17] Ibid. p. 13.

[18] Ibid. p. 19.

Konody imagined Nevinson emptying himself of the basic human responses to horror, in such a way that, anticipating Eliot's later split of personal suffering and poetic self, pity and sympathy could be winnowed away to leave only the medic's professional curiosity. Konody labelled it a 'cruel objectivity', a 'cruel realism', one 'without a vestige of sentimentality'.[19] According to another advocate, J. E. Crawford Flitch in *The Great War Fourth Year by C. R. W. Nevinson* (1918), Nevinson was the first 'uncorrupted witness'. By 'sift[ing] the evidence of the eye, selecting from its prolix and confusing report just that residuum of form which has vital significance', Nevinson had found, according to Crawford Flitch, a means of giving form to contemporary history that was lost in the 'undigested record of the camera' and 'the emotional version of the popular illustrator'.[20] This art was an early intimation of the inert chamber in which art could be synthesised.

As Nevinson's exhibition closed, *Poetry* published Isaac Rosenberg's 'Trench Poems', 'Marching' (*December 1915*) and 'Break of Day in the Trenches' (*June 1916*), in its December edition. Although there is no definitive evidence, it is unlikely that those modernist poets who remained in London did not read them that winter, especially since Rosenberg was already well known in modernist circles.[21] The latter of these poems still is particularly remarkable. As it opens it reveals a soldier looking at 'A queer sardonic rat'. He plucks 'the parapet's poppy' to stick behind his ear in a high degree of camp. The poet tells us the rat is 'Droll'. It seems an unlikely observation to make. Cynicism and self-mockery in a rat? So obvious are these personifications that we refocus on the narrator as it becomes increasingly unclear in the poem what is a description of the rat and what of the soldier. The two seem to fuse as this composite being also 'Bonds to the whims of murder'.[22] The narrator does confess to the 'seem[ing]' nature of these thoughts, but this is the darkest of humours, a macabre joke which seems to be partly laughing at its own dalliance with poetic convention. Who is it that the poem is bonding to murder? The combatants? They are legally

[19] Ibid. pp. 21, 26.

[20] *The Great War Fourth Year by C. R. W. Nevinson, with an Introductory Essay by J. E. Crawford Flitch* (London: Grant Richards, 1918), pp. 9, 10.

[21] Mark Gertler introduced Rosenberg to Hulme in November 1913, and Pound sent Rosenberg's poems from *Youth* (1915) to Monroe. Jean Moorcroft Wilson, *Isaac Rosenberg: The Making of a Great War Poet, A New Life* (Evanston, IL: Northwestern University Press, 2008), pp. 105, 186–8. John Rodker sent Rosenberg's trench poems to Monroe. Eliot did not know Rodker until 1918 though and the earliest evidence for Eliot's appreciation of Rosenberg is 'A Brief Treatise on the Criticism of Poetry' (*Chapbook*: March 1920) where Eliot aligned him with Hulme. Others have noticed similar classical affinities. Joseph Cohen, 'Isaac Rosenberg: From Romantic to Classic', *Tulane Studies in English*, 10 (1960), 129–42.

[22] Isaac Rosenberg, 'Break of Day in the Trenches', in *The Collected Works of Isaac Rosenberg*, ed. by Ian Parsons (London: Chatto & Windus, 1979), pp. 103–4 (p. 103).

bound to wage war. Or the rat, biochemically attracted to the spoils of flesh? Or are the bonds here economic, references to the financing of war by interest-bearing civilian war notes? These images are themselves bound together into a metaphor of the event as a very public premeditated sacrifice, the vision of a landscape amounting to no more than an open grave.

These reflections lead to the pivotal question. What might the battle look like from the Other's perspective?

> What do you see in our eyes
> At the shrieking iron and flame
> Hurled through still heavens?
> What quaver—what heart aghast?[23]

The combatant aims the question at the rat, but the stress on 'do' implicates the reader in the 'you'. In an appalling and grotesque reversal of the romantic love conceit, the eyes of the combatant become a cinematic screen, for the rat literally and for the public metaphorically. The inhumanity of the carnage beyond the trench parapet is then projected on to this screen. What can we interpret from these staring eyes? The poem invites us to take a step inside the combatant's mind. It is the same step the solider took into the rat. The doubling up of rhetorical questions, added to the manuscript by Rosenberg in June 1916 to replace the uneven set of lines which appeared in the *Poetry* version, raises the inherent problem of the knowability of the trembling and fleshy horror of combat.[24] That uncertainty leaves us with little purchase on the poem's closing lines. They are hermetic. Are we left with anger? Or a way of protecting the self from existential threat? Is it a man shocked into insensitivity? Is it even sardonic or droll?[25] There seems no way of knowing: the monosyllabic simplicity waterproofs the final clause against any attempt to make it mean. The lyrical self closes at the very moment we expect and demand it to fully reveal itself.

THE GNOSTICISM OF GERTRUDE STEIN

The choice of these three masculinist modernisms – the trench memoir, a Futurist-inflected war art and a form of the trench lyric – is deliberate. It sets up the question of the gendered nature of combat gnosticism to now destabilise it. Take the first part of Mary Borden's 'At the Somme', titled 'Where is Jehovah?', written at the field hospital Borden founded for the French army at Bray-sur-Somme. Here too we find Borden structuring the central motif according to a

---

[23] Ibid.

[24] The version in *Poetry* has several variants including the reflected image of the battlefield. Isaac Rosenberg, 'Break of Day in the Trenches', *Poetry*, 9.3 (December 1916), 128–9 (p. 129).

[25] Rosenberg, 'Break of Day in the Trenches', in *The Collected Works of Isaac Rosenberg*, pp. 103–4.

division between the here of grotesque direct experience (of men 'going mad, jabbering, bleeding, twisting') and the absence of Jehovah from the chaos. 'He ought to be here,' the poem claims, while in contrast the 'he' that is 'here' (a word repeated over half a dozen times) is the 'he' that is the soldier: 'He is dirty. He is tired. His stomach is empty –'. Borden quite deliberately opposes the reality of the world before the eyes ('he stands there') with the absent god ('where is Jehovah'). The addition of 't' and 'w' to 'here' deliberately changes the hereness of the poem. This hereness stands in contrast to the afterwardness of Chapter 1. Borden wrote this explicitly into the text through the addition of one note to the poem. It reminds us that she drafted the poem 'Under the Tricolour'.[26] It is the mark of the poem's right to speak authentically.

The more intriguing example is Gertrude Stein's 'Lifting Belly' (1953). Stein began this extended prose poem following departure from Paris in March 1915 for the Balearics to 'forget the war a little', Stein said later in *The Autobiography of Alice B. Toklas* (1933).[27] Several images suggest it was mostly drafted in 1917, and this is the consensus arising from Stein's Beinecke manuscripts and the bibliography published in *transition* (February 1929).[28] The poem's incorporation of one particular scene, discussed later in this section and taken from *The Autobiography of Alice B. Toklas* where it is dated to after the Armistice, suggests to me that Stein worked on it at least into 1919.[29]

Structured as an elliptical and unresolved dialogue between unnamed persons and parts of the same self, 'Lifting Belly' charts Stein's relationship with Alice B. Toklas on Mallorca and their time together as volunteers with the AFFW, the American Fund for the French Wounded.[30] The poem takes its name from what is a very enigmatic act. Stein intends it to be both literal and metaphorical. It encompasses coded moments of sexual intimacy, the ecstatic moment of orgasm and the minutiae and erotics of pillow-talk, alongside the daily routine of eating and growing and the swelling of pregnancy. This latter suggestion Stein links also to the poem's emergence into the world. As Rebecca Mark (1989) describes best, 'lifting belly' has no singular meaning. Punctured by oblique references to the fighting in France, the flotsam and jetsam of history, it comes to stand in as a more general synonym for a way of life based on relationship in its multifarious forms, a mixing of voices. It is, Mark says, a kind of synonym for 'collaboration, dialogue, response, [and] love' which,

---

[26] Borden, pp. 77–8.

[27] Gertrude Stein, *The Autobiography of Alice B. Toklas* (New York: Harcourt Brace, 1933; repr. New York: Vintage, 1990), p. 161.

[28] Rebecca Mark, 'Introduction', in Gertrude Stein, *Lifting Belly*, ed. by Rebecca Mark (Tallahassee: Naiad Press, 1989), pp. xi–xxxiii (p. xvi).

[29] Stein, *Autobiography of Alice B. Toklas*, pp. 184–7.

[30] On the background see David M. Owens, 'Gertrude Stein's "Lifting Belly" and the Great War', *Modern Fiction Studies*, 44.3 (Fall 1998), 608–18 (pp. 608–9).

emanating from the outside of war, serve to stand against the fission of human feeling going on within it.[31] Stein's words capture the complexity: 'Lifting belly is a language. It says island. Island a strata. Lifting belly is a repetition.' Although it might appear then to be an isolated act it emerges in the poem as a third part of the Stein-Toklas relationship.[32] 'Three eggs in lifting belly. / Éclair. / Think of it. Think of that,' the poem asks its reader.[33] We are to see this alternative war consciousness not through the singularity of egotistical presence but as a tripartite meeting point, the pastry filled with cream and topped with fondant, the inseparable entity that becomes Stein, Toklas and the manuscript, an image surely designed to function as the literal translation of *éclair* or a flash of lightning.

It was then a very radical attempt to redefine the entire concept of identity and what fundamentally constituted war writing. Yet, even here, we find the hard and resistant kernel of combat gnosticism:

> I can't express the hauntingness of Dugny.
> I can't express either the obligation I have to say say it.
> Lifting belly is so kind.
> Dear me lifting belly is so kind.
> Am I in it.
> That doesn't affect it.
> How do you mean.
> Lifting belly and a resemblance.
> There is no resemblance.
> A plain case of misdeed.
> Lifting belly is peacable.[34]

Etymologically 'haunt' derives from habituation, from an obsessive frequenting, a traumatic revisitation. Here, Stein links it to both a physical site inhabited by ghosts and the state of the ego in which the absence of exorcism goes with ineffability. As Ross Chambers defines it in *Untimely Interventions*, the quality of haunting can be best conceived 'as the manifestation of liminal areas of consciousness that, because they can be neither fully ignored nor fully identified, seem spectral and elusive'.[35] Or as Avery F. Gordon suggests in *Ghostly*

---

[31] Mark, p. xvii.
[32] Gertrude Stein, 'Lifting Belly', in *The Unpublished Writings of Gertrude Stein*, ed. by Carl Van Vechten and others, The Yale Edition, 8 vols (New Haven: Yale University Press, 1951–8), III: *Bee Time Vine and Other Pieces [1913–1927]* (1953), pp. 62–115 (p. 78).
[33] Ibid. p. 110.
[34] Ibid. p. 75.
[35] Chambers, p. 34.

Matters (1997), 'being haunted draws us affectively, sometimes against our will and always a bit magically, into the structure of feeling of a reality we come to experience, not as cold knowledge, but as a transformative recognition'.[36] Stein's idea is then a form of gnosis. It raises the question, precariously unbalanced by the sense of shame on 'misdeed', of what it means to be 'in it', of what participation and 'affect' means within war when the public shares affect.[37]

The original site of the experience in this stanza of 'Lifting Belly' was Dugny-sur-Meuse, the headquarters of the *Région Fortifiée de Verdun*. It was a crucial town in the system of forts and *ouvrages* set up around the strategically important region of Verdun. It was also a front-line supply station sitting at the interface between the standard gauge railway and local front-line spurs. Stein and Toklas travelled down the road to Dugny as they headed for Alsace in the spring of 1919, and this sublime object of memory would seem to be the same site recorded by Stein in *The Autobiography of Alice B. Toklas*:

> Soon we came to the battle-fields and the lines of trenches of both sides. To anyone who did not see it as it was then it is impossible to imagine it. It was not terrifying it was strange. We were used to ruined houses and even ruined towns but this was different. It was a landscape. And it belonged to no country.
>
> I remember hearing a french nurse once say and the only thing she did say of the front was, c'est un paysage passionant, an absorbing landscape. And that was what it was as we saw it. It was strange.[38]

Translating (and misspelling) 'passionant' as 'absorbing' underplays the interplay of excitement and horror that results in 'strange'. It wonderfully exposes the primal *jouissance* that accords with the encounter with the real. It introduces that menacing point outside both the symbolic and imaginary orders where the drives coalesce as *das Ding*. The misspelling only adds to the effect.

Ineffability is only part of the story though. 'Lifting Belly' is intent on making another point too. Take the line already cited: 'I can't express either the obligation I have to say say it.' One meaning is that there is an ethical responsibility to give voice to the ineffability of gnosis. Another meaning is that this responsibility can find itself mute. The repetition on 'say' (itself repeated in the *Autobiography*'s need to say the same thing twice: 'it was strange') suggests

---

[36] Avery F. Gordon, *Ghostly Matters: Haunting and the Sociological Imagination* (Minneapolis: University of Minnesota Press, 1997), p. 8.

[37] Similarly, see the language used in Gertrude Stein, 'J.R.' and 'J.R. II' (*Vanity Fair*: March 1919), in *The Previously Uncollected Writings of Gertrude Stein*, ed. by Robert Bartlett Haas, 2 vols (Los Angeles: Black Sparrow Press, 1973), I: *Reflection on the Atomic Bomb*, p. 38.

[38] Stein, *Autobiography of Alice B. Toklas*, p. 187.

something that is also hard to admit into the poem. The feelings seem to stick in the throat, they die on the tongue and the lips. Stein must spit them out. Say it! The obligation then appears as the responsibility to say to the *ars poetica* that expression can fail. It is a recognition that repeatedly haunts the poem as a gnawing problem. It is the thing that the poem's 'lifting belly' must work against in its movement from fission to relationship.

The poem's strategy to achieve relationship reveals a process which must first redefine the notion of veterancy. It does this by repeatedly opposing images of violence, patriotism and defence – Verdun, the conquistadors, prize-fighters, fortified European cities and the American flag for example – to the compassionate action of 'lifting belly':

> Lifting belly is so kind.
> What shall you say about that. Lifting belly is so kind.
> What is a veteran.
> A veteran is one who has fought.
> Who is the best.[39]

The absence of question marks here is a signpost to meaning. As Stein explained in *Wars I Have Seen* (1945) the Stein-Toklas pairing was a composite being with 'a veteran mentality'.[40] And to that end 'Lifting Belly' repeatedly reminds us that Stein-Toklas did 'go there and back again', that 'By going to it. / We will go. / For them'.[41] This results in a glimpse inside Stein's proposed poetic:

> Big Caesars.
> Two Caesars.
> Little seize her.
> Too.
> Did I do my duty.
> Did I wet my knife.
> No I don't mean whet.[42]

Margaret Dickie's *Stein, Bishop, and Rich* (1997) helps us to unpick Stein's codewords here.[43] The transformation of the warmongering of emperorship into its demasculinised homonym links to the Stein-Toklas codeword for orgasm. It becomes a somatic image of the physical act of lovemaking. In the

---

[39] Stein, 'Lifting Belly', pp. 76, 79, 90, 81–2.
[40] Gertrude Stein, *Wars I Have Seen* (London: B. T. Batsford, 1945), p. 48.
[41] Stein, 'Lifting Belly', pp. 69, 115.
[42] Stein, 'Lifting Belly', pp. 83–4.
[43] Margaret Dickie, *Stein, Bishop, and Rich: Lyrics of Love, War, and Place* (Chapel Hill: University of North Carolina Press, 1997), pp. 28, 34.

process it breaks apart the opposition of 'wet' and 'whet' and the question of what duty means, of how we ought to think about a life on Mallorca lived amidst the paroxysms of sexual excitement and one lived out alongside the sharpening of blades. The aggression of the 'Two Caesars', the sense of aggressive entrapment, pivots on that lonely 'Too' to introduce alternative histories.

The poem's opacity makes these points difficult to approach. Readers rejecting the difficulty may well shy away from its deliberately anxiogenic effects. This is always one of the problems faced by intra-war modernist poetics. There are however strong grounds for recognising the extraordinary nature of Stein's vision:

> Lifting belly is anxious.
> Not about Verdun.
> Oh dear no.
> The wind whistles that means it whistles just like any one. I thought it
>   was a whistle.
> Lifting belly together.
> Do you like that there.[44]

The ambivalence in the third line unnerves the reader. It matters a great deal how we read this. What kind of island is 'lifting belly'? Do the lovers return to the intimacy of sexual touch in the final line with the dead forced out of or into mind? It is surely the latter rather than the former. 'Oh dear no' is not a dismissive response to a surprise question, but a register of shock. It is a return of the repressed, a sympathetic registering of the scale of the death at Verdun, of the potential invasion and occupation of France. Stein transforms the 'whistle', a whistling that repeatedly punctuates the poem and follows here so soon after the reflection on slaughter, into the echo of the trench whistle used to signal attack. It is not the dead the poem brings into the poem. The poem hides the body in pieces; it does not take us to the battlefield. Instead, Stein asks us to inhabit the hauntedness. The poem catches soldiers in the trench in the beingness of their fear. They are the soon to die. The poem brings them compassionately into the act of sexual union; they are all 'Lifting belly together'.

David A. Owens (1998) rightly suggests that 'Lifting Belly' was a deliberate attempt to come to terms with the relationship between its isolated nature and the war.[45] We might add to this the need to come to terms with combat gnosticism. It is a poem that hankers after a language that can arbitrate between the perpetually haunting nature of strange experience and the limits of the sympathetic imagination. Few intra-war modernist poems come close to its clarity

---

[44] Stein, 'Lifting Belly', p. 71.
[45] Owens, p. 617.

of vision. This makes it feel very out of place in any intra-war history. Whilst we might note stylistic similarities to Eliot's work, what marks the poem out is Stein's sense for compassionate action. It sees the need to simply recognise that the Other is in pain, the need that is to hold those in pain as opposed to the need to apply the mechanics of pity, sympathy or empathy to examine that pain. To think then of all combat gnosticism entirely through a pejorative gender lens is not especially constructive. In 'Lifting Belly' the reciprocity of sexual relationship and of compassion for the Other arises out of Stein's distinct understanding of the unique nature of otherness, an understanding in turn stemming from the idea that combat is an ineffable unique order of experience. The poem aims to create an overarching metaphor of relationship in which the public can counter violence with a sense for the radical nature of alterity.

The Ends of the Image

Although Stein's peers lacked both the audacity and scope of vision that we can find in 'Lifting Belly' something had markedly changed during these months. Whereas in Chapter 1 *The Egoist* lauded John Gould Fletcher's work exposing the fakery of war verse, in December 1916 Fletcher raised the pressing need to deal with the war. 'Has a poet a right to make use of the war as a subject? And if so, how should it be treated?' Fletcher now asked. This was a sharp generic turn, introducing what Fletcher described as the 'knotty' problem of the war and the lyric. It was a problem originating in the free position on subject matter taken by the Imagists.[46] In *Some Imagist Poets* (May 1916) Aldington claimed that '"Imagism" refers to the manner of presentation, not to the subject'. This was an appeal to an alleged radical sincerity. It enabled the poem to bring the effect of an object to the reader's mind as it had presented itself to the poet's mind when the poet first sat down to write it.[47] The Imagists grounded this sincerity in *vers libre*'s faith in the rise and fall of cadence, in the strophe that is rather than the foot or the emphasis on a spoken rather than a written poetry. As Fletcher explained, these rules resulted in the subject choosing the Imagist. The subject was the thing through which the poet expressed emotion and mood. This left Fletcher wondering then how the Imagist ought to deal with the war.

Fletcher rejected the jingoism and syrupy sentimentalism of Rupert Brooke and John Masefield. He even rejected Nevinson's cruel realism which he felt was too objective and efficient. Instead, Fletcher demanded 'some poetry that puts the reader face to face with the imaged reality, perplexing, horrible, and

---

[46] John Gould Fletcher, 'On Subject-Matter and War Poetry', *The Egoist*, 3.12 (December 1916), 188–9 (p. 189).

[47] [Richard Aldington], 'Preface', in *Some Imagist Poets 1916: An Annual Anthology* (Boston: Houghton Mifflin, 1916), pp. v–xii (pp. v, vi).

yet at times curiously beautiful'. It is unclear how Fletcher intended the Imagists pull this off. On the one hand he insisted that neither the ordinary nor daily matters need restrict the poet.[48] On the other hand, though, Imagism had clearly come to rest on a concept of presence grounded in the act of composition as the stamp guaranteeing the authenticity of the emotion the poem hoped to recover. Fletcher was unable to avoid Aldington's demands, expressed in this essay as the need for 'a man [who] looks out of a window', who 'consults his mood', who sees 'one single dead leaf'.[49] The gendering here is again a symptom. It signals a reluctance to recognise other perspectives.

It is possible that Imagism constitutively lacked an answer to war. The core of Hellenistic deadness at its heart, the artifice and lack of dynamism, was eventually mortifying. As Tim Armstrong summarises in *Modernism: A Cultural History* (2005), the Image's prioritisation of instantaneity perversely demanded certain regimes of elimination and prohibition that, after the gradual clipping away of dead matter, left behind only the overly sculptured, the plastic and the abstract, a non-being rather than being.[50] Tellingly, just a few weeks after Fletcher's article, Aldington was in France writing to Amy Lowell that were it not for H.D. he was looking forward to the whole experience of war, seemingly in search of a handful of that newly minted currency of immediate experience.[51]

We can read Wallace Stevens's 'Metaphors of a Magnifico' (*Little Review*: June 1918; *1917*) as a graphic illustration of this fault line in Imagism. It mockingly describes the multiple perspectives a poet might use to visualise a scene of twenty combatants crossing a bridge into a village. It suggests the use of metaphor. It also suggests an etymological play on the metaphor's Greek origins, that is on *metapherein* or metaphor as a form of transfer, the carrying across or bridging of meaning which alters and changes it. There is then a clear sense of parody. The magnifico's attempts to connect with what is real all seem to fail. They cannot ever take shape. The meaning simply 'will not declare itself', it consistently escapes.[52] It reveals a nebulous and unstable poetic imagination. It is not the imagination Pound would describe in a letter to his father in 1927 as one capable of the pursuit of 'the "magic moment" or moment of metamorphosis, bust thru from quotidien into "divine or permanent world"'.[53] Stevens's riff on

---

[48] Fletcher, 'On Subject-Matter and War Poetry', p. 189.

[49] Ibid.

[50] Armstrong, *Modernism*, p. 31. See also Tiffany, pp. 148–58.

[51] Richard Aldington, letter to Amy Lowell (4 January 1917), qtd in Doyle, p. 61.

[52] Wallace Stevens, 'Metaphors of a Magnifico', *Little Review*, 6.2 [5.2] (June 1918), 4. See also Wallace Stevens, 'Metaphors of a Magnifico', in *Harmonium* (New York: Alfred A. Knopf, 1923), p. 35.

[53] Pound, letter to Homer L. Pound (11 April 1927), p. 285.

this theory of imagination suggests it might be a form of sorcery. The great or regal *magnus* of the mocking meta-title becomes then a *magus*, a skilled magician or an astrologer, as the poem resolves itself into a *haiku*: 'The first white wall of the village / Rises through fruit-trees'. This does not work either and leaves behind it a question, 'Of what was it I was thinking?'[54] All connection with reality seems lost. The Imagists' error here lies in the glorification of the imagination, the sense of the poetic self as a shaman or shapeshifter.

There are similar concerns in F. S. Flint's poetry.[55] 'War-time' (*Poetry*: February 1916) argues that a poet might usefully follow one of two creative paths. The first is an old route. It lures him with 'the bovine quiet of houses / Brooding over the cud of their daily content'. It is an aesthetic of the everyday, a simple metaphor for the pre-war avant-garde. The closing image in this section of 'the almond blossom shaming / The soot-black boughs' would seem to clinch that interpretation, an ironic allusion to Pound's earlier meditations at the metro station. The second route goes into 'the dust, the tattered paper', the 'rattling noise of the motor-'busses' and 'clangorous tram-cars'. It is a messy world of human frailty and judgement. Here Flint can 'feel the heat of Europe's fever', but only at the cost of an emotional overload that leaves him 'burning'. The spectatorial distance required by a Kantian aesthetic collapses and the poet 'can make / As each man makes the beauty of the woman he loves, / No spring and no woman's beauty'.[56] The poem's demand that the everyday immerse it seems to refute poetry. Except, of course, as in Stevens's critique, for the awkward fact that it has produced yet again a poem.

Flint showed little interest in the imagined experience of combat. We find instead a concerted desire that prevents the imagination taking flight into battle. 'Soldiers' (*The Egoist*: September 1916), its definitive version dedicated to Aldington, imagines the poet standing at ease with a battalion as he watches his fellow Imagist march by: 'Brother, I saw you in a muddy road in France'. Before the war, the two had 'climbed the Devon hills together', and here we find their 'eyes met, startled' at that same shared experience. It leads only to a recognition of the differences in their futures:

---

[54] Stevens, 'Metaphors of a Magnifico', *Little Review*, 4.

[55] Flint did not serve on the battle front. Debarred by health from overseas action with the same C1 rating as Eliot, he served out the period August 1918 to June 1919 in England and Scotland. Michael Copp, 'Introduction', in *The Fourth Imagist: Selected Poems of F. S. Flint*, ed. by Michael Copp (Madison, NJ: Fairleigh Dickinson University Press, 2007), pp. xxi–xlv (pp. xxi–xxv), Google ebook.

[56] F. S. Flint, 'War-time', *Poetry*, 7.5 (February 1916), 231–2.

you went on, you went on,
into the darkness;
and I sit here at my table,
holding back my tears,
with my jaw set and my teeth clenched,
knowing I shall not be
even so near you as I saw you
in my dream.[57]

The opposition is stark. The pen cannot and does not follow Aldington into a darkness that simply swallows him. The two soldiers take their own paths. With Flint clearly in pain and yet refusing to imagine Aldington's pain in turn, we sense only the space that now lies between them.

Flint's later poem 'Zeppelins' (*Some Imagist Poets*: April 1917) attempts to give expression to the unknowability of total technological war from the home front. A series of cries and alarms awake the lyric I. In the heat of the moment, it registers only a vague awareness of events. 'How long have I slept?' it asks. It can make no sense of its own body: 'I shiver: chill? excitement? fear?' We learn the actual nature of this disaster once this confused consciousness gives way to a journalistic account:

Yet something slinks overhead through the sky;
men will say that they saw it pass, and then
a flash, a thud, —
a house has been cleft through three stories, and burns;
and children burn in their beds[.][58]

This is an account that comes to the poet's consciousness only in aftermath however:

But we do not know this yet;
we have only heard explosions,
and have seen the glow of fires in the sky,
quickly gone.

A world structured by the scientific laws of cause and effect breaks apart. The story of what has happened is the account the community pieces together after

---

[57] F. S. Flint, 'Soldiers', *The Egoist*, 3.9 (September 1916), 134. Flint added the dedication to Aldington in *Some Imagist Poets 1917* and kept it in *Otherworld: Cadences* (1925).
[58] F. S. Flint, 'Zeppelins', in *Some Imagist Poets 1917: An Annual Anthology* (Boston: Houghton Mifflin, 1917), pp. 57–9 (p. 58).

the attack. Only then is there a causal relationship between 'a flash, a thud' and the burnt corpses. In the moment, the self knows only its own confusion. The narrator can feel that 'the silence and stillness are sinister', he can sense the lurking unseen presence of the Zeppelin, but there is no consummation of that free-floating essence in knowledge. The poetic consciousness climbs to the top of the house to search for clues, but this is also unrevealing: 'There is nothing to see . . .' The world is merely *unheimlich*, even 'Brick and stone have become unreal'. As the imagination searches for the Zeppelin, the poem reveals 'A flame-coloured circle of light that glows'.[59] There are however no zeppelins, they deliver their cargo unseen; the glow is just the moon.

In the contemporaneous 'Star Sentinel' (2013; *November–December 1916*), Lawrence used the moon and the heavens as permanent witnesses to history. They are planetary objects able to unite disparate human experience.[60] A lover thinks of a betrothed partner in Mesopotamia, one Lawrence probably modelled on Kut Al Amara where the British Army garrison found itself besieged the previous spring. The hope is that the lovers will both turn to look at the canopy of stars at the same moment, allowing the phenomenological gap to be forded through a proxy: 'Oh, as you stand and gaze, do you know it is I? / Do I see your bayonet twinkle with answering love?'[61] It is a tenuous and unlikely prospect and the sexual metaphor again hardly subtle, but Lawrence makes a poetry from the unknowing of it all. Rather than aping shock, Lawrence's emphasis is on the intersubjective ruptures of war, the fragility of the imagination as it tries to connect with bodies that have become separated by violence.

'Star Sentinel' is part of Lawrence's recently published manuscript entitled 'All of Us' (2013). This is a poetry of war of quite a different order from those discussed in Chapters 1 and 2. As its preliminary title suggests it was a sequence in which Lawrence aimed to ignore the distinctions created by fronts and national alliances to rebind humanity. It signals a change in mood in Lawrence's work which we can date. Lawrence sent the manuscript to J. B. Pinker and Cynthia Asquith on 11 December 1916 from Cornwall. It had taken shape six years earlier following his engagement to Louie Burrows and as part of Lawrence's translation of several Egyptian 'Fellah songs' (*fellaheen* or peasant) from the German.[62] Lawrence obtained a copy of the German translations,

---

[59] Ibid. p. 59.

[60] See also Thomas Hardy's '"I looked up from my writing"' (1917; *1916*), which echoes both Flint's *in medias res* strategy of 'Soldiers' and the emphasis on the moon in 'Zeppelins'. The poem uses the contrast between the poet's inactivity and the need to write to create an unresolved bind between indifference and the accusation of callousness.

[61] D. H. Lawrence, 'Star Sentinel', in Lawrence, *The Poems*, I: *Poems* (2013), p. 139.

[62] D. H. Lawrence, letter to Louie Burrows (6 December 1910), in *The Letters of D. H. Lawrence*, I: *September 1901–May 1913*, ed. by James T. Boulton (1979), pp. 195–8 (p. 196).

originally written down by the Egyptologist Heinrich Schäfer during archaeological excavations, from his uncle Fritz Krenkow, the Arabic scholar.

Catherine Brown (2017) persuasively argues that the poems in 'All of Us' were Lawrence's attempt to build Anglo-German relations.[63] It is certain that by the time Lawrence returned to the sequence in late 1916 he did so amidst a growing disillusion with what he thought was a monstrous and contemptible war that was testing his faith in sympathetic communion. He told J. B. Pinker in November 1916 that the war had destroyed the unity of mankind (Lawrence's term). It had frayed the bonds between men and pushed each individual into their own peculiarly isolated perspective. 'Now, one can only submit, they are they, you are you, I am I – there is a separation, a separate, isolated fate,' he said, accepting that even Brooke's dislikeable sonnets were true for Brooke and his fellow soldiers.[64] Nervous that the poems in 'All of Us' may be technically naive, Lawrence nonetheless saw them as an alternative form of war literature and he believed they would be a popular success.[65] They told the war from the perspective of the civilian's isolated fate. Cyril Beaumont disagreed, however, and he rejected them for publication in March 1918. In part Beaumont's decision reflected his intention to publish a different collection of Lawrence's war poems, *Bay* (November 1919; *April 1918*). It may also have reflected, as Lawrence himself suggested, that they were slightly wicked.[66] Lawrence would press on in March 1919. Beaumont's loss of the manuscript forced Lawrence to rework the poems from his notebooks and he eventually unglamorously retitled it as 'Bits' (1964). Harriet Monroe published just under half of the thirty poems as 'War Films' in the 'After-the-War Number' of *Poetry* in July 1919.

This detailed textual history paves the way to return later to Lawrence's notion of a poetry rooted in the present moment. Here it emphasises two consistent features to imagining the broad theatre of war. On the one hand, the poems again redefine what the experience of war meant in a way that is consistent with today's understanding of the concept of war writing. The poet takes us to Africa and to the Levant rather than to Flanders. We see lovers, mothers, fathers, children, labourers, prisoners, nurses, suburbs and munitions factories. Without exception, these poems move away from trying to imagine the combat zone. They are about broken relationships. Their subject is the unbridgeable gaps

---

[63] Catherine Brown, 'Anglo-German Relations and D. H. Lawrence's "All of Us"', <http://catherinebrown.org/anglo-german-relations-and-d-h-lawrences-all-of-us/> [accessed 30 March 2022], para. 22 of 152.

[64] D. H. Lawrence, letter to Lady Cynthia Asquith (15 November 1916), in *The Letters of D. H. Lawrence*, III, pp. 32–3.

[65] D. H. Lawrence, letter to J. B. Pinker (11 December 1916), in *The Letters of D. H. Lawrence*, III, p. 51.

[66] D. H. Lawrence, letter to Lady Cynthia Asquith (8 March 1918), in *The Letters of D. H. Lawrence*, III, p. 221.

between people caused by war. Yet on the other hand, Lawrence's method relied on a retrospective methodological apparatus, particularly the use of translation to rediscover a contiguity in human experience. Whereas *Cathay* used Chinese, Lawrence opted for Egyptian to give shape and meaning to contemporary experience. Both felt the need for an external model to bring authenticity to an experience not felt on the skin. We might add however that these poets worked to different ends. Lawrence created a highly personal poetic. In contrast to Pound, it shows little hankering after the epic. It held a genuine sense of compassion for lives blighted and frustrated by war.

Combat Agnosticism: H.D. and Edward Thomas

In the work of Stevens, Flint and Lawrence there was a tentative recognition of the essential insularity of the Image. We can also note in these poets, and in the work of Stein, a noticeable shift towards the positions of H.D., Mina Loy and Helen Saunders, a turn that is towards home front cultures. Here there appeared a reluctance to imagine the body in pieces, an obvious anxiety about the deforming abilities of imagination and a sense for war as relational rupture. There was a willingness in these writers to concede to the soldier, the ambulance driver and the nurse their combat gnosticism. It is not the beginnings of a poetry of resignation though but, as exemplified by Stein, a tentative programme for the imagination's reconstruction, a theory of poetry that predicted our own turn to war writing. It is a shift that reached its fullest expression in the work of H.D. and Edward Thomas, two poets, both non-combatants at the time of composition, without any direct experience of the battle front at all.

In July 1916 H.D. moved to Corfe Castle, a small village close to the English south coast overlooked by the ruins of a Norman fortress and the site of a besieged Royalist stronghold during the English Civil War. Wareham Camp, where Aldington undertook basic training following enlistment in May, lay to the north. Here H.D. drafted the poems in *The Islands* series, the sequence later entitled 'The God' and work now lost to fire in late 1917.[67] This distinctive turn

---

[67] The poems written between July and December 1916, many of which were collected in *Hymen* (1921) and *Heliodora* (1924), include (1) 'Fragment Thirty-six' (*Poetry*: 1921) and 'The Lookout' (*The Egoist*: July 1917); (2) *The Islands* series; the title taken from H.D.'s typescript, which includes 'Amaranth' (1983, in part as Sappho translation 'Fragment Forty-one' (1924)), 'Eros' (1983, in part as 'Fragment Forty' (1924)), 'Envy' (1983, in part as 'Fragment Sixty-eight' (1924)) and, presumably, although not part of this typescript, 'The Islands' (*North American Review*: January 1920); (3) 'The God' sequence, created by H.D. for *Collected Poems* (1925), which includes 'The Tribute' (*The Egoist*: November 1916), 'Circe' (*The Egoist*: December 1916), 'Adonis' and 'The God' (*The Egoist*: January 1917), 'Pygmalion' (*The Egoist*: February 1917) and 'Eurydice' (*The Egoist*: May 1917). Within *Collected Poems* (1925), 'The God' sequence includes earlier poems from 1913–14. See Michael Boughn, *H.D.: A Bibliography 1905–1990* (Charlottesville: University Press of Virginia, 1993), p. 10.

in H.D.'s work took shape over the summer and into the autumn of 1916 before she returned to London and to Mecklenburgh Square in December. These poems written at the site of earlier battles and surrounded by military camps chart the anxiety of Aldington's departure for France. We see the impact of illness, the trauma of a lost child and the consequences of Aldington's open affair with Flo Fallas. They also reflect H.D.'s broadening involvement in London's literary culture as the new assistant editor at *The Egoist*. Written after the introduction of conscription and encompassing the same time span as the unfolding of events at the Battle of the Somme (1 July–18 November 1916), these are indisputably a war poetry. Here Imagism did splinter; the shift that H.D. acknowledged to Lowell in August the following year had begun.[68]

Unlike in *Sea Garden*, the overt focus on violence slips away now the poet finds herself in the very midst of militarism and enmity. In 'Fragment Thirty-six' (1921) there are still suggestions of the older painful self-division – 'My mind is quite divided, / my minds hesitate' – and that H.D. might resolve the division through complete surrender to the shattering experience of breakdown.[69] There is a fragility to that confidence though. In 'Eros' (1969, in full 1983) the hope of recovery seems to fade. 'I had thought myself frail,' the poem tells us, 'about to fall shattered, / with flame spent', but the self recovers sufficiently to reflect that 'to sing love, / love must first shatter us'.[70] 'The Islands' (1920) however questions whether Hellenism might survive a lover's death, whether beauty is set apart:

> In my garden
> the winds have beaten
> the ripe lilies;
> in my garden, the salt
> has wilted the first flakes
> of young narcissus,
> and the lesser hyacinth,
> and the salt has crept
> under the leaves of the white hyacinth.
>
> In my garden
> even the wind-flowers lie flat,
> broken by the wind at last.[71]

---

[68] H.D., letter to Amy Lowell (10 August 1917), qtd in Caroline Zilboorg, 'Introduction', in *Richard Aldington and H.D.: Their Lives in Letters 1918–61*, ed. by Caroline Zilboorg, new collected edn (Manchester: Manchester University Press, 2003), pp. 1–39 (p. 28).

[69] H.D., 'Fragment Thirty-six', in *Collected Poems*, pp. 165–8 (p. 167).

[70] H.D., 'Eros', in *Collected Poems*, pp. 315–19 (pp. 318–19).

[71] H.D., 'The Islands', in *Collected Poems*, pp. 124–7 (pp. 126, 127).

This feels like another deliberate contrast to *Sea Garden*. In 'Sea Lily' (1916), although 'slashed and torn' and 'shattered / in the wind', petals 'cut' and furrowed by sand, the flowers are still 'lifted up'.[72] In comparison, in 'The Islands' they seem finally 'beaten' and the tone dies with them. Whereas in 'Hermes of the Ways' (*Poetry*: January 1913) the 'salt-crusted grass / answers', here it only wilts.[73] This wind bleaches the hyacinths, while in 'The Gift' (*The Egoist*: March 1916) and 'Sea-Gods' (*The Egoist*: June 1916) those flowers remained violet despite the violence. This is not now a scattering of pieces, a weakening or impairment of fragments that can come back together. It is a breaking (*brecan*, violent division or destruction), a violation from violence that causes a laying down. H.D. brings the dreamlike world of *Sea Garden* up short against the realities of history in a way that complicates the mechanics of personal recovery from breakdown. In 'The Tribute' (*The Egoist*: November 1916) imagining the self as if 'veiled as the bud of the poppy / in the poppy-sheath' leads to the suggestion that 'our hearts will break from their bondage / and spread as the poppy-leaf— / leaf by leaf, radiant and perfect'.[74] Broken though, we might ask, in what way?

There is a self-conscious sense of reappraisal in all these poems. Take the narrator's covetousness of the lover's 'chance of death' in 'Envy' (1969, in full 1983) and the playing with death in 'Eurydice' (*The Egoist*: May 1917) for example.[75] This problematises the certainty of the position in H.D.'s contemporaneous essays. In the essay on 'Marianne Moore' (*The Egoist*: August 1916) H.D. sets out the determination of a resilient group of artists 'who do not for one moment believe that beauty will be one whit bruised' by the war's 'turmoil and distress'.[76] Despite her opposition to the masculinist rhetoric in Vorticism this sounds uncannily like Lewis in *Blast*. In the essay on W. B. Yeats, H.D. went further and claimed that 'we, <u>les jeunes</u>' were 'sick of self-analysis, self-torture, self-appreciation'.[77] However, this was precisely the ground of H.D.'s poetry. As 'Fragment Thirty-six' puts it, 'so my mind waits / to grapple with my mind'.[78] In the poet's voice we find fear. The poems seem to lack the self-confidence of the essays and give full voice to the latent fear in the essays that it will be not only the combatants who are 'broken by the bitterness of their experience', to use H.D.'s words from the review of Yeats, but those too 'crouched as in a third line of battered trenches', those tenaciously

---

[72] H.D., 'Sea Lily', in *Collected Poems*, p. 14.

[73] H.D., 'Hermes of the Ways', in *Collected Poems*, pp. 37–9 (p. 38).

[74] H.D., 'The Tribute', in *Collected Poems*, pp. 59–68 (p. 64).

[75] H.D., 'Envy', in *Collected Poems*, pp. 319–21 (p. 319).

[76] H.D., 'Marianne Moore', p. 119.

[77] H.D., 'Typescript corrected by H.D. of unpublished review of *Responsibilities and Other Poems*', p. [67].

[78] H.D., 'Fragment Thirty-six', p. 167.

'hanging on against all odds'.[79] In the horrifying introspection of 'Amaranth' (1969, in full 1983) – 'my flesh is scorched and rent, / shattered, cut apart, / and slashed open' – H.D.'s self-appointed responsibility as a torch carrier for beauty came aground on the isolation and sense of loss.[80]

There is clear support here for H.D.'s sapphic modernism. The historicisation of war in 'The Tribute' as the product of capitalism's ethics of squalor for example.[81] And especially in the essay on Yeats where H.D. identified war as the product of 'the devil of machinery' complicit with 'the black-magic of triangles and broken arcs' found in *Blast* and the Futurist manifestos.[82] There is however another feature to highlight in H.D.'s concept of 'a third line of battered trenches' as a type of war poetry made by one knowingly outside the battlefield. A great deal of non-combatant poetry of war tends towards a predominant structural motif, a shift from immediate sensory experience to metaphor to dramatise the shuttling of imagination between fronts. In a classic example, Margaret Postgate Cole's 'The Falling Leaves' (1918; *November 1915*) uses the simile of leaves falling '*like snowflakes wiping out the noon*' as the propellent that brings to mind '*a gallant multitude*' now '*withering*', imagined in turn through simile, '*strewed / Like snowflakes falling on the Flemish clay*'.[83] These similes are not, as they are in the trench lyric, a licence to speak but rather a struggling after expression. There is as Stevens proposed something of a *magus* in this process, a subtle unexplained shift subsumed by the figurative.

In contrast H.D.'s poetry of war never attempts this leap. The soldiers in these poems we see askance through the narrator's consciousness. He is 'adrift on the great sea', taking 'fright' facing 'the terror', aboard 'the purple ships'.[84] It is an absent you that is emphasised, the war-torn effects of relationship, the fragile memory of touch ('My mouth is wet with your life') and of orgasm ('In my body were pearls cast, / shot with Ionian tints').[85] This anticipates the position H.D. took two years later in 'Notes on Thought and Vision' (1982; *July 1919*), where love is the precondition for artistic vision:

---

[79] H.D., 'Typescript corrected by H.D. of unpublished review of *Responsibilities and Other Poems*', p. [67].

[80] H.D. 'Amaranth', in *Collected Poems*, pp. 310–15 (p. 311).

[81] H.D., 'The Tribute', p. 59.

[82] H.D., 'Typescript corrected by H.D. of unpublished review of *Responsibilities and Other Poems*', pp. [68], [69].

[83] Margaret Postgate [Cole], 'The Falling Leaves: November 1915', in *Margaret Postgate's Poems* (London: George Allen & Unwin, 1918), p. 34.

[84] H.D., 'Circe', in *Collected Poems*, pp. 118–20 (p. 118); H.D., 'The Islands', p. 127; H.D., 'Amaranth', p. 314.

[85] H.D., 'Eros', p. 316.

We begin with sympathy of thought.

The minds of two lovers merge, interact in sympathy of thought.

The brain, inflamed and excited by this interchange of ideas, takes on its character of over-mind, becomes (as I have visualised in my own case) a jelly-fish placed over and about the brain.[86]

This 'jelly-fish' is a form of reaching out, a tentacular manifestation of the sympathetic imagination grounded in spiritual and sexual love. As in Lawrence's work, separation is the critical combat wound here. 'How shall I call you back?' Circe asks.[87] There is no inside or outside to H.D.'s war; we are as Lawrence suggested 'all of us' in it together:

Panther and panther,
then a black leopard
follows close—
black panther and red
and a great hound,
a god-like beast,
cut the sand in a clear ring
and shut me from the earth,
and cover the sea-sound
with their throats,
and the sea-roar with their own barks
and bellowing and snarls,
and the sea-stars
and the swirl of the sand,
and the rock-tamarisk
and the wind resonance—
but not your voice.[88]

Circe is ringed by circling beasts, the braying uproar of contest. The distant voice, the absent Other, calls from the other side.

Alongside H.D. in this 'third line of battered trenches' we can find Thomas's version of war poetry. We can date his entire poetic corpus to the period December 1914 to January 1917, from his criticism of war poetry as a genre discussed in Chapter 1 to shortly before he left military training. Like the weather and the natural world, history seeped into the landscape of this poetry repeatedly and

---

[86] H.D., 'Notes on Thought and Vision', in H.D., 'Notes on Thought and Vision' and 'The Wise Sappho' (San Francisco: City Lights Books, 1982), pp. 17–53 (p. 22).

[87] H.D., 'Circe', p. 118.

[88] H.D., 'Circe', p. 119.

effortlessly; the war entered the lyric not as an epic catastrophe that the poet must shape and give meaning but as a consuming power infecting the entire structure of private feeling, one that penetrated consciousness and language at every ordinary turn.

Thomas's idiosyncratic poetic owes part of its strategy to his friendship with Robert Frost. Faced with war in 1916 Frost had opted for silence. If he was unable to enlist, Frost told Thomas in November 1916, then he would not turn to sympathy.[89] In his one concerted poetic discussion of the war, 'On Talk of Peace at This Time' (1974; *1916*), Frost decided to remain a watcher of those fighting because he could not directly know the specificity of their pain.[90] The distance created by Frost's return to the United States in February 1915 may well have made that position easier to maintain. It left Thomas's poetry, always aware of its proximity to battle, to arbitrate between the quintessentially Frostian emphasis on locality, his particularity for actual experience and the pressing demands of history.

Thomas's is a poetry that turns repeatedly to agnosticism. The desire to know and the simultaneous impossibility of knowing are its main drivers. Take one of the first of Thomas's poems, 'March' (December 1918; *December 1914*), with its longing for the return of spring:

> What did the thrushes know? Rain, snow, sleet, hail,
> Had kept them quiet as the primroses.
> They had but an hour to sing. On boughs they sang,
> On gates, on ground; they sang while they changed perches
> And while they fought, if they remembered to fight[.]

These birds squeeze their song into an hour of dusk, 'they cared not what they sang or screamed'. Whilst setting up the expectation of revelation, the poem never reveals the 'Something they knew'. This 'something' the poem wraps in 'silence'.[91] Thomas's deliberate refusal of anthropocentrism makes the point that the birds are their silence. They are their refusal to yield their inner mysteries. Yet the reference to screaming, a metaphor that links the poetic song to birdsong and to a scream of pain, especially coming so soon after the repetition of the verb to fight, on the seeming pointlessness of fighting, is an awful

---

[89] Robert Frost, letter to Edward Thomas (6 November 1916), qtd in Matthew Hollis, *Now All Roads Lead to France: The Last Years of Edward Thomas* (London: Faber and Faber, 2011), p. 302.

[90] Robert Frost, 'On Talk of Peace at This Time', in Robert Frost, *Collected Poems, Prose, and Plays*, ed. by Richard Poirier and Mark Richardson (New York: Library of America, 1995), p. 531. For analysis see George Monteiro, 'Robert Frost's "On Talk of Peace at This Time": A Third Version of an Uncollected Manuscript Poem', *ANQ*, 7.1 (1994), 26–8.

[91] Edward Thomas, 'March', in Edward Thomas, *Collected Poems*, ed. by R. George Thomas (London: Faber and Faber, 2004), pp. 8–9.

reminder of what is at stake. Briefly the poem shuttles from the frosty English soil to a diorama of Flanders, to what also lies ahead in the following spring. It is the briefest of glimpses of an unknown world, conjured up through fear, one left like the thrushes in their alterity. The contrast to Pound's method in *Cathay* could not be more extreme. Thomas's is a poetry grounded in a refusal of totality. It is, as Michael Kirkham (1986) elegantly puts it in his examination of Thomas's imagination, the means to make a world out of the mysteries of uncertainty.[92]

This deft interlacing of public and private was a hallmark of Thomas's poetry. Although it is steeped in nature, its moods are elegiac rather than pastoral. These poems hold a profound sense of compassion for the combatant. Take 'In Memoriam [Easter, 1915]' (October 1917; *6 April 1915*), written weeks before Pound's imagining of St Eloi:

> The flowers left thick at nightfall in the wood
> This Eastertide call into mind the men,
> Now far from home, who, with their sweethearts, should
> Have gathered them and will do never again.[93]

The flowers are an appalling reminder of rupture. They tell us of a literal absence, of how far this home front has changed. The narcissi are also a metaphor for those mown down in battle. The tone and mood here suggest an aftermath, a word etymologically drawn from the Old English *mæð*, a mowing or cutting of grass. Thomas binds two imaginary spaces, one of love and one of war, the private world and the public world, wood and mud. The effect is so gentle that it is just perceptible. 'Left thick at nightfall in the wood' interlaces romantic love metaphor with the fragile suggestion of corpses piled up before burial, an image that breaks against the enjambement of 'should / Have gathered them'. The conditionality unbalances easy conclusions. The awkwardness of 'home, who, with' further complicates things. Who is the fallen and who is the gathered? Everyone is suddenly falling; everyone ought to be held. For the briefest of moments, the introduction of 'and will do' holds sway in the rhythm of the final line suggesting that we might recover these lost bodies, just before that optimism comes aground on the awful and simple finality of 'never again'. The poem introduces the war as an echo into poetry, eschewing the wrecking-ball grandeur of epic.

Thomas's description of this method – the 'call into mind' – is especially revealing as a counter strategy to Cole's simile. It is a call to imaginary arms, an invitation to the figurative by the literal. It leans on imagination but there

---

[92] Michael Kirkham, *The Imagination of Edward Thomas* (Cambridge: Cambridge University Press, 1986), pp. 205–6.

[93] Edward Thomas, 'In Memoriam [Easter, 1915]', in *Collected Poems*, p. 63.

is a pre-cognitive element to it that is more primitive than the sympathetic apparatus. It is introjective and projective, the world presses in on the reluctant self as the lamp of the imagination pushes out to meet and create the world. In 'The Owl' (October 1917; *February 1915*) Thomas uses the call-to-mind process to investigate the universality of basic human feeling (incidentally also the theme of *Cathay*). The poem repeats the three most simple human states, 'how hungry, cold, and tired was I', three times in the first two stanzas. It then pivots by reversing the discomfort into assuagement through 'food, fire, and rest'. It is the owl's 'most melancholy cry' that acts as the call-to-mind, reminding the lyrical I of a more profound sense of guilt, 'telling me plain what I escaped / And others could not, that night':

> And salted was my food, and my repose,
> Salted and sobered, too, by the bird's voice
> Speaking for all who lay under the stars,
> Soldiers and poor, unable to rejoice.[94]

The repetition of 'salted' undermines any idea that hospitality will assuage need. Salt seasons and preserves; it heals and aids rest. It can nonetheless ruin a meal and invariably stings open flesh. Whereas *Cathay* relied on a permanent and unchanging ground to human affective experience, by holding together two ideas simultaneously without resolution Thomas's poem sets up a much more complex picture. The evening is both 'Salted and sobered', dialled up in affect and yet dialled down. The persona gets food and rest, but as the owl's cry brings the relief of safety, even the compensations of *Schadenfreude*, it rubs salt into guilty wounds.

In 'The sun used to shine' (October 1917; *May 1916*), the catalyst is Lawrence's unchanging and all-seeing moon:

> The war
> Came back to mind with the moonrise
> Which soldiers in the east afar
> Beheld then. Nevertheless, our eyes
>
> Could as well imagine the Crusades
> Or Caesar's battles. Everything
> To faintness like those rumours fades –
> Like the brook's water glittering
>
> Under the moonlight[.][95]

---

[94] Edward Thomas, 'The Owl', in *Collected Poems*, p. 44.
[95] Edward Thomas, 'The sun used to shine', in *Collected Poems*, pp. 114–15.

The moonrise is the ready-made convention. It is the catalyst for the imagination to move to the historical Other. It invites analogy – the poem suggests great battles at places like Antioch, Acre, Bibracte or Vosges – as the means to frame the contemporary, to set chaos in its right and proper place. Thomas however refuses that imaginative act. Here vicarious events are no more than doubtful truths, barely perceptible foundations that cannot be relied on. They are beguiling reflections that dissolve in the moon's glow. Contrast it with the remarkably similar yearning for past battles and the heat of battle at Thermopylae in Eliot's 'Gerontion'. As discussed in more depth in Chapter 5, Eliot used Gerontion's yearnings for combat as a straw objective correlative. He was the butt of Eliot's art, his desire for fleshwitnessing revealing the essential need for poetic impersonality. In contrast, Thomas's poetry speaks only of the problem. Its topic is the ineffable and contingent feeling of modernity, the awareness of a fundamental separation from those 'in pain or thus in sympathy', those 'Helpless', 'Like a cold water among broken reeds' as Thomas puts it in 'Rain' (October 1917; *January 1916*).[96] The difference again is compassion. It is the decision to simply suffer with rather than to imagine with.

'As the team's head-brass' (October 1917; *May 1916*) is the clearest illustration of method. Here Thomas's narrator sits amidst 'the boughs of the fallen elm' sharing snatched pieces of conversation with a ploughman at each turn of the machine:

> So the talk began –
> One minute and an interval of ten,
> A minute more and the same interval.
> 'Have you been out?' 'No.' 'And don't want to, perhaps?'
> 'If I could only come back again, I should.
> I could spare an arm. I shouldn't want to lose
> A leg. If I should lose my head, why, so,
> I should want nothing more . . . . Have many gone
> From here?' 'Yes.' 'Many lost?' 'Yes: a good few.[']

The rhythm not only mimics the broken nature of the conversation but reminds us of the patterned forms of a traditional way of life on the land. That cyclical and slow-moving form of life makes for a stark contrast to the macabre fear of the body in pieces. One of the ploughman's '"mates"' is already dead, and he cannot now move the felled elm until the end of the war. The play on losing one's head, upended by the 'why, so' clause, suggests both the insanity of a war and the possibility that the narrator might use shock to excuse participation. The repetition of 'should' and 'could' – five times – suggests the poet's psychological

---

[96] Edward Thomas, 'Rain', in *Collected Poems*, p. 95.

entrapment between what one feels bound to do and what free will might dictate. We get a keen sense of the war's long-range physical and psychical effects, of a world turned upside down, '"another world"' as the narrator says, reflecting on the chance encounter.[97]

The poem is doing something more than reflecting on the indecision of enlistment. It begins and ends with the image of lovers entering and then re-emerging from a surrounding wood. The narrator watches their return:

> Then
> The lovers came out of the wood again:
> The horses started and for the last time
> I watched the clods crumble and topple over
> After the ploughshare and the stumbling team.

As with the thrushes, we never find out what happens in the wood. Perhaps the lovers conceived a new future for this rural idyll. Perhaps not. The images, forming a bracket around the dialogue about the war, point us towards the inevitable gaps in our knowledge about the world, the constructed nature of truth especially in relation to events that are separate from the immediacy of our own *qualia*. We are to piece it all together between the moments of silence. Reflecting on the poet's hankering after a world without the war, the plough-man gnomically observes the crucial point: '"Ay, and a better, though / If we could see all all might seem good."'[98] The possibility of a totalising experience runs aground on the double conditionality of 'could' and 'might', the uncertainty of 'seem' and the repetition of 'all'. It is an echo of the 'should' and 'could' of the poet's indecision.

The poem questions whether anything can be known beyond the local. Our ability to visualise everything – the symbolic importance of the lovers, of the war – might help us, but equally it might hinder. It brings the narrator back to the war in closing. As Peter Howarth rightly observes in *British Poetry in the Age of Modernism*, 'topple over' here suggests going over the top.[99] We see the same double meaning in 'clods' implying the idiocy of enlistment. The war is there in 'crumble' too as a metaphor for psychological breakdown; it is also there in the reference to steel that makes both plough and ammunition. We can see its shape in 'horses', 'last time', 'stumbling' and 'team'. Each word becomes suddenly dynamic. This allows the final image to constantly oscillate between the literal and the figurative, backwards and forwards cinematically from English field to Flanders field, from the breaking of mud to the falling

---

[97] Edward Thomas, 'As the team's head-brass', in *Collected Poems*, pp. 115–17 (p. 116).
[98] Ibid. pp. 116–17.
[99] Howarth, *British Poetry in the Age of Modernism*, p. 104.

bodies of soldiers, from ploughman to a vision of the poet's destiny and the possibility of his own death. Again, without seeming intent on transporting us to Stein's strange trench landscape, we find that Thomas has fashioned a poetry of war, one able to dramatise the war's most pernicious, devastating and far-reaching effects.

Modernist Doubts

During 1916 the arrival of the moral witness served to challenge an established poetic credo. The moral witness claimed there had come into being a new real, a modernity marked by the rending of flesh and the scarring of mind, the real of the body in pieces, a real that was unimaginable to anyone not there. How could this seminal truth about the new technological modernity be known by anyone else? The poetry of H.D. and Thomas shied away from imagining the wounded combatant's mind. It accepted the gnosis of combat, and it suggested that gnosis might be a feature of all human experience especially at the extremes when the commonality of affect breaks down. This poetry of absence rather than presence, an agnosticism, took refuge in a more private elegiac space that effectively conceded combat representation to the moral witness. This is a distinct change from the poems of 1914 and 1915. Those poets prioritised a lyrical I that could use the sympathetic imagination to know even shock.

As illustration of the change, take two further examples as support for the dating of this rupture. The first is from Ford Madox Ford writing about writer's block at the Ypres Salient on 15 September 1916 in a short piece called 'Arms and the Mind/War and the Mind' (1980–9), collected in his *War Prose* (1999). Ford explained that he had spent a good deal of time wondering why he could not write about the psychological content of his combat experience. He felt he had lost the ability to evoke the Somme.[100] The position was a formidable challenge to literary impressionism's foregrounding of sensation. His true skill, Ford said, was not just the ability to evoke the things he had seen, but 'still better', his words, anything he had not seen.[101] In contrast, Ford went on that whilst he could call images of the battle front to mind, even the appalling image of human liquefaction, 'as for putting them – into words! No: the mind stops dead, and something in the brain stops and shuts down'.[102] Ford concluded that there must be some form of invisible barrier inside the brain between the profession of soldiering and the act of putting experience into words.

To explain this in the absence of a language of shock, Ford turned instead to an unnamed article in the *New Age*. Ford does not say which article, but it

---

[100] Ford Madox Ford, 'Arms and the Mind/War and the Mind' (1980–9), in Ford Madox Ford, *War Prose*, ed. by Max Saunders (Manchester: Carcanet, 1999), pp. 36–48 (p. 36).

[101] Ibid. pp. 36–7.

[102] Ibid. p. 37.

was probably Ernest A. Boyd's 'The Imperviousness of Literature to War' of January 1916.[103] Boyd said he could find no evidence following the Franco-Prussian War that war changed literature. Boyd's logic was simple: the major novelists working in the Flaubertian tradition remained impersonal; the Symbolists guided poetry with only care for beauty and rhythm; war must then be the field of very minor writers. The creative mind in contrast rejected war because of its relationship to destruction. Ford's much better summary of Boyd's position was that 'lookers on see most of the Game'.[104] This view argued that the non-participants to war best document its psychological impact, a theory that led Ford to the broader conclusion that authorship in general must require a privileged or objective vantage point from which to represent extreme individual experience.

The second example is from H.D.'s *Bid Me to Live* (1960). Although we cannot precisely date the scene in question, the evidence presented by Mark Kinkead-Weekes (1996) suggests March 1917, contemporaneous with Ford's essay.[105] In this section of H.D.'s memoir Rico has written to Julia to discuss a poem. He advises that Julia '"stick to the woman speaking"'. '"How can you know what Orpheus feels?"' Rico asks, '"it's your part to be woman, the woman vibration, Eurydice should be enough. You can't deal with both."'[106] Julia responds:

> Rico could write elaborately on the woman mood, describe women to their marrow in his writing; but if she turned round, wrote the Orpheus part of her Orpheus-Eurydice sequence, he snapped back, 'Stick to the woman-consciousness, it is the intuitive woman-mood that matters.' He was right about that, of course. But if he could enter, so diabolically, into the feelings of women, why should not she enter into the feelings of men? She understood Rafe, really understood that he loved her – that he desired *l'autre*.[107]

---

[103] Ernest A. Boyd, 'The Imperviousness of Literature to War', *New Age*, 18.10 (6 January 1916), 227–8.

[104] Ford, 'Arms and the Mind', p. 37. This quintessentially English proverb, traceable to John Palsgrave and Francis Bacon, has its origin in the difference between a bystander watching a game of chess or draughts and the player within the melee of action. 'LOOKERS-ON see most of the game', in *The Oxford Dictionary of Proverbs*, ed. by Jennifer Speake, 6th edn (Oxford: Oxford University Press, 2015), p. 192. James Joyce used it, suitably, in the voyeuristic 'Nausicaa' episode of *Ulysses* (1922). James Joyce, '*Ulysses*: (Episode XIII concluded)', *Little Review*, 7.2 (July–August 1920), 42–58 (p. 47).

[105] Mark Kinkead-Weekes, *D. H. Lawrence: Triumph to Exile 1912–1922*, The Cambridge Biography, II (Cambridge: Cambridge University Press, 1996), pp. 418–20.

[106] H.D., *Bid Me to Live: A Madrigal* (Redding Ridge, CT: Black Swan Books, 1983), p. 51.

[107] Ibid. p. 62.

Julia's 'of course' is like Ford's 'still better'. They reveal an unstated ideology. Julia accepts that value must exist in an intuitive investigation of personal embodiment. Yet, she is unable to accept what one ought logically to extrapolate from that truism, namely the suggestion that her own art is either aesthetically incapable of the act or proscribed from it. Julia's understanding of Rafe's desire for the Other suggests the possibility of a theory of ego that is permeable to the sympathetic imagination. Yet H.D. published 'Eurydice', despite the stated suspicion of Lawrence's theoretical position on sexuality, in *The Egoist* in May 1917 as a dramatic monologue without Orpheus's perspective, rather than as the dialogue originally written, the memoir states, for Lawrence.[108]

We can use both scenes to illustrate other points. Ford's perplexed conclusions on the act of looking on was one of the earliest and most illustrative examples of shock, the numbing of affect and the mind's automaticity in a battle zone.[109] Similarly, the Rico-Julia exchange raises the question of what society allowed a woman to write in the 1910s. It also exposes the extreme double standards of Lawrence's androgynous vision, exemplified in the first version of *Women in Love*, 'The Sisters' (2002), drafted in the spring of 1916. The point here however is more mundane. We see the certainty of early modernist aesthetics falling apart. For if the writer in it cannot easily write about the embodied experience of it, and the writer out of it cannot easily imagine themselves into it, how was art to incorporate the seminal event of modernity? How can one be sufficiently proximate to know enough and to write authentically, and yet sufficiently distanced to represent cause, meaning and consequence? Where is the right place of balance, the right point of focus between zoom and pan?

It is telling that in 1916 the first signs of doubt appeared in Pound's development. Such doubts are at odds with our current understanding of his work and his plain disregard for all things related to the war. James Longenbach does describe Pound as being deeply affected by the practicalities of war despite the decision 'to maintain an aristocratic indifference'.[110] The death of Gaudier-Brzeska in June 1915 had pushed Pound towards a gradual conversion through which he came to see the war, as he told Monroe in May 1915, as 'the struggle for free life and free thought', the force that blights the lives in 'Canto XVI' (1925).[111] The essential Pound of the opening years of the war however was the one who wrote in the autumn of 1915 that 'war is a dirty and disgusting annoyance, it is an interruption of everything that matters'.[112] It was a man disengaged

---

[108] Ibid. p. 173.

[109] See especially Ford's conclusion in this section of the essay; Ford, 'Arms and the Mind', pp. 36–7.

[110] Longenbach, *Stone Cottage*, p. 108.

[111] Pound, letter to Monroe (May 1915), qtd in Longenbach, *Stone Cottage*, p. 120. On Pound's conversion see Peter Wilson, *A Preface to Ezra Pound* (Abingdon: Routledge, 2014), p. 226.

[112] Ezra Pound, 'On America and World War I (presented by Timothy Materer)', *Paideuma*, 18.1–2 (Spring and Fall 1989), 205–14 (p. 208).

from the actualities of history, one determined according to A. David Moody in *The Young Genius* (2007) to press on regardless, to promote a realist oriented writing as his personal contribution to the war effort.[113]

This too is a bit neat as a summary though. Pound's attempts to enlist, as with Eliot's in Chapter 4, attest to a much deeper set of confusions about the war. According to Pound's account he tried to volunteer at least once. The military rejected his application on the grounds of his being a foreigner. This left him excluded altogether Pound said because there was no foreign legion to join.[114] This is hardly persuasive. Pound would have known that other Americans, such as Alan Seeger and Kiffin Rockwell, had chosen to go to war with the French Foreign Legion, and of the long history of international brigades fighting in European wars. Pound knew Allen Upward had been a volunteer soldier in Crete and Turkey.[115] If fighting was Pound's goal, then fighting was available. By the time America entered the war in April 1917 Pound told his father he was '"too old tew fight"', falling just outside the age limits imposed by the Selective Service Act of 1917.[116] When the US government expanded these age limits in August 1918, Pound directed his efforts towards obstruction rather than the facilitation of conscription despite a brief flirtation with intelligence work for the American Embassy in London. It is a mark of Pound's strange position in London in these years that in February 1916 one or more governments suspected he was a spy.[117]

In a much later letter to Bryher, H.D. also pinned the blame for Pound's withdrawal from London in 1919 on the war:

'I wonder so much what DID HAPPEN. It may have been confusion about the last war, being there and not being in it, and E was made much of by many people; I know how they changed tempo during the first war, and he may have felt they were no longer interested in the same way. He appears to me now, to have BEGUN the down-curve at the end of or just after World War I. . . . Anyway I feel there was some definite break or repercussion or even percussion in or at the end of War I, that sent him back to the old shock of being asked to leave Hamilton College.'[118]

---

[113] Moody, *The Young Genius*, p. 278.
[114] Ezra Pound, letter to Milton Bronner ([1915 or 1916]), qtd in Moody, *The Young Genius*, p. 462 n. 261.
[115] [Harriet Monroe], 'Notes', *Poetry*, 2.6 (September 1913), 228–9 (p. 228).
[116] Ezra Pound, letter to Homer Pound (23 August 1917), qtd in Moody, *The Young Genius*, p. 329.
[117] Moody, *The Young Genius*, pp. 294, 342.
[118] H.D., letter to Bryher (13 October 1948), qtd in *Between History and Poetry: The Letters of H.D. and Norman Holmes Pearson*, ed. by Donna Krolik Hollenberg (Iowa City: University of Iowa Press, 1997), p. 110 n. 8.

This was a retrospective and psychological attempt to understand Pound's politics made in 1948 at a time when Pound's friends were trying to prevent the death penalty.[119] H.D. also confuses Hamilton College in New York, where Pound studied from 1903 to 1905, with Wabash College in Crawfordsville, Indiana, where Pound taught during 1907 and 1908, as the site of dismissal on the grounds of sexual scandal. However, H.D. knew Pound as well as anyone and knew at first hand Pound's enduring sense of isolation. Pound claimed to have left Crawfordsville because it was one of the circles of hell, mediocre, amateurish and moralistic.[120] H.D. also later identified the antipathy Pound experienced in Philadelphia and his overwhelming sense of loneliness.[121] Pound it would appear left London for these reasons. He had become aware of his isolation, the exclusion from a society that had initially welcomed the American's eccentricity but now saw it as repugnant. The war had made the sense of expatriation in the world more real. This casts the '"being there and not being in it"' into an interesting light.

If there did appear a tone of uncertainty in Pound's method in 1916 then it was a return of the repressed. Pound was aware, at least conceptually, of the nature of the imaginative problem prior to the war. It is clear from the record of his 1912 walking tour in Provence, published posthumously as *A Walking Tour in Southern France* (1992), where Pound's praise of the troubadours rests on the immediacy of their involvement in history. 'Their testimony', Pound said in 'A Retrospect' (1918), 'is of the eyewitness, their symptoms are first hand.'[122] Pound theorised that the organic poetic consciousness could bridge the gaps of intersubjectivity through a triangulation involving philological research, focused acts of recreation and embodied acts of the sympathetic imagination. He explained in the essay 'Troubadours – Their Sorts and Conditions' (1913) that to gain 'emotional, as well as intellectual, acquaintance with an age so out of fashion as the twelfth century', one could read the original manuscripts or the historical record in the *razos* or *vidas*, perhaps listen one's way into a period through its music. Or 'a man may walk the hill roads and river roads'.[123] And yet, the fragmentary journal of that very journey is remarkable because Pound did not find what he sought. We are left only with an elegiac sense of the past as irrecoverable.[124] 'Going my way amid this ruin & beauty it is hard for me

---

[119] A. David Moody, *Ezra Pound: Poet, A Portrait of the Man and his Work*, III: *The Tragic Years 1939–1972* (2015), pp. 224–5.

[120] Moody, *The Young Genius*, p. 59.

[121] Carr, *The Verse Revolutionaries*, pp. 83–4.

[122] Ezra Pound, 'A Retrospect', in *Literary Essays of Ezra Pound*, ed. by T. S. Eliot (New York: New Directions, 1968), pp. 3–14 (p. 11).

[123] Ezra Pound, 'Troubadours – Their Sorts and Conditions', in *Literary Essays of Ezra Pound*, pp. 94–108 (pp. 94–5).

[124] Richard Sieburth, 'Introduction: "To Set Here the Roads of France"', in Ezra Pound, *A Walking Tour in Southern France: Ezra Pound among the Troubadours*, ed. by Richard Sieburth (New York: New Directions, 1992), pp. vii–xxi (pp. xv–xvi).

at times not to fall into the melancholy regarding that it is gone, & this is not the emotion that I care to cultivate for I think other poets have done so sufficiently.'[125] Pound repeatedly found himself, he admitted, no more than a dealer 'in garments for the dead', amidst a 'land so thick with ghosts' that it could hardly be rethought as a living presence.[126]

Timeline 3.2 January–August 1917

	Composition	*Publication, Exhibition, Event*
January	Pound, drafts of 'Three Cantos' Lawrence, 'Horse-Dealer's Daughter' (*English Review*: April 1922)	H.D., 'The God', 'Adonis' (*Egoist*) Pound/Fenollosa, '*Noh*', or, *Accomplishment: A Study of the Classical Stage of Japan* War dead: Silvertown munitions explosion
February	Gurney, 'Pain' (November 1917)	H.D., *The Tribute and Circe* (American ed.), 'Pygmalion' (*Egoist*) Monroe and Henderson, *The New Poetry* Pound, 'Rev. G. Crabbe' (*Future*) Thomas, poems including 'Old Man' (*Poetry*)
March	Eliot, quatrain poems and poems in French Woolf, *Night and Day*	Aldington, 'Thanatos' (*Little Review*) Eliot, 'Reflections on *Vers Libre*' (*New Statesman*); begins employment at Lloyds Bank February Revolution in Russia Lawrence, 'Thimble' (*Seven Arts*), 'Samson' (*English Review*) Stein leaves Paris with AFFW Thomas, poems in *Annual of New Poetry* Woolfs order printing machine
April	Lewis, 'The Bull Gun' (1991)	*The Blindman* 1 Loy, 'Songs to Joannes' (*Others*) *Some Imagist Poets* Anderson, 'The War' (blank page in *Little Review*) United States enters the war War dead: Arthur Graeme West, Thomas Wounded: Gurney, Sassoon

---

[125] Pound, *A Walking Tour in Southern France*, p. 22.
[126] Ibid. pp. 28, 35.

	Composition	*Publication, Exhibition, Event*
May	Lewis, 'Cantleman's Spring-Mate' Pound, redrafts 'Three Cantos' for *Lustra* (American ed.); 'MS Ur2' a further draft fragment of *The Fourth Canto* Rosenberg, 'Dead Man's Dump' (1922), 'Daughters of War' (1922)	*The Blind Man* 2 Eliot, 'Eeldrop and Appleplex [I]' (*Little Review*) H.D., 'Eurydice' (*Egoist*) Hulme and Lewis at the front line Pound, 'Editorial' as Foreign Editor of *Little Review* Pound/Lewis, serialisation of 'Imaginary Letters' (*Little Review*) Sassoon, *Old Huntsman* Woolf, 'Sassoon's Poems' (*TLS*) Wounded: Owen evacuated
June	Joyce, 'Lotus-Eaters', 'Hades', 'Aeolus', 'Proteus' Eliot, 'Mélange Adultère', 'Lune de Miel', 'Hippopotamus'	Eliot, *Prufrock* Haigh-Wood letter to Eliot; letter by Eliot to *Nation* H.D. (and Aldington) step down as Assistant Editors at *Egoist* and replaced by Eliot Lawrence, 'Resurrection' (*Poetry*) Owen at Craiglockhart Pound, serialisation of 'Three Cantos' (*Poetry*) Yeats, 'Wild Swans at Coole' (*Little Review*)
July	Sassoon, 'Repression of War Experience' (1918), Counter-Attack' (1918)	Aldington returns from France until the spring 1918; moves to Lichfield; H.D. moves to Lichfield Battles: Passchendaele begins Barbusse, *Under Fire* H.D., 'The Look-out' (*Egoist*) Eliot's poems finished in June 1917 (*Little Review*); review of Hulme's (1916) translation of Sorel's *Reflections on Violence* (1908) Lawrence, 'The Mortal Coil' (*Seven Arts*) Sassoon, 'Declaration' drafted with the help of Murry and Russell; at Craiglockhart Woolfs, *Two Stories*
August	Borden, 'Unidentified' Owen, 'Song of Songs' Stevens, '"Lettres d'un Soldat"'	Borden, 'At the Somme' (*English Review*) Eliot, review of Pound's '*Noh*' (*Egoist*) Joyce, *Exiles* Pound, 'Eliot' (*Poetry*)

Guide to Timelines

Works arranged in alphabetical order within each month.

Publication dates given in parenthesis, except if given in the main text, endnotes or elsewhere in timelines.

Titles shortened for brevity.

These anxieties upset the sense of conviction in the most closely related poem, 'Provincia Deserta'.[127] This poem presents the reader with a forsaken province, one that withholds from Pound any definitive answer to his almost neurotic insistence that there might be a hidden riddle in Bertran de Born's poem 'Dompna pois de me no'us cal'. The poem hopes to overcome this historical and poetic desertion.[128] And yet its incantatory beat – 'I have walked there', 'I have crept over', 'I have seen' – always offers the hope that we might connect with the past only to deflate those growing expectations. At Aubeterre we see only 'a garrulous old man at the inn', at Mareuil 'an old woman / glad to hear Arnaut'.[129] It is not a living past that Pound recreated. It is just image after image of the elderly. Each of the poem's claims on testimony, each 'I have said', 'I have looked', 'I have lain', rises with an expectation that falls back to sterile ground.[130]

Pound attempts an answer to this problem at the poem's closure. He does so by setting up a meta-poesis or a self-aware dramatisation of the poem's own method:

> That age is gone;
> Pieire de Maensac is gone.
> I have walked over these roads;
> I have thought of them living.[131]

'I have thought of them' functions in both the past and the present tenses. It is not a simple reimagining of this Auvergnat knight as if he were living. It is an act of thinking within the immediacy of current being: I have, or I possess thought in the here and now. It is a holding in mind. The past is to come alive through the embodied act of looking, feeling and moving in the present moment, as it had at the end of both '1915: February' and 'Trenches: St Eloi'.

This solution is developed in 'Near Perigord' as Pound rehearses the different modes of the historian, historical novelist and lyric poet and their respective abilities to locate objective truth.[132] It ends, as do many of the poems between

---

[127] It is possible that Pound began 'Provincia Deserta' as early as 1912. As Kenner (p. 321) suggests, however, the winter of 1914 seems the most likely date of composition. Pound later claimed the technical advances of 'Provincia Deserta' pre-dated *Cathay*. Ezra Pound, letter to Kate Buss (4 January 1917), in *The Letters of Ezra Pound*, p. 154. Pound began *Cathay* on 30 November and finished it by 20 December 1914. Longenbach, *Stone Cottage*, p. 288 n. 107.

[128] Sieburth, pp. xiv–xv.

[129] Ezra Pound, 'Provincia Deserta', *Poetry*, 5.6 (March 1915), 251–4 (pp. 251, 252) (*Poems and Translations*, pp. 297–9 (p. 297)).

[130] Pound, 'Provincia Deserta', p. 253 (*Poems and Translations*, p. 298).

[131] Pound, 'Provincia Deserta', p. 254 (*Poems and Translations*, p. 299).

[132] Moody, *The Young Genius*, pp. 304–6.

late 1914 and early 1916, by bringing imagination into play with fact, with the visionary-imaginative poet seeming to triumph over the sceptic.[133] The inherent uncertainty in both poems though gave way, albeit briefly, in the middle years of the war. This is clear in the changes Pound made to his 'Three Cantos', first published between June and December 1917.[134] 'I walk Verona. (I am here in England.) / I see Can Grande. (Can see whom you will.),' Pound insisted in the 'Three Cantos' completed by January 1917 and published in *Poetry*.[135] That insistence withered in the revisions he made soon after sending the poems to Monroe and during the summer of 1917 for the American edition of *Lustra* (October 1917) and for publication in *Future*. We can already glimpse the change in another of the unused drafts of *The Fourth Canto*, Froula's 'MS Ur2'. Here we have a narrator questioning his purpose: '"What do I mean by all this clattering rumble?" / Bewildered reader, what is the poet's business?'[136] In the revised 'Three Cantos' we see these doubts about the sympathetic imagination leaking into the poem:

> What have I of this life?
> > Or even of Guido?
> A pleasant lie that I knew *Or San Michaele*,
> Believe the tomb he leapt was Julia Laeta's,
> Do not even know which sword he'd with him in the street-charge.
> I have but smelt this life, a whiff of it,
> The box of scented wood
> Recalls cathedrals.   Shall I claim;
> Confuse my own phantastikon
> Or say the filmy shell that circumscribes me
> Contains the actual sun;
> > > confuse the thing I see
> With actual gods behind me?
> > > Are they gods behind me?[137]

---

[133] Longenbach, *Modernist Poetics of History*, pp. 91–2.

[134] There are three distinct versions of these poems. The '*Poetry* Three Cantos [I–III]' (*Poetry*: June–August 1917), the '*Lustra* Three Cantos' (rewritten in the summer of 1917 as soon as *Poetry* began publication, and published in autumn in the American edition of *Lustra*) and the '*Future* Three Cantos' (published February–April 1918 in *Future* as 'Passages from the Opening Address in a Long Poem', 'Images from the Second Canto of a Long Poem' and 'An Interpolation taken from the Third Canto of a Long Poem').

[135] Ezra Pound, 'Three Cantos I', *Poetry*, 10.3 (June 1917), 113–21 (p. 115).

[136] Ezra Pound, 'MS Ur2', qtd in Froula, *To Write Paradise*, p. 74. Froula dates 'MS Ur2' to autumn 1916–summer 1917.

[137] Ezra Pound, 'Three Cantos of a Poem of Some Length', in *Lustra of Ezra Pound with Earlier Poems* (New York: privately printed, 1917), pp. 179–202 (pp. 186–7).

This is not the measured certainty of Pound before 1915 or after 1919. Not until Pisa will we find again a poetic consciousness wracked by the fear that its basic and foundational assumptions are flawed. Pound's belief in the Neoplatonic concept of imagination, one borrowed from Yeats, an instrument of the *magus*, a tool that symbolises within the idea of one great universal mind, began to fray here.

It was during these months that Pound became Lewis's agent and, in case of the new recruit's death, executor. With Lewis's enlistment there began a correspondence that gave Pound his most immediate and prolonged access to the historical reality of warfare. Pound was acutely aware of their separation. He wrote to Lewis in the summer of 1916 in response to the new recruit's anxieties:

> Judging the matter from the depths of my moderately comfortable arm chair, with the products of your brush, pen and the reproductory processes of the late publisher M. Goschen before me—or from free seats at the opera—I can not see that the future of the arts deamns that you should be covered with military distinctions. It is equally obvious that you should not be allowed to spill your gore in heathen and furrin places.[138]

Pound's separation is clear in the injury (ironic or otherwise) he fears for Lewis. It is from Waterloo, a bayonet rather than a shell. In response to Pound's advice Lewis pointed to the difference in their roles. 'If you knew exactly how it was in the Ranks—the many reasons why it is desirable to be an officer' then 'you would understand my being anxious to change my state'.[139]

These gaps in experience grew once Lewis took position with the artillery during 1917. From the Messines Ridge on 14 June, Lewis asked Pound to visualise the scene: 'imagine a stretch of land one mile in depth sloping up from the old German first-line to the top of a ridge, & stretching to right & left as far as you can see.' Lewis's description then moved on to the *unheimlich*, the feeling, despite the frenzy of the fighting, that 'a watchfulness, fatigue and silence penetrates everything':

> Shall I or shall I not ask to go up there again tomorrow? There is nothing there you cannot imagine: but it has the unexpected quality of reality. Also the imagined thing and the felt are in two different categories. This category has its points. I will write you further on the subject of War. Do not expect my compositions to be well-worded, as letters (my letters) are only meant to be chat and slop.[140]

---

[138] Ezra Pound, letter to Wyndham Lewis (24 June 1916), in *Pound/Lewis*, pp. 39–40 (p. 39).
[139] Wyndham Lewis, letter to Ezra Pound (25 June 1916), in *Pound/Lewis*, pp. 42–3 (p. 42).
[140] Wyndham Lewis, letter to Ezra Pound (14 June 1917), in *Pound/Lewis*, pp. 75–6 (pp. 75, 76).

Lewis understood this to be important in Pound's hands, hence the caveats. Lewis wanted to make a crucial point about the phenomenological encounter with fear and the way it changes the perceptual contents of reality. It is 'chat and slop' because it is not clear Lewis fully understood it either. 'This category' presumably indicates the felt, not the imagined, and the idea that it has 'its points', or rather it has its points too. This suggests Lewis was proposing the felt as a category in its own right. Lewis knew how Pound might take the accusation that the scene was impossible to imagine.

Lewis had read *Le Feu* shortly after leaving the Messines Ridge. In August Pound told the combatant that 'I have not read Le Feu, Dorothy has and I got a breath off the top, when she quoted chunks of it'.[141] Pound was reluctant to pick it up and told Lewis that 'I have not read Barbeuse, Dorothy did. Baker dont feel like reading it either.' He went on, 'I dont see what the hell any writer can add to one's imagination of things. However.. that's no reason for not trying. And again neither Baker nor I can be taken as types of average imagination. All these books should ultimately be very useful.'[142] 'What the hell': Pound had sent *Cathay* to Gaudier-Brzeska for this very reason, to validate trying to imagine combat experience through a Chinese model using the raw material of the soldier's letters. Here was Lewis denying that achievement or at least questioning it.

The combatant was nonetheless stubbornly insistent. In October Lewis wrote again:

> Barbusse says in his book, & this surprised me with the French, that 'trés peu d'artistes ou de riches ont risqués leur figures dans les tranchées', or something like that; those were the words I think. Well, I dont, as you know, aspire to be a military hero. I shall shortly have 6 months service in France to my credit, during which time I have risked my 'figure' many times; more than you think.[143]

It is the concept of risk that Margalit uses to conceptualise the moral witness. The moral witness takes on the risk of evil to record it. Lewis was making a direct accusation. It was an accusation Pound could hardly have failed to take personally, especially at a time when his own method was subject to such personal scrutiny.

---

[141] Ezra Pound, letter to Wyndham Lewis (17 August 1917), in *Pound/Lewis*, pp. 94–5 (p. 94).

[142] Ezra Pound, letter to Wyndham Lewis (25 August 1917), in *Pound/Lewis*, pp. 98–100 (p. 99).

[143] Wyndham Lewis, letter to Ezra Pound (18 October 1917), in *Pound/Lewis*, pp. 109–10 (p. 109). The French translates as 'very few artists or the rich have risked their features in the trenches'.

Non-combat Gnosticism: Wallace Stevens and Citation

Stevens's poetry had also begun to move in a different direction in a second and lengthier attempt at an imagined war poem. The poem was 'Lettres d'un Soldat (1914–1915)', a series of seventeen poems, thirteen of which are extant, first published in part in *Poetry* during May 1918 and in full in 1989.[144] Stevens chose as his source material Eugène Lemercier's *Lettres d'un soldat (août 1914–avril 1915)* (1916), a series of exchanges between a new soldier and his mother.

Lemercier disappeared, presumed dead, in April 1915. In the following August, the *Revue de Paris* published *Lettres d'un soldat* and Theodore Stanton translated the sequence into English, publishing it anonymously as *A Soldier of France to his Mother* (June 1917).[145] For the readers of *Poetry* this history was hard to unpick. Its cover announced Stevens's interpretation as 'Poems on a French Soldier's Letters from the Front'.[146] Monroe also supplied extensive background in the notes to the edition to make sense of this array of sources.[147] This was entirely necessary. That Stevens's poems are variations on someone else's letters is not at all self-evident to the casual reader. The contents page and the poem's headnote in *Poetry* give it the title '"Lettres d'un Soldat"', suggesting but not making at all clear that the title referred to the citations accompanying each poem.[148] *Harmonium* (1923), *Collected Poems* (1954) and *Opus Posthumous* (1957; rev. 1989), the later collected editions of Stevens's poetry, all complicate the question of what is Stevens's work and what is Lemercier's. In these texts Stevens's sequence appears piecemeal. There is little or no supporting context and many of the citations from Lemercier's original disappear entirely. The title of Stevens's poem has even started to lose its double quotation marks.[149]

---

[144] *Poetry* published nine sections after Monroe sorted the good from the weak in the sequence. Wallace Stevens, '"Lettres d'un Soldat" I–IX', *Poetry*, 12.2 (May 1918), 59–65. For the publication background see Wallace Stevens, letter to Elsie Stevens (14 March 1918), in *The Letters of Wallace Stevens*, ed. by Holly Stevens (Berkeley: University of California Press, 1996), p. 205.

[145] Longenbach argues Stevens read Lemercier in French (in the *Revue de Paris* or a collected edition published by Chapelot) at Woodstock in the summer of 1917. Longenbach, *Plain Sense of Things*, p. 48.

[146] [Anonymous] [Harriet Monroe], 'Poetry: A Magazine of Verse edited by Harriet Monroe. May 1918', *Poetry*, 12.2 (May 1918), [cover].

[147] [Anonymous] [Harriet Monroe], 'Notes, *Poetry*, 12.2 (May 1918), 115–16 (p. 115).

[148] [Anonymous] [Harriet Monroe], 'Poetry for May, 1918', *Poetry*, 12.2 (May 1918), [contents page]; Stevens, '"Lettres d'un Soldat" I–IX', p. 59.

[149] Milton J. Bates, 'Notes to "Lettres d'un soldat (1914–1915)"', in Wallace Stevens, *Opus Posthumous*, ed. by Milton J. Bates, rev. edn (New York: Knopf, 1989; repr. New York: Vintage, 1990), p. 319.

There is no question of plagiarism here. The complexity and the process of re-citation is Stevens's point. He took great care to state his sources in the pre-publication correspondence with Monroe.[150] Monroe had little choice though but to add the clarification on *Poetry*'s cover and in the notes. The journal ran into trouble with readers, as discussed in Chapter 4, on this ground with other poetries of war. By 1918, the eager reading public had forced publishers to make clear the precise form of witnessing contained in their texts. That is the issue at stake in Stevens's sequence.

Lemercier's letters are remarkable on their own as source material. Echoing the poetries of Lawrence and H.D., they reveal a tender relationship forced to feel its way into communication across distance. We might detect Stevens's principal interest in them through their repeated turn to the relationship between experience and the imagination:

> I have no longer any desires. When the trials are really hard, I simply accept my unhappy lot and try and keep my mind a blank. Then, when things grow pleasanter, I begin to think again and dream, when throng back to me the bonny hours of the past tinged with the old touch of distant poetry, which led my thoughts in those happy days into the strange paths of the imagination.[151]

Repeatedly Lemercier turns to epic to structure the nightmarish experience.[152] At times this is profoundly lyrical:

> I forgot to tell thee that during the battle of the other day I saw in the evening the cranes coming back north, and a lull in the fight made it possible even to hear their cries. It seems so long since I saw them depart on their southern journey. I remember that when they left us at the beginning of winter everything appeared to grow sadder afterwards. Their coming back is like a dove from Noah's ark[.][153]

The soldier tells his mother, 'I am made very happy, too, by thy admirable letters. As regards our sufferings here on earth I think they are not so unbearable as you seem to imagine.'[154] He begs her to 'imagine the tender emotions' of the

---

[150] Wallace Stevens, letter to Harriet Monroe (1 September 1917), in *The Letters of Wallace Stevens*, p. 202. Stevens sent Monroe a copy of the French original and recommended the translated edition as a source.

[151] Anonymous [Eugène Lemercier], *A Soldier of France to his Mother: Letters from the Trenches on the Western Front*, trans. by Theodore Stanton (Chicago: A. C. McClurg, 1917), pp. 117–18.

[152] See for example Lemercier's use of Dante. Ibid. p. 142.

[153] Ibid. p. 155.

[154] Ibid. p. 112.

soldier in the Loire, asked to understand the specific state of his mind. She is warned against what it might not be possible to imagine.[155] Lemercier implores: 'You must call on your imagination a little.'[156] 'I don't want you to imagine that I haven't good friends here', 'please don't imagine that I rest insensible to the heart-rending spectacle in which we are plunged'.[157] Slowly there opens a gap between the felt and the imagined revealing a blank space between two humans previously bound by their Catholic piety.

Whilst seeking salvation in the divine, the soldier's letters slowly begin to deny the mother those same consolations. 'You cannot imagine how much longer a day is without home news.'[158] 'You cannot imagine how ashamed I would be', 'you cannot imagine my longing', 'you cannot imagine how much comfort I get', 'you can not imagine our state of despair', 'you cannot imagine how the forests have suffered', 'you cannot imagine how this upsets our whole existence', 'you cannot imagine, dear Mother, what awful things man can do to man'.[159] It erodes his faith. If his mother cannot imaginatively share his experience whose testimony can he believe? By the end of his letters, Lemercier is a broken man who 'cannot even imagine what a new life might be'.[160]

Stevens's reflections on Lemercier's manuscript are astonishingly opaque. Their piecemeal publication, and Stevens's willingness to let Monroe prune them, suggest personal concern as to their value. As in 'Phases', the overriding theme is far from clear, the irony too mobile. There is also a tendency to moralise. In *The Modern Dilemma* (2008), Leon Surette suggests Lemercier's interest in the consolations of piety when faced with death piqued Stevens's interest.[161] In contrast, Paul Mariani (2016), Stevens's biographer, suggests Stevens had found a kindred spirit seeking glimpses of beauty amidst hell.[162] Longenbach's position in *The Plain Sense of Things* is the most persuasive, however. Stevens found in Lemercier someone who shared his vision of the imagination's limits when faced with raw experience. This was especially powerful for Stevens in a modern world robbed of the promise of an afterlife.[163] It is especially noticeable that the fragments of Lemercier's letters chosen by Stevens are indeed those in which imagination found itself face to face with

---

[155] For example, ibid. p. 9.

[156] Ibid. p. 75.

[157] Ibid. pp. 48, 52.

[158] Ibid. p. 35.

[159] Ibid. pp. 8, 38, 43, 66, 87, 107, 140.

[160] Ibid. p. 118.

[161] Leon Surette, *The Modern Dilemma: Wallace Stevens, T. S. Eliot, and Humanism* (Montreal: McGill-Queen's University Press, 2008), p. 119.

[162] Paul Mariani, *The Whole Harmonium: The Life of Wallace Stevens* (New York: Simon & Schuster, 2016), pp. 112–13.

[163] Longenbach, *Plain Sense of Things*, pp. 58–9, 72.

reality looking for the consolations of beauty, justice and spectacle.[164] It was the reflective combatant that interested Stevens, the one consoled by the night, not the one 'in the zone of horrors', amidst 'the screaming of the shells' or subject to 'nervous reaction'.[165]

Stevens's poetic model pivots on the issue of citation, of what is found, borrowed and imagined. In doing so it looks backwards to Pound's found poem at St Eloi and forwards to Eliot's use of tradition in his theory of impersonality. Stevens placed a long citation at the beginning of his sequence. He took it from André Chevrillon's French preface to Lemercier's letters. In turn, Chevrillon took it from the *Bhagavad Gita*. It speaks of Krishna's instruction to Arjuna to fight on the field of battle with open eyes but without hope of glory or gain.[166] Arjuna was to turn away from the absolute towards reality. He was to be dutiful as a warrior but without any attachment to the result and despite his compassion for those he must fight. Eliot would use the same image when faced with a similar dilemma in the Second World War. *The Dry Salvages* (1941) tells of Krishna instructing Arjuna to face the mixed feelings of the battlefield with *nishpala karma* or disinterested action.[167] We might wonder with Pierre Bourdieu in *Practical Reason* (1994) whether such an act is ever really plausible.[168] Here, it suggests that Stevens was leaning towards a position that intertwined the ethical with the aesthetic, a perspective of disinterest achieved through the irony of multiple layers of quotation that could arbitrate between the objectivity of the eyewitness and the subjectivity of the fleshwitness.

Take as example the first poem in Stevens's sequence, 'Common Soldier', a poem Monroe and Stevens chose not to print. The poem returns to the theme of 'Phases' and the jaunty excitement of the early pals battalions. Stevens's opening epigraph from Lemercier serves as the newly found object, the raw commodity excavated from the site of original feeling. It speaks of the soldier's naivety, of an event the soldier hoped to experience as an adventure and without any overwhelmingly strong personal feeling. Religiously schooled and face

---

[164] Wallace Stevens, 'Lettres d'un Soldat (1914–1915)', in *Collected Poetry and Prose*, pp. 538–45 (pp. 539, 541, 542).

[165] [Lemercier], pp. 14, 15, 16.

[166] Stevens, 'Lettres d'un Soldat', p. 538.

[167] T. S. Eliot, *The Dry Salvages*, in *Collected and Uncollected Poems*, pp. 193–200 (p. 198). See Christopher Ricks, *T. S. Eliot and Prejudice* (Berkeley: University of California Press, 1988), pp. 252–3. By the 1930s Eliot had come to the view that at least some artists should remain isolated from the Spanish Civil War, a position that led him toward the Hindu model. 'T. S. Eliot', in *Authors Take Sides on the Spanish War* (London: Left Review, 1937), p. [27]. For analysis see Christopher Ricks and Jim McCue, 'Commentary: *The Dry Salvages*', in Eliot, *Collected and Uncollected Poems*, pp. 959–88 (p. 980 n. III lines 33–44).

[168] Pierre Bourdieu, *Practical Reason: On the Theory of Action* (1994) (Stanford: Stanford University Press, 1998), pp. 75–91.

turned very much to the absolute (unlike Arjuna), this combatant takes the world at face value. He learns only by rote. In aggregate, this harks back to the senselessness of the Belgian mood isolated by Ford in *Antwerp*, but this is a much more stylised poem. Through a change in font, a break in title and jarring changes in pronouns the found object becomes an aesthetic object as the poem begins. Stevens exaggerates the coming together of these two consciousnesses, combatant and poet, with the use of a colon to end the first line. It acts to demarcate the two personalities. As in 'Trenches: St Eloi', it is as if out of the chaos of introspection there appears a new composite personality, one that keeps a residue of the original set of feelings and yet can bring them into a shape and meaning that they lacked in their original form.

Stevens's method suggests then that this might be a tentative solution to the overreaching possibilities of the *magus*. 'If I should fall, as soldier,' Stevens's common combatant says, 'I know well / The final pulse of blood from this good heart / Would taste, precisely, as they said it would.'[169] The reference is surely to Brooke. 'If I should die, think only this of me,' begins the most famous example of the very spirit that took people, such as Lemercier, to war. Brooke's poem imagines the warrior's body as 'A dust' that becomes 'some corner of a foreign field', a place 'for ever England', 'this heart' but 'A pulse in the eternal mind'.[170] Stevens transforms that image into 'If I should fall'. It is a falling that gives rise not to the combatant's body becoming a dust richer than the earth but to a gruesome pumping out of the blood. Again, as in Ford's *Antwerp*, it becomes a stain on the earth, although in Stevens's poem the victim eats his own words. He is force-fed the very structure of feeling that sent him to war in the first place.

This is certainly not the agnosticism of H.D. or the partnership with unknowingness in Thomas's work. By 1917 Stevens had twice tried to follow the soldier into battle. His poem is effectively a development of Pound's model. It is a meta-poem. It is a series of quotes speaking about quotes, a poem reflecting on citations, a text that deliberately confuses authorship and authenticity. Form replaces experience. We might go further by suggesting that form appears as an alternative form of compensation. It confers the ability to bring chaos into perspective, a pay-off for not having been up to the neck in it all. Bringing the found object into the poem allows the looker-on to see the game, to be knee deep in things, or rather to see the things that need seeing. In its appeal to form, this modernism claimed to be able to set content in its proper context by taking public images out of the cultural marketplace. It was then a gnosticism of a different sort, one that demanded the disinterested outside rather than the vested interest of the inside, a non-combat gnosticism that foundationally depended on not having fought at all.

[169] Stevens, 'Lettres d'un Soldat', p. 538.
[170] Brooke, '1914: V. The Soldier', p. 23.

4

AN EMERGENT CRITIQUE OF
WAR EXPERIENCE:
AUTUMN 1917–SPRING 1919

Transmutations into Poetry

The problems raised by Wallace Stevens's sequence were already widely clear within modernist cultures. In 1918 *Poetry* awarded the Helen Haire Levenson Prize to John Curtis Underwood for his Serbian war poem, 'The Song of the Cheechas' (*Poetry*: June 1918).[1] It appeared with a group of poems entitled 'War Times' which gave vent to Underwood's antagonism towards the Central Powers. Methodologically, it followed the process Underwood developed in the 1917 collection *War Flames* and took as its source material poems covering each of Europe's main theatres of war that relied on the first-hand experience of soldiers and other combat witnesses. Underwood went to great lengths to make this method clear. He highlighted reuse of material from a range of sources which included May Sinclair's *A Journal of Impressions in Belgium*.[2] Harriet Monroe singled out this approach when praising *War Flames*, calling it 'a crowded frieze showing the marching of all nations through the terrors and agonies of the cataclysmic struggle'.[3]

Underwood did not however cite a source for his poem on the Cheechas and in January 1919 Paul Fortier Jones alleged Underwood had unduly paraphrased

---

[1] [Harriet Monroe], 'Announcement of Awards [1918]', *Poetry*, 13.2 (November 1918), 108–14 (p. 112).

[2] John Curtis Underwood, *War Flames* (New York: Macmillan, 1917), [front papers].

[3] H.M. [Harriet Monroe], 'War Poems', *Poetry*, 10.5 (August 1917), 271–8 (p. 275).

his memoir *With Serbia into Exile* (1916).[4] Jones went to Serbia in September 1915 as part of a humanitarian relief effort and was the only American with the local army as it catastrophically retreated through the Albanian mountains. As Jones explained, *cheecha* means uncle, and in Serbia it was a term given to men over the age of thirty. Jones found however that many of the *cheechas* were well over forty. He felt that Underwood had taken his core point, that the Serb seems never too old to fight, without due attribution.[5] Jones complained that Underwood had 'contrived to add so little to the original source of his verse that only simple honesty must have impelled him to give due credit to that source'. Without that acknowledgement, Jones concluded, Underwood wanted to deceive the reading public about his own combat credentials.[6]

The accusation was not entirely unfounded. Underwood's poem lifted whole phrases and images verbatim from Jones's text.[7] Monroe defended *Poetry's* award of the Prize on the administrative ground that it was irrevocable, and that in any case Underwood had already donated his prize money to the United War Work Campaign. The most crucial element of her defence however was the reassertion of the evolving modernist poetic of the *magus*. Having quoted Jones, Monroe said:

> The passages above quoted are prose; deriving from them his basic material and his inspiration, Mr. Underwood made a poem. It was manifest that this poet, a native American who had never travelled in Serbia, must have drawn his material from printed or oral accounts. In our opinion, *The Song of the Cheechas* is not a mere paraphrase of Mr. Jones' excellent prose, but a transmutation into poetry.[8]

This makes two separate points. First, it links meaning to the reader's understanding of the circumstances of the poem's publication and the accompanying apparatus. These are to function as a manifest guarantee of authenticity. Second, Monroe follows the May Sinclair–Ezra Pound method of composition, setting aside the paraphrase for a process that creates the artefact from found material by changing its essential form. The poet removes the unprocessed material from its original prosaic context and places it into a new figurative

---

[4] Paul Fortier Jones, 'Correspondence: About Mr. Underwood's Prize', *Poetry*, 13.4 (January 1919), 228–30 (p. 228).

[5] [Paul] Fortier Jones, *With Serbia into Exile: An American's Adventures with the Army that Cannot Die* (New York: Grosset & Dunlap, 1916), p. 47. The wording is also uncannily like the wording used by Pound in Chapter 3. Pound, letter to Homer Pound (23 August 1917).

[6] Jones, 'Correspondence: About Mr. Underwood's Prize', p. 228.

[7] See for example Jones, *With Serbia into Exile*, p. 61; John Curtis Underwood, 'The Song of the Cheechas', *Poetry*, 12.3 (June 1918), 117–18 (p. 117).

[8] [Harriet Monroe], 'Note by the Editor', *Poetry*, 13.4 (January 1919), 230.

life through the act of transmutation. In a further anticipation of T. S. Eliot's alchemical metaphors, something that is base becomes that which is precious.

The fracas is an obvious sign that combat experience had become a distinctive category of experience that readers recognised and respected. By 1918 authors and publishers had to make their sources clear or risk accusations of inauthenticity or plagiarism. Was the text authentic or found? We can see this dynamic at work in the modernist's own publication practices. Despite being extremely critical of the Georgian deification of Rupert Brooke, each major modernist coterie sought a dead combatant as a totem of its art. Richard Aldington, John Cournos and Ford Madox Ford all tried to lay claim to the discovery of Henri Gaudier-Brzeska, even after Pound's memoir of 1916.[9] Eliot dedicated *Prufrock and Other Observations* (June 1917) to Jean Verdenal and he emphasised his dead friend's battle credentials in post-war editions of poetry.[10] In doing so poets were situating their work within a cultural context that demanded the forging of allegiances with the combatant. *Poetry*, the journal that initiated the genre of the imagined war poem back in 1914 with its $100 competition, gradually identified itself with Joyce Kilmer and Alan Seeger following their deaths in France.[11] The Sitwells marked the death of Wilfred Owen in the same way that *Georgian Poetry* had the death of Brooke.[12] These poetries felt the growing need of a combatant's corpse on which they might ground their craft.

T. S. ELIOT'S WAR, F. H. BRADLEY'S LEGACY

Despite the appearance of Verdenal in *Prufrock*, prior to 1918 the accents of war are easy to miss in Eliot's poetry. In the poems written during late 1914 and early 1915 at Oxford, there is little sense Eliot was in a country only miles from war. In poems such as 'Paysage Triste' (1996; *February 1915*), 'Afternoon' (1988; *February 1915*) and 'To Helen' (1996; *April 1915*) we see only voyeuristic narrators drifting in a Laforguian metropolis, strangely eyeing women.[13] The self-conscious draw and disdain for mass commercialisation in 'In the Department Store' (1996; *February 1915*) remains largely consistent

---

[9] Richard Aldington, 'Remy de Gourmont, After the Interim', *Little Review*, 5.10–11 (February–March 1919), 32–4 (p. 34); John Cournos, 'Discussion: The Death of Vorticism', *Little Review*, 6.2 (June 1919), 46–8 (p. 48); Ford Madox Ford, 'Henri Gaudier, The Story of a Low Tea-shop', *English Review*, 26 (October 1919), 297–304.

[10] T. S. Eliot, *Prufrock and Other Observations* (London: Egoist, 1917), [front papers].

[11] H.M. [Harriet Monroe], 'Comment: Joyce Kilmer', *Poetry*, 13.1 (October 1918), 31–4.

[12] *Wheels: Fourth Cycle*, ed. by Edith Sitwell and others (Oxford: B. H. Blackwell, 1919), [front papers].

[13] T. S. Eliot, 'Paysage Triste', in *Collected and Uncollected Poems*, p. 267; T. S. Eliot, 'Afternoon', in *Collected and Uncollected Poems*, pp. 267–8; T. S. Eliot, 'To Helen', in *Collected and Uncollected Poems*, p. 271.

with Prufrock's much earlier reflections on society.[14] Even after the disastrous events in the spring of 1915, the war emerged as only a shadow. We can see it, perhaps, in 'Mr. Apollinax' (*Poetry*: September 1916; *July 1915*) via the emergence of the figure of the drowned man after the sinking of the *Lusitania* as Eliot crisscrossed the Atlantic in July and August.[15] Even in poems where analogy with the war might be expected, such as 'The Death of Saint Narcissus' (1950; *April 1915*), sexuality is very much the focus.[16] Whilst Eliot's narrator in 'Hysteria' (*Catholic Anthology*: November 1915; *March 1915*) imagined a distinctly feminised hysteria staring into the mouth of a socialite, in 'XXVII: A Sonnet' (1916) Charles Sorley was seeing 'millions of the mouthless dead' across his dreams.[17]

Eliot's biography resists the conclusion that he played possum.[18] His letters during 1914 and 1915 to Eleanor Hinkley, Conrad Aiken and Isabella Gardner speak of the enormous personal impact of the war.[19] By 1916 the death of Verdenal in the Dardanelles and the disappearance of the poet Martin Armstrong in the Artists Rifles brought the war even closer to home.[20] These same letters though also reveal a rather unnerving sense of excitement. Eliot the poet seemed equally to be relishing these conditions. They gave him the material for a series of long poems, he told Aiken.[21] He conveyed the same sense of excitement to Charlotte Eliot in May 1917, describing the alarming experience of being amidst a war with its constant news of the dead and the wounded.[22]

In *The Imperfect Life of T. S. Eliot* (2012) Lyndall Gordon describes Eliot's subsequent efforts to enlist in 1918 as mildly frantic.[23] He was eventually rejected for front-line duty due to a hernia and a heart rhythm disorder, and

---

[14] T. S. Eliot, 'In the Department Store', in *Collected and Uncollected Poems*, p. 268; T. S. Eliot, 'The Love Song of J. Alfred Prufrock' (*Poetry*: June 1915; *July 1910*), in *Collected and Uncollected Poems*, pp. 5–9 (p. 5).

[15] T. S. Eliot, 'Mr. Apollinax', in *Collected and Uncollected Poems*, p. 25. Similarly, T. S. Eliot, 'The Engine' (1996; *July 1915*).

[16] T. S. Eliot, 'The Death of Saint Narcissus', in *Collected and Uncollected Poems*, pp. 270–1 (p. 270).

[17] T. S. Eliot, 'Hysteria', in *Collected and Uncollected Poems*, p. 26; Charles Sorley, 'XXVII: A Sonnet', in Charles Sorley, *Marlborough and Other Poems*, 2nd edn (Cambridge: Cambridge University Press, 1916), p. 69.

[18] See the claims in Froula, 'War, Empire and Modernist Poetry', p. 219.

[19] T. S. Eliot, letter to Eleanor Hinkley (8 September [1914]), in *The Letters of T. S. Eliot*, I, pp. 60–2 (p. 62); T. S. Eliot, letter to Conrad Aiken (25 February [1915]), in *The Letters of T. S. Eliot*, I, pp. 95–6 (p. 95); T. S. Eliot, letter to Mrs Jack [Isabella] Gardner (4 April [1915]), in *The Letters of T. S. Eliot*, I, pp. 100–3 (p. 101).

[20] T. S. Eliot, letter to Conrad Aiken (10 January 1916), in *The Letters of T. S. Eliot*, I, pp. 137–9 (p. 137).

[21] Ibid. p. 138.

[22] T. S. Eliot, letter to Charlotte Eliot (13 May 1917), in *The Letters of T. S. Eliot*, I, pp. 198–9 (p. 199).

[23] Lyndall Gordon, *The Imperfect Life of T. S. Eliot*, rev. edn (London: Virago, 2012), p. 134.

the saga weighed heavily on him.[24] Subsequent medical advice required Eliot to rest until the spring of 1919, a period of drought broken by the composition of 'Gerontion'.[25] Eliot repeatedly defended his failed attempt to serve, especially to his parents.[26] It suggests insecurity, perhaps a fear that he may be labelled a slacker, the pejorative term used to justify raids on Americans avoiding military service.[27] Peter Ackroyd (1993), Daniel J. Childs (2001) and Robert Crawford (2015) suggest other perfectly understandable motives: duty, class anxiety, a natural fear of death or injury, the financial consequences of conscription and the impact on Vivien Eliot's failing health.[28] As with Pound, the matter seems difficult to simplify. On the one hand Eliot told Herbert Read in June 1920 that his unfit-for-service grading left a Kantian hue to life, a certain disinterestedness in war and its aftermath.[29] And yet Eliot told Graham Wallas in December 1918 that it had been the struggle with the administrative procedures of enlistment, along with both the pandemic and failed peace, that had left him with a very great interest in the war.[30]

It is Eliot's existential historicism that especially complicates the war as an intellectual problem. Whereas F. H. Bradley's *Appearance and Reality* (1893) has tended to take centre stage in studies of Eliot's development as a poet, in *T. S. Eliot's Intellectual and Poetic Development* (1982) Piers Gray rightly emphasised the influence of Bradley's peculiar brand of scepticism in *The Presuppositions of Critical History*.[31] *The Presuppositions of Critical History* is grounded in Bradley's interest in the Bible as historical evidence and, particularly, the authority of its testimony in the face of miracles that violated the ordinary laws of nature. In *The Idea of History* (1946; rev. 1994), R. G. Collingwood termed Bradley's book 'the Copernican revolution in the theory of historical knowledge'.[32] More recently Richard Niland (2009) argues for it

[24] T. S. Eliot, letter to Henry Ware Eliot (4 November 1918), in *The Letters of T. S. Eliot*, I, pp. 286–9 (p. 289); T. S. Eliot, letter to Charlotte Eliot (13 November 1918), in *The Letters of T. S. Eliot*, I, pp. 300–1 (p. 300).

[25] T. S. Eliot, letter to John Rodker (9 December 1918), in *The Letters of T. S. Eliot*, I, p. 307.

[26] For example, see Eliot, letter to Charlotte Eliot (13 November 1918), p. 301.

[27] Christopher Capozzola, *Uncle Sam Wants You: World War I and the Making of the Modern American Citizen* (Oxford: Oxford University Press, 2008), pp. 21–54.

[28] Daniel J. Childs, *Modernism and Eugenics: Woolf, Eliot, Yeats, and the Culture of Degeneration* (Cambridge: Cambridge University Press, 2001), pp. 110–11; Crawford, *Young Eliot*, pp. 303–6. Both Childs and Crawford suspect the real reason to be Eliot's financial concerns since his income risked reduction as a private. Peter Ackroyd, *T. S. Eliot* (London: Penguin, 1993), p. 87 comes down on the side of patriotism.

[29] T. S. Eliot, letter to Herbert Read (20 June 1920), in *The Letters of T. S. Eliot*, I, pp. 469–70 (p. 469).

[30] T. S. Eliot, letter to Graham Wallas (14 December 1918), in *The Letters of T. S. Eliot*, I, p. 308.

[31] Piers Gray, *T. S. Eliot's Intellectual and Poetic Development 1909–1922* (Brighton: Harvester Press, 1982), pp. 102–7.

[32] R. G. Collingwood, *The Idea of History*, ed. by Jan van der Dussen, rev. edn (Oxford: Oxford University Press, 1994), p. 240.

as the neo-Hegelian moment when history became understood as inevitably constructed.[33] In Chapter 5, Bradley's attempt to understand the nature of the evidence presented in the Bible will help us to understand Eliot's protracted meditation on the sympathetic imagination in 'Gerontion'. It particularly helps to explain Eliot's dramatic and disorientating move in that poem from imagined trench experience to the question of belief through the image of the Magi.

Here the point of focus is Bradley's assertion in *The Presuppositions of Critical History* that 'history rests in the last resort upon an inference from our own experience, a judgement based upon our own present state of things'.[34] Bradley understood that history was always fatally flawed at its source, inescapably biased by the standpoint of its author's prejudices. This was the basis for Bradley's important distinction between the uncritical amateur who prejudicates without knowing it and the self-conscious or critical historian 'who consciously orders and creates from the known foundation of that which for him is the truth'.[35]

As Collingwood rightly noted this leads us to the crux of the problem. Bradley's critical version of history depended on a major assumption, 'the assumption of the essential uniformity of nature and the course of events'.[36] What of, Collingwood asked, the moment when the critical historian finds no analogy in personal experience?[37] Bradley's solution to that problem takes us to the core of Eliot's imaginative project:

> By inferences, however complicated yet in the end resting on personal observation, we have so apprehended and possessed ourselves of the consciousness of others, that we are justified in assuming the identity of their standpoint with our own; i.e. we can be assured that the already systematized world, which was brought as a canon by the witnesses to the observation and to the subsumption of the mesmeric phenomena, was practically the same as that which we ourselves should have brought. We thus are certain that the men can see for us, because we know that they are able to think for us.[38]

When analogy breaks down the self can fall back on a canon of witnesses, the plurality of voices within a common system of intersubjectivity, as the means to approximate to what the self would have felt in the same situation. There

---

[33] Richard Niland, *Conrad and History* (Oxford: Oxford University Press, 2009), p. 73.
[34] F. H. Bradley, *The Presuppositions of Critical History* (Oxford: James Parker, 1874), p. 19.
[35] Ibid. p. 13.
[36] Ibid. p. 15.
[37] Collingwood, p. 137.
[38] Bradley, *The Presuppositions of Critical History*, pp. 22–3.

is the spirit of John Stuart Mill's analogical inference here. We can see the self-consciously tenuous nature of Bradley's solution since in the final reckoning the problem of the Other's mind rests on the assumption that its mind holds a cosmos that is subject to the same laws as one's own:

> Testimony goes beyond individual experience, but not beyond *our* experience; or it takes us beyond our experience if it takes *us* with it. It is not uncriticised; it stands, if at all, on the basis of our world. It has been subject to the laws of, and has been connected with and become part of, our personal experience, not in its own right *as* testimony, not in the right of the witness *as* witness, but in the right of and on the guarantee of our own intelligence.[39]

'Not in the right of the witness *as* witness': witnessing itself has no preferential access to truth. It only achieves its power through a process of cultural agglomeration.

The question of war was then subtly different for Eliot and Pound. We can use Eliot's observations in 'Eeldrop and Appleplex' (*Little Review*: May and September 1917) to illustrate the distinction. According to Eliot, 'Eeldrop was a sceptic, with a taste for mysticism, and Appleplex a materialist with a leaning toward scepticism'.[40] The materialist is Pound. The tag fits his grounding in *Lebensphilosophie* and philological faith in hermeneutics as the means of recapturing *virtù*. Pound's search for the troubadours revealed the scientific monist, one who believed in a deeper essence or a common physical reality inherent to all objects. In contrast, Eliot is the classical sceptic, one who sees that knowledge of essences might never be possible. A philosophical education had made Eliot acutely aware that the alleged truths of *Verstehen* ignored their own mediation, resulting in a bias the only corrective for which was the pragmatism of scientific method.

Defined this way, it is natural that the sceptic should hanker after mysticism. Mystical experience holds out to the sceptical mind the fragile possibility that

---

[39] Ibid. p. 24.
[40] T. S. Eliot, 'Eeldrop and Appleplex', in *Apprentice Years, 1905–1918*, pp. 525–32 (pp. 525–6). The relationship between Eeldrop–Appleplex and Eliot–Pound is moot. Longenbach, *Modernist Poetics of History*, pp. 152–5 argues it is a satiric portrait emphasising Eliot's view of Pound and leaving out Pound's occultism. James E. Miller Jr, *T. S. Eliot: The Making of an American Poet, 1888–1922* (University Park: Pennsylvania State University Press, 2005), p. 284 suggests Appleplex is a Pound–Russell composite, objecting that Pound had not studied the physical and biological sciences referred to in Eliot's essay. Eliot's reference however was to Pound's knowledge of Remy de Gourmont's vast project of ideas that aimed to reconcile Symbolism with science especially through physiology and psychology. Glenn S. Burne, 'Remy de Gourmont and the Aesthetics of Symbolism', *Comparative Literature Studies*, 4.1/2 (1967), 161–75.

a rarefied sensibility might be able to bridge knowledge and experience. It is equally natural, as we have seen with Pound's doubts, that the conviction of the materialist be occasionally tested, especially when the *magus* senses that the apparatus of reason presupposes its own supremacy. As Eliot neatly summarised it, the sceptic is a pessimist. Their lives see brief moments breaking through the gloom. The materialist is in contrast an optimist. Brief spells of doubt puncture their lives. It was in epiphany and doubt rather than in their theories of imagination that these two poets could find common ground.

If Eliot's assessment here is correct, then it leads us to two alternative aesthetic approaches to the moral witness. In Pound's case, if all organic life is but one substance of some sort then the very idea that there might be a gnosis associated with combat would be to insert a spooky second substance or spirit into life. It would be a vitalism, a return to Bergsonism. The materialist denies the combat gnostic hypothesis on the grounds that the imagination must be able, *a priori*, to move freely throughout the commonality of one substance. In contrast, in Eliot's case, the moral witness confirms the Bradleyean position that all accounts are prejudicated *a priori*. His clamouring for presence is just another example of Bradley's description of a world structured by intellectual white noise, by 'the divergent accounts of a host of jarring witnesses, a chaos of disjoined and discrepant narrations'.[41] To bring felt experience into poetry the imagination must work not by trying to reach across a gap the sceptic knows already is too wide to be bridged, but by rebuilding the commonality of human experience throughout the ages. It was an approach, as Stevens's meta-poem in Chapter 3 suggested, that aimed at an objective phenomenology using the multiplicity of witnessing as its source. If Pound's poet needed a shard of authentic found experience, then Eliot's needed literary taste and sufficient leisure time to crowdsource the evidence.

In *The Matrix of Modernism*, Sanford Schwartz gives a clear example of this difference. In his copy of Remy de Gourmont's *Le Problème du style* (1902), Pound highlighted one particular observation which begins 'I do not disapprove of the imaginary notation of things "not seen"', but ends with de Gourmont's idea that 'to imagine is to associate images and fragments of images; that is not creating'.[42] Pound, irked, responded in the margin that '"it is quite possible, nevertheless, that the imagination does create"', and he cited as counter example, '"I can not remember metalic architecture—i.e. interior decoration—bronze— from life, etc."'[43] As Schwartz rightly observes, Pound strenuously believed in

---

[41] Bradley, *The Presuppositions of Critical History*, p. 5.

[42] Remy de Gourmont, 'Selections from *The Problem of Style*', in Remy de Gourmont, *Selected Writings*, ed. and trans. by Glenn S. Burne (Ann Arbor: University of Michigan Press, 1966), pp. 108–29 (p. 125).

[43] Qtd in Schwartz, p. 108.

the ability of art to create an atom of an idea, or at the very least in its ability to expose the falsity of past ideas.[44] There can be no limit to the sympathetic imagination since everything shares the same substrate of life. For Eliot, the moral witness was more of a genuine philosophical challenge, a reminder of the urgent necessity to redefine the law, to create the new *Summa Theologiæ*.

Tom, Maurice and the Corridor into *The Waste Land*

This fundamental difference is manifest in Eliot's reuse of Pound's corridor as a metaphor for the shocked mind. Unlike Eliot's other draft poems in this period, 'In silent corridors of death' (1996) did not form part of the original Berg Notebook and the associated loose leaves bought by John Quinn in 1922. The manuscript belonged to Maurice Haigh-Wood, Eliot's brother-in-law, a Second Lieutenant in the 2nd Battalion of the Manchester Regiment. This is supportive of the case made by both Carl Krockel (2011) and George Simmers (2017) that this short and fragmentary poem was a war poetry.[45] Although Crawford is somewhat more circumspect, given Eliot and Haigh-Wood shared a lengthy correspondence during the war, it might be argued, at this stage hypothetically, that if Ezra's first-hand experience of the body in pieces came from his friends Henri and Wyndham then Tom's came from Maurice.[46]

We can sense Eliot's fascination with Haigh-Wood's combat experience when he described it to Charlotte Eliot during November 1915. Eliot picked out not only the attractions of Haigh-Wood's class but also the range of his experiences for one so young. He chose to emphasise the young soldier's loneliness, his insomnia, encounters with giant rats and the nature of his underground sunless trench.[47] When the army invalided Haigh-Wood, for the insomnia according to Eliot, the poet was again interested in the abnormality of the combatant's experience. He wrote to Hinkley in September 1916 telling her of Haigh-Wood's breakdown and his encounter with the body in pieces. It left Eliot feeling very immature in comparison.[48]

Christopher Ricks and Jim McCue (2015) placed the composition of 'In silent corridors of death' towards the end of 1916.[49] They cite the fragment's

---

[44] Schwartz, p. 108.

[45] Krockel, p. 93; George Simmers, 'T. S. Eliot's Letter to "The Nation"', *Great War Fiction*, <https://greatwarfiction.wordpress.com/tseliots-letter-to-the-nation/> [accessed 22 March 2022].

[46] Crawford, *Young Eliot*, p. 277.

[47] T. S. Eliot, letter to Charlotte Eliot (18 November 1915), in *The Letters of T. S. Eliot*, I, pp. 131–3 (p. 132).

[48] T. S. Eliot, letter to Eleanor Hinkley (5 September 1916), in *The Letters of T. S. Eliot*, I, pp. 161–3 (p. 162).

[49] Ricks and McCue place Eliot's fragment in the (chronologically arranged) 'Uncollected Poems', after 'The Engine', 'Hidden under the heron's wing' (1996; *undated*) and 'O lord, have patience' (1996; *undated*), but before 'Airs of Palestine, No.2' and 'Petit Epître' (both 1996; *March– October 1917*).

references to a 'Dry airless sweet scent' suffocating its protagonist and the idea that Eliot may have taken this from *The Times* of 28 December 1916.[50] The specific nature of these images and the history of gas warfare makes this conclusion difficult to confirm. We can make arguments for and against.[51] What is clear is that the dating of Ricks and McCue would be inconsistent with the trajectory of Eliot's career. Between the composition of 'Introspection' (1996) in July–August 1915 and his French poems, most probably begun around March 1917, we have little to no record of any significant poetic output.[52] Eliot was otherwise well occupied: finishing his doctoral dissertation, working on a series of lectures that began in October 1916 and focused on finding a solid salary. This would support the idea, without being definitive, that Eliot wrote his imagined war poem sometime after his return to criticism in March 1917.

The most compelling evidence is Eliot's correspondence with Haigh-Wood. On 8 June 1917, the combatant sent the poet a letter in response to an article by H. M. Tomlinson, the War Correspondent for the *Daily News*. Haigh-Wood had read Tomlinson's article in the previous week's *Nation*. It focused on the split between those who return with direct testimony of the battle front and those with second-hand experience. 'You really have come back from another world [. . .] these people will never know what you know,' Tomlinson argued.[53] The contrast between the indefiniteness of 'these people' and the 'you' that owns the power to know sets up a powerful experiential opposition. Eliot received Haigh-Wood's letter and read Tomlinson's piece around 13 June. On the same day Eliot described his brother to his father, as a man who was himself immature,

[50] T. S. Eliot, 'In silent corridors of death', in *Collected and Uncollected Poems*, pp. 275–6 (p. 276). In *The Times*, the image is '"the sickly sweet scent of the rolling gas-cloud"' of the battle front. Cited in Christopher Ricks and Jim McCue, 'Commentary: "In silent corridors of death"', in Eliot, *Collected and Uncollected Poems*, pp. 1167–8 (p. 1168 nn. 12–13).

[51] On the one hand, sulphur-based gases are typically associated with the sweet smell of mustard, garlic and horseradish but neither side deployed these chemicals until July 1917. The gases used earlier in the war – chlorine, phosgene and tear gas – are pungent not sweet recalling mown hay, grass or fruit. Yet, the poem's focus on the physiological problems of breathing do suggest the effects of phosgene, a chemical that reacts with the lungs and kills by constriction. The sweet mustard gases were less deadly than phosgene and their effects included blistering and burning, closer to the injuries of the despised landlord in 'Gerontion'. John Terraine, *White Heat: The New Warfare* (London: Sidgwick & Jackson, 1982), p. 160.

[52] Lawrence Rainey dates 'The Death of the Duchess' (1971) to September 1916. The evidence for 1919 is however more persuasive. Lawrence Rainey, *Revisiting 'The Waste Land'* (New Haven: Yale University Press, 2005), pp. 200–1; Christopher Ricks and Jim McCue, 'Commentary: "The Death of the Duchess"', in Eliot, *Collected and Uncollected Poems*, pp. 1180–3 (p. 1180). Rainey, *Revisiting 'The Waste Land'*, pp. 198–201 dates 'After the turning of the inspired days', 'I am the Resurrection and the Life' and 'So through the evening, through the violet air' (all 1971) to October 1913, and 'The Burnt Dancer' (1996), 'Oh little voices of the throats of men' (1988) and 'The Love Song of St Sebastian' (1988) to June–July 1914.

[53] H.M.T. [Henry Major Tomlinson], 'On Leave', *The Nation*, 21.9 (2 June 1917), 220.

Timeline 4.1 September 1917–May 1918

	Composition	Publication, Exhibition, Event
1917		
September	Eliot, 'In silent corridors of death', *Pound: His Metric and Poetry* Owen, 'Anthem for Doomed Youth' (1920)	Eliot, 'Eeldrop and Appleplex II' (*Little Review*), 'Reflections on Contemporary Poetry I' (*Egoist*), begins lectures in Sydenham on Victorian literature for London County Council Lewis, 'Inferior Religions' (*Little Review*) Owen and Sassoon poems in *Hydra* Pound, 'L'Homme Moyen Sensuel' (*Little Review*) War dead: Hulme Wounded: Gurney at Saint-Julien
October	Eliot, 'Cooking Egg', 'Dans le Restaurant', 'Petit Epître', 'Airs of Palestine', 'Tristan Corbière' (1996) Lewis, 'King of the Trenches' (1967) Mansfield, 'Prelude' Owen, 'Dulce et Decorum Est'	1917 Club founded Eliot begins second Southall lecture series on *Modern English Literature*; 'Reflections on Contemporary Poetry II' (*Egoist*) Lawrences expelled from Cornwall, move into H.D.'s flat in Mecklenburgh Square, Arabella York moves into Cournos's upstairs flat Lewis, 'Cantleman's Spring Mate' (*Little Review*) Pound, *Lustra* (American ed.) Richardson, *Honeycomb* Thomas, *Poems* including 'The Combe', 'Adlestrop', 'Tears', 'The Owl', 'The Glory'
November	Joyce sends 'Telemachus' to Sykes Owen, 'The Show', 'Insensibility' (1920)	Battles: Cambrai Eliot, 'Reflections on Contemporary Poetry III' (*Egoist*) *Georgian Poetry 1916–1917* Gurney, *Severn & Somme* Hardy, *Moments of Vision* Lawrence, *We Have Come Through* Osborn, *Muse in Arms*
December	Ford, 'Footsloggers' Owen, 'Hospital Barge', 'Exposure' (1920) Joyce sends 'Nestor' and 'Proteus' to Sykes	Battles: capture of Jerusalem Borden, 'Unidentified' (*English Review*) Eliot, pseudonymous letters to the *Egoist* Lewis, 'A Soldier of Humour' (*Little Review*) Pound receives *Ulysses* opening chapters Stein, 'Relief Work in France' (*Life*) War dead: Shaw Stewart

	Composition	*Publication, Exhibition, Event*
1918		
January	Gurney, 'To His Love' (1919) Owen, 'Miners' Pound redrafts '*Future* Three Cantos'	Ford, serialisation of 'Women and Men' (*Little Review*) H.D. burns lyrics and long poem Owen, 'Miners' (*Nation*)

February	Mansfield, 'Bliss'	Pound, *s.* versions of 'Three Cantos'
		    (*Future*)
		West, serialisation of *The Return of*
		    the Soldier (*Century*)

March	H.D. in Cornwall, 'Song' (1921),
	    'Lethe' (1920), 'Leda'
	Eliot, 'Sweeney Among the
	    Nightingales'
	Owen, 'Strange Meeting'
	Rosenberg, 'Through pale cold days'
	    (1937)
		Battles: Spring Offensives
		Joyce, 'Telemachus' (*Little Review*)
		Pound receives Joyce, 'Calypso'
		Stein, 'A Patriotic Leading' (*Sun*)

April	Lawrence, *Bay*	Aldington returns to France Ford, *Poems Written on Active Service* Joyce, 'Nestor' (*Little Review*) Ridge, 'The Ghetto' (*New Republic*) Sinclair, 'Novels of Dorothy Richardson' (*Egoist* and *Little Review*) War dead: Rosenberg

May	Owen, draft Preface, 'Futility'	Jepson, 'Recent US Poetry' (*English*
		    Review)
		Joyce, 'Proteus' (*Little Review*)
		Lewis, 'The Ideal Giant' (*Little*
		    Review)
		Pound receives Joyce, 'Hades'
		Stevens, '"Lettres d'un Soldat"'
		    (*Poetry*)
		Strachey, *Eminent Victorians*

Guide to Timelines
Works arranged in alphabetical order within each month.
Publication dates given in parenthesis, except if given in the main text, endnotes or elsewhere in timelines.
Titles shortened for brevity.

a man who had seen but one world, someone whose restlessness resulted from a more generalised desire for experience. Eliot's letter implied that such distance left Henry twice removed from raw experience, while he in contrast could engage with the war directly through the senses of the men returning from battle.[54]

[54] T. S. Eliot, letter to Henry Ware Eliot (13 June 1917), in *The Letters of T. S. Eliot*, I, pp. 202–4 (p. 203). Eliot's stoicism in this letter mimics Pound's accusation of a widespread ignorance blocking literature. Ezra Pound, 'American Chaos I', *New Age*, 17.19 (9 September 1915), 449.

On 17 June Eliot sent Haigh-Wood's letter to *The Nation*. It appeared anonymously on 23 June. Oddly, Eliot felt the need to highlight the combatant's education and age. Even more oddly, Eliot signed his own letter, an uncharacteristic moment in an otherwise carefully executed career marked by a clear sense of tact in relation to English mores. By this date both the public and the establishment saw *The Nation* as a dangerously partisan outlet. The War Office informed its editor in the spring following allegations of German propaganda that the state would restrict its distribution abroad. Battle-front narratives and atrocity stories had already fanned widespread fears throughout the spring and summer. In April 1917, the British press falsely reported the use of corpses in Germany for oil, fertiliser and animal food, a misunderstanding of the word for the bodies of horses and cattle rather than of humans. *The Lancet* published an article on 21 April discussing the technicalities of corpse use in industrial processes, with *The Nation* itself responding to the controversy on 19 May.[55]

Haigh-Wood's letter gave full support to Tomlinson's position. It argued that it was categorically impossible for those outside the battle to imagine what it was like for those in it. The letter is in effect a manifesto of combat gnosticism. It divides the world into ineffable and ordinary realms of experience, denigrates the power of images (whilst resorting to them) and reifies the soldier's ownership of an arcane knowledge. It ends with a highly figurative account of the grotesque nature of combat focused on rotting flesh and the disembowelled.[56] Who was Haigh-Wood's intended audience? The readers of *The Nation*, clearly. Was Haigh-Wood also delivering a message to Eliot? Either way, Eliot could hardly ignore the implication. Shortly after this letter, Haigh-Wood returned to London on a training exercise. He played tennis with Eliot and a letter to Hinkley of July suggests the differences in experience still occupied Eliot.[57]

The late summer of 1917 would seem then the date Eliot drafted his imagined war poem. It leads off where Pound's 'Trenches: St Eloi' ended by extending the corridor motif that first appeared in the *Catholic Anthology*. Eliot certainly knew the image. He appeared in the same volume and often referred to it affectionately.[58] This was an act of literary baton-passing. It took the combatant from a Vorticist trench system and pitched him straight into the

---

[55] Tate, pp. 70–1.

[56] T. S. Eliot, letter to the Editor of *The Nation* (17 June 1917), in *The Letters of T. S. Eliot*, I, pp. 204–5 (p. 205).

[57] T. S. Eliot, letter to Eleanor Hinkley (23 July 1917), in *The Letters of T. S. Eliot*, I, pp. 210–11 (p. 210).

[58] See, for example, Eliot, letter to Conrad Aiken (10 January 1916), p. 137. It is however unclear whether Eliot understood Hulme or Pound to be the author of 'Trenches: St Eloi'. See Ricks and McCue, 'Commentary: "In silent corridors of death"', p. 1168 n. 1 for the connection. It was Hulme's early lyrics that Eliot had in mind when he thought of Hulme as a poet. T. S. Eliot, letter to

dark and claustrophobia of a subterranean world. The poem's central conceit is based on the transformation of this narrow and suffocating corridor into a vision of Dante's hell. In the *Inventions of the March Hare* (1996), Ricks also proposed analogy with the solipsism of prison, suggesting Oscar Wilde's *The Ballad of Reading Gaol* (1898) as a source.[59] That is right. These tight spaces – trench system, prison and hell – become intertwined in a world populated by souls lost in 'the alleys of death'.[60] It is an extended riff on the idea of Bradley's closed mind cut off from the world. Although Eliot takes us straight into the psychological frame of shock, he replaces Pound's two-dimensional angular landscape with irregular iambic lines and antonymic rhymes. These emphasise constriction in both the external and internal worlds and Eliot exaggerated this in lines later added to the manuscript.[61] The extremely visceral sense of claustrophobia may be traceable to the autumn of 1917 when Vivien Eliot took shelter from Zeppelin attack in the cellar at Crawford Mansions. Eliot's core point however is that the ego of this moral witness collapses as it wanders through hell. It does not gain suffering or profit from its suffering. The lyric I is ghostly and disembodied. It has no concrete relationship with its bodily senses, no contact with what ought to be audible or tactile. It can only smell the pungency of death. Desire and fear dissipate into numbness as the self becomes lost amidst the breathing, sighing and crying of lost souls.

The specific binding conceit here is the allusion to the journey into the underworld in *Aeneid* VI.[62] Among Vivien Eliot's papers are two typescripts – *'Perque Domos Ditis Vacuas'* (2015) and *'Necesse est Perstare?'* (1925) – by F. M., presumed to be Vivien Eliot. As Ricks and McCue note, the title of the first of these, from section VI of the *Aeneid*, reuses images and phrases from 'In silent corridors of death'. As with Stevens's play on Brooke's youthful optimism, this obviously suggests a formalism trying to transform the chaotic and ineffable privacy of immediate experience into meaning through the

Mary Hutchinson ([9? July? 1919]), in *The Letters of T. S. Eliot*, I, pp. 371–2 (p. 371). A letter to Samuel Hynes of 23 March 1954 (KHULF 8) states that Eliot had read only the poems in *Ripostes* and Hulme's preface to Georges Sorel's *Reflections on Violence* (1908) prior to the publication of *Speculations* (1924). Eliot's view, at least by the 1950s, was that Hulme's work, whilst stimulating for a generation, was immature and undeveloped.

[59] Christopher Ricks, 'Editor's Notes to "Silent corridors of death"', in T. S. Eliot, *Inventions of the March Hare, Poems 1909–1917*, ed. by Christopher Ricks (London: Faber and Faber, 1996), pp. 301–3 (p. 301).

[60] Eliot, 'In silent corridors of death', pp. 275–6.

[61] Christopher Ricks and Jim McCue, 'Textual History: "In silent corridors of death"', in *The Poems of T. S. Eliot*, II, *Practical Cats and Further Verses*, p. 591 [nn. 8–9]; Crawford, *Young Eliot*, p. 285.

[62] See Virgil, *Aeneid Book VI*, trans. by Seamus Heaney (London: Faber and Faber, 2016), p. 16; Ricks and McCue, 'Commentary: "In silent corridors of death"', pp. 1167–8.

public sphere of culture. Given Eliot gave the manuscript to Haigh-Wood, we can suggest it was yet another modernist attempt to evaluate the authenticity of a poem's account of combat experience. Pound had sent *Cathay* to Henri Gaudier-Brzeska for the same purpose.

Unlike Pound who stood and watched, Eliot appears to have tried to give Haigh-Wood a clue to the route out of his personal hell. This comes in the poem's fourth line and its reference to Proverbs (19: 18) and its chastening of the son and the soul's crying. This tentatively suggests that Haigh-Wood was the poem's intended I. Alone and psychologically disorientated, unable to piece together his experience, Haigh-Wood's distress reflected, as Arianna Antonielli (2011) suggests, his lack of a guiding Virgil.[63] We might guess that this was the day-to-day spiritual role Eliot intended to fill for this moral witness. The problem at stake was not, then, as it had been in Pound's investigation of the corridor, shock's impact on expressivity. It was Haigh-Wood's lack of an ethical or spiritual system, one that might order the disruptive outbursts of affect and protect the ego from annihilation.

Without this compositional background 'In silent corridors of death' is a gnomic and unyielding draft. Eliot's decision to abandon it might owe something to the advice he gave to Mary Hutchinson about her short story 'War' (*The Egoist*: December 1917). Hutchinson's story had got inside affect, Eliot said, but had failed to then get back out again.[64] In other words, by getting too close to the specific felt experience Hutchinson had lost sight of its wider meaning. Eliot's gift of the manuscript to Haigh-Wood may well then have been a gesture or a token designed to preserve the meaning that did remain in the draft fragment between those who knew its origins best.

The *Waste Land* manuscripts suggest however Eliot did try to get out of the claustrophobia at least once more. He would rework parts of 'In silent corridors of death' into 'The Burial of the Dead' as dead souls flow across London Bridge. Eliot's manuscript revisions to this section of the poem bring into sharp focus the struggle to link expiry and exhalation with the death of these tortured souls.[65] Pound jotted James Joyce's initials alongside this section in the manuscript, a move Eliot's editors interpret as recognition of a correspondence with the 'Hades' episode (*Little Review*: September 1918; *June 1917*) in *Ulysses*.[66]

---

[63] Arianna Antonielli, 'Dantesque Perspectives in T. S. Eliot's *Inventions of the March Hare*', in *T. S. Eliot, Dante, and the Idea of Europe*, ed. by Paul Douglass (Newcastle upon Tyne: Cambridge Scholars, 2011), pp. 63–74 (pp. 69–70).

[64] T. S. Eliot, letter to Mary Hutchinson (19 September 1917), in *The Letters of T. S. Eliot*, I, pp. 219–20 (p. 220).

[65] T. S. Eliot, *'The Waste Land': A Facsimile and Transcript of the Original Drafts Including the Annotations of Ezra Pound*, ed. by Valerie Eliot (Orlando: Harcourt, 1971), p. 9.

[66] Ibid.; Christopher Ricks and Jim McCue, '*The Waste Land*: Commentary', in Eliot, *Collected and Uncollected Poems*, pp. 587–709 (p. 614 n. [I] lines 60–3).

Pound however hardly needed to flag the underlying reference to Dante's first circle. Instead, the referent may well have been to 'Scylla and Charybdis' (*Little Review*: April 1919; *October 1918*), and specifically Stephen Dedalus's interpretation of the ghost in *Hamlet* (1603). Pound had seen the direct connection between Eliot's lines and the ghost's appearance in the first act of Shakespeare's play. In *Hamlet*, the ghost returns from its own confinement 'To tell the secrets of my prison-house' with a tale that will 'harrow up thy soul, freeze thy young blood'.[67] The allusion is consolidated through the ghost's image of the poison that 'courses through / The natural gates and alleys of the body'.[68] Indeed, Eliot's distorted ghostly I, like that of Shakespeare, retains only one of its senses, the sense of smell.[69]

We can take the correspondence of these images further by examining Joyce's reflections on the nature of the ghost and of the haunted. Responding to his own question, Stephen proposes a ghost is one 'who has faded into impalpability through death, through absence, through change of manners'. He then asks, 'who is the ghost, returning to the world that has forgotten him? Who is king Hamlet?'[70] In the first full printing of *Ulysses* Joyce amended the penultimate line, in typescript or printed proof, to 'who is the ghost from *limbo patrum*, returning to the world that has forgotten him?'.[71] The annotations on Eliot's draft long poem suggest then that Pound had correctly ascertained Eliot's reference in *The Waste Land*, as it had been in 'In silent corridors of death', was to the Limbo of the Patriarchs, the first circle of hell populated by virtuous but non-Christian souls, those who die in original sin without being assigned to the damned. As Eliot's letters detailed, Haigh-Wood was a good man and well-bred, but he was an unbeliever, one lost, following Bradley, because of a refusal to have faith in anything beyond the immediate felt contents of consciousness. Eliot made Haigh-Wood into one of the lost; lost in the same way that we will find Gerontion is lost, in the latter case because of an insistence that there be eyewitness proof of the Magi's encounter with Christ as a precondition for faith. Both Haigh-Wood and Gerontion insist on having felt before they can know. Had Eliot ignored Pound's advice to use 'Gerontion' as a prelude to *The Waste Land* these

---

[67] William Shakespeare, *Hamlet*, ed. by Harold Jenkins, The Arden Shakespeare (London: Methuen, 1982; repr. London: Routledge, 1989), I, v, 216.

[68] Ibid. 219.

[69] In *Hamlet*, the ghost can 'scent the morning air' that presages the 'sulph'rous and tormenting flames'. Ibid. 219, 215.

[70] James Joyce, 'Ulysses: Episode IX [part I]', *Little Review*, 5.11 [5.12] (April 1919), 30–43 (p. 34).

[71] James Joyce, *Ulysses* (Paris: Shakespeare and Company, 1922), p. 180; James Joyce and Clive Driver, *'Ulysses': The Manuscripts and First Printings Compared, Annotated by Clive Driver* (London and Philadelphia: Faber and Faber and Philip H. & A. S. W. Rosenbach Foundation, 1975), p. 180.

highly coded intellectual connections to the war, its witnessing practices, its dead and the theme of modern alienation would have been significantly more obvious.[72]

'*Limbo patrum*' was an often-used form of Elizabethan slang for prison and this returns us to Ricks's insightful connection of 'In silent corridors of death' to Wilde's prison ballad. If Eliot was to be Virgil to Haigh-Wood, there needed to be a form of release that the poet had not found in the suffocating lines of the 1917 fragment. We can find that instead in lines 412–15 of *The Waste Land* with its opaque meditation on the prison and its key. It is here that we see the full importance of the earlier fragment as Eliot turned to the *Upanishads* to understand the relationship between compassion and solipsism. Allyson Booth's *Reading 'The Waste Land' from the Bottom Up* (2015) provides us with the clearest description of these lines.[73] Eliot invokes the Sanskrit invocation to sympathy through the allusion to Dante's Count Ugolino. Archbishop Ruggieri has nailed him into a tower where he will starve. With no possibility for escape, it is *limbo patrum*, and Ugolino is a version of the suffocated Haigh-Wood in the trenches. In turn, Eliot took Ugolino as a model for Bradley's concept of the existential self, a closed circle impervious to any act of sympathy.[74] Ugolino is a literary surrogate for the category of experience described in this and the previous chapter, the experience passed by Wyndham Lewis to Pound, by Haigh-Wood to Eliot, someone in pain with whom one naturally wants to sympathise and yet someone whose pain is unreachable. Eliot's tentative way out of the prison follows the changing verb constructions as the stanza moves from the present perfect through a static notion of the present to a perpetual moment of here and now in which the participle becomes active. It is the same way out that Pound used in 'Provincia Deserta' to recreate a living past. It is through the act of self-conscious thinking that the self confirms the world. It is Eliot's glimmer of a route out of solipsism: glimpsing that imprisonment is a communal experience of imprisonment confirms intersubjectivity. Whether Eliot succeeds in presenting this vision or whether the overall tone of *The Waste Land* mitigates against it is highly debatable. Eliot's point is that the airless space need not be without a door. The poem might confirm the waste land of the prison, but the fact that individual points of view are themselves felt seems to confirm the existence of other points of view. It is a communality the poem secures by working through the testimony of Bradley, Dante and Joyce. It is certainly a form of sympathy albeit of quite different sorts.

[72] Ezra Pound, letter to T. S. Eliot ([28? January 1922], in *The Letters of T. S. Eliot*, I, pp. 630–1 (p. 630).

[73] Allyson Booth, *Reading 'The Waste Land' from the Bottom Up* (New York: Palgrave Macmillan, 2015), pp. 224–6.

[74] F. H. Bradley, *Appearance and Reality: A Metaphysical Essay* (London: Swan Sonnenschein, 1893), p. 346.

JOHN MIDDLETON MURRY'S CRITIQUE OF CRYING ALOUD

This jumps ahead in the genealogy. How did Eliot move from the poet of the abandoned fragment to the one behind the formalist masterpiece? A pivotal essay in his development was John Middleton Murry's 'Mr. Sassoon's War Verses'. It was the first concerted attempt to speak out against the moral witness, provocatively appearing in *The Nation*. It was a ruthlessly unforgiving and divisive piece, and it gave Eliot the coded vocabulary he needed for mounting his own attack on modern poetry. In the three back-to-back essays titled 'Reflections on Contemporary Poetry', published in *The Egoist* during the autumn of 1917, Eliot had begun to mark out his position in the emergent modernist canon. After Murry's essay Eliot was to turn his attention to the moral witness.

Published on 13 July 1918 as a review of Siegfried Sassoon's *Counter-Attack*, Murry's essay was a prompt intervention into the developing discourse of combat gnosticism. Ivor Gurney published *Severn and Somme* in November 1917. *Century Magazine* serialised *The Return of the Soldier*, a novel focused on the problem of imagining the battle front, in February 1918. Ford Madox Ford's '*On Heaven' and Poems Written on Active Service* appeared two months later. Isaac Rosenberg died in action at the same time and his poems received posthumous praise. *The Nation* published Wilfred Owen's 'Hospital Barge' and 'Futility' in June. Thomas Sturge Moore's essays on combatant poetry, *Some Soldier Poets* (1919), began serialisation in the *English Review*. *Georgian Poetry 1916–1917* appeared in November 1917. It was an edition dedicated by Edward Marsh in his preface to the 'newcomers' amongst 'the younger generation'.[75] According to J. C. Squire, this third instalment of the annual caused a small literary sensation precisely because of its inclusion of the war poetries of Robert Nichols, Robert Graves and Sassoon.[76] It also included Wilfrid Wilson Gibson's poetic tribute to Brooke as a sacrificial figure, 'Ablaze', a man who 'burned, a flame of ecstasy', immolated 'flame to flame, and fire to fire'.[77] It was an image Eliot would later lampoon.

Murry published his essay anonymously. It showed little regard for Sassoon's courage, moral strength or suffering. Although Murry was not to know it, one of Sassoon's men mistaking a returning raiding party for a German attack shot Sassoon in the head on the day of the review's publication. The coincidence of Murry's anger and Sassoon's hospitalisation gave the article symbolic significance in public circulation. Murry certainly knew the psychological hurt the review might cause. The combatant openly admired Murry as a critic. Through

---

[75] E.M. [Edward Marsh], 'Prefatory Note', in *Georgian Poetry 1916–1917* (London: Poetry Bookshop, 1917), p. [i].

[76] [J. C. Squire], 'Georgian Poetry', *New Statesman*, 14.346 (22 November 1919), 224, 226 (p. 224).

[77] Wilfrid Wilson Gibson, 'Rupert Brooke', in *Georgian Poetry 1916–1917*, p. 117.

Philip Morrell, and then Henry Massingham, Sassoon met with Murry on 11 June, and then with Bertrand Russell two days later. Together they helped clarify the drafts of Sassoon's incendiary 'Finished with the War: A Soldier's Declaration' amidst widespread speculation of a pacifist revolution in Britain.[78] This would lead Sassoon to Craiglockhart Hospital, but it also made the case for gnosis, criticising 'the callous complacence with which the majority of those at home regard the continuance of agonies which they do not share, and which they have not sufficient imagination to realize'.[79] 'Callous' – from *callus* or hardened skin – points to the affective dimension of the divide, of the perceived impermeability of bodies, each in its own prison.

Bloomsbury had brought Sassoon into its circle during 1917. In the *TLS* on 31 May Virginia Woolf wrote positively of Sassoon's *The Old Huntsman and Other Poems* (May 1917) in an essay titled 'Mr Sassoon's Poems'. Woolf said that 'what Mr Sassoon has felt to be the most sordid and horrible experiences in the world he makes us feel to be so in a measure which no other poet of the war has achieved'.[80] The title of Murry's essay was surely a deliberate play on Woolf's and to make matters worse Ottoline Morrell had initially encouraged the review.[81] In Sydney Janet Kaplan's *Circulating Genius* (2010) Murry's overt censure of Sassoon is identified as an act of outright betrayal.[82] Russell, writing from prison and initially unaware of Murry's hand in affairs, was irked by the essay's '"safe smugness"' and 'ancient and respectable' 'dogmas'.[83] Russell countered that if art was to survive then it had to be truthful, it must be an argument about the nature of reality not a statement about empirical fact or a theory.[84] It was precisely because Sassoon's verses were so bitter, Russell told Morrell, lacking any reconciliation in a higher harmony, that they were so

---

[78] Paul Moeyes, *Siegfried Sassoon, Scorched Glory: A Critical Study* (Basingstoke: Macmillan, 1997), p. 44; Sydney Janet Kaplan, *Circulating Genius: John Middleton Murry, Katherine Mansfield and D. H. Lawrence* (Edinburgh: Edinburgh University Press, 2010), p. 101; Richard A. Rempel and others, 'Chronology: Russell's Life and Writings, 1916–1918', in Bertrand Russell, *Pacifism and Revolution, 1916–18*, ed. by Richard A. Rempel and others (London: Routledge, 1995), pp. lxv–lxxxii (p. lxxii).

[79] Qtd in Stallworthy, *Wilfred Owen*, p. 206.

[80] Virginia Woolf, 'Mr Sassoon's Poems', in *The Essays of Virginia Woolf*, II, pp. 119–22 (p. 120).

[81] Woolf nonetheless feared that public opinion had placed her on Murry's side of the debate. Virginia Woolf, diary entry (Monday, 29 July 1918), in *The Diary of Virginia Woolf*, I, pp. 173–6 (p. 174).

[82] Kaplan, p. 101.

[83] Bertrand Russell, letter to Ottoline Morrell (14 July 1918), qtd in Richard A. Rempel and others, 'General Headnote to Part X', in Russell, *Pacifism and Revolution*, pp. 411–18 (p. 415); Bertrand Russell, 'On a Review of Sassoon' (*The Nation*: 27 July 1918), in *Pacifism and Revolution*, p. 428.

[84] Russell, 'On a Review of Sassoon', p. 428.

likeable. Upon discovering the identity of the essay's author, Russell inevitably attributed Murry's vitriolic tone to his sexual jealousy.[85]

The article's vicious streak stuck in the craw of cultural memory. In *The Athenæum* in late 1919, J. W. N. Sullivan, reviewing an advance copy of Murry's *The Evolution of an Intellectual* in which Murry chose to reprint 'Mr. Sassoon's War Verses', identified an obsessive disillusion with writers unable to simply endure and suffer the pain of war.[86] In his 1920 essay 'The Poetic Futility of Flanders', Thomas Moult, a rival editor at *Voices* and a veteran, targeted the essay and its impact on combatant poetries of war. It was, he said, the one essay responsible for the unanimously negative critical attitude towards war poetry in the British press.[87]

Even a century later the severity of Murry's assessment is really striking:

> It is the fact, not the poetry, of Mr. Sassoon that is important. When a man is in torment and cries aloud, his cry is incoherent. It has neither weight nor meaning of its own. It is inhuman, and its very inhumanity strikes to the nerve of our hearts. We long to silence the cry, whether by succour and sympathy, or by hiding ourselves from it. That it should somehow stop or be stopped, and by ceasing trouble our hearts no more, is our chief desire; for it is ugly and painful, and it rasps at the cords of nature.[88]

Murry's target here, as it is in James Campbell's critique of combat gnosticism, is Sassoon's phonocentrism. Crying aloud releases a voice that the poet cannot silence; it stands against the world, not for it, an image Murry achieves by deftly conflating the rasping of the ties that bind the natural world with those of the vocal cords. Although Murry could not have read Owen's preface at this time, it was an astute assessment. He may have taken this image from the screams in Owen's 'Hospital Barge'. Whatever the source, Murry rightly highlighted the central terms of the moral witness's claim, his *warnian* to the world, that primal existential cry that tries to claim selfhood and authenticity from the dissociating experience of pain. Alec Waugh reused Murry's terms in

---

[85] Bertrand Russell, letter to Ottoline Morrell (25 July [1918]), in *The Selected Letters of Bertrand Russell*, ed. by Nicholas Griffin, 2 vols (Harmondsworth and London: Penguin and Routledge, 1992–2001), II: *The Public Years, 1914–1970* (London: Routledge, 2001), pp. 160–4 (pp. 160, 161).

[86] J.W.N.S. [J. W. N. Sullivan], 'The Dreamer Awakes', *The Athenæum*, 4677 (19 December 1919), 1364–5 (p. 1364).

[87] Moult, 'The Poetic Futility of Flanders', p. 68.

[88] John Middleton Murry, 'Mr. Sassoon's War Verses', in Murry, *The Evolution of an Intellectual*, pp. 70–9 (p. 70).

his bibliography of modern poetry for the *Chapbook* when he categorised the awfulness of Sassoon's emotional outpouring.[89]

The critique of a phonocentric art however lies much deeper in modernist literary culture. Arthur Davison Ficke and Eunice Tietjens used it in the *Little Review* during 1914.[90] It is a motif in *Blast* 1 through Pound's censored poem 'Fratres Minores' (June 1914).[91] Woolf used it in a later review of Sassoon's poetry, describing a 'bawling' gramophone too raw for poetry.[92] In 'Reflections on *Vers Libre*' (*New Statesman*: March 1917) Eliot described free verse as 'a battle-cry of freedom', recommending the need for some limitation on emotion through metre and rhyme to order the flux.[93] Several weeks before Murry's article, Pound criticised the 'logopoeia' of the poets published in *Others* as 'the utterance of clever people in despair, or hvoering upon the brink of that precipice'. He said this poetry was 'a mind cry'.[94] William Carlos Williams's later critique of the war poems of Richard Aldington and D. H. Lawrence used the same trope. 'Poetry is not a despairing cry of defiance,' Williams said.[95]

The persistence of the motif reflects the modernist's confused relationship to emotional intensity. In 'A Few Don'ts by an Imagiste' (*Poetry*: 1913) Pound stated that the Image was no more than an 'emotional complex'.[96] Only progressively did theorists add the intensity.[97] In *The Egoist* during June 1914, Pound described one of Lewis's works as exemplary of Vorticism's modernity: 'I could point to that design and say "That is what I mean" with more satisfaction than I could point to any other expression of complex intense emotion.'[98] In the *New Age* of January 1915 this had shifted to an 'intense emotion' which caused patterns to form in the mind.[99] 'Constantia Stone' (most probably

---

[89] [Anonymous] [Alec Waugh], 'A Bibliography of Modern Poetry with Notes on Some Contemporary Poets (Compiled and Edited by Recorder)', *Chapbook*, 2.12 (June 1920), 38.

[90] Arthur Davison Ficke, 'Of Rupert Brooke and Other Matters', *Little Review*, 1.5 (July 1914), 17–21 (p. 18); Eunice Tietjens, 'The Spiritual Dangers of Writing Vers Libre', *Little Review*, 1.8 (November 1914), 25–9 (pp. 25–6).

[91] Ezra Pound, 'Fratres Minores', *Blast*, 1 (June 1914), 48.

[92] Virginia Woolf, 'Two Soldier-Poets' (*TLS*: 11 July 1918), in *The Essays of Virginia Woolf*, II, pp. 269–72 (p. 270).

[93] T. S. Eliot, 'Reflections on *Vers Libre*', in *Apprentice Years, 1905–1918*, pp. 511–18 (pp. 512, 514).

[94] Ezra Pound, 'A List of Books', *Little Review*, 5.11 [4.11] (March 1918), 54–8 (pp. 57–8).

[95] Williams, 'Four Foreigners', p. 37.

[96] Ezra Pound, 'A Few Don'ts by an Imagiste', *Poetry*, 1.6 (March 1913), 200–6 (p. 200).

[97] I can find only one other expression of the emotion as intense. Ezra Pound, letter to Alice Corbin Henderson ([8–9] August 1913), qtd in Moody, *The Young Genius*, p. 227.

[98] Ezra Pound, 'Wyndham Lewis', *The Egoist*, 1.12 (15 June 1914), 233–4 (p. 234).

[99] Ezra Pound, 'Affirmations IV. As for Imagisme', *New Age*, 16.13 (28 January 1915), 349–50 (p. 349).

Pound) demanded in response 'a new definition of intense emotion'.[100] It is notable that Aldington's 1915 preface to *Some Imagist Poets* carefully avoided the word 'emotion' altogether, focusing instead on moods, the tonal state of mind rather than Pound's developing notion of complex emotion.[101]

As the war progressed, intense emotion became commonplace in Pound's vocabulary. He used it in letters to John Quinn and posing as William Atheling in the *New Age*.[102] It reappeared in Edgar Jepson's controversial attack on American poetry in 'Recent U.S. Poetry' (*English Review*: May 1918), one of the central essays considered in the next chapter. Jepson defended Eliot's 'La Figlia Che Piange' (*Poetry*: September 1916; *1911–12*) as a 'delicate, beautiful, intense emotion'.[103] This was Edmund Wilson's position in an important 1922 review of *The Waste Land*. Forget the notes, Wilson claimed, there was no need of erudition in order 'to feel the force of the intense emotion which the poem is intended to convey'.[104] Intensity was part of the modernist remit. It was a self-awarded licence and one zealously regulated.

In Murry's essay, Sassoon's problem is precisely his loss of control over affect. The soldier cannot keep intense emotion within the strictures of form. Again, the basic model is from Pound and his metaphors of disgust and containerisation. In the fourth of the 'Affirmations' series for the *New Age* in January 1915, Pound concluded:

> Where the voltage is so high that it fuses the machinery, one has merely the 'emotional man' not the artist. The best artist is the man whose machinery can stand the highest voltage. The better the machinery, the more precise, the stronger; the more exact will be the record of the voltage and of the various currents which have passed through it.

---

[100] Constantia Stone [Ezra Pound?], 'Letters to the Editor: Imagisme', *New Age*, 16.14 (4 February 1915), 390. 'Stone' wrote again in response to an article by Ramiro de Maeztu y Whitney, the Spanish theorist/journalist, a regular at Hulme's Frith Street salons. 'Letters to the Editor: What Is a Nation?', *New Age*, 16.15 (11 February 1915), 413–14. Constantia is a form of Jurassic limestone and, as discussed later, Pound (and Eliot) often turned to female pseudonyms to pose as frustrated members of the public in a state of bewilderment at the avant-garde's antics.

[101] [Richard Aldington], 'Preface', in *Some Imagist Poets: An Anthology* (Boston: Houghton Mifflin, 1915), pp. v–viii (p. vi).

[102] Ezra Pound, letter to John Quinn (13 July 1916), in *Ezra Pound and the Visual Arts*, ed. by Harriet Zinnes (New York: New Directions, 1980), p. 239; William Atheling [Ezra Pound], 'Music', *New Age*, 24.7 (19 December 1918), 107–8 (p. 107).

[103] Edgar Jepson, 'The Western School', *Little Review*, 5.5 (September 1918), 4–9 (p. 9). This is a truncated version of the original article in the *English Review* and included Pound's commentary. A further example of the trope of intensity is R. Herdman Pender, 'John Gould Fletcher', *The Egoist*, 3.11 (November 1916), 173–4 (p. 174).

[104] Edmund Wilson Jr, 'The Poetry of Drouth' (1922), in *T. S. Eliot: The Contemporary Reviews*, ed. by Jewel Spears Brooker (Cambridge: Cambridge University Press, 2004), pp. 83–90 (p. 86).

In contrast to Eliot's later lexicon of industrial chemistry, this is a resource-based model taken from physics. It has more than a hint of masochism. The successful artist 'can, within limits, not only record but create', claimed Pound; 'he can move as a force; he can produce "order-giving vibrations"; by which one may mean merely, he can departmentalise such part of the life-force as flows through him'. 'Departmentalise': the ability to organise or divide so that the self can quarantine emotion and mediate it through style. Or as Pound put it, 'energy, or emotion, expresses itself in form'.[105]

Murry's attack also returned to de Gourmont's conclusion on the shocked mind. Murry notes that Sassoon's 'language is over-wrought, dense and turgid, as a man's mind must be under the stress and obsession of a chaos beyond all comprehension'.[106] Murry does not then deny the gnosis of combat. Rather, gnosticism is the problem. The unknowable immediacy of war shocks the mind out of the individuality that is the hallmark of style into a broken language over-loaded by the fight-flight-fright response. The trench lyric simply externalises emotion without any guiding intervention. Murry illustrates by taking an image of the body in pieces from Sassoon's 'Counter-Attack', 'The place was rotten with dead; green clumsy legs / High-booted, sprawled and grovelled along the saps'.[107] Murry responds:

> That is horrible, but it does not produce the impression of horror. It numbs, not terrifies, the mind. Each separate reality and succeeding vision is, as it were, driven upon us by a hammer, but one hammer-beat is like another. Each adds to the sum more numbness and more pain, but the separateness and particularity of each is lost.

'We are given', Murry went on, 'the blurred confusion, and just because this is the truth of the matter exactly rendered we cannot apprehend it any more than the soldier who endures it can.'[108]

Murry turns the arguments made by the moral witness upside down. Being there is the very problem not the solution. It results in an all too truthful account of what happens to the shocked mind. It is a mimesis of confusion, incoherence and numbness. It is not a testimonial that confers knowledge. It is unprocessed emotion, a crystallisation of endocrinology into *logos*, words rearranged in such a way that they appeal to a common conception of what poetry ought to be. As Murry says, 'these verses express nothing, save in so far as a cry expresses pain.'[109]

---

[105] Pound, 'Affirmations IV', p. 350.

[106] Murry, 'Mr. Sassoon's War Verses', p. 71.

[107] Siegfried Sassoon, 'Counter-Attack', in Siegfried Sassoon, *Counter-Attack and Other Poems*, third printing (New York: E. P. Dutton, 1920), pp. 11–13 (p. 11).

[108] Murry, 'Mr. Sassoon's War Verses', p. 72.

[109] Ibid. p. 71.

Murry's ultimate purpose in the essay, as Russell's criticism rightly high-lighted, was to use this material to set up a contrast. For 'there is another truth more valuable still' than that of the body in pieces, Murry said:

> The unforgettable horror of an inhuman experience can only be rightly rendered by rendering also its relation to the harmony and calm of the soul which it shatters. In this context alone can it appear with that sudden shock to the imagination which is overwhelming. The faintest discord in a harmony has within it an infinity of disaster, which no confusion of notes, however wild and various and loud, can possibly suggest.[110]

It is the being-not-in-it rather than the being-in-it that becomes the necessary condition for poetry. The extreme experience within the gnosis is set against this other state, a non-gnosis, a notion of selfhood that is permanent and uni-versal. The poet achieves this through an undefined act of composition, the awkwardness of which is manifest in that stumbling phrase 'rightly rendered by rendering also'. Murry was stepping towards a model of complex and intense emotion in poetry according to which the poet gives back a form of shock to the reader's feeling. There must be a dramatic re-enaction of the original shock, a shattering, a suddenness that overwhelms the reader. This not only dialled up modernism's claim over intense and complex emotion, but it also made the case that it might do something more than just speak about the body in pieces. It might be possible to recreate that experience by becoming itself a form of shocking experience. It proposed a poetry that might masquerade as its own form of shell attack.

The most important part of this for Eliot was Murry's idea that only the uncompromised psyche, the non-combat mind, could approach a comparison of states of being. Murry's argument was based entirely on the necessity of distance, on the hypothesis that only the looker-on, to return to Ford's phrase-ology, the one not stupefied by the game, could supply a readerly shock. Murry hardly needed to tell us the Romantic antecedent of this idea:

> It is on this that the wise saying that poetry is emotion recollected in tranquillity is so firmly based, for the quality of an experience can only be given by reference to the ideal condition of the human consciousness which it disturbs with pleasure or with pain. But in Mr. Sassoon's verses it is we who are left to create for ourselves the harmony of which he gives us only the moment of its annihilation.[111]

---

[110] Ibid. p. 73.
[111] Ibid. pp. 73–4.

This returns us to Chapter 1 and the earliest critiques of war verse. Except, Murry twisted the theory of expressivity to focus on the quality of experience and moved from the production of emotion to its reception, from the wound to the disturbance within the onlooker. This allowed him to propose an alternative to the moral witness:

> The experiences of battle, awful, inhuman, and intolerable as they are, can be comprehended only by the mind which is capable of bringing their horror and their inhumanity home to the imagination of others. Without the perspective that comes from intellectual remoteness there can be no comprehension, no order and no art. Intellectual remoteness is not cold or callous; it is the condition in which a mind works as a mind, and a man is fully active as a man.[112]

Since this is the state in which a mind works as a mind, Sassoon, we must assume, is quite out of his mind. To the combatant's gnosis Murry theorised what had been latent in Stevens's return to war, a non-combatant gnosis, an obviously masculinist way of knowing from the outside. He was an electrified man channelling the world's voltage at its highest possible setting. Distanced, rooted in reason, able to understand if not to know the pain of combat, this was (allegedly) sanity itself. It was a poesis now beginning to take shape as the essential mechanics of impersonality.

REDEFINING AGE AND WISDOM, COUNTERING *THE NEW ELIZABETHANS*

In summary form, Murry's essay claimed that the figurative, the evocative and the gestural aspects of language were the principal means of understanding the timelessness of wounding and not the existential cry of pain. It reaffirmed tranquillity in such a way that immersion in an event served to prevent the accumulation of knowledge. Sassoon's language was, Murry said, an archival method with only numbing effects. It merely collated data. It was no more than 'a barely sufficient entry in a log-book'.[113] Murry complained that Sassoon's 'Hark! Thud, thud, thud,—quite soft . . . they never cease— / Those whispering guns—O Christ' in 'Repression of War Experience' (*The Lancet*: February 1918; *July 1917*) was awful precisely because it refused figuration and instead dissolved into onomatopoeia, ellipsis and exclamation mark.[114] In contrast, Murry's essay made literary language the key to unconscious wounding. It was a primitive trauma aesthetic, one that set *écriture* firmly against *parole*.

---

[112] Ibid. p. 78.
[113] Ibid. pp. 74, 75.
[114] Siegfried Sassoon, 'Repression of War Experience', in Sassoon, *Counter-Attack and Other Poems*, pp. 51–3 (p. 53).

Murry's alternative poetic owed a good deal to his reading of French war writers for the *TLS* during 1917 and 1918. In 'The Discovery of Pain' (*TLS*: June 1917) Murry recorded finding in the work of Henri Barbusse, Georges Duhamel and Romain Rolland an existential honesty, a language that recognised the full discovery of pain and of death.[115] In *A Critical Difference* (1998), David Goldie suggests this insistence was personal for Murry, an early indication of Murry's much later idea that suffering was the route to integrity.[116] If it was such an indication it feels confused given Murry's venom. Murry's affinity for the French accounts of war rested on their ability to use the trained 'eye of the imagination' rather than the one that reacted only to 'torn flesh and the stench of wounds'.[117] The truly shamanic poet, in this case Duhamel, Murry argued, was a moral menial rather than a moral witness, one 'fronting on our behalf that which we have not dared to look upon'.[118] In 'What Is Realism?' (*The Nation*: October 1918, reprinted as 'Realism'), Murry made the case that the contemporary mind, judged by the literature and art before and during the war, had 'proved itself inadequate to the real—worse, careless of the real'.[119] It was not imitation that was important but the '"heightened sense"' of reality derived from the personal idiosyncrasies of the artist's world view or *Weltanschauung*.[120] On 16 May 1919, Murry traced the origins of the deterioration in English intra-war poetry to Brooke 'becoming a national hero' and covering his fellow poets in undeserved accolades.

They became heroes in a national movement, Murry said.[121] Instead, on 23 May 1919, he anointed Jules Romains's *Europe* (December 1916) as the poem of the war, despairing of any proper English response. Romains 'voiced the outraged *mind* of Europe, not her outraged body', Murry said. He reiterated the point of his earlier essay: 'the mind stands apart from the event. It alone lends to the event the terror and pity without which it is merely a thing that happens. It alone makes transitory things unforgettable.'[122] *Europe* was 'the tormented cry of the European soul made articulate', the reinsertion of meaning into the

---

[115] John Middleton Murry, 'The Discovery of Pain', in Murry, *The Evolution of an Intellectual*, pp. 39–49 (p. 39).

[116] David Goldie, *A Critical Difference: T. S. Eliot and John Middleton Murry in English Literary Criticism, 1919–1928* (Oxford: Clarendon Press, 1998), pp. 32–3.

[117] Murry, 'The Discovery of Pain', pp. 44, 47.

[118] Ibid. p. 48.

[119] John Middleton Murry, 'Realism', in Murry, *The Evolution of an Intellectual*, pp. 80–97 (p. 95).

[120] Ibid. pp. 85, 86.

[121] J.M.M. [John Middleton Murry], 'Modern Poetry and Modern Society', *The Athenæum*, 4646 (16 May 1919), 325–6 (p. 325).

[122] J. [John] Middleton Murry, 'The Poet of the War', *The Athenæum*, 4647 (23 May 1919), 376–7 (p. 377).

Timeline 4.2 June 1918–April 1919

	Composition	Publication, Exhibition, Event
1918		
June	Lawrence, 'Seven Seals' (1918) Yeats, 'In Memory of Robert Gregory', 'An Irish Airman foresees his Death'	Joyce, 'Calypso' (*Little Review*) Lawrence, poems from *Bay* (*English Review*) Lowell, 'Dreams in War Time' (*Little Review*) Owen, 'Hospital Barge', 'Futility' (*Nation*) Sassoon, *Counter-Attack* (English ed.) Stein, 'The Great American Army' (*Vanity Fair*) Stevens, 'Metaphors of a Magnifico' (*Little Review*) Sturge Moore, 'Soldier Poets' (*English Review*)
July	Eliot, 'Ode' (1920) Owen, 'Mental Cases' (1920), 'Parable of the Old Man and the Young' (1920), 'Spring Offensive' (1920) Woolf, redrafts *Kew Gardens*	Joyce, 'Lotus-Eaters' (*Little Review*) Lewis, *Tarr* Mansfield, *Prelude* Murry, 'Sassoon's War Verses' (*Nation*) War dead: Kilmer, Chilwell factory explosion Wounded: Sassoon
August	Eliot, 'Sweeney Among the Nightingales', 'Mr. Eliot's Sunday Morning Service', 'Whispers of Immortality', 'Burbank', 'Sweeney Erect'	Eliot, 'The Hawthorne Aspect' (*Little Review*) Pound receives Joyce, 'Aeolus' Yeats, 'In Memory of Robert Gregory' (*English Review*)
September	Ford, 'True Love and a GCM' (1999) Williams, *Kora in Hell*	Eliot, poems finished in August 1918 and 'Dans le restaurant' (*Little Review*) Joyce, 'Hades' (*Little Review*) Lawrence Derby medical examination Pound, 'Three Cantos III extract' (*Egoist*) Yeats, 'In Memory of Robert Gregory' (*Little Review*)
October	Joyce, 'Scylla and Charybdis' Lawrence, *Touch and Go* (1920)	Eliot begins Elizabethan lecture series Joyce, 'Aeolus' (*Little Review*) Lawrence, *New Poems* (English ed.) Pound receives Joyce, 'Lestrygonians'
November	H.D., *Choruses from the Hippolytus of Euripides* Woolf, *Night and Day*; 'Solid Objects' (1920)	Armistice Eliot and Woolf first meeting H.D./Pound, 'Choruses' (*Little Review*) War dead: Owen

	Composition	Publication, Exhibition, Event
December	Lawrence, 'Tickets Please', 'The Blind Man', 'The Fox' (1920) Lewis, 'War Baby' Pound, 'Homage to Sextus Propertius'	Rodker, 'Hymn to Death' (*Egoist*) Sassoon, *Counter-Attack* (American ed.) Thomas, *Last Poems*, including 'Digging' War dead: Apollinaire
1919		
January	Joyce, 'Wandering Rocks' Lawrence, 'The Wintry Peacock' (1921) Yeats, 'The Second Coming' (*Dial*: November 1920)	*Art and Letters* relaunched; *Voices* 1 *Canadian War Memorials* exhibition begins Joyce, serialisation of 'Lestrygonians' (*Little Review*); serialisation of 'Nestor' (*Egoist*) Lewis, 'War Baby' (*Art and Letters*) Paris Peace Conference begins
February	Lawrence, *Movements in European History* (1921)	Lawrence, 'Poems' from *Bay* (*Poetry*) Moult, 'Old Men' (*Voices*) Pound receives Joyce, 'Wandering Rocks' Richardson, *The Tunnel*
March	Eliot, 'Sweeney Erect', 'Burbank', 'Death of the Duchess' (1971) Lawrence, 'Adolf' (1920), 'Rex' (1921); redrafts 'All of Us'	Joyce, serialisation of 'Proteus' (*Egoist*) Pound, 'Propertius I–IV' (*Poetry*) Stein, 'J.R.', 'J.R. II', 'A Deserter' (*Vanity Fair*) Yeats, *Wild Swans at Coole*
April	Pound, *The Fourth Canto*, 'Fifth Canto' (1921) Sassoon, 'Everyone Sang' (*Owl*: October 1919)	Aldington, *Images of War* Eliot, 'New Elizabethans and Old' (*Athenæum*) Joyce, serialisation of 'Scylla and Charybdis' (*Little Review*) Lawrence, 'Tickets Please' (*Strand*) Valery, 'Crisis of Mind' (*Athenæum*)

Guide to Timelines
Works arranged in alphabetical order within each month.
Publication dates given in parenthesis, except if given in the main text, endnotes or elsewhere in timelines.
Titles shortened for brevity.

scream.[123] Murry was signalling a refusal of the idea poetry ought to move in the agnostic direction:

> The experience of modern war is held by those who suffer it to be unique, and, since they are of necessity the final arbiters, our duty is to endeavour to apprehend it from their angle and, if we are poets who will

[123] Ibid. p. 376.

not acquiesce in a disability, to make an expression congruous with their experience.[124]

We can characterise this modernism then by its unwillingness to accept a disability, by its refusal to accept the imagination's limits, its unwillingness to accept that an experience might exist beyond its ken.

The echo of that position is in Eliot's contemporaneous 'Sweeney among the Nightingales' (*Little Review*: September 1918; *March–August 1918*).[125] Echoing both Stevens's 'Phases' and Murry's emphasis on crying aloud, Eliot bracketed his poem with Agamemnon's death cry. This sets up the ironic contrast with Sweeney the modern foot soldier home on leave. This might in turn explain the existence of a typescript of this poem in the Lewis archives.[126] Lewis had left front-line artillery service at Passchendaele in the autumn of 1917, returning with the Canadian War Memorials Fund in January 1918. Eliot's respect for Lewis's work had steadily increased, especially between the publication of Lewis's 'Inferior Religions' (*Little Review*: September 1917) and *Tarr* (July 1918). Eliot reviewed the novel for *The Egoist* in the June/July and September issues. Perhaps Eliot evaluated this imagined war poem using another combatant home on leave that summer? Perhaps for inclusion in the never-completed third instalment of *Blast*?

Either way, the poem's coldness functions as a perfect tribute to Murry's poetic demands, especially its total resistance to psychological interpretation. It takes an obvious relish in the macabre. There is a sense of intellectual foolishness in its forced metaphors, in the awkward sense of sound and in the overemphasis on bathos. The rhymes are overtly jarring ('laugh' and 'giraffe', 'withdraws' and 'paws') and many flirt, surely consciously, as in Ford's *Antwerp*, with amateurism ('coffee-cup' and 'stocking up', 'leaning in' and 'golden grin').[127] The focus is on what is made rather than what is found, on the written

---

[124] [John Middleton Murry], 'M. De Régnier's War Poetry', *TLS*, 890 (6 February 1919), 66.

[125] Eliot returned to verse from critical work in May 1918 and agreed, at the latest by 23 June, to publish four poems which then appeared in September's *Little Review*. Two of these Eliot had completed, 'Whispers of Immortality' (*March 1917–August 1918*) and 'Dans le Restaurant' (*March–October 1917*). The remaining two, 'Mr. Eliot's Sunday Morning Service' and 'Sweeney among the Nightingales', can be dated to March–August 1918. Eliot later connected the atmosphere of the latter to a period marked by air-raids on London. T. S. Eliot, 'The Tendency of Some Modern Poetry', in *The Complete Prose of T. S. Eliot, IV: English Lion, 1930–1933*, ed. by Jason Harding and Ronald Schuchard (2015), pp. 840–5 (p. 843). Gotha bombers conducted attacks in London on both 13 June and 7 July 1918.

[126] Christopher Ricks and Jim McCue, 'Textual History: "Sweeney among the Nightingales"', in Eliot, *Practical Cats and Further Verses*, pp. 356–8 (p. 356 ts3).

[127] T. S. Eliot, 'Sweeney among the Nightingales', in *Collected and Uncollected Poems*, pp. 51–2 (pp. 51–2).

rather than the spoken.[128] The poem deliberately blocks acts of speech, restricting vocalisation to affective disruptions from inside the Lewisian wild body. The title suggests the poem ought to be cacophonous, whether we take the birds as literal or as a brothel metaphor. Yet it is utterly silent, a slow-motion film reel, images with captions. Perhaps taking inspiration from Lewis's contemporaneous obsession with the human face caught in an agonised or ecstatic grimace, Eliot's poem parts the lips for everything but speech. Sweeney laughs, a woman yawns, Agamemnon cries and the nightingales sing. Yet each act is ultimately cauterised, the sound is evacuated. Eliot hushes the seas. Anything resembling a human, Eliot silences. The storms of the heavens, Rachel's savage tearing, what should be deafening Eliot drains of sound to leave only indistinct conversations.[129] This satire of *parole* Eliot accentuated with the excision of the poem's original second epigraph focused on speech acts. Following initial publication in *Poems* (May 1919) and in *Ara Vus* [*Vos*] *Prec* (1920) it disappeared.[130] No one it seems is to speak.

There is no evidence that Eliot and Murry met before the latter offered the former the *Athenæum* assistant editorship in the spring of 1919. When they first met is hard to pin down.[131] They clearly did overlap in several shared interests. They both chose the partisan *Nation* as the forum for their views on combat gnosticism. They shared a respect for the French intellectual reaction to combat. Eliot recommended to his students in Ilkley in the early winter of 1916 those French conservatives struggling with their faith amidst combat (especially those associated with *Action française*) and pacifist works such as Rolland's *Au-dessus de la mêlée* (1914).[132] Eliot had already taken Murry's later line when he anointed Ford's *Antwerp* as the only good poem of the war in 'Reflections on Contemporary Poetry [III]', his review of Harriet Monroe and Alice Corbin Henderson's *The New Poetry*

---

[128] Lawrence Rainey makes a similar point about 'Whispers of Immortality'. See Lawrence Rainey, 'Pound or Eliot: Whose Era?', in *The Cambridge Companion to Modernist Poetry*, ed. by Alex Davis and Lee M. Jenkins (Cambridge: Cambridge University Press, 2007), pp. 87–113 (p. 95).

[129] Eliot, 'Sweeney among the Nightingales', pp. 51–2.

[130] For various revisions (and misspellings in *Ara Vos Prec*) see Ricks and McCue, 'Textual History: "Sweeney among the Nightingales"', p. 357, *Second epigraph*.

[131] Murry had just six weeks to prepare April's *Athenæum* after offering the role to Eliot. Kaplan, p. 105. Peter Brooker suggests a first meeting at Garsington, but Eliot's first recorded visit there was not until early May. Vivien Eliot, letter to Mary Hutchinson ([10 May 1919]), in *The Letters of T. S. Eliot*, I, p. 346; Peter Brooker, 'Harmony, Discord, and Difference: *Rhythm* (1911–13), *The Blue Review* (1913), and *The Signature* (1915)', in *The Oxford Critical and Cultural History of Modernist Magazines*, ed. by Peter Brooker and Andrew Thacker, 3 vols (Oxford: Oxford University Press, 2009–13), I: *Britain and Ireland 1880–1955* (2009), pp. 314–36 (p. 315).

[132] T. S. Eliot, 'Syllabus of a Course of Six Lectures on Modern French Literature' (1999), in *Apprentice Years, 1905–1918*, pp. 471–7 (p. 476).

(February 1917). This anthology had made war poetries a critical part of its editors' bold claim to having identified a poetry 'of absolute simplicity and sincerity', one that 'looks out more eagerly than in'.[133] Amongst other war poems, and alongside Ford's *Antwerp*, it included Stevens's 'In Battle' taken from 'Phases', Harold Monro's 'Youth in Arms', Pound's 'Coming of War: Actaeon' and several poems from Gibson's *Battle*. Apart from singling out Ford, Eliot only drily noted that Brooke's poetry was 'not absent'.[134]

Eliot quickly followed 'Reflections on Contemporary Poetry [III]' with a pseudonymous letter to *The Egoist* pretending to object to the slur on Brooke's reputation:

> Brooke's early poems exhibit a youthful exuberance of passion and an occasional coarseness of utterance, which offended finer tastes; but these were but dross which, as his last sonnets show, was purged away (if I may be permitted this word) in the fire of the Great Ordeal which is proving the well-spring of a Renaissance of English poetry. Helen B. Trundlett Batton, Kent.[135]

The editors of Eliot's collected prose suggest that this and the five other pseudonymous pieces in the December 1917 *Egoist* were whimsical pieces designed to fill space.[136] This is generous. Trundlett's sentiments are echoed by 'Muriel A. Schwarz' of '60 Alexandra Gardens, Hampstead' who objects to another 'slur upon the cheery philosophy of our brave boys in the trenches', this one made by Lewis.[137] Both Trundlett and Schwarz are women out of their depth, stereotypes like 'J. A. D. Spence, Thridlingston Grammar School', 'Charles James Grimble, The Vicarage, Leays' and 'Charles Augustus Conybeare, The Carlton Club, Liverpool'.[138] Sentimental women inspired by war verse, the dusty classics tutor, the moralising vicar and the clubbable old-Oxonian were Eliot's version of the blasted. Amidst a carefully crafted career, this surely serves as something of a lapse, a dropping of the mask that tells us a great deal about Eliot's personal views on 'the fire of the Great Ordeal' as a revolutionising force in poetry.

The coded reference here is to Gibson's sacrificial image of the burning Brooke referred to earlier in this chapter published in *Georgian Poetry 1916–1917*. It also

---

[133] H.M. [Harriet Monroe], 'Introduction', in *The New Poetry: An Anthology*, ed. by Harriet Monroe and Alice Corbin Henderson (New York: Macmillan, 1917; repr. 1918), pp. v–xiii (p. vi).

[134] T. S. Eliot, 'Reflections on Contemporary Poetry [III]', in *Apprentice Years, 1905–1918*, pp. 608–12 (p. 610).

[135] T. S. Eliot, 'Pseudonymous letters for *The Egoist*', in *Apprentice Years, 1905–1918*, pp. 613–14 (p. 613).

[136] Ibid. p. 614 n. 1.

[137] Ibid. p. 614.

[138] Ibid. pp. 613–14.

suggests Edward Osborn's *The Muse in Arms*. Osborn was one of the earliest pro-
ponents of combatant war poems, especially in the *TLS*.[139] Published in November
1917, and a commercial success reprinted in February 1918, *The Muse in Arms*
was the first major anthology to introduce the collective testimony of Brooke,
Graves, Gurney, Nichols, Sassoon, Sorley and Osbert Sitwell. Its subtitle made
clear its theme: '*A Collection of War Poems, for the Most Part Written in the
Field of Action, by Seamen, Soldiers, and Flying Men Who Are Serving, or Have
Served, in the Great War*'.[140] Osborn's stated aim was confessedly voyeuristic:

> The object of this Anthology is to show what passes in the British war-
> rior's soul when, in moments of aspiration or inspiration, before or after
> action or in the busy days of self-preparation for self-sacrifice, he has
> glimpses of the ultimate significance of warfare. [. . .] [T]he selection
> [. . .] presents a picture of the visible imagery of battle as mirrored in
> his mind.[141]

These combat gnostics have been through 'the great ordeal', Osborn argued.[142]
They 'know war from within'.[143] It was Osborn's focus on the young, and
especially the idea of the young gaining experience unavailable to the old, that
deserves particular emphasis since it takes us back to Eliot's earlier reflections
on Haigh-Wood. It is also a reminder of Goldie's crucial point that until the
summer of 1919 Murry's influence meant that it was not history or tradition
that denoted approval in Eliot's vocabulary but maturity and rhetoric, terms
he used in opposition to immaturity and sentimentality.[144] Eliot, and Murry,
could use this language to speak about the contemporary poetic scene. In
Eliot's 'Murmuring of Innumerable Bees' (*The Athenæum*: October 1919) and
Murry's 'The Condition of English Literature' (*The Athenæum*: May 1920) we
can see this in full flow.[145]

We can trace the terms isolated by Goldie to at least 'Reflections on
Contemporary Poetry, I' (*The Egoist*: September 1917). Eliot states there

---

[139] [E. B. Osborn], 'The Soldier Patriot', *TLS*, 798 (3 May 1917), 205–6 (p. 205); E. B. Osborn, 'To
the Editor: A Soldier's Song-Book', *TLS*, 850 (2 May 1918), 208–9 (p. 208).

[140] *The Muse in Arms: A Collection of War Poems, for the Most Part Written in the Field of Action,
by Seamen, Soldiers, and Flying Men Who Are Serving, or Have Served, in the Great War*, ed.
by E. B. Osborn (London: John Murray, 1917), [front matter].

[141] E. B. Osborn, 'Introduction', in Osborn, ed., pp. vii–xxiii (p. vii).

[142] Ibid. p. viii.

[143] Ibid. p. ix.

[144] Goldie, p. 42.

[145] T. S. Eliot, 'Murmuring of Innumerable Bees' (*The Athenæum*: October 1919), in *The Perfect
Critic, 1919–1926*, pp. 129–31 (p. 129); J.M.M. [John Middleton Murry], 'The Condition of
English Literature', *The Athenæum*, 4697 (7 May 1920), 597–8 (p. 598).

that contemporary verse had tried to escape its natural tendency to rhetoric, abstraction and moralising in its recovery of the rhythms of ordinary or
direct speech by focusing on the trivial and ordinary.[146] Although Eliot named
Edward Marsh and other allies as his primary target, he was taking broader
aim at the conservative mood of modern poetry. He linked the Georgians to
their immediate contemporaries through a shared respect for the pastoral
and for patriotism.[147] The younger poets were 'Georgian' according to Eliot
because Georgianism was but a symptom of a much wider failure to build
bridges between the local and the universal, a failure that resulted in turn
from the failure to develop a unifying philosophy about the world. In this
sense Haigh-Wood was very much a 'Georgian'.

Repeatedly in Eliot's prose we find phrases such as 'the last few years' and
'young writer' subtly attempting to characterise the verse of the war.[148] The
rhetorical edge to this is bitter. His review of 1917's *Georgian Poetry* – 'Verse
Pleasant and Unpleasant' (*The Egoist*: March 1918) – drily noted 'the fresh
recruits'.[149] In 'Reviews of Contemporary Poetry' (*The Egoist*: August 1918),
Eliot recorded of one war poet, the surviving half of the future Faber and Gwyer
publishing house, that 'Captain Faber did not observe very much of importance
In the Valley of Vision [(1918)]'.[150] In 'Whether Rostand Had Something about
Him' (*The Athenæum*: July 1919), Eliot critiqued the 'many modern writers,
who sometimes disingenuously hide their emotions behind obscure simplici-
ties'.[151] In *The Sacred Wood* the nod towards Murry's essay here would be more
obvious. It became 'some writers appear to believe that emotions gain in intensity through being inarticulate. Perhaps the emotions are not significant enough
to endure full daylight.'[152] It also suggests dialogue with Aldington's foreword to
War and Love (1915–1918) (August 1919) which affirmed itself as an example
of 'the often inarticulate feelings of the ordinary civilized man thrust suddenly
into [. . .] extraordinary and hellish circumstances'.[153]

Eliot levelled the accusations of immaturity and simplicity in quick succession
in the spring of 1919 in the pages of *The Athenæum*. In April 1919 he targeted

---

[146] T. S. Eliot, 'Reflections on Contemporary Poetry, I', in *Apprentice Years, 1905–1918*, pp. 573–7
(p. 573).

[147] Ibid.

[148] Eliot, 'A Brief Treatise on the Criticism of Poetry', p. 202; T. S. Eliot, 'Reflections on Contemporary
Poetry [IV]' (*The Egoist*: July 1919), in *The Perfect Critic, 1919–1926*, pp. 66–71 (p. 66).

[149] T. S. Eliot, 'Verse Pleasant and Unpleasant', in *Apprentice Years, 1905–1918*, pp. 679–85 (p. 679).

[150] T. S. Eliot, 'Reviews of Contemporary Poetry', in *Apprentice Years, 1905–1918*, pp. 733–5 (p. 734).

[151] T. S. Eliot, 'Whether Rostand Had Something about Him', in *The Perfect Critic, 1919–1926*,
pp. 83–91 (p. 91 n. 3).

[152] Ibid. pp. 86–7.

[153] Richard Aldington, *War and Love (1915–1918)* (Boston: Four Seas, 1919), p. 6. See the
response and citation of this foreword in Marjorie Allen Seiffert, 'Soldier and Lover', *Poetry*,
14.6 (September 1919), 338–41 (p. 338).

a group of pre-war poets.[154] At the beginning of May it was Rudyard Kipling; at the month's end it was Henry Adams.[155] One article takes the same line and precedes these, an unsigned review of Osborn's second collection, *The New Elizabethans* (1919), entitled 'The New Elizabethans and the Old' (*The Athenæum*: 4 April 1919). Genealogically it occupies an interesting position. It was the first article for Murry, Eliot's new editor at *The Athenæum*. Although Eliot eventually declined the offer of the assistant editorship after great handwringing, he took pride in the offer and clearly wanted to impress both his new editor and his new audience. It was a marked public step-up. *The Athenæum* sold 3,000 to 3,500 copies per week compared to *The Egoist*'s circulation of 150–500 copies per issue. As a sign of its heft, Arnold Rowntree's backing ensured Murry received a salary in inflation-adjusted terms of over £40,000.[156] 'The New Elizabethans and the Old' was also Eliot's first significant essay after a medically recommended sabbatical during the winter of 1918 to 1919. This was the consequence of either a physical or nervous breakdown after his attempts to enlist. The death of his father in January certainly compounded Eliot's distress.[157] Eliot had much to say, then, much to gain and a platform from which to say it.

Eliot told Jepson in March 1919 that Osborn's work was laden with sentiment.[158] That is not without truth. Osborn designed the volume as a follow-up to the success of *The Muse in Arms*. He changed the focus however to make it '*A First Selection of the Lives of Young Men Who Have Fallen*'. It was an anthology of doomed youth, the book's cover adorned with an image of Julian Grenfell in front of Taplow Court. It interlinked art and biography, critical commentary with poetic excerpt. It included sections on Grenfell, Seeger and Sorley alongside a series of lesser-known poets. Its predominant mood, suggested by its epigraph from Ewart Mackintosh's mournful 'The Ship of the Soul' (1918), was deeply melancholic.[159] 'These golden lads', as Osborn collectively referred

---

[154] T. S. Eliot, 'The Post-Georgians' (*The Athenæum*: 11 April 1919), in *The Perfect Critic, 1919–1926*, pp. 16–20 (p. 17).

[155] T. S. Eliot, 'Kipling Redivivus' (*The Athenæum*: 9 May 1919), in *The Perfect Critic, 1919–1926*, pp. 33–9 (p. 35); T. S. Eliot. 'A Sceptical Patrician' (*The Athenæum*: 23 May 1919), in *The Perfect Critic, 1919–1926*, pp. 41–7 (pp. 43–4).

[156] Michael H. Whitworth, 'Enemies of Cant: *The Athenæum* (1919–21) and *The Adelphi* (1923–48)', in Brooker and Thacker, eds, pp. 364–88 (p. 367); Peter White, 'Literary Journalism', in *T. S. Eliot in Context*, ed. by Jason Harding (Cambridge: Cambridge University Press, 2011), pp. 93–104 (p. 96).

[157] Eliot began the essay after 12 March and 'Marivaux' (*Art and Letters*: Spring 1919), which precedes it in Eliot's collected critical prose, sometime after 29 March. T. S. Eliot, 'Marivaux', in *The Perfect Critic, 1919–1926*, pp. 1–9 (p. 6 n. 1).

[158] T. S. Eliot, letter to Edgar Jepson (12 March 1919), in *The Letters of T. S. Eliot*, I, p. 328.

[159] E. A. Mackintosh, ['The Ship of the Soul'], qtd in E. B. Osborn, *The New Elizabethans: A First Selection of the Lives of Young Men Who Have Fallen in the Great War* (London: John Lane, 1919), p. [iii].

to them, formed 'a group bound together by ties of personal friendship and, what is even more, a common confidence that life and love are inexhaustible'.[160]

Osborn detected two characteristically Elizabethan features in the work he collected. First, an 'instinct of brotherliness'. Second, a sense that the soldiers believed 'their land was the Gloriana they glorified in their deeds'.[161] It seems high-flown, but the comparison was not unusual at the time. Margaret Wynne Nevinson, for example, suggested the same idea in the *English Review* in September 1919.[162] Crucial for Eliot at this stage of his poetic development was Osborn's focus on age. The word 'young', or words associated with it, appear more than once every three pages in *The New Elizabethans*, 120 times in total. The essential message Osborn wanted to convey was that *'youth knows more about the young than middle age or old age'*.[163] The 'elder generations' needed, Osborn argued, to 'stand aside when the young men come back from the War' and allow them 'the task of rebuilding' civilisation. 'For this is the chief lesson of the War,' Osborn said, 'that age is not wiser than youth, as we used to think in the former peace-time.'[164] The effective consignment of anyone over the age of thirty to the scrap heap was precisely what Eliot's review aimed to debunk.

Eliot's first move in 'The New Elizabethans and the Old' is to debunk the idea of innovation in Osborn's tentative school of poets. Plato had already dealt with the theme of youth cut prematurely short, Eliot said. In any case, the poets in Osborn's collection were not poets but writers of a very juvenile and low-quality verse. Osborn was then no more than a charlatan, a snake-oil seller exposing the gullible. As Eliot put it cuttingly, the work of these poets was 'hardly more than a means of exploiting their charm, and in the charm is the danger'.[165] Again, we might note in Eliot's prose an uncharacteristic lack of reserve whilst we also register the total absence of compassion. 'As for the subjects of these memoirs, we are quite prepared to believe that they were delightful persons, and that their loss is a public misfortune,' Eliot drily observed, before adding that 'none of the heroes, if we may judge from the verse and prose extracts from their works, was favoured with remarkable genius (unless what is called the "genius for living")'.[166] The insertion of the words 'the heroes' tips things firmly towards cruelty. It returns us to the academic sniggering of Trundlett's mock defence of

---

[160] Osborn, *The New Elizabethans*, pp. 1, 3.

[161] Ibid. p. 4.

[162] Margaret Wynne Nevinson, 'Some of our Young War Poets', *English Review*, 29 (September 1919), 224.

[163] Osborn, *The New Elizabethans*, p. xi.

[164] Ibid. p. 7.

[165] T. S. Eliot, 'The New Elizabethans and the Old', in *The Perfect Critic, 1919–1926*, pp. 10–15 (p. 10).

[166] Ibid. p. 11.

Brooke. Whilst it might masquerade as the cool objectivity of a peer review process, it is really a takedown. Eliot stages it in a manner that explains the need, as with Murry's essay, for the cover of anonymity.

Eliot's point was that the young struggle to produce genuine poetry. 'Important truth', as opposed we must conclude to merely commonplace or simple truths, 'comes to the young only in rare flashes of genius,' Eliot recorded. He asks us to think about the type of experience that matters to the poet, not as the series of moments of extreme affective overload which precipitate poetry but as the marination of the self within intellectual life. Osborn's poets, Eliot's finds, are all lacking here. He summarises the position clearly:

> there are no flashes; some of the men had a nice honesty in detail, in accounting for their lives in France – but not that great honesty of the general scheme, that super-human honesty which is realized only by years of observation and thought and which constitutes the genius of middle age.[167]

The Romantic ideal is oddly repositioned. Eliot keeps the concept of mental reflection and egoistic tranquillity, but the myth of the boy genius, of Thomas Chatterton in the garret, he replaces with a model of experience based on mental calisthenics rather than fleshy experience. There appear two types of truth, both subtly linked to age. There is the specific and local detail of immaturity and the great and general scheme of middle age, particulars versus universals we might say in Aristotelian terms.

Notably Eliot picked out Seeger from Osborn's collective as a representative of these youthful versifiers. Born in Staten Island, Seeger attended Harvard and possibly shared a room with Eliot; he died on the Somme in July 1916.[168] Eliot reviewed Seeger's poems in another unsigned review for *The Egoist* in December 1917, calling them 'out of date', 'high-flown, heavily decorated and solemn', not a posture, Eliot said, having known the man, but entirely sincere.[169] Others had already made the link between Seeger and Brooke as popular icons of doomed youth, especially after publication of Seeger's letters home in the *New York Sun*. Eliot's argument, premised on personal intimacy he said, was that Seeger could not avoid undiluted, self-conscious aestheticism. Seeger 'seems to us to have lived always in a violet mist', Eliot said, by which he meant a melodramatic brain fog.[170] That fault left Seeger too general and lacking in the right kind of detail. In contrast, Eliot took a man over the age of forty, Walter Raleigh,

---

[167] Ibid.
[168] Crawford, *Young Eliot*, pp. 110–11.
[169] T. S. Eliot, 'Unsigned reviews of poetry by Alan Seeger, Guy Rawlence, Joseph Campbell, and Edward Thomas', in *Apprentice Years, 1905–1918*, pp. 619–22 (p. 619).
[170] Eliot, 'The New Elizabethans and the Old', p. 11.

as a counter example of how to write about war. It was a clarion call to middle age that could hardly be anything other than self-serving. Eliot, Lewis and Pound were all in their early to mid-thirties.[171] For Eliot action becomes contiguous with pure or unmoderated emotion and he suggests that whenever a writer takes art from direct experience there is always the risk that it becomes constitutively contaminated by contemporary artistic failings. It always risks the lack of proper perspective that comes with a mature vision. Such a move allowed Eliot to set out a comprehensive genealogy linking together these New Elizabethans with the Victorians through his distaste for the vulgarity of the Wilde and Brooke periods. 'To a person of any real feeling', Eliot said, 'the heroes might have been all the more interesting had they been less articulate.'[172] Taking Murry's original critique of crying aloud, Eliot had linked Victorian sentimentality through decadence to the Georgians and into war verse to create one seamless tradition.

The stinging cruelty in that final line of 'The New Elizabethans and the Old' is hard to read. It upends what Eliot took real feeling to mean. He meant taste and not the ability to experience the Other. There was no 'lifting belly' here, on the contrary. If we can trace the essay's critical energy to Murry, this new openness of tone in Eliot's work, its withering assessment of idealism, owes something to Lytton Strachey. He was Eliot's newest acquaintance in the spring of 1919 and Eliot had read Strachey's *Eminent Victorians* (May 1918), widely recognised as a major stylistic departure, as a text that had introduced a new honesty into the English arts.[173] We can find an unusual and respectful intimacy in the correspondence between Strachey and Eliot in these months.[174]

---

[171] Also note Eliot's characteristic insertion of seriousness into the debate, emphasising the need for care, sincerity and maturity. Leonard Diepeveen, 'Taking Literature Seriously: Essays to 1927', in *A Companion to T. S. Eliot*, ed. by David E. Chinitz (Chichester: Wiley-Blackwell, 2009), pp. 263–74.

[172] Eliot, 'The New Elizabethans and the Old', p. 13.

[173] The book sold 1,000 copies in nine impressions by February 1920, and by 1932 (the date of Strachey's death) 35,000 copies in the United Kingdom and 55,000 in the United States. Michael Holroyd, *Lytton Strachey: The New Biography* (New York: Farrar, Straus, and Giroux, 1994; repr. New York: W. W. Norton, 2005), pp. 419–30.

[174] Eliot had read *Eminent Victorians* by 7 November 1918 at the latest. T. S. Eliot, to Mrs Jack [Isabella] Gardner (7 November 1918), in *The Letters of T. S. Eliot*, I, pp. 290–2 (p. 292). It was during April and May 1919, as Pound left England for France under a hail of opprobrium, that Eliot moved closer to the coterie at Garsington Manor. The Eliots dined with the Woolfs in January and April 1919 as the publication of the Hogarth edition of *Poems* approached. On 11 May 1919 Eliot dined with Strachey, although Strachey privately expressed frustration with Eliot's reserve. Holroyd, p. 455. On their intimacy see Vivien Eliot, letter to Mary Hutchinson ([undated]), in *The Letters of T. S. Eliot*, I, p. 292 n. 2; T. S. Eliot, letter to Lytton Strachey (1 June 1919), in *The Letters of T. S. Eliot*, I, p. 357; T. S. Eliot, letter to Mary Hutchinson ([7 January 1920?]), in *The Letters of T. S. Eliot*, I, p. 429; T. S. Eliot, letter to Lytton Strachey (17 February 1920), in *The Letters of T. S. Eliot*, I, p. 445 (p. 445 n. 2). Strachey was on Eliot's postcard list from France in August 1919. T. S. Eliot, postcard to Lytton Strachey ([25? August 1919]), in *The Letters of T. S. Eliot*, I, p. 388.

Eliot casually likened the longer-range intent of the project in *The Athenæum* to Strachey's biographical method and took time to explain to him the strategic direction of 'Gerontion' days after its first draft.[175]

If Strachey had sensitively tapped into a public tired of state control, Eliot's lack of compassion for both the dead and the grieving feels misjudged and ideological. Compare it to Woolf's 'These Are the Plans', a notably signed *Athenæum* review of 1 August 1919 covering poems by two other dead poets, Donald Johnson and Charles Sorley. Like Eliot, Woolf recognised that this verse was often prose ordered into irregular lines. Yet Woolf saw that its confessional quality enabled it to avoid socially imposed constraints. They 'evidently wrote poetry because it allowed them to express their feelings without a sense of irreticence', Woolf rightly observed.[176] Osborn had made this a central editorial premise in his anthology. He sensed a classless 'instinct of brotherliness'.[177] He never went as far as Cole, Das or Adrian Caesar in *Taking It Like a Man* (1993), but Osborn's suggestion does anticipate recent academic work on the homosocial and homoerotic aspects of the trench lyric.[178] Woolf sensed that poetry offered these soldiers a repository. The rhyme, metre and hackneyed phrases served as a mask, Woolf said, behind which the poet could hide from the blushes he would experience in prose. For Woolf, the poetry was in the act of 'disguise'.[179]

It seems improbable that Eliot did not see this too. Eliot could diagnose the coercive forces present in Osborn's sentimentalism and was aware of the value in poetic confession. As the next chapter illustrates, the subtlety of Eliot's mind is consistently fascinating. So why did Eliot choose this text of all texts for his inaugural *Athenæum* review? The Elizabethan theme was certainly bait. Osborn was also a rival literary editor at the *Morning Post* and Eliot coveted publication in the *TLS*. It was nonetheless an obviously odd and uneven collection to begin from. There were plenty of other examples of war writing for Eliot to review, all of which have stood the test of time better than Osborn's collection: Aldington's *Images of War* (April 1919), illustrated by Paul Nash, Gurney's *War's Embers* (May) and Sassoon's *Picture Show* (July) for example. Woolf opted to review texts such as these. Eliot also had form in opting for easy targets. He picked out Faber's *In the Valley of Vision* only to dismiss it out of

---

[175] T. S. Eliot, letter to Lytton Strachey (6 August 1919), in *The Letters of T. S. Eliot*, I, p. 388. On 'Gerontion' see Eliot, letter to Lytton Strachey (1 June 1919), p. 357.

[176] Virginia Woolf, 'These Are the Plans', in *The Essays of Virginia Woolf*, III: *1919–1924*, ed. by Andrew McNeillie (London: Hogarth Press, 1988; repr. Orlando: Harcourt Brace Jovanovich, [undated]), pp. 73–7 (p. 73).

[177] Osborn, *The New Elizabethans*, p. 4.

[178] Adrian Caesar, *Taking It Like a Man: Suffering, Sexuality and the War Poets, Brooke, Sassoon, Owen, Graves* (Manchester: Manchester University Press, 1993).

[179] Woolf, 'These Are the Plans', p. 73.

hand. In 'Reflections on Contemporary Poetry [IV]' (*The Egoist*: July 1919), he used *Naked Warriors* (1919) to illustrate Read being 'handicapped by his imperfection of musical sense, in the production of *tone*'.[180] That was unfortunate wording. Tortured by anxiety and lacerated by barbed wire, a brother killed in action, Read was eventually awarded the Distinguished Service Order and the Military Cross.[181] And it is notable that on 11 April in the week following Eliot's essay, Murry returned to praise of Duhamel: 'He did not merely cry with pain, as did the most sincere of our own writers on the war; he steeled his sanity and used it to make vocal and intelligible the cries of pain which he had heard through the long night of four interminable years.'[182] Eliot's choice of Osborn's anthology looks then like another modernist straw strategy. It bore all the ideological fingerprints of the partnership with Murry at *The Athenæum*. It was a continuation of the same critical pivot against the likes of Brooke that began in 1915.

---

[180] Eliot, 'Reflections on Contemporary Poetry [IV]', p. 68. Others praised Read's work for expressing the grotesque nature of combat. [Anonymous], 'List of New Books', *The Athenæum*, 4641 (11 April 1919), 188.

[181] Hugh Cecil, 'Herbert Read and the Great War', in *Herbert Read Reassessed*, ed. by David Goodway (Liverpool: Liverpool University Press, 1998), pp. 30–45 (pp. 32–8).

[182] J. [John] Middleton Murry, 'The Gospel of M. Duhamel', *The Athenæum*, 4641 (11 April 1919), 184.

5

THE FORM AND PRACTICE OF
MODERNIST DISTASTE:
SUMMER–AUTUMN 1919

Although 'The New Elizabethans and the Old' never found its way into *The Sacred Wood* and scholars have disregarded it, the essay was important for T. S. Eliot. A few weeks following its publication in *The Athenæum* he mentioned to his mother an upcoming lecture on 31 May at London University. Eliot either abandoned it or we have lost the manuscript, but Eliot planned, he said, to cover the younger generation of poets. It may well have been a version of the lecture he finally gave to the Arts League in October 1919, discussed later in this chapter. However, given Eliot wagered his London University lecture was to be on a delicate subject it is unlikely it merely attacked the Georgians. Poetries of war were the especially delicate subject in London during 1919. It was a society marked by the mass demobilisation of its armies, the tending of its wounded and the commemoration of its dead.[1]

On 9 July Eliot sent 'The New Elizabethans and the Old' to John Quinn. He recommended it for inclusion in the volume Alfred Knopf would eventually publish as *Poems* (February 1920). Initially this was to be a volume entitled *A Book of Verse and Prose*. Eliot told Quinn that the essay might address the interest of the American public in the war.[2] Although the combined volume of

---

[1] T. S. Eliot, letter to Charlotte Eliot (25 May 1919), in *The Letters of T. S. Eliot*, I, p. 353.
[2] T. S. Eliot, letter to John Quinn (9 July 1919), in *The Letters of T. S. Eliot*, I, pp. 373–5 (p. 373). Eliot wanted to add essays written for *The Athenæum* to those written for *The Egoist*. T. S. Eliot,

prose and poetry never happened, Eliot ensured the link to the war in *Poems* (1920) via its dedication to Jean Verdenal. Eliot had originally published the same dedication in *Prufrock and Other Observations* but felt it was unnecessary in *Ara Vos Prec*, the English edition of *Poems*, where he used Dante instead. The reference to Dante differentiated, as in 'In silent corridors of death', between those souls forced to suffer and those souls wishing to suffer as penitents as they journeyed through purgatory.[3]

What American interest was Eliot referring to when he sent 'The New Elizabethans and the Old' to Quinn? There was certainly no straightforward evidence of that interest in the internationalist oriented *Little Review*. There is a clear shallowness to the single blank page that Margaret Anderson inserted into the April 1917 edition of the magazine as the United States entered the war. Anderson's caveat that the *Little Review* might be censored for this non-statement is not redemptive.[4] Anita Helle (2007) argues that there were some issues of the journal given over to the war.[5] This is a difficult argument to sustain as the journal became increasingly separated from lived European history and committed to Ezra Pound's protégés in the last years of the war. Rupert Brooke, who featured extensively in the March, April, July and December 1914 editions, disappeared after June 1915. Those quasi-war poems the journal did publish – Carl Sandburg's 'Graves' (April 1916), Richard Aldington's

---

letter to John Quinn (25 May 1919), in *The Letters of T. S. Eliot*, I, p. 354. Quinn, seeking a publisher, requested more poems and essays suggesting the subsequently abandoned title. John Quinn, letter to T. S. Eliot (30 June 1919), in *The Letters of T. S. Eliot*, I, p. 368 (p. 368 n. 1). The essays Eliot wanted published were 'A Romantic Patrician' (*The Athenæum*: 2 May 1919), 'A Sceptical Patrician', 'The New Elizabethans and the Old' and 'American Literature'. Eliot, letter to John Quinn (9 July 1919), p. 373. By late August, Knopf decided to publish only Eliot's poetry. John Quinn, letter to T. S. Eliot (26 August 1919), in *The Letters of T. S. Eliot*, I, pp. 389–92 (p. 389).

[3] T. S. Eliot, *Prufrock and Other Observations*, [front matter]; T. S. Eliot, *Poems* (New York: Alfred A. Knopf, 1920), [front matter]. For discussion see Christopher Ricks and Jim McCue, 'Commentary: *Poems* (1920)', in Eliot, *Collected and Uncollected Poems*, pp. 455–67 (pp. 464–5). There is no dedication in the Hogarth Press edition of *Poems* (May 1919). In *Poems 1909–1925* (London: Faber and Gwyer, 1925), p. 9, Eliot used both the dedication to Verdenal and the quotation from Dante as an introduction to his early poetry. Eliot also made clear the battle-front location of Verdenal's death in the Dardanelles. The post-*Prufrock* poems received no separate dedication. Ricks and McCue note the similarity to Arthur Davison Ficke's dedication in 'To Rupert Brooke', a poem published in the same issue of *Poetry* as 'The Love Song of J. Alfred Prufrock'. Arthur Davison Ficke, 'To Rupert Brooke I–V', *Poetry*, 6.3 (June 1915), 113–16 (p. 113). For Eliot's translation of and reflections on the quote from Dante see T. S. Eliot, *Dante* (1929), in *The Complete Prose of T. S. Eliot*, III: *Literature, Politics, Belief, 1927–1929*, ed. by Frances Dickey and others (2015), pp. 700–45 (p. 715).

[4] Margaret C. Anderson, 'The War', *Little Review*, 3.10 (April 1917), 4. The journal used the same strategy for different purposes in September 1916.

[5] Anita Helle, '"Blasé Sorrow": Ultramodernity's Mourning at the *Little Review*, 1917–20', in *Modernism and Mourning*, ed. by Patricia Rea (Lewisburg, PN: Bucknell University Press, 2007), pp. 118–35 (pp. 120, 131 n. 9).

'Thanatos' (March 1917) and Eliot's 'Whispers of Immortality' (September 1918; *March 1917–August 1918*) for example – deal with war very obliquely if at all. Only with the publication of Elsa von Freytag-Loringhoven's 'Poems' in March 1920 did the war enter the magazine with any real commitment, leaving the *Little Review*'s blank space as a rather frank representation of its non-position, the page on which '"the Men of 1914"', to borrow Wyndham Lewis's phrase in *Blasting and Bombardiering* (1937), could write their own intra-war histories.[6]

In contrast, *Poetry* took a much more definite interest. Despite its propagation of what Pound had term 'the war poem scandal', Harriet Monroe initially followed her English peers, and criticised the early war versifiers and their glamorisation of the savagery and horror.[7] Unlike those critics however Monroe foresaw the opportunity for a new poetry of war, a mode which might strip away the masculinist admiration of power, murder and big stakes.[8] Alice Corbin Henderson also sensed that the emerging American poetical response to war might amount to a local breakthrough. *Poetry* would gradually recover the war as a seminal moment in the genesis of a distinctly American poetic voice, one marked by a spirit of protest and common sense.[9] In *Poetry*, American neutrality became a form of Kantian distance on the brutality of affairs.

Take *Poetry*'s shifting relationship to Brooke, the poet who gradually disappeared in the *Little Review*. Monroe recognised the double nature of his legacy. She was quite willing to award him honour whilst also accepting that he had glorified all the old illusions of war.[10] Yet *Poetry* was equally guilty of perpetuating the Brooke mythology. Monroe imagined him dying of sunstroke like 'those Homeric heroes whom some god wrapped in golden mist and bore from the bloody field' in another singularly grotesque distortion of the facts.[11] Repeatedly Brooke's poems appear in *Poetry* as a gold standard, the art that all other war verse must first overcome.[12] To read *Poetry* through the war is to find

---

[6] Wyndham Lewis, *Blasting and Bombardiering* (London: Eyre & Spottiswoode, 1937), pp. 251–2.

[7] H.M. [Harriet Monroe], 'The Poetry of War', *Poetry*, 4.6 (September 1914), 237–9 (p. 237).

[8] Ibid. p. 238.

[9] A.C.H. [Alice Corbin Henderson], 'Poetry and War', *Poetry*, 5.2 (November 1914), 82–4 (pp. 83, 84).

[10] H.M. (*for the Jury*), [Harriet Monroe], 'Announcement of Awards [1915]', *Poetry*, 7.2 (November 1915), 102–6 (p. 104); H.M. [Harriet Monroe], 'The Death of Rupert Brooke', *Poetry*, 6.3 (June 1915), 136–8 (p. 137).

[11] [Monroe], 'The Death of Rupert Brooke', p. 138.

[12] A.C.H. [Alice Corbin Henderson], 'The Great Adventure', *Poetry*, 10.6 (September 1917), 316–19 (p. 316); H.M. [Harriet Monroe], 'A Decade of Gibson', *Poetry*, 9.2 (November 1916), 93–5 (p. 94); H.M. [Harriet Monroe], 'Will Art Happen?', *Poetry*, 10.4 (July 1917), 203–5 (p. 204); A.C.H. [Alice Corbin Henderson], 'War Poetry Again', *Poetry*, 12.5 (August 1918), 284–5 (p. 284); [Monroe], 'Announcement of Awards [1918]', p. 108; Marsden Hartley, 'Tribute to Joyce Kilmer', *Poetry*, 13.3 (December 1918), 149–54 (p. 152).

Brooke's corpse used yet again by discourse. He was a model soldier-poet, one who died both ecstatically and glamorously for a greater cause.[13] The Brooke that appeared in *Poetry* was someone utterly sincere, someone whose value lay in naivety. This was a cinematic version of Brooke. As Isaac Rosenberg intuited in 'Break of Day in the Trenches' the soldier had become the screen on to which others could project their own emotional lives.

After America entered the war, *Poetry* moved to canonise its own heroes. Marsden Hartley explicitly linked these figures to Brooke's alleged passion for the ideals of poetry and life.[14] Initially it was Alan Seeger who took centre stage.[15] *Poetry* added Joyce Kilmer later, to make, Monroe announced, the 'two gold stars [that] shine at the top of the flag which hangs in the poets' window'.[16] It later added the Cromwell sisters, volunteer nurses with the Red Cross, who, tortured by their experiences, committed suicide.[17] In contrast to the positions of John Middleton Murry and Eliot, in *Poetry* the cry of pain brought weight to the poetic voice. Here, as Monroe said in praise of Kilmer, 'death in battle is for a poet an accolade—it ennobles him, gives him a high significance.'[18] Salomón de la Selva argued that immediate affective experience ennobles and enriches.[19] Combat was not a retreat into idealism, but a rite of passage.[20] In *Poetry* the combatant's cry was as an act of supreme resistance in the face of the worst of the world. It was individual standing and screaming at the malevolent forces of the world. Monroe called it a gesture of 'incredible power and pride, an attitude of almost impossible heroism, the lonely uprising of a naked pigmy between overpowering hordes and the abyss'.[21] This was surely the interest that Eliot wanted to address when he asked Quinn to reprint his scathing attack on the younger generation for an American audience.

---

[13] H.M. [Harriet Monroe], 'Great Poetry', *Poetry*, 13.4 (January 1919), 219–24 (pp. 220, 221); H.M. [Harriet Monroe], 'A Radical-Conservative', *Poetry*, 13.6 (March 1919), 322–6 (p. 322). Similarly, A.C.H. [Alice Corbin Henderson], 'Reviews: *The Collected Poems of Rupert Brooke*', *Poetry*, 7.5 (February 1916), 262–4 (p. 263); H.B.F. [Henry B. Fuller], 'The Brooke Letters', *Poetry*, 8.3 (June 1916), 155–7 (p. 157).

[14] Hartley, 'Tribute to Joyce Kilmer', p. 152.

[15] A.F., 'Youth at War', *Poetry*, 10.1 (April 1917), 38–41. Similarly, [Henderson], 'The Great Adventure', p. 316; [Henderson], 'War Poetry Again', p. 284.

[16] [Monroe], 'Comment: Joyce Kilmer', p. 31.

[17] Notably, Monroe placed them on *Poetry*'s roll-of-honour 'just under [. . .] Alan Seeger, Joyce Kilmer and the other poet-heroes who died in battle'. H.M. [Harriet Monroe], 'A Gold Star for Gladys Cromwell', *Poetry*, 13.6 (March 1919), 326–8 (p. 327).

[18] [Monroe], 'Comment: Joyce Kilmer', p. 32.

[19] Salomón de la Selva, 'Strains of Yesterday', *Poetry*, 11.5 (February 1918), 281–2 (p. 282).

[20] H.M. [Harriet Monroe], 'The War and the Artist', *Poetry*, 11.6 (March 1918), 320–2 (p. 321).

[21] Ibid. p. 322.

Timeline 5.1 May–December 1919

	Composition	Publication, Exhibition, Event

May	Eliot, 'Gerontion'
	Ford, 'English Country'
	Freud, 'Beyond the Pleasure
	  Principle' (1920); 'Uncanny'
	  (1919)
	Lawrence, 'Last Straw' (1921),
	  'Monkey Nuts' (1922)
	Mirrlees, Paris (1920)
		Anderson, Winesburg, Ohio
		Coterie 1, Owl 1
		Eliot, Poems (Hogarth ed.),
		  'Cooking Egg' (Coterie)
		Gurney, War's Embers
		Little Review 2nd seizure
		Woolf, Kew Gardens

June	Joyce, 'Cyclops'; shifts focus in
	  Ulysses from Dedalus and
	  Bloom
	Lawrence, 'Hadrian' (1920),
	  preface to Touch and Go
	Pound, 'Sixth Canto' (1921)
		Aldington, Images of Desire
		Babbitt, Rousseau and
		  Romanticism
		Joyce, serialisation of 'Wandering
		  Rocks' (Little Review)
		Richardson, serialisation of
		  Interim (Little Review)
		Treaty of Versailles

July	Eliot, 'Tradition and the Individual
	  Talent'
	H.D., 'Notes on Thought and
	  Vision'
	Lewis, The Caliph's Design
	Joyce, draft of 'Sirens'
		Eliot, 'Burbank', 'Sweeney Erect'
		  (Art and Letters)
		H.D., 'Leda' (Monthly Chapbook)
		Joyce, serialisation of 'Hades'
		  (Egoist)
		Lawrence, Bay poems (Voices and
		  Monthly Chapbook), 'War
		  Films' (Poetry)
		Monthly Chapbook 1
		Peace Day (London)
		Sassoon, Picture-Show

August	Lawrence, 'Verse Free and Unfree'
	Lewis proposes Blast 3
		Eliot holidays with Pound in
		  France
		Ford, serialisation of 'English
		  Country' (New Statesman)
		Joyce, serialisation 'Sirens' (Little
		  Review)

September	Eliot, 'Gerontion'
	Lawrence, foreword to Women in
	  Love (1920)
	Pound, 'Seventh Canto'
		Aldington, Images
		H.D., Choruses from the
		  Iphigeneia in Aulis and the
		  Hippolytus of Euripides
		Eliot, 'Tradition and the Individual
		  Talent I' (Egoist), 'Hamlet'
		  (Athenæum)
		Freytag-Loringhoven, 'Cast-Iron
		  Lover' (Little Review)
		Shaw, Heartbreak House
		Stein, 'A League' (Life)
		Williams, 'Four Foreigners'
		  (Little Review)

	Composition	Publication, Exhibition, Event
October	Pound, 'Fifth Canto' (1921)	Eliot lecture at Arts League Lawrence, 'Verse Free and Unfree' (*Voices*) Lewis, *Caliph's Design* Pound, *The Fourth Canto, Quia Pauper Amavi* including 'Propertius' Sassoon, *War Poems* Woolf, *Night and Day*
November	H.D., 'I Said' (1982) Eliot considers long poem Joyce, 'Nausicaa' (1920) Pound 'Sixth Canto' (1921)	*Georgian Poetry, 1918–1919* Joyce, serialisation of 'Cyclops' (*Little Review*) Lawrence, *Bay;* leaves England Lewis, 'Prevalent Design' (*Athenæum*) *London Mercury* 1 Owen, poems (*Wheels*) including 'The Show', 'Strange Meeting'
December	Pound, 'Seventh Canto'; *Hugh Selwyn Mauberley*	Eliot, 'Tradition and the Individual Talent II' (*Egoist*); reads Pound's draft 'Seventh Canto' Keynes, *Consequences of the Peace* *Nation's War Paintings* exhibition begins Owen, 'Mental Cases' (*Coterie*) Richardson, *Interim*

Guide to Timelines
Works arranged in alphabetical order within each month.
Publication dates given in parenthesis, except if given in the main text, endnotes or elsewhere in timelines.
Titles shortened for brevity.

A COUNTER VERSE OF THE PRESENT MOMENT

From Eliot's perspective this desire to attack war verse coexisted with the desire to challenge *Poetry*'s claim on poetic tradition. In *Poetry*'s case, as Henderson suggested in November 1914, it had explicitly linked war verse to the appearance of a new American voice in modern poetry. By the end of the war, this had solidified to the extent that the two genres seemed indistinct, war verse becoming in its pages an extremely specific manifestation of an indigenous poetics of immediacy rooted in a language of the direct and the particular. It traced its origins to Walt Whitman and found its most cogent theorisation in the work of D. H. Lawrence as part of the research he undertook for *Studies in Classic American Literature* (1923). In the 'Preface to *New Poems*', drafted in August 1919 and published standalone in both *Voices* (as 'Verse Free and Unfree', October 1919) and *Playboy: A Portfolio of Art and Satire* (as 'The Poetry of the Present', Summer–Fall 1919), Lawrence called for an instant poetry to oppose the emergent modernist formalism. It was a poetry ranged against 'the crystalline, pearl-hard jewels, the poems of the eternities'.[22] Lawrence said he wanted to feel 'the heavy, silting, sucking mud' of the world in pure naked-ness. He wanted nothing that was unmoving, abstract, infinite or eternal. He demanded 'the still, white seething, the incandescence and the coldness of the incarnate moment: the moment, the quick of all change and haste and oppo-sition: the moment, the immediate present, the Now'.[23] It was a poetry with roots in modernity rather than in the classics and in tradition. As Eliot and Pound looked to Europe, Lawrence followed them back to America. Lawrence's verse functions, probably unconsciously, as critical inversion of T. E. Hulme's classicist pivot. In the posthumously published lecture given at Clifford's Inn Hall during 1912, Hulme defined Romanticism as 'spilt religion', likening its messiness and blurring of human experience to pouring treacle over the din-ner table.[24] In contrast, Lawrence wants to explore the treacle. He is fascinated with the beguiling and amorphous nature of the mud's slipperiness, its dual nature, part liquid and part solid, a fascination that can be set against Hulme's crystalline dryness.[25] His poetry wanted to celebrate the outpouring passion of the fleshy moment, the very instability of it all, its opposition to a poetry recol-lected in tranquillity.

Poetry placed its emphasis on the locality of language. In March 1919, for example, Vachel Lindsay reviewed *Yanks: A.E.F. Verse* (1919), an anthology taken from *Stars and Stripes*, the journal of the American Expeditionary Force. Like Edward Osborn's *The New Elizabethans*, *Yanks* was an odd and uneven anthology. It began with an introduction that apologised for its disjointed metre and amateurish rhymes. None of this was to matter though because, like Brooke's work, it was veridical. 'It was', its editor said, 'inspired by mud and cooties and gas and mess-kits and Boche 77's and home and mother.'[26] The specificity of the language and the lack of technical virtuosity was the point. It was a poetry that offered access to unmediated fleshy experience, a direct route

---

[22] D. H. Lawrence, 'Preface to *New Poems*', in *The Poems*, I, pp. 645–9 (pp. 646–7). From 1916 to 1917 Lawrence worked on the essays collected as *Studies in Classic American Literature*. Several appeared in the summer of 1919 in the *English Review*.

[23] Lawrence, 'Preface to *New Poems*', p. 646.

[24] T. E. Hulme, 'Romanticism and Classicism', in *The Collected Writings of T. E. Hulme*, pp. 59–73 (p. 62).

[25] It also predicts the reflections on mud in Jean Paul Sartre, *Being and Nothingness: An Essay on Phenomenological Ontology*, trans. by Hazel E. Barnes (London: Methuen, 1958; repr. Abingdon: Routledge, 2003), pp. 628–9 (first published in French as *L'Être et le néant*, 1943).

[26] John T. Winterich, 'Foreword', in *Yanks: A.E.F. Verse* (New York: G. P. Putnam's Sons, 1919), pp. v–vii (p. v).

into biochemistry unencumbered by the scaffolding of poetics. As a source book of A.E.F. emotion it was in effect a guidebook to the combatant's soul.[27]

Lindsay, looking to move things on from Whitman's legacy, saw the anthology as a foundational moment in modern American verse. He suggested it developed Edgar Lee Masters's creation of an authentic and local language in *The Spoon River Anthology* (April 1915):

> It is written in the American language. It is colloquial, without too much slang, the easy American dialect of college boys and farm-hands alike. This is a step toward the future idiom for our informal verse [. . .] It has not the least notion it is poetry. It is all an embarrassed refusal to be aesthetic, heroic or stoical.[28]

Monroe agreed. In 'A Year After' (*Poetry*: July 1919) she appealed to American combatants to use their experience so 'they may prepare and enrich the soil, so that the seed may not fall on rocky or barren ground; and they may give the sapling a fair chance at healthy growth'.[29] These earthy images in *Poetry* are borrowed from Brooke's war sonnets. They are the same images Wallace Stevens used to choke the throat of his reimagined recruit. What had served an English nationalism in 1915, though, *Poetry* reutilised for an American poetic patriotism. Murry and Eliot had shifted to the idea that poetry was anathema to event. In contrast, for Lindsay, Monroe and Lawrence it was technique that was anathema to the particular. They reconfigured the cultural inflections of style as a revolt against aboriginality, a position intended to ostracise the London-based expatriates from the succour of native soil.

Eliot had associated the vices of American poetry with those of the poetries of war for some time. He had, deliberately it would seem, singled out Seeger from Edward Osborn's cohort in 'The New Elizabethans and the Old'. This made the essay the perfect material to publish in Knopf's volume. Eliot had also subtly titled his April 1918 review of Amy Lowell's *Tendencies in Modern American Poetry* (1917) as 'Disjecta Membra'. He took the phrase from his 1916 letters home describing Maurice Haigh-Wood's experience of the body in pieces. In 'Disjecta Membra' the key vice of the American poet, Eliot said, was the 'provinciality of point of view'.[30] Eliot did not name Monroe, but it is hard to think *Poetry* was not his object.

The immaturity and narrow-mindedness of the American Renaissance was one of Eliot's recurrent themes in the months leading to the composition of

---

[27] Ibid. p. vi.
[28] Vachel Lindsay, 'A Doughboy Anthology', *Poetry*, 13.6 (March 1919), 329–35 (p. 329).
[29] H.M. [Harriet Monroe], 'A Year After', *Poetry*, 14.4 (July 1919), 209–11 (p. 211).
[30] T. S. Eliot, 'Disjecta Membra', in *Apprentice Years, 1905–1918*, pp. 695–7 (p. 697).

both 'Gerontion' and 'Tradition and the Individual Talent'. In preparation for its publication in the *Little Review*, for example, Eliot added back to 'Whispers of Immortality' a fourth stanza originally written in 1917. It argues, in the same vein as Murry, for a poetry that shows its expertise through its craft rather than through the narrow confines of experience.[31] The final line of the fifth stanza of 'A Cooking Egg' (*Coterie*: May 1919; *March–October 1917*) also changed at least twice in the spring of 1919. In the poem's early typescripts, Eliot simply stated the contrast between Lucrezia Borgia's anecdotes and those of the less glamorous Pipit. The comparison had no ancillary detail. In May's edition of *Coterie*, however, Eliot pinned the difference on Pipit's memory. It was the empty mental faculty. The matter needed saying much more plainly though and Eliot finally settled in *Ara Vos Prec* on experience itself, the paucity of it, being Pipit's problem.[32] She simply had nothing interesting to say because she had done nothing interesting. These issues are again emphasised by Eliot's deliberations over the poem's epigraph. He settled on one from François Villon, cited in both 'The New Elizabethans and the Old' and 'A Romantic Patrician' (*The Athenæum*: May 1919), which emphasised the difference between age and intellectual maturity.

Raymond Williams's differentiation in *Keywords* (1976, rev. 1983) between 'experience past' and 'experience present' helps to unpick Eliot's meaning. The first usage Williams links to arguments deployed against rashness, of learning from experience through experiment and observation. The concept opposes the expert to the lay person according to an index of innocence. In contrast, the second usage connotes experience understood as an act of conscious awareness, an authenticity encompassing bodily and psychic affect.[33] Eliot's change from anecdote to memory to experience in 'A Cooking Egg' deliberately scorns 'experience present' and makes emptiness the essence of Pipit's entire being. The poem's obviously disdainful attitude to a certain kind of society points towards that accumulative, economic type of experience which Eliot would firmly deride in 'The Problems of the Shakespeare Sonnets' (1927) when he

---

[31] T. S. Eliot, 'Whispers of Immortality', in *Collected and Uncollected Poems*, pp. 47–8 (p. 47); Christopher Ricks and Jim McCue, 'Textual History: "Whispers of Immortality"', in Eliot, *Practical Cats and Further Verses*, pp. 350–5.

[32] Christopher Ricks and Jim McCue, 'Textual History: "A Cooking Egg"', in Eliot, *Practical Cats and Further Verses*, pp. 344–5 (p. 345 n. 20); T. S. Eliot, 'A Cooking Egg', in *Collected and Uncollected Poems*, pp. 38–9 (p. 38). We can date the late changes to early July when Eliot sent a draft to Rodker with 'Gerontion'. T. S. Eliot, letter to John Rodker (9 July 1919), in *The Letters of T. S. Eliot*, I, p. 372.

[33] Raymond Williams, *Keywords: A Vocabulary of Culture and Society*, rev. edn (London: Fontana Press, 1983), p. 126.

contrasted experience for the poet and for the stockbroker, and again in the same terms in *After Strange Gods* (1934).[34]

This experiential distinction was the theoretical basis of Eliot's critique of American poetry and prose. In 'American Literature' (*The Athenæum*: 25 April 1919), Eliot judged that the American artist was destined to always fall short of literary greatness because they had the wrong type of experience:

> Their world was thin; it was not corrupt enough. Worst of all it was secondhand; it was not original and self-dependent – it was a shadow. Poe and Whitman, like bulbs in a glass bottle, could only exhaust what was in them. Hawthorne, more tentacular and inquisitive, sucked every actual germ of nourishment out of his granite soil; but the soil was mostly granite.[35]

This partly explains Eliot's enthusiasm for being amidst the alarums of war and the critique of his brother's immaturity. In 'The Education of Taste' (*The Athenæum*: 27 June 1919) Eliot appropriated William James's concept of 'the *Apperzeptionsmass*' to conceptualise the real value in experience.[36] For James the *Apperzeptionsmass*, borrowing from Johann Friedrich Herbart, was the psychological means by which a new idea became sensible through assimilation into the existing body of possessed ideas. In 'Reflections on Contemporary Poetry [IV]', published weeks later, Eliot transformed this into a cultural model:

> It is not true that the development of a writer is a function of his development as a man, but it is possible to say that there is a close analogy between the sort of experience which develops a man and the sort of experience which develops a writer. Experience in living may leave the literary embryo still dormant, and the progress of literary development may to a considerable extent take place in a soul left immature in living.[37]

The context for these reflections was Herbert Read's war book *Naked Warriors*.[38] Eliot's point was that Read's experience, as with the Americans, was not the kind

---

[34] T. S. Eliot, 'The Problems of the Shakespeare Sonnets', in *Literature, Politics, Belief, 1927–1929*, pp. 36–9 (p. 37); T. S. Eliot, *After Strange Gods: A Primer of Modern Heresy*, in *The Complete Prose of T. S. Eliot*, V: *Tradition and Orthodoxy, 1934–1939*, ed. by Imran Javadi and others (2017), pp. 15–55 (p. 28).

[35] T. S. Eliot, 'American Literature', in *The Perfect Critic, 1919–1926*, pp. 21–5 (p. 24). In 'The Hawthorne Aspect' (*Little Review*: August 1918) Eliot had briefly granted Hawthorne antennae as the means of accessing psychological truth. T. S. Eliot, 'The Hawthorne Aspect', in *Apprentice Years, 1905–1918*, pp. 736–44 (p. 739).

[36] T. S. Eliot, 'The Education of Taste', in *The Perfect Critic, 1919–1926*, pp. 60–5 (p. 64).

[37] Eliot, 'Reflections on Contemporary Poetry [IV]', p. 66.

[38] Herbert Read, letter to T. S. Eliot ([March?] 1919), qtd in *The Letters of T. S. Eliot*, I, p. 329 n. 3.

of experience that was necessarily the basis of poetry. Instead, Eliot said that it was through the body of existing images stored within European civilisation that the poet could reveal the truth about violence to a reader.[39] For Eliot, this was really a form of self-promotion. He illustrated his point using lines from George Chapman's *Bussy D'Ambois* (1607) and their dialogue with Seneca. Eliot had adapted the same lines with their reflections on Ursa Major during the previous month in the early drafts of 'Gerontion' to speak about the chthonic origins of the waves of post-war violence.[40]

What Eliot in effect proposed in 'Reflections on Contemporary Poetry [IV]' was an alternative form of gnosticism. He asked that poetry ground itself on a corpse. Not on Osborn's brotherhood of death-in-combat. Rather, poets should ground their art on 'a feeling of profound kinship, or rather of a peculiar personal intimacy, with another, probably a dead author'. Not then the experience that transformed Read, but an intellectual encounter. Eliot proposed that 'when a young writer is seized with his first passion of this sort he may be changed, metamorphosed almost, within a few weeks even; from a bundle of second-hand sentiments into a person'. Not Whitman's wound-dressing as the prelude to poetic personality, but the recognition, in keeping with the conclusions of Pound's journey into France in search of the troubadours, of one's living mind as having previously lived in another. This was to be a non-sentimental encounter with the dead, one creating, in Eliot's own words, 'an unshakeable confidence', an alternative 'secret knowledge' amounting to an 'intimacy, with the dead man'.[41]

Eliot meant the intimacy of a close and private friendship, a feeling of detailed knowledge with a body of work. It is unlikely he consciously meant the intimacy of a sexual encounter. The connotation hangs there nonetheless and there is a real sense of a pillaging of the dead.[42] Eliot wanted to reformulate the charged physical contact of combat, the type of battle-front tactility best described for example by Santanu Das (2002), into a reaching out that touched the Other through *écriture*.[43] Having set aside Osborn's account of trench brotherhood, then, Eliot had then merely created a counter fraternity. The being-there and the being-in-it, the secret or ciphered encounter with the body in pieces, became a different encounter. It was an encounter marked by the instant of recognition of the poetic self in the poetic Other, a glimpse from the rubble of profanity inside the core of the sacred. This was a psycho-cultural version of the *Apperzeptionsmass* with its own form of mystical knowledge,

---

[39] Eliot, 'Reflections on Contemporary Poetry [IV]', pp. 67–8.

[40] Ibid. pp. 68, 70 n. 3.

[41] Ibid. p. 66.

[42] Sarah Cole, 'Modernism, Male Intimacy, and the Great War', *ELH*, 68 (2001), 469–500.

[43] Santanu Das, '"Kiss me, Hardy": Intimacy, Gender, and Gesture in World War I Trench Literature', *Modernism/modernity*, 9.1 (2002), 51–74.

one that argued for a non-combat gnosticism as the only antidote to Read's combat gnosticism.

'ALL LIFE IN A LIFE' AND T. S. ELIOT'S RACIAL SLUR

The most graphic illustration of Eliot's engagement with these ideas and with American poetics comes from his central position in a transatlantic exchange of essays and letters that precedes the composition of 'Gerontion' and 'Tradition and the Individual Talent'.[44] Edgar Jepson precipitated the debate in a damning response to Monroe's request for an article celebrating the winners of *Poetry*'s annual poetry prize. It became known in modernist circles as the 'Sheep's Wool correspondence'. This followed from Jepson's criticism of the flat line – 'his hair was black as sheep's wool that is black' – in Masters's poem 'All Life in a Life' (*Poetry*: March 1916). 'All Life in a Life' is a modern retelling of the First Gospel and it won *Poetry*'s Levenson Prize for 1915–16.[45] After *Poetry* refused to print Jepson's article, it found its way into the *English Review* in May 1918, a condensed version following with Pound's annotations in the *Little Review* in September 1918 under the title 'The Western School'. Pound simultaneously printed Eliot's 'Sweeney among the Nightingales' and 'Whispers of Immortality' to illustrate Jepson's argument.

Jepson described the development of the new school of American poetry based in Chicago. He described its overt focus on 'steel rails, journalism, moving pictures, popular tales and songs, local festivals, world's fairs, clamorous cities'.[46] Contrary to its stated goals and *Poetry*'s aims, Jepson concluded that these poets were not at all securely rooted in their native soil: 'they create no new diction, no new idiom. They create nothing. There is no new, authochthonous note in them. They are as rancid as *Ben Hur*.'[47] American poems 'were punk', he said.[48] As a contrast, Jepson took Pound's line that Eliot was a poet who did what the American school professed to do. 'His poetry', Jepson said, was 'securely rooted in its native soil; it has a new poetic diction; it is as autochthonous as Theocritus. It is new in form [. . .] it is musical with a new music.'[49] As Jepson emphasised in a later tit-for-tat exchange, the art was a matter of handling and not of content.

The debate pulled in participants on both sides. Pound said Jepson had not gone far enough in the description of the awfulness of the American mood, somewhat ironically we should note because Jepson had not lived and suffered

---

[44] T. S. Eliot to Edgar Jepson (22 September 1919), in *The Letters of T. S. Eliot*, I, p. 397.

[45] Edgar Lee Masters, 'All Life in a Life', *Poetry*, 7.6 (March 1916), 292–300 (p. 292).

[46] Jepson, 'The Western School', p. 4.

[47] Ibid. p. 8.

[48] Edgar Jepson, 'That International Episode', *Little Review*, 5.10–11 (February–March 1919), 62–[5] (p. 62).

[49] Jepson, 'The Western School', p. 9.

there.[50] Monroe countered that *Poetry* had rejected Jepson's article because of its 'cheap incompetence'.[51] Hartley ambivalently likened reading Eliot's poetry to 'lemon juice [. . .] running through the optical nerve, down the marrow of my spine'.[52] Williams took up the debate in the prologue to *Kora in Hell* (1920; *September 1918*), finding the final stanza of 'La Figlia Che Piange' 'warped out of alignment, obscured in meaning even to the point of an absolute unintelligibility by the inevitable straining after a rhyme'.[53] The debate ran through to May 1919 when Conrad Aiken responded in the *New Republic*. For Aiken American poets glorified recording the ordinary in a way that turned poetry into a yawn.[54] He illustrated his point by suggesting Louis Untermeyer was a poet who simply could not detach his ego from the here and now.[55] Untermeyer responded by questioning the Olympian impersonality of an Anglo-American modernism that had become a linguistic conjuring trick, a poetic always at risk that it be defrauded. Eliot's cerebral irony was the problem. The emotions of 'despair, hate, longing, any hunger' will find words, he said, but the process Aiken described and sponsored worked in the opposite direction. Words set out to find emotions.[56] Whether Untermeyer knowingly reversed Murry's terms in this article is moot. Nonetheless his critique rightly targeted the same point. Rather than Murry's idea in which the emotional content of immediate experience burst into and then out of words, Untermeyer suggested that the very hankering after words left poems that were no more than empty husks of meaning, husks with no original emotional content.

Eliot was very aware of his position in the correspondence. He boasted of it to Charlotte Eliot upon publication. He told Quinn of Aiken's article on 9 July 1919. Quinn took the hint and promised on 26 August to suggest that Knopf use it as commentary on the jacket of *Poems*. Eliot and Jepson also became quite close. On 11 July Eliot asked Jepson's view of the poems he had published in the latest instalment of *Art and Letters*. On 22 September it would appear he intended to ask for it on two further poems in development, most probably 'Gerontion' and 'The Death of the Duchess' (1971).[57] It was to Jepson that Eliot confessed the transatlantic debate had given him much pleasure. It had ended just as 'I wanted to join in', Eliot said.[58]

---

[50] Ezra Pound, letter to Edgar Jepson ([? May] 1918), in *The Letters of Ezra Pound*, pp. 194–5 (p. 194).

[51] H.M. [Harriet Monroe], 'An International Episode', *Poetry*, 13.2 (November 1918), 94–5 (p. 95).

[52] Marsden Hartley, 'Breakfast Resume', *Little Review*, 5.7 (November 1918), 46–50 (p. 47).

[53] William Carlos Williams, *Kora in Hell: Improvisations* (Boston: Four Seas, 1920), p. 27.

[54] Conrad Aiken, 'The Ivory Tower – I', *New Republic*, 19.236 (10 May 1919), 58–60 (p. 59).

[55] Ibid. p. 60.

[56] Louis Untermeyer, 'The Ivory Tower – II', *New Republic*, 19.236 (10 May 1919), 60–1 (p. 61).

[57] T. S. Eliot, letter to Edgar Jepson (11 July 1919), in *The Letters of T. S. Eliot*, I, p. 379.

[58] Eliot, letter to Edgar Jepson (22 September 1919), p. 397.

Eliot did clearly join in though. Compare side by side the opening section from Masters's prize-winning poem and lines from 'Gerontion':

Masters	Eliot
His father had a large family	My house is a decayed house,
Of girls and boys, and he was	And the Jew squats on the window-
born and bred	sill, the owner,
In a barn or kind of cattle shed.	Spawned in some estaminet of
But he was a hardy youngster,	Antwerp,
and grew to be	Blistered in Brussels, patched and
A boy with eyes that sparkled	peeled in London.
like a rod	The goat coughs at night in the field
Of white-hot iron in the black-	overhead;
smith shop.	Rocks, moss, stonecrop, iron,
His face was ruddy like a rising	merds.[60]
moon,	
And his hair was black as	
sheep's wool that is black[.][59]	

Jepson claimed Masters's poem was just 'bad, bald, prosy prose'.[61] Eliot's poem is far more damning of Masters's attempt to update the Gospels. Amidst the decay of modernity, Jesus is no longer *Iēsus Nazarēnus, Rēx Iūdaeōrum*. Rather, in the earliest drafts and versions of the poem, he was notably a decapitalised Jew, a shift designed to emphasise the tone of degradation within the poem.[62] Masters's 'large family' gives way to a spawning. 'Born and bred' devolves into that ugly 'squat'. Eliot's swaddled child comes from 'some estaminet' (etymologically from the Walloon *stamina*, a cow shed), not 'a barn or kind of cattle shed'. The 'hardy youngster' has grown up, but not to be a 'smith'. He is an agent of profit, in Gerontion's eyes the illegitimate owner of his rented property. The 'iron' of artisanship has given way to a broken wasteland of rootless bog plants, sedums sucking nourishment from granite, a world of excreta. It is an appalling image. Eliot's Jew shits on Gerontion.

Two features of the anti-Semitism need to be emphasised. First, the nature of it. Eliot's poem is invoking Thomas Aquinas's *maxime praeter naturam* and in turn Pound's notion of the usurious loan as a perverted instrument of exchange. The Aristotelian and Christian opposition to usury meet here as the

---

[59] Masters, 'All Life in a Life', p. 292.
[60] Eliot, 'Gerontion', p. 31.
[61] Jepson, 'The Western School', p. 7.
[62] Christopher Ricks and Jim McCue, 'Textual History: "Gerontion"', in Eliot, *Practical Cats and Further Verses*, pp. 339–41 (p. 339 n. 8).

racist links one unnatural divine birth, contrary to the laws of nature, to the unnatural creation of money, of money begetting money in the rentier's hands. As a symbol of that transformation, Masters's romantic notion of the 'sheep' as lamb of god becomes Eliot's lustful 'goat' Baphomet, the satanic figure of the Tarot. This is not the saviour of humankind at all, but the destroyer of worlds.

The point in 'Gerontion' is that Masters's poem is no way at all to speak about modernity. The earlier poem is the object of fun. It is *this* that Jesus has become during war and not *that*, 'Gerontion' says. Eliot's poem satirised Masters's out-of-touch poetic just as reciprocally it attested to a counter wisdom. There is a perverse logic to it that reflects modernist anti-Semitism of the time. It can be seen in Virginia Woolf's confession in June 1918 that 'there is something condensed in all Jews'. She said she felt about Mark Gertler, as she did 'about some women, that unnatural repressions have forced him into unnatural assertions'.[63] Woolf imagines the persecuted Jew having evolved in such a way that Gertler hands back to the world the violence perpetrated against him. He is a concentrated embodiment of the world's malevolent forces.[64]

The second point to emphasise is the historical circumstance of these obviously racist slurs. Eliot knew quite well the dire geopolitical situation in 1919 having taken on a role in a new department at Lloyds Bank. He was effectively a foreign exchange analyst, examining the changing economic landscape as the basis for understanding the bank's status as international creditor. Eliot ought to have known, and probably would have known, of the appalling position of Europe. In *The Cambridge History of the First World War* (2013), Bruno Cabanes graphically illustrates the state of the world: the ongoing violence in British colonies, the large-scale displacement of refugees in Poland and the Baltic states following the defeat of the White Armies in Russia, the mass repatriation of soldiers from foreign soils, the liberation of prisoners of war, the growing necessity of aid to avert a humanitarian crisis, the urgent need to control a global pandemic, the emergence of a new post-war framework of international law.[65] Eliot would also have known that the situation was grave closer to home. Jon Lawrence (2003) explains that during 1919 the threat of imminent violence amidst a precipitous economic slump, growing post-demobilisation unemployment, the increasing demand for rent controls, recurrent outbreaks of barrack

---

[63] Virginia Woolf, diary entry (Monday, 24 June 1918), in *The Diary of Virginia Woolf*, I, pp. 158–60 (pp. 158–9).

[64] That Woolf had an acid tongue and was married to a Jew is a weak defence. Janet Wolff, *AngloModern: Painting and Modernity in Britain and the United States* (Ithaca, NY: Cornell University Press, 2003), p. 126.

[65] Bruno Cabanes, '1919: Aftermath', in *The Cambridge History of the First World War*, ed. by Jay Winter, 3 vols (Cambridge: Cambridge University Press, 2013), I: *Global War*, pp. 172–97 (pp. 186–90).

rioting and the widespread targeting of war profiteers accumulated and threatened to unleash the forces of brutalisation on the British establishment.[66]

Inevitably racial prejudice stoked the violent spiral. Throughout the spring and summer rioting took place in London's East End, Cardiff and Liverpool. Rioters targeted their anger at non-white employees and especially at the lascar community of sailors from across Southeast Asia and East Africa serving an understaffed British merchant fleet. West Indians employed in the munitions industry were also a target.[67] Street battles in Glasgow, Salford and Hull redeployed ugly stereotypes of the Chinese community as alleged opium smugglers, black seamen as bent on miscegenation and Jews as importers of Bolshevism.[68] David Cesarani (1993) cites one article of April 1919 in which the *East London Observer* criticised British Parliament for its inadequate response: '"nothing at all is intended to be done to meet the demand of the country to be protected from floods of alien spies, enemies and traitors, the mentally, morally and physically diseased and the parasitical scum of the earth."'[69]

The British Nationality and Status of Aliens Act of August 1918 had granted the government powers to revoke individual naturalisation certificates, but anti-alien rhetoric was the dominant feature of the December 1918 election. According to Cesarani, the Aliens Restriction (Amendment) Bill introduced in early 1919 went further and managed to elevate anti-alienist sentiment 'to a new level of viciousness'.[70] It allowed the government to deport enemy 'aliens' unless a new advisory committee exempted them. Incitement to disaffection or unrest was one ground for deportation. 'Aliens' were not permitted to enter the country for five years, hold land or stakes in key industries or to serve on British ships. The government even prohibited those who had been resident since 1914 from changing their name, from joining the civil service, from serving on juries and from acting on merchant vessels. Parliament strengthened the legislation with the Aliens Order of 1920. It required any 'alien' seeking work to have permission from the Ministry of Labour and granted unprecedented powers to police discretion.

---

[66] Jon Lawrence, 'Forging a Peaceable Kingdom: War, Violence, and Fear of Brutalization in Post-First World War Britain', *Journal of Modern History*, 75.3 (September 2003), 557–89.

[67] Humayun Ansari, *'The Infidel Within': Muslims in Britain since 1800* (London: Hurst & Company, 2004), pp. 40–3. On the lascar as a symbol of alterity in 1919, see T. S. Eliot, 'A Foreign Mind' (*The Athenæum*: July 1919), in *The Perfect Critic, 1919–1926*, pp. 72–6 (p. 73).

[68] Jacqueline Jenkinson, 'The 1919 Race Riots in Britain: A Survey', in *Under the Imperial Carpet: Essays in Black History 1780–1950*, ed. by Rainer Lotz and Ian Pegg (Crawley: Rabbit Press, 1986), pp. 182–207; Jacqueline Jenkinson, *Black 1919: Riots, Racism and Resistance in Imperial Britain* (Liverpool: Liverpool University Press, 2009).

[69] Qtd in David Cesarani, 'An Alien Concept? The Continuity of Anti-Alienism in British Society before 1940', in *The Internment of Aliens in Twentieth Century Britain*, ed. by David Cesarani and Tony Kushner (Abingdon: Routledge, 1993), pp. 25–52 (p. 38).

[70] Ibid. p. 39.

By 1919, non-naturalised East European Jews, most having arrived before 1914, were the largest body of 'aliens' in Britain. The state expelled many for alleged subversive activities, the Jew becoming an ugly synonym for anarchism, espionage and Bolshevism.[71] This was a microcosm of a broader international tilt back towards anti-Semitism, most evidentially in the widely publicised persecution of and pogroms aimed at the Jewish community in Lviv and Kielce (November 1918), Minsk (April 1919) and Kiev (June–September 1919). On 21 May, shortly after Eliot put pen to paper on the first draft of 'Gerontion', several thousand people gathered in Madison Square Garden to protest against the pogroms in Poland. Protesters held similar events across the Northeast and Midwest.[72] On 28 June, as Eliot revised the second version of his poem, the League of Nations signed the Little Treaty of Versailles, a treaty designed to give some protection to Polish minorities alongside its more famous sibling.[73] At much the same time, Henry Morgenthau began investigating the Polish atrocities against the Jewish community. He finally issued his report shortly after Eliot finished the final draft of 'Gerontion'.[74] The compositional history of 'Gerontion' sits then within an enormous wave of virulent nationalism and amidst widespread anti-immigrant feeling with a renewed emphasis on the figure of the Jew as a homeless, threatening economic parasite. It is simply implausible to believe that Eliot deployed his racial slur in 'Gerontion' without purpose.[75] But what purpose?

A Theory of Non-combat Gnosticism: 'Tradition and the Individual Talent'

Before addressing that question, we need to first examine 'Tradition and the Individual Talent' in relation to the evolving evidence. In particular, we need to take more account of its historical context and especially of the silent Other

---

[71] Ibid. pp. 38–40.

[72] On the dating see typescript 1 (ts1) in Ricks and McCue, 'Textual History: "Gerontion"', p. 339. For detailed discussion of 'Gerontion' and its compositional history see Jamie Wood, '"Here I Am": Eliot, "Gerontion", and the Great War', *Biography*, 41.1 (2018), 116–42. For discussion of the protests and the pogroms see C. S. Monaco, *The Rise of Modern Jewish Politics: Extraordinary Movement* (New York: Routledge, 2013), p. 173.

[73] See ts2 in Ricks and McCue, 'Textual History: "Gerontion"', p. 339.

[74] See ts3 in ibid. By 9 July Eliot had sent drafts to Mary Hutchinson and Sydney Schiff, asking Hutchinson for the return of the manuscript before leaving for a French walking holiday with Pound on 9 August. Eliot then added lines 69–73 to the verso of the second leaf (Ricks and McCue, 'Textual History: "Gerontion"', p. 339) before allowing Pound to annotate the poem as the pair travelled together through the Dordogne and Corrèze. Eliot returned to England on 31 August, finished the poem and sent it to Quinn. Lewis had already discussed it with Quinn.

[75] See also the contemporaneous anti-Semitism in 'A Cooking Egg' and its use of an apostrophe in Golders Green. Jon Silken discusses this in *The Life of Metrical and Free Verse in Twentieth-Century Poetry* (Basingstoke: Macmillan, 1997), p. 53 n. 1.

that is its target. It is certainly exemplary of Eliot's emergent critique of direct experience and sentimentality and of the amateurism in the emergent modernism of Chicago. We might also read it as the culmination of the five-year-long modernist response to the ideology of war verse. That it does not mention the war or war verse directly, especially given it is a product of its aftermath, ought to raise our suspicions and remind us, as Eliot told his mother, that this was a delicate subject in the summer of 1919. On 5 July, for example, troops marched by his office at Lloyds Bank in Cornhill as part of the extensive preparations for Peace Day. Eliot began 'Tradition and the Individual Talent' around six days later. Like W. B. Yeats in 1914, Eliot needed to speak in whispers.

The essay begins where Eliot's critique of the American Renaissance and the recalibration of the *Apperzeptionsmass* ended. Eliot wants us to understand that the individuality of a poet's work comes directly from those parts of his mind where the dead poets are most active as influence. The gendered terms are Eliot's here. He suggests that there is a quasi-telepathy at play in which dead voices assert themselves through the medium of the living poet. He reinforces the point made in 'The New Elizabethans and the Old' that he means by this not the adolescent poet but the one in his maturity.[76] We can see this as the moment, following David Goldie, that Eliot's earlier emphasis on immaturity finally gave way to the concept of tradition. It suggests 'The New Elizabethans and the Old' as an important bridge in that process. It may also explain why that earlier essay never found its way directly into *The Sacred Wood*. Its core themes are in effect so thoroughly digested in that volume that Eliot need never mention the war, not once on any page.

Eliot introduces the relationship with the dead poet as a relationship with tradition. It is a form of gnosis from the first moment it arrives in the essay. Like combat gnosticism, it too is a knowledge that 'cannot be inherited'. The poet must acquire it. Whereas the fleshwitness's suffering confers the ability to speak of evil directly, Eliot's poet gains wisdom as compensation for his journey into the sacred wood of literature. Both gnosticisms are tough rites of passage. To progress 'beyond his twenty-fifth year', Eliot argued, the poet must understand the past and the continuous present of that past by having read everything since Homer.[77] Since most estimates put the average age of the First World War soldier at somewhere between twenty-three and twenty-six years, and the average age of death was twenty-seven, it is again difficult to see how this did not function in a post-war society as an oblique reference to the soldier.[78] We might accuse Eliot of many things, but he was not without sensitivity. He had

---

[76] T. S. Eliot, 'Tradition and the Individual Talent', in *The Perfect Critic, 1919–1926*, pp. 105–14 (p. 106).

[77] Ibid.

[78] On the ages of combatants see [Anonymous], 'WW1 Age at Enlistment', <https://mq.edu.au/on_campus/museums_and_collections/australian_history_museum/online_exhibitions/oua_anzac_unit/wwi_age_at_enlistment> [accessed 25 March 2022].

not cut himself off from society in the way Pound had at this time. Lloyds Bank paid him to analyse the world economy and he toured England's smaller cities in 1919 at their request. He knew the state and mood of the nation.

Eliot places value in 'Tradition and the Individual Talent' on critical reading, on a broad library of the classics, as Eliot told Mary Hutchinson in an elucidative letter written at the same time as the essay.[79] In so doing, he replaces the combatant's journey into the mutism of affective experience with what he calls, following F. H. Bradley, the historical sense. This intellectual wisdom arises from maturity and enables the individual to see the proper relations of affect and the world. It is, as Eliot wrote to Hutchinson, the means to create a mind that is a balanced arbiter between the demands of feeling and reason.[80]

This historical sense, whilst wearing Bradley's clothes, is however just a more formal version of Murry's original solution to the problem of Sassoon. By becoming traditional, in Eliot's positively valenced sense of that word, the writer becomes more aware of his own situation. He can order the local and particular. War, with its morass of immediate sense data, the chaos of disturbed dreams and the disorder of shattered limbs, is one obvious example of data that needs ordering. Eliot reinforces that reference when he insists that no poet stands alone. The poet cannot mean anything except in relative terms.[81] The solitary poet, the one stranded in the mud, howls at the storm with Lear, while Eliot's poet hears the cries of a universal pain because he is outside that maelstrom.

We can now see the full extent of Eliot's restructuring of William James's *Apperzeptionsmass* in *Talks to Teachers* (1899) by placing the two texts side by side:

James	*Eliot*
In this gradual process of interaction between the new and the old, not only is the new modified and determined by the particular sort of old which apperceives it, but the apperceiving mass, the old itself, is modified by the particular kind of new which it assimilates.[82]	The existing monuments form an ideal order among themselves, which is modified by the introduction of the new (the really new) work of art among them. The existing order is complete before the new work arrives; for order to persist after the supervention of novelty, the *whole* existing order must be, if ever so slightly, altered.[83]

[79] T. S. Eliot, letter to Mary Hutchinson ([11? July 1919], in *The Letters of T. S. Eliot*, I, pp. 377–9 (p. 378).

[80] Ibid.

[81] Eliot, 'Tradition and the Individual Talent', p. 106.

[82] William James, *Talks to Teachers on Psychology and to Students on Some of Life's Ideals*, in William James, *Writings 1878–1899*, ed. by Gerald E. Myers (New York: Library of America, 1992), pp. 705–887 (p. 805).

[83] Eliot, 'Tradition and the Individual Talent', p. 106.

James is speaking of the fusion between a new impression and the mind as it existed prior to the receipt of that impression, of the intermingling of Williams's experience past and experience present. James wants us to understand the mind's inherent resistance to the new thing, its inherent tendency to what he calls an '"old fogyism"' which acts as a self-protection mechanism or polices the established internal set of laws.[84] Notably, such '"fogyism"' begins according to James at twenty-five, Eliot's chosen age for the decisive emergence of the historical sense. James thinks of this economically. The bigger the stock of ideas the more capable is the man and the more likely that he will balance his behaviour.[85] This really is, following but inverting the target of James Campbell, a phallic discourse. It is the size of the *Apperzeptionsmass* that governs value, and this makes it the perfect tool for Eliot's notion of the types of experience that matter for poetry. It allows Eliot to take James's oppositions and simply change the words. 'Impressions' and 'mind' are substituted for 'artworks' and 'tradition'.

Eliot's poet is then a true innovator. His role is to insert innovation into the existing order. He takes care of the established canon. He improves it and passes it on, a development yes, but one which does not 'superannuate' or retire the past with the laurels of a pension.[86] Naturally, Eliot must defend himself against the obvious criticism that this gnosticism, this cultural *Apperzeptionsmass*, requires enormous erudition. To which Eliot responds in a beg, borrow or steal fashion, insisting the poet must get this through 'a continual surrender of himself as he is at the moment to something which is more valuable'. 'As he is at the moment': not a poetics of presence at the site of the body in pieces, but an 'Impersonal theory of poetry' that amounts to the loss of presence. With that letting go of the ego – a 'depersonalization' – comes Eliot's famous image of the platinum in the test tube magically producing acid from gaseous origins.[87] This amalgamates the tropes discussed in earlier chapters, especially those focused on containerisation and the *magus*. As Eliot made much clearer in 'Modern Tendencies in Poetry' (1920), an essay that began as a lecture to the Arts League of Service in October 1919, the crucial point in this chemical process is that 'the platinum does not enter into the combination but merely looks on'.[88] It is, to return to Edward Thomas in 1914 and then Ford Madox Ford in 1916 and then Murry in 1918, the looking on that is the absolute key.[89] It is afterwardness that defines the poet in relation to action.

---

[84] James, *Talks to Teachers*, p. 803.

[85] Ibid. p. 806.

[86] Eliot, 'Tradition and the Individual Talent', p. 107.

[87] Ibid. pp. 108, 109.

[88] T. S. Eliot, 'Modern Tendencies in Poetry', in *The Perfect Critic, 1919–1926*, pp. 212–25 (p. 215).

[89] We can note similar concepts at the time of Eliot's essay. See 'remote imaginativeness' in Padraic Colum, 'Rilke's Poems', *Poetry*, 14.3 (June 1919), 168–70 (p. 168). See also 'the looker-on' in Marsden Hartley, 'The Business of Poetry', *Poetry*, 15.3 (December 1919), 152–8 (p. 157).

The entire modernist distaste for war verse in the intra-war years had been based on a model of bodily overflow. Murry had seen it as a spilling out of the body beyond its harder boundaries. Eliot's position is more subtle than that. His poet is 'a more finely perfected medium' for containment. What the immature poet lacks in Eliot's schematic is the ability to synthesise because he is too active and caught up in things. The act of proper affective containment is inactive. It is not a surrendering to Lawrence's seething moment. The moral witness's experience is then no more than the abundant gases of the everyday world, free-floating emotions and feelings that are grist in Eliot's poetic mill. This returns us again to the tropes in Chapter 1 from the beginning of the war and the images of digestion. Eliot's immature poet, the one who stands alone raging against the gods, is simply unable to 'digest' the bolus of passions inside himself.[90] In contrast, Eliot's poet creates an unstable, toxic and pungent compound that can dissolve the bolus.

This act of containerisation is worth dwelling on a moment. Eliot's chemical reaction takes place in a 'receptacle'. It suggests the container as a store of energy and a site from which the poet can tap energy. Eliot may have had in mind the Harvey Hubbell receptacle patented in 1904 to allow an easy and safe way to connect electrical appliances to a wall-mounted socket. That would nod back to Pound's electro-physics. There is also a return of the sexual connotation, a sense of fecundity that stems from the poet's ability to seize and store what Eliot calls 'numberless feelings, phrases, images', for holding them in a free-floating liquid 'suspension' until 'the proper combination' arrives. It suggests a sexual act, one capable of a great 'variety of types of combination'.[91] And in this sense, we might detect in Eliot's receptacle a subconscious need to put the body in pieces back together again. It would be an attempt to recontainerise the emotion that has overflowed the body's limits, to re-encapsulate and cage the danger of the feminine within the crystalline certainty of the masculine.

One way to conceptualise that psychological act would be using Wilfred Bion's concept of 'nameless dread'.[92] In his account of emotional survival during the First World War, *The Secret Battle* (2009), Michael Roper uses the term to describe an extremely specific but widespread fear amongst combatants of imminent death.[93] In Bion's *Learning from Experience* (1962), an infant projects its unbearable anxieties, especially those related to a symbolic or literal death, on to the mother in the expectation that the mother will return them shorn of terror. That inchoate anxiety can however result in an excess

---

[90] Eliot, 'Tradition and the Individual Talent', p. 109.

[91] Ibid.

[92] Wilfred R. Bion, *Learning from Experience* (Lanham, MD: Rowman & Littlefield, 1962; repr. 2004), p. 96

[93] Roper, p. 250.

of empathy on the mother's part. The mother then projects the terror backwards. The mother does not hold the emotion in a way in which, even if the
original emotion remained unpleasant, the infant/mother could make it meaningful and integrated. Esther Bick (1986) traces the emergence of this intoler-
able dread to the earliest moments of life as the infant leaves the container
of the womb and experiences the body as if in pieces or as an entity liquefy-
ing.[94] In Jacques Lacan's *Écrits* (1966) this experience is referred to as the frag-
mented body or '*corps morcelé*', those infantile anxieties associated with the
disjunction between a unified notion of selfhood and a body experienced as an
assemblage.[95] Thomas Ogden (1989) implicates aesthetics in the related term
'*formless dread*', a fear of shapelessness or the fear of a lack of context, fear of
a world in which things ought to be separate but in which they actually flow
together.[96] Eliot's letters with his own mother provide ample material to support this reading, but here the more important point is that Eliot's receptacle
functions as the means to ward against an excess of empathy that threatens
to shatter the poetic container. By inserting the demand for balance between
object and subject it posits that it can make a coherent world from the rubble
of it all.

Eliot is especially interested in 'Tradition and the Individual Talent' in what
he terms the pressure exerted by this act of containerisation. He refers to it
clearly as an act of fusion, again emphasising the sexual.[97] It is the pressure, the
continuous application of intellectual force, which allows the poet to become
a very unusual type of container, what we can only term a consciousness that
has managed to get rid of its presence. Only then can it ignore the body in
pieces and instead refocus itself on the medium of self by foregrounding the act
of storing and fusing the fragments of ordinary experience. It is to be a hall of
mirrors, the consciousness of one's own self-consciousness. As Pound's narrator suggested in 'Provincia Deserta', it is not a single consciousness living the
past in the present but a strange plurality of egos.

Eliot positions this as a very radical theory. However, the conservatism of
the approach is clear as the essay closes. Eliot insists that the emotions arising
from 'particular events' are of no value no matter what they are. It is a fallacy,
he suggests, for us to look for any particular or new emotions. To do so would
be perverse. Instead, Eliot concludes:

---

[94] Esther Bick, 'Further Considerations on the Function of the Skin in Early Object Relations.
Findings from Infant Observation Integrated into Child and Adult Analysis', *British Journal of
Psychotherapy*, 2.4 (June 1986), 292–9 (p. 296).

[95] Jacques Lacan, *Écrits* (1966), trans. by Bruce Fink (New York: W. W. Norton, 2006), p. 774 nn.
97.3 and 78.

[96] Thomas H. Ogden, *The Primitive Edge of Experience* (Lanham, MD: Rowman & Littlefield,
1989; repr. 2004), p. 39.

[97] Eliot, 'Tradition and the Individual Talent', p. 109.

The business of the poet is not to find new emotions, but to use the ordinary ones and, in working them up into poetry, to express feelings which are not in actual emotions at all. And emotions which he has never experienced will serve his turn as well as those familiar to him.[98]

Emotions he has never experienced are just as good as those he knows from personal experience. The idea sneaks into the paragraph when it ought to be in bold. It betrays Eliot's pessimism about the world. It shows the hold of Hulme's conceptualisation of original sin and the influence of Pound's theory of universal emotions in *Cathay*. To these early modernist theories Eliot had added the theoretical psychological weight of William James's *Apperzeptionsmass*. It is the host of witnesses from history and not the moral witness in history who authenticates the felt world.[99]

Appropriately, as this body of theory began with William Wordsworth in the essays of Harold Monro and Thomas in 1914, so it ends in 1919. Eliot tells us that the concept of tranquillity is but 'an inexact formula'.[100] Not wrong then. Not not a formula. Updating the idea, Eliot said poetry is an amalgamation of experiences, an amalgamation beyond ordinary ken, a divination rather than a simple conscious act.[101] It is tranquil only in that the poet is passive in the attention he pays to the event in question. Poetry is to be then the instinctual amalgamation of the entire contents of intellectual life, an agglomeration of fragments which act on the poet without any reciprocal force or resistance in an act of supreme attention. It is a definition that reinserts a deeply metaphysical notion of presence into a poetics of absence, an entirely new form of occasional poetry. Gone is the process of a unified subjectivity in the act of memory. So too the notion of moving from the hurly burly to a position of greater reflectivity. Instead, the poet is *always* outside, he is a spectator that *can never be* within the maelstrom. He must be betwixt and between, neither nor. This poet makes poetry from non-participation, a poetry constituted by the state of expatriation or separation from the world. Everything else is verse.

Following the completion of 'Tradition and the Individual Talent' Eliot made this argument in a much less abstract and less guarded form in 'Modern Tendencies in Poetry', the lecture to the Arts League.[102] Here Eliot instructed

---

[98] Ibid. p. 111.

[99] See similarly Eliot, 'The Problems of the Shakespeare Sonnets', pp. 37–8.

[100] Eliot, 'Tradition and the Individual Talent', p. 111.

[101] Miller, *T. S. Eliot*, p. 93 suggests William Allan Neilson's notion of concentration as a model here.

[102] On the lecture see T. S. Eliot, letter to Charlotte Eliot (10 November 1919), in *The Letters of T. S. Eliot*, I, pp. 415–16 (p. 416). Murry famously told Katherine Mansfield the lecture marked the start of a fight between the array of intellectuals he had gathered around him and the Georgians. John Middleton Murry, letter to Katherine Mansfield (29 October 1919), qtd in J. Matthew Huculak, '*The London Mercury* (1919–39) and Other Moderns', in Brooker and Thacker, eds, pp. 240–59 (p. 241).

his audience to turn against the idea that poetry was 'the mere ebullition of a personality'.[103] Instead, Eliot defined great poetry as a poetry in which personality is completely '*déversée*' ('poured out') in such a way that all the great poets occupied one mind working across time and space.[104] Eliot had purged the singular mind of Pound and Yeats of its most occult tendencies with the science of the *Apperzeptionsmass*, but the two ideas are still closely related. Eliot illustrated his point using two antithetical poets, 'the Emotional, and the Unemotional', sited, he said, between the ideal or virtuous poet 'in conversation with the other artists, with a few scientists, and with Aristotle in a corner of the room'.[105] The 'Unemotional' Eliot dealt with quickly. He was the Dadaist who appeared to have given up on emotion altogether. From the 'Emotional' camp Eliot quoted the first two stanzas of James Stephens's 'The Snare' (1915):

> I hear a sudden cry of pain!
> There is a rabbit in a snare:
> Now I hear the cry again,
> But I cannot tell from where.
>
> But I cannot tell from where
> He is calling out for aid;
> Crying on the frightened air,
> Making everything afraid.[106]

On one level this is just an exemplary pre-war poem, first published in *Songs from the Clay* (1915) and then reprinted in *Georgian Poetry 1913–1915* (1916 [November 1915]). It was an old target. Eliot referred to it in 'Reflections on Contemporary Poetry, I' as illustrative of vague emotion.[107] In 'Modern Tendencies in Poetry', Eliot deliberately chose the one passage that evoked Murry's essay of July 1918. Stephens's fault, he said, is that 'instead of *making* the cry make everything afraid, he tells you that it does'.[108] That is, 'he gives you some *idea* of what he means, but the catharsis, the pity and terror, he means to produce from the association of a rabbit and a snare, is no more inevitable a result than the thought of rabbit-pie'.[109] It is quite funny, at least for Eliot. Except it was far easier to speak of 'snare' and 'rabbit-pie' than the dead meat of combatants. The

---

[103] Eliot, 'Modern Tendencies in Poetry', p. 213.

[104] Ibid. p. 214.

[105] Ibid. pp. 219, 221.

[106] James Stephens, 'The Snare', in *Georgian Poetry 1913–1915* (London: Poetry Bookshop, 1916), p. 190.

[107] Eliot, 'Reflections on Contemporary Poetry, I', p. 574.

[108] Eliot, 'Modern Tendencies in Poetry', p. 219.

[109] Ibid. p. 220.

reappropriation of Murry's argument is nonetheless obvious as Eliot moved from Stephens to another unnamed school of poets:

> There are writers much more modern, and trying to do something much more difficult and interesting than this, whose weakness is at bottom the same. They wish to evoke an emotion for which they have not found the sensory equivalent. They may *feel* the emotion, but you cannot put mere feelings into language; the thing is to *cease to feel* the emotion, to *see* it as the objective equivalent for it.[110]

This is Murry's argument against Sassoon cut, redrafted, given theoretical basis and incorporated into a more complete genealogy. It served to set war verse against the objective correlative, the one method, according to Eliot, able to transform the mania of a private passion into a public good.

IMPERSONALITY IN PRACTICE: 'GERONTION'

This is not however the end of things although it is the beginning of the New Critical hegemony. We might now draw a distinction between Eliot's theory, with its formal and cold certainties, and his poetic practice. We can see there was doubt in Eliot's work. We can see the perpetual possibility that Eliot harboured thoughts that the moral witness really did have a point, that the appeal to compassion was not without value, that the complex machinations of impersonality were simply too contorted. The singular problem with 'Gerontion', the poem most associated with the emergence of Eliot's poetics in *The Sacred Wood*, is that it does not conform to the theoretical blueprints set out in 'Tradition and the Individual Talent' and 'Modern Tendencies in Poetry'. Instead, it makes manifest the highly structured and abstract nature of impersonality, destabilising it in such a way that the private space of suffering refuses to quite separate itself from the act of creation. In other words, in 'Gerontion' (the poem as formal construct), Tom (the man), Eliot (the poet) and Gerontion (the satirised narrator) do not come apart as cleanly in the catalytic process as the theory tells us they should. Whilst the poem clearly tried to bring together the host of straw figures Eliot had exposed in the previous two years, to make one large bonfire of them from which the phoenix of a counter poetic would appear, his satire seems to stick, the willingness to lampoon, the desire to mock bends back viciously on the poet profoundly destabilising the didactic intentions. This will necessarily return us to Eliot's anti-Semitism.

The satiric intention in 'Gerontion' begins with an epigraph from *Measure for Measure* (1603–4) which yet again focuses on age, death and the afterlife. The reference is arcane. Eliot was self-consciously writing for an exceedingly

---

[110] Ibid.

small audience within an enclave of the cognoscenti. The Ovid Press issued *Ara Vos Prec* in an edition of only 264 copies, of which Eliot signed just thirty. The epigraph is a clear continuation of the private and coded language in 'The New Elizabethans and the Old'. It served Eliot well because it also signalled his intention to intervene in the Jepson fracas and to make Masters the butt of the joke in the opening stanza. Jim McCue (2014) has noted similar connections.[111] Masters's poem 'O Glorious France' (April 1916) and its refrain 'Nor love, nor youth's delight, nor manhood's power' is uncannily similar to the epigraph Eliot chose from Shakespeare. 'O Glorious France' is also an imagined war poem, one that transports readers to 'trenches where the dead / Clog the ensanguined ice' before it retreats into images of combatants becoming 'Prophetic and enraptured souls' wrapped up in 'the keen ecstasy of fated strife'.[112]

The obscure epigraph functions, then, at least for Eliot's ideal reader and the close coterie around him, as the perfect prelude to Gerontion's own attempt at the trench lyric:

> I was neither at the hot gates
> Nor fought in the warm rain
> Nor knee deep in the salt marsh, heaving a cutlass,
> Bitten by flies, fought.[113]

This is to be the first symptom of Gerontion's alleged madness. Participation in combat is the first of Gerontion's thwarted desires. As the next stanza of the poem suggests, it is part of the wider demand that Gerontion places on the evidence of the senses as a prelude for religious faith. In Eliot's terminology, Gerontion, like Haigh-Wood before him, is set up to be an example of the uncritical or imperfect historical consciousness, a man without the ability to synthesise knowledge into a system. To have knowledge, Gerontion insists he must have the fleshwitness's evidence, hence the demands he places on the Magi as witnesses to the birth of Jesus.

Here the *magus* is clearly trying to show impersonality at work. It comes through that awkward use of joint denial, the neither-nor construction that

---

[111] Jim McCue, 'T. S. Eliot, Edgar Lee Masters and Glorious France', *Essays in Criticism*, 64.1 (January 2014), 45–73.

[112] Edgar Lee Masters, 'O Glorious France', in Edgar Lee Masters, *Songs and Satires* (New York: Macmillan, 1916), pp. 71–3 (p. 71).

[113] Eliot, 'Gerontion', p. 31. Eliot may also have had in mind the distanced, indecisive, comfortable middle-class man in the British recruitment poster, '"Daddy, what did YOU do in the Great War?"' That image presents us with a boy playing with toy soldiers spread out on the floor whilst the girl reads. Gerontion is playing with images of battle taken from myth and from second-hand stories he has heard and reconstructed.

blocks our steady progress through the stanza. In *The Great War and the Language of Modernism* Vincent Sherry reads this as Eliot's irony exposing Gerontion's senescent politics, an example of the way modernists 'reenact the disestablishment of a rationalistic attitude and practice in language'.[114] We can read these lines instead as the imposition of a perfect logic system. Originating in the pragmatist development of a Boolean algebra, initially in the work of Charles Sanders Peirce during the 1880s, joint denial is the means by which we can produce a truth system. As a mark of its claim on rationality joint denial deploys the same form of logical NOR that powered the decision-making system on board the Apollo Lunar Module in 1969.[115] Two negatives in a logic system make a positive. To put it another way, the construct p NOR q, or $p \downarrow q$ to use Peirce's notation, is true when both p and q are false. In Eliot's poem p and q – 'at the hot gates', 'in the warm rain', 'in the salt marsh' – are false. This is what Gerontion lacks. For Eliot's ideal reader, one able to wring the culturally dense allusions from the parody, that lack becomes though a new form of life, a truth system that appears out of the figuration. Eliot dramatises the process by bracketing 'fought' in the chiasmus.[116]

Eliot designed this parody of the trench lyric as a denial not of combat gnosticism per se but of the combat gnostic's ability to represent experience. Eliot subtly linked his poem to the essay 'The New Elizabethans and the Old'. Typically, we trace the allusions in Gerontion's war fantasy to Sidney Lanier's 'marsh-grass, waist-high' and Alfred Tennyson's 'knee-deep in mountain grass', amongst others.[117] No doubt these are present as Eliot boasted when he sent a draft of the poem to Hutchinson.[118] However, these opening references also suggest Osborn's *The New Elizabethans*. There we find Canadian poet Guy Drummond who died in glory at Langemarck, 'one of the most glorious episodes in the war', according to Osborn 'a greater Thermopylæ'.[119] Gerontion's rain comes from Julian Grenfell's communion with nature in 'The Hills', a poem

---

[114] Sherry, *The Great War and the Language of Modernism*, p. 14.

[115] Yves Nievergelt, *Logic, Mathematics, and Computer Science: Modern Foundations with Practical Applications*, 2nd edn (New York: Springer, 2015), pp. 66–7.

[116] There are other oblique allusions to the war here. The cutlass was an important symbol for the United States Navy, reissued and purposively redesigned in 1917. Harold L. Peterson, *The American Sword 1775–1945* (Philadelphia: Ray Riling Arms Books, 1965; repr. Mineola, NY: Dover, 2003), p. 55. Wyndham Lewis found himself holed up in a whitewashed cottage under a hail of artillery fire amidst the dunes and marshes at Oostduinkerke in August 1917. Hulme died there a month later.

[117] Sidney Lanier, 'Hymns of the Marshes: IV. The Marshes of Glynn' (1907), in *Poems of Sidney Lanier*, ed. by Mary D. Lanier (New York: Charles Scribner's Sons, 1920), pp. 14–18 (p. 16); Alfred Tennyson, 'Mariana in the South' (1832–42), in Alfred Tennyson, *Poems*, 2 vols (London: Edward Moxon, 1842), I, pp. 87–93 (p. 89); Christopher Ricks and Jim McCue, 'Commentary: "Gerontion"', in Eliot, *Collected and Uncollected Poems*, pp. 467–86 (pp. 471–2).

[118] Eliot, letter to Mary Hutchinson ([9? July? 1919], p. 372.

[119] Osborn, *The New Elizabethans*, p. 278.

Osborn had first anthologised in *The Muse in Arms*.[120] The image of being 'knee deep' in marshland finds similarity in William Hodgson's sketch of the sodden Festubert marshes.[121] The 'cutlass' is in Hodgson's juvenilia amidst fantasies of smuggling, piracy and romance in the Far East. Osborn equated it with Hodgson's lust for war experience.[122] The stinging of death is in Donald Hankey.[123]

Eliot tells us in 'Tradition and the Individual Talent' to move from content to form. We must see the multiplicity of imagery, of both Hodgson and Mariana simultaneously 'knee deep' in it all for example. We are to take it as a direct illustration of the enduring and necessary ordinariness of poetic emotion. Wars – whether it be Festubert or Mylae, the First World War or the Punic War – are all the same. The new emotions that Gerontion yearns to experience are then simply perverse and unoriginal, the result of a failure to understand the systematised nature of the world, the inability to call upon the hosts of history to speak about universals.

Eliot wrote this method very deeply into the poem. Take the poem's opening syllables: 'Here I am'.[124] They are a direct summoning of the words we hear from the combatant in the 'Song of the Bowmen of Shu': 'Here we are, picking the first fern-shoots'.[125] Eliot twists the knife though. Pound's collective 'we' from the inside of battle has given way to Gerontion's solitary rumination from outside the war. He becomes the torpid old man of *The Fourth Canto*, completed as Eliot began 'Gerontion': 'And by the curved carved foot of the couch, claw-foot and lion head, an old man seated / Speaking in the low drone . . .'.[126] And a prototype for the one in 'The Seventh Canto', begun as Eliot finished his poem: 'And the old voice lifts itself / weaving an endless sentence.'[127]

We can trace Eliot's use of joint denial in his mock trench lyric to Pound's unwillingness to sacrifice the ideals of poetry to the martial state in 'Homage to Sextus Propertius':

> Thus much the fates have alloted me, and if, Maecenas,
> I were able to lead heroes into armour, I would not,
> Neither would I warble of Titans, nor of Ossa spiked onto Olympus,
> Nor of causeways over Pelion[.][128]

---

[120] Ibid. pp. 307–8.

[121] Ibid. p. 261.

[122] Ibid. p. 251. For background see Charlotte Zeepvat, *Before Action: William Noel Hodgson and the 9th Devons* (Barnsley: Pen and Sword Books, 2015), pp. 9–10.

[123] Osborn, *The New Elizabethans*, p. 190.

[124] Eliot, 'Gerontion', p. 31.

[125] Pound, 'Song of the Bowmen of Shu', p. 249.

[126] Ezra Pound, *The Fourth Canto* (London: Ovid Press, 1919), p. 2.

[127] Ezra Pound, 'The Seventh Canto', *Dial*, 71.2 (August 1921), 178–81 (p. 179).

[128] Ezra Pound, 'Homage to Sextus Propertius', in *Poems 1918–21, including Three Portraits and Four Cantos* (New York: Boni and Liveright, 1921), pp. 11–34 (p. 21) (*Poems and Translations*, pp. 526–45 (p. 534)).

In Gerontion's return to Thermopylæ there is the echo of Ford's *Antwerp*, of 'scars / Won in many wars . . . / Punic, / Lacedæmonian, wars of Napoleon'.[129] And the echo of Ford's 'Footsloggers' (April 1918; *December 1917*), where shocked soldiers struggle with the insensate meaninglessness of 'mud to the knees / And khaki and khaki and khaki . . .'.[130] There is most crucially also the allusion to Yeats's attempt to understand what took one soldier to war in 'An Irish Airman Foresees his Death' (March 1919; *June 1918*). In 'Gerontion', the chiasmus of the mock trench lyric, structured around the repetition of the intransitive 'fought', formally dramatises Gerontion's solipsism. It brackets the present participle – 'heaving' – between past participles. It is the action that he can never complete, the perpetual state of swinging that cutlass. In Yeats there is first the joint denial – 'Nor law, nor duty bade me fight, / Nor public men, nor cheering crowds' – as the poem unsuccessfully explores Gregory's decision to fight. Second there is also the chiasmus as the poem settles on the abstract idea that Gregory's motivation to fight was 'A lonely impulse of delight':

> I balanced all, brought all to mind,
> The years to come seemed waste of breath,
> A waste of breath the years behind
> In balance with this life, this death.[131]

The plane's trajectory, reinforced by the yaw of the cadence, is a metaphor for Gregory's motivation and his need to feel the intensity of lived experience. Gregory's solitariness might seem unreflective, except Yeats mythologises it into another act of 'balance' which appears at the centre of the chiasmus as a kind of ecstasy in the moment. In 'Gerontion', the echo of Yeats's utopianism, really always a fragile and evanescent compromise for not understanding what took Gregory to war, comes firmly aground on Gerontion's grounded stasis. He is the very antithesis of the airman's projectile arc.

Finally, there is Whitman on the battlefield too. May 1919 marked the centenary of Whitman's birth and Monroe devoted May's edition of *Poetry* to him.[132] In the most famed of the *Drum-Taps* series, the poem placed at its centre, 'The Wound-Dresser' (1865), Whitman begins: 'An old man bending I come among new faces'.[133] Bending versus waiting. Whitman's participle is one of action.

---

[129] [Ford], *Antwerp*, p. [2].

[130] Ford Madox Hueffer [Ford Madox Ford], 'Footsloggers', in Ford Madox Hueffer [Ford Madox Ford], *'On Heaven' and Poems Written on Active Service* (London: John Lane, 1918), pp. 58–76 (p. 66).

[131] W. B. Yeats, 'An Irish Airman Foresees his Death', in *The Poems*, pp. 135–6 (pp. 135, 136).

[132] H.M. [Harriet Monroe], 'Walt Whitman', *Poetry*, 14.2 (May 1919), 89–94.

[133] Walt Whitman, 'The Wound-Dresser', in Walt Whitman, *Complete Poetry and Collected Prose*, ed. by Justin Kaplan (New York: Library of America, 1982), pp. 442–5 (p. 442).

He is tending to the wounded and dressing wounds. Gerontion's participle is one of disengagement. Whitman returns to the battlefield as nurse 'With hinged knees', adopting the position of worship before rotting flesh, amputated limb and crushed skull, a metaphor for the poem's humility before suffering.[134] His poem is keenly aware of its almost voyeuristic desire for experience, for the rich stuff that would prove to be, according to Whitman, 'the most profound lesson of my life'.[135] According to Eliot's poem, it is precisely the absence of humility, the insistence on an empirical basis to knowledge rather than a willingness simply to have faith, that blocks Gerontion's passage to redemption.

This allows us to better understand the poem's most obscure shift of perspective as it moves from reflections on war, housing and social deterioration in the first stanza to the second's arcane reflections on religion and Lancelot Andrewes's Christmas sermons of 1618 and 1622.[136] As Marjorie Perloff says in *Differentials* (2004), when Gerontion uses the word 'fought' he is using it partly metaphorically. He really means '"lived" or "had intense experiences"' in a much wider sense than merely combat.[137] He means liminal moments of human experience, such as those moments of mystical enlightenment explored by Andrewes. Gerontion's thoughts have run from imagining war to the nature of the Incarnation, through the image of God as the tenant of the body of Christ. The decay in this house is the failure of faith, a splitting of intellect from belief and passion, one figured through the image of the Pharisees determined to take all signs of divinity as only miraculous wonders. The introduction of the gentle hands of a Mr Silvero suggests Christ's healing of the man with the withered hand in St Matthew. The obvious link backwards to the 'estaminet' and to Christ's birth as the ultimate sign of divinity, the poem develops through the images of the swaddled babe and the oncoming of the hunted tiger.

Eliot introduces Andrewes then as a direct contrast to Gerontion's need (and that of the trench lyric) to see, hear or touch, the need to be there, to be in it. Instead, the Christmas sermons to which the poem alludes place emphasis on the humility inherent in the act of finding the child in its natural surroundings and thereby simply accepting its divinity. We are to understand that we need not ground religious belief on a sensory encounter with God, but instead build it on the metaphysical buttress of the *logos*. As in Eliot's fragmentary imagined

---

[134] Ibid. p. 443.

[135] Walt Whitman, *Specimen Days* (1882), in Whitman, *Complete Poetry*, pp. 689–926 (p. 776).

[136] For detailed analysis of the references see Jewel Spears Brooker, *Mastery and Escape: T. S. Eliot and the Dialectic of Modernism* (Amherst: University of Massachusetts Press, 1994), pp. 94–8; Rick de Villiers, 'Banishing the Backward Devils: Eliot's Quatrain Poems and "Gerontion"', in *The New Cambridge Companion to T. S. Eliot*, ed. by Jason Harding (Cambridge: Cambridge University Press, 2017), pp. 55–70 (pp. 67–9).

[137] Marjorie Perloff, *Differentials: Poetry, Poetics, Pedagogy* (Tuscaloosa: University of Alabama Press, 2004), p. 21.

war poem given to Haigh-Wood, the problem of combat gnosticism and the problem of faith become the same problem. They lead to an agonising inwardness that eventually results in the loss of contact with the world.

If this is the way the poem wants us to read it then it is also the way we have most often read it. In the 1940s, Eliot claimed 'Gerontion' was merely a way to express a mood associated with old age, something of an experiment devoid of intellectual content.[138] That position is consistent with Eliot's unsubstantiated statement in the 1930s that *The Waste Land* was merely grumbling in a rhythmic manner.[139] In the work of Robert S. Lehman (2009) and Rick de Villiers (2017) attention has shifted back to a formalist account of Eliot's work in this period and demanded that we read the poetry as direct expressions of Eliot's prose project.[140] This may in part be a response to the publication of Eliot's complete prose. We might also see it as an antidote to the revelatory publication of Eliot's complete letters and the idea, most widely popularised by Cynthia Ozick (1989), that Eliot's poetry served as a confessional mask that used the false front of irony.[141] These polar regions of Eliot research – the formalist and the biographical – have proven highly resistant to even sensitive attempts, such as Ronald Schuchard's *Eliot's Dark Angel* (1999), that have aimed at a reintegration of art and life.[142]

Both approaches threaten to ossify 'Gerontion' as they wring either Eliot or Tom from the mix. This returns us to the poem's anti-Semitism and its irrefutable use of a racial slur. The argument that the use of the racial slur, whatever the context or the use, is damaging is well made.[143] We can imagine that readers of Eliot's work have used it in many harmful ways. We cannot whitewash this. We can think about Eliot's historical intention here though in one of two ways. If the poem's irony works only on its content, shuttling between parody and impersonality, then this anti-Semitism is, given the historical circumstances set out in this chapter, deeply unsettling and macabre. It would suggest that amidst widespread Jewish persecution and amidst widespread resistance and opposition to that persecution, Eliot was guilty of using a nasty Jewish stereotype to categorise the ruination of post-war capitalist society.

---

[138] T. S. Eliot, letter to Seán Ó'Faoláin (21 February 1944), qtd in Ricks and McCue, 'Commentary: "Gerontion"', p. 468; T. S. Eliot, letter to Diana Captain (3 January 1945), qtd in Ricks and McCue, 'Commentary: "Gerontion"', p. 468.

[139] Henry Eliot, *Excerpts from Lectures 1932–1933*, qtd in Christopher Ricks and Jim McCue, '*The Waste Land*: Headnote', in Eliot, *Collected and Uncollected Poems*, pp. 547–86 (p. 577).

[140] Robert S. Lehman, 'Eliot's Last Laugh: The Dissolution of Satire in *The Waste Land*', *Journal of Modern Literature*, 32.2 (2009), 65–79 (p. 67); de Villiers, pp. 55–70.

[141] Cynthia Ozick, 'T. S. Eliot at 101', *The New Yorker*, 20 November 1989, pp. 119–54 (p. 121).

[142] Ronald Schuchard, *Eliot's Dark Angel: Intersections of Life and Art* (New York: Oxford University Press, 1999).

[143] Anthony Julius, *T. S. Eliot, Anti-Semitism, and Literary Form*, new edn (London: Thames & Hudson, 2003), pp. 302–35.

There is an alternative reading. This centres on the question of whether the poem's irony resists the very processes it hopes to demonstrate. As we have seen throughout this narrative, there are simply too many biographical overlaps between Gerontion and Eliot – their ages, the crisis of faith, the tortured desire to enlist, the sexual frustration, the sense of public humiliation, the isolation leading to breakdown – to be quite content that this is entirely parody. We must recognise just how much of Eliot's life did not burn in the flame of art here. Take something as mundane as the weather. As Eliot sat down to write 'Gerontion' the British Meteorological Office recorded that London was in the grip of 'an absolute drought' that left corn crops 'short, yellow, and dry'.[144] Thermometers close to London's Kensington Palace (close that is to the Hotel Constance where Eliot moved around 4 May to await the redecoration of his flat) recorded peak temperatures of twenty-seven degrees Celsius.[145] It was 'abnormally dry'; only millimetres of rain fell on the parched soil of southeast England, levels unprecedented in the prior forty to fifty years. The early frosts common in late spring all but disappeared. There were dewless mornings with dry thunderstorms, spells of unusual visibility following periods of dense fog and mist. From across the country came reports of solar and lunar coronas, halos and sun-pillars. The aurora danced into view.[146] The pervasive sense of aridity in the poem, its wait for the deluge, the cosmic displays and the vision of the heavens sundered to atoms by chthonic waves of violence were not merely figurative constructs in 'Gerontion'. They were an exact meteorological description of May 1919.[147]

The poem also displays an unusual sense of sympathy for the difficult postwar environment faced by non-combatants like Eliot and Gerontion. The day prior to Eliot's move to the Constance the dominion troops from Australia, Canada, New Zealand and South Africa gathered across the street in Hyde Park before parading through the capital, the start of that summer's peace celebrations across European and American cities.[148] The month marked a peak in the demand for a rapid demobilisation; 11 May was the six-month anniversary of the Armistice and a date chalked on military equipment as an *aide-mémoire* by British combatants who mistakenly believed it to be the final backstop for a return home. For Eliot it was a dry month in other ways as he

---

[144] *Monthly Weather Report of the Meteorological Office*, 36.5 (May 1919), p. 1.

[145] Vivien Eliot was staying close by in Inverness Terrace at the Sayes Court Hotel.

[146] *Monthly Weather Report of the Meteorological Office*, p. 1.

[147] On the observation of the solar eclipse at Principe on 29 May 1919 as proof of the general theory of relativity see Michael Whitworth, 'Pièces d'identité: T. S. Eliot, J. W. N Sullivan and Poetic Impersonality', *English Literature in Transition, 1880–1920*, 39.2 (1996), 149–70.

[148] Jacqueline Jenkinson, '"All in the Same Uniform?" The Participation of Black Colonial Residents in the British Armed Forces in the First World War', in *The British Empire and the First World War*, ed. by Ashley Jackson (Abingdon: Routledge, 2016), pp. 379–402 (p. 384).

returned to creative work following a breakdown and the death of his father. In the spring Eliot and Vivien dealt with the lease on a house in Marlow shared with Bertrand Russell, shared tenants in a *ménage à trois* to which only astonishing innocence could protect Eliot from the awareness of his cuckolding. They nursed their domestic servant back to health from pneumonia, the result of the H1N1 influenza pandemic sweeping across England.[149] The maid in 'Gerontion' sneezes as she stokes the fire. The virus struck down Lewis and Lawrence along with the Eliots. Even the goat in 'Gerontion' coughs.

This interlacing of fiction and fantasy suggests there is alongside the parody a trope of personal trial in the poem. Its first draft typescript took the title 'Gerousia'.[150] The *gerousia* was the name given to a Greek judicial council of elders, usually men over the age of sixty. It was also the periodic Jewish council in the Talmud convened on the most momentous occasions in the history of a nation.[151] It was through the Sanhedrin, the priestly form of the *gerousia*, that Pontius Pilate judged and condemned Jesus for making false claims to be the King of the Jews. In 'Gerontion' the title's emphasis shifted to the combination of the suffix '-ion' (the action or condition of being) with the stem 'geront-' (from the Greek, old man). This foregrounded senescence. In contrast, in 'Gerousia' the title problematises judge, jury, victim and perpetrator. Is Gerontion an emissary of the *gerousia*? Is he standing before it accused? Who is it that is doing the judging?[152]

The most obvious connection to make here is John Henry Newman's *The Dream of Gerontius* (1865), a poem originally conceived as consolation for dead souls stranded in purgatory. Newman's Gerontius finds himself, like Gerontion,

---

[149] Vivien Eliot, letter to Charlotte C. Eliot (7 April 1919), in *The Letters of T. S. Eliot*, I, pp. 335–6 (p. 335); Tom [T. S. Eliot], to Charlotte Eliot (27 February [1919]), in *The Letters of T. S. Eliot*, I, pp. 324–5 (p. 324).

[150] Ricks and McCue, 'Textual History: "Gerontion"', p. 339 n. *Title*.

[151] Lawrence H. Schiffman, *From Text to Tradition: A History of Second Temple and Rabbinic Judaism* (Hoboken, NJ: Ktav Publishing House, 1991), pp. 68–70.

[152] We can note parallels to Thomas Moult, 'The Old Men', *Voices*, 1.2 (February 1919), 93–5 (p. 93). Moult's poem highlights the divisive nature of the split between the young and the old, the innocent and the guilty, the judged and the jury in post-war English society. It was a provocative poem, especially since Moult launched *Voices* in the previous month to serve as a vehicle for combatants to voice their experience. Mark S. Morrisson, 'The Cause of Poetry: Thomas Moult and *Voices* (1919–21), Harold Monro and *The Monthly Chapbook* (1919–25)', in Brooker and Thacker, eds, pp. 405–27 (pp. 408–15). The poem most notably presents the old as voyeuristic bystanders masturbating over the dead. Since *Voices* published Murry's 'The Daughter of Necessity' in April 1919 it would seem the *Athenæum* circle read the journal and was aware of its rival intent. Noticeably, Eliot's old man originally shared the rheumatic and spasmodic condition of Moult's old man in lines he initially added but then dropped from the manuscript in the summer of 1919. Ricks and McCue, 'Textual History: "Gerontion"', p. 341 n. 73. On age-based prejudice in the period 1919–20 more generally, see Toby Thacker, *British Culture and the First World War: Experience, Representation and Memory* (London: Bloomsbury, 2014), p. 8.

before a court of judgement, a demonic *gerousia*. It tells him that thought is what blocks his path to God as he finds that his earthly guilt prevents any final beatific vision on the night of trial. So popular was Newman's poem and its theme of consolation for those dispossessed by death that John Lane reissued it during 1916 in a lavish edition illustrated by Stella Langdale. Edward Elgar's choral setting of Newman's poem was extensively performed throughout Britain during the war, accompanied by settings of Laurence Binyon's poems, including those famous lines 'They shall grow not old, as we that are left grow old'.[153] Popular demand led to a Newman revival at the Festival Gerontius in May 1916 in the shadow of Verdun, a time when large-scale concerts in London had all but ceased under threat of Zeppelin attack. Jeremy Crump (2014) cites the alto Clara Butt, who organised the Festival, asking if it was not finally '"time that art in England should try to express a new attitude of the English mind towards life after death"'.[154]

We can see Eliot's private fears about the afterlife in 'Gerontion' beyond the naming of its protagonist. Between its first and second drafts it lost a second epigraph taken from Friar Alberigo in *The Divine Comedy* ('Inferno', Canto XXXIII'). We see Alberigo lurking in the circle of hell reserved for those who have betrayed (in his case murdered) their guests.[155] This might suggest Eliot's own betrayal by Russell and the link to the shared lease at Marlow. More likely, as Eliot told Pound on 15 August when the two were walking through France, it suggests that he too was very much afraid of life after death, an emotion that might partly explain the perplexed attitude of the Confucian to the early drafts of 'Gerontion'.[156]

Do the poem's repeated attempts to impose tradition reveal impersonality at work? Does it simply play out the mechanics of 'Tradition and the Individual Talent'? Or does it reintroduce the very personality the poem sets out to avoid, emphasising its meta-nature to such an extent that the poem's self-consciousness deteriorates into self-parody? This need not be a statement about Eliot's later work. It may just be a statement about 'Gerontion' and its historical context.

---

[153] Laurence Binyon, 'For the Fallen', in Laurence Binyon, *The Four Years: War Poems* (London: Elkin Mathews, 1919), pp. 42–3 (p. 43).

[154] Qtd in Jeremy Crump, 'The Identity of English Music: The Reception of Elgar 1898–1935', in *Englishness: Politics and Culture 1880–1920*, ed. by Robert Colls and Philip Dodd, 2nd edn (London: Bloomsbury, 2014), pp. 189–216 (p. 201).

[155] Dante Alighieri, 'Inferno, Canto XXXIII', in Dante Alighieri, *The Divine Comedy*, trans. by C. H. Sisson (Oxford: Oxford University Press, 1993; repr. 2008), pp. 186–90 (p. 189).

[156] Ezra Pound, 'Canto XXIX', in *The Cantos of Ezra Pound*, 4th edn (London: Faber and Faber, 1987), pp. 141–6 (p. 145). Eliot later expanded on the fear, claiming he had encountered it before when at the house shared with Russell in Marlow. T.S.E. [T. S. Eliot], letter to William Force Stead (9 August 1930), in *The Letters of T. S. Eliot*, V: *1930–1931*, ed. by Valerie Eliot and John Haffenden (2014), pp. 287–9 (p. 287). For one interpretation see Schuchard, *Eliot's Dark Angel*, pp. 119–21.

To illustrate these alternatives, take two alternative potential sources for the poem's anti-Semitism. Eliot certainly knew of Pound's propensity to use the lower-case Jew in an insulting fashion. Well before his retreat from London and flirtation with economics, Pound had the 'jews' conspiring with 'editorial maggots' who 'drive a snout still deeper in the swim-brown of the mire'.[157] As Adam McKible explains in *The Space and Place of Modernism* (2002), in Pound's increasingly paranoid world the Jew was parasitical, a necessary Other in which to embody cultural confusion.[158] In Lewis's world too we should add. 'Cantleman's Spring-Mate' (*Little Review*: October 1917; *May 1917*) underwent, like 'Gerontion' after it, a silent capitalisation of its reference to 'the quarrels of jews'.[159] Does this then make Eliot's decapitalised Jew yet another clubroom joke? It might seem so.[160]

Contrast these usages however with those of James Joyce, who placed the same words in Mr Deasy's mouth in 'Ulysses: Episode II' (*Little Review*: April 1918), the 'Nestor' chapter. Deasy is a racist, a fool and a pedant. He fears "'England is in the hands of the jews"'.[161] Joyce does not want us to like him. When we first meet him, we do so through Stephen's eyes immediately after Stephen has with great tenderness and sensitivity helped his student, Sargent, with arithmetic. Joyce wanted to expose Deasy's anti-Semitism. He constructed it in the same way as it appeared in Pound's work as a delusional paranoia, a prejudice moving from the very private sense of isolation from power to the bizarre and illogical conclusion that someone must therefore control the apparatus of finance and the press. We know Eliot read Joyce in 1919. *The Egoist* reprinted the Deasy dialogue at the beginning of the year. 'Gerontion' hints at the connection too. In the *Iliad* Nestor is Gerenian Nestor. He is the archetype of ageing, an Argonaut famed for fighting the centaurs, a charioteer whose fighting days lay in the past but still a wise adviser to Agamemnon and mentor to Telemachus. We know that Joyce's work also served as a reference point elsewhere in 'Gerontion'. The opening words of the poem mimic the narrator in 'Telemachus' (*Little Review*: March 1918; *November 1917*) who tells us of 'the man that was drowned. A sail veering about the blank bay waiting for a swollen bundle to bob up, roll over to the sun a puffy face, saltwhite.

---

[157] Ezra Pound, 'An Anachronism at Chinon', *Little Review*, 4.2 (June 1917), 14–21 (p. 15). The 'thin pale Russian Jew' – J.H. [Jane Heap], 'Push-Face', *Little Review*, 4.2 (June 1917), 4–7 (p. 6) – in the same edition of the *Little Review* was notably capitalised. See also Ezra Pound, 'Editorial on Solicitous Doubt', *Little Review*, 4.6 (October 1917), 20–2 (p. 21).

[158] Adam McKible, *The Space and Place of Modernism: The Russian Revolution, Little Magazines, and New York* (New York: Routledge, 2002), pp. 90–5.

[159] Wyndham Lewis, 'Cantelman's Spring-Mate', *Little Review*, 4.6 (October 1917), 8–14 (p. 9).

[160] In support of this see especially Rodger Kamenetz, 'The Lower Case Jew', *Jewish in America (Part Two)*, 42.1 (Winter 2003), <http://hdl.handle.net/2027/spo.act2080.0042.120> [accessed 24 March 2022].

[161] James Joyce, 'Ulysses: Episode II', *The Egoist*, 6.1 (January–February 1919), 11–14 (p. 14).

Here I am.'[162] Gerontion is a prototype for Eliot's other drowned figures, those sunk by carnal cravings, by a life given over to immediate experience that only serves to confirm isolation.

If we read the poem in this way the poem's anti-Semitism begins to shift from an ugly private joke between friends towards a narrative exposing the historicity of anti-Semitism in the aftermath of war. Was it then a parody of the racisms propagated in the work of Pound and Lewis? Was Eliot developing Joyce's parody of Deasy? Was it even a guilty parody of the racism widespread in the Eliot household? Eliot's mother, in the most extreme of many examples, confessed to likening Jews to animals.[163]

Take the poem's use of the 'estaminet' image, the infamous site of origin for the squatting property owner. It comes at once after the mock trench lyric: 'My house is a decayed house'.[164] There seems no obvious link between the trench lyric and these reflections. What does not fighting have to do with living conditions? Gerontion can only mean to implicate two thoughts in an unsaid comparison: my house is a decayed house, whereas or but . . . The Housing and Town Planning Act was passed into British law in June 1919 to mark the return of those that did fight as part payment of David Lloyd George's original promise to build 'homes fit for heroes'.[165] It is somewhat contorted but with a grain of logic then that Gerontion arrives here. His rented tenement is neither fit for nor the safe harbour of any hero, his sense of shame transforming itself into a spiteful targeting of the landlord who 'squats on the window-sill, the owner, / Spawned in some estaminet of Antwerp, / Blistered in Brussels, patched and peeled in London'. The word 'house' becomes a vortex of images: Gerontion's tenanted room, the household of neighbouring 'aliens', the animal sty, the inn, the brothel, the Stock Exchange, the temple, the *gerousia* itself as a form of assembly and the House of Jacob. Signed in January 1919, The Faisal-Weizmann Agreement put in place the basis of the Arab-Jewish cooperation that would prove necessary for the development of Palestine.[166]

Is the anti-Semitism in 'Gerontion' a reflection of anti-alien sentiment in the summer of 1919 or an expression of it? The bitterness of the images, the proposed inhumanity of it all – the squatting and spawning, the blistering and peeling – certainly draws in those infamous estaminets of ill-repute in late-nineteenth-century French impressionism, the working-class bars of Émile Zola's *Germinal* (1884–5), hay-strewn floors covered with coal dust, dirt and

---

[162] James Joyce, 'Ulysses: Episode I', *Little Review*, 5.11 [4.11] (March 1918), 3–22 (p. 21).

[163] Charlotte Eliot, to T. S. Eliot (1 August 1920), in *The Letters of T. S. Eliot*, I, pp. 479–82 (p. 482).

[164] Eliot, 'Gerontion', p. 31.

[165] Mark Swenarton, *Homes Fit for Heroes: The Politics and Architecture of Early State Housing in Britain*, reissue (Abingdon: Routledge, 2018), p. 1.

[166] Herbert Samuel notably reviewed Nahum Sokolow's *History of Zionism* (1919) in *The Athenæum* on 16 May 1919.

spittle.[167] It also suggests the war, the drinking houses and brothel culture of Ivor Gurney's 'The Estaminet' (1917). Jonathan F. Vance (1997) argues for the estaminet as the single most important recurring image in First World War texts.[168] 'Gerontion' certainly encourages us to read the unitalicised 'estaminet' as slang as we stumble through the piling up of vowels and agonise over how to pronounce it. It is combatant patois taken over from French into English.[169]

Gerontion is connecting the Jew to the war, even configuring the stereotype as a manifestation of the war's violent effects. In what way though? Those blisters might be another stereotype, this time from a ghetto, a horrifying sense of the Jewish body as a harbour for disease. However, the 'patch', which we might link to that metaphor, could also be a reference to the *Judenstern*, the yellow-starred badge the racist hangs on the Jewish body.[170] The composite nature of

---

[167] Hollis Clayson, *Painted Love: Prostitution in French Art of the Impressionist Era* (Los Angeles: Getty, 2003), pp. 28–9. Jules Laforgue compared the colourless winter sun to 'un crachat d'estaminet' or bar-room spittle. Jules Laforgue, 'L'hiver qui vient' (1886), in *Oeuvres complètes de Jules Laforgue*, 3 vols (Paris: Mercure de France, 1902), I: *Poésies*, pp. 289–92 (p. 290). Instead, Christopher Ricks identifies the French Cubist André Salmon's 'Anvers' (1910), set in '*l'Estaminet de l'Etoile Polaire*' and owned by 'une veuve hilaire et sans pudeur' as an important source. André Salmon, 'Anvers', in André Salmon, *Le Calumet* (Paris: Henri Falque, 1910), pp. 96–9 (p. 97); Christopher Ricks, 'A l'envers ou à Anvers? A Source for Eliot's Estaminet', *TLS*, 4902 (14 March 1997), 14. Others suggest 'estaminet' was intended as a (close) anagram of anti-Semite. David Spurr, 'Myths of Anthropology: Eliot, Joyce, Lévy-Bruhl', *PMLA*, 109.2 (March 1994), 266–80 (p. 279).

[168] Jonathan F. Vance, *Death So Noble: Memory, Meaning, and the First World War* (Vancouver: UBC Press, 1997), pp. 79–80. In April 1919, in the weeks leading up to the composition of the first drafts of Eliot's poem, Katherine Mansfield reviewed Sarah Macnaughton's *My War Experiences in Two Continents* (1919) for *The Athenæum*. Her essay followed Eliot's 'American Literature'. Macnaughton was almost fifty when she arrived in Antwerp with the Red Cross, and Mansfield singled out her sacrifice at the end of her life. K.M. [Katherine Mansfield], 'Portrait of a Little Lady', *The Athenæum*, 4643 (25 April 1919), 238.

[169] On 23 May 1919 there began a long-running commentary in *The Athenæum* describing the emergence of a post-war soldier patois. Ernest A. Baker, 'English in War-Time', *The Athenæum*, 4647 (23 May 1919), 359–60; 'Ernest A. Baker, 'Slang in War-Time', *The Athenæum*, 4654 (11 July 1919), 582–3; R. W. King, 'Correspondence: Slang in War-Time', *The Athenæum*, 4658 (8 August 1919), 729.

[170] There is also the suggestion of the stereotype of the Jew as a coward. Tony Kushner, *The Persistence of Prejudice: Antisemitism in British Society during the Second World War* (Manchester: Manchester University Press, 1989), pp. 122–3. For examples of such prejudice see Telemachus Thomas Timayenis, *The American Jew: An Exposé of his Career* (New York: Minerva, 1888), pp. 84–92; G. K. Chesterton, 'At the Sign of the World's End: The Jew and the Journalist', *New Witness* (11 October 1917), 562–3; Ezra Pound, 'Pastiche. Regional. XVI', *New Age*, 26.1 (6 November 1919), 16. On the image of the Jew as a sexual coward see D. H. Lawrence, 'An Elixir' (2013; *November 1916*) and its revised version, 'The Jewess and the V.C.' (*Poetry*: July 1919; *March 1919*). For examples of the counter narrative to this see Anonymous, 'We Jews', *New Age*, 24.18 (6 March 1919), 292–4. Notably an anonymous article (and response by Lily Montagu) in *The Nation* (2 and 9 June 1917) entitled 'What Is a Jew?' appeared alongside Tomlinson's 'On Leave', the essay that precipitated Haigh-Wood's letter to Eliot.

---

these metaphors certainly suggests the Hebrew *tzaraath*, an affliction of the skin (and of garments or a house), one often associated in the Old Testament with leprosy as spiritual retribution for sin. This language oscillates so consistently between the unconscious revelation of racism and the self-conscious exposure of the racist that it is hard not to think that racism is one of its topics.

It is worth considering whether the racial slur in 'Gerontion' is after all Eliot's private recognition of the inevitability of racism for those postulating unchanging views about human emotion. Michael Leiris's reflections in his afterword to *Manhood: The Journey from Childhood into the Fierce Order of Virility* (1992) seem especially relevant here:

> 'Is not what occurs in the domain of style valueless if it remains "aesthetic", anodyne, insignificant, if there is nothing in the fact of writing a work that is equivalent (and here supervenes one of the images closest to the author's heart) to the bull's keen horn, which alone—by reason of the physical danger it represents—affords the *torero*'s art a human reality, prevents it from being no more than the vain grace of a ballerina?'[171]

Eliot's concept of impersonality depended on a very dark recognition. If poetic representation was able to unseat the artistic claims of combat gnosticism it could only do so by effectively denying the plurality of affect. We can read 'Gerontion', uniquely in Eliot's oeuvre, as an intensely biographical poem, one that reveals the risk of violence in any systematising approach. As Perloff acutely observes of the tone, steady concentration and passion of the poem's opening lines, there was something very important at stake here for Eliot, something that needed to be resolved.[172] As Edward Brunner (2009) argues, there may then be a terrible honesty to it, a final doubling back of the irony in this hall of mirrors that reveals Gerontion to be the man – the non-combatant, the anti-Semite, the solipsist – that Eliot feared he was or could become, a fear that in practice poetry might fall short of its theoretical goals.[173]

The poem deserves then a much more prominent position in the genealogy of modernist poetics than we have so far granted to it. It is not merely one of those obscure quatrains that mark the later part of Eliot's early career. It complicates Eliot's poetic development. What, for example, should we make of the copy of the poem in Nancy Cunard's commonplace book? Was Cunard editor,

---

[171] Michael Leiris, 'Afterword: The Autobiographer as *Torero*' (1946), in Michael Leiris, *Manhood: The Journey from Childhood into the Fierce Order of Virility*, trans. by Richard Howard (Chicago: University of Chicago Press, 1992), pp. 153–64 (p. 154).

[172] Perloff, *Differentials*, p. 24.

[173] Edward Brunner, '"Gerontion": The Mind of Postwar Europe and the Mind(s) of Eliot', in Chinitz, ed., *A Companion to T. S. Eliot*, pp. 145–56 (p. 154).

lover or friend?[174] Eliot placed great weight on this poem. It was to be Eliot's poem, not a collaboration with Pound. Although Pound saw the poem in draft form as the two walked together through France in August 1919, Eliot mostly ignored the suggestions of his poetic master this time.[175] Pound questioned the opening stanza, proposed deletions and said the poem's opening lines were disorientating. These were all set aside by Eliot.[176] Such was his faith in the poem that Eliot insisted it headline both *Poems* and *Ara Vos Prec* when both Knopf and Quinn expressed their preference to begin with earlier poems.[177] Although everyone except Murry ignored the poem upon publication, Eliot still suggested, in the face of Pound's continued opposition, that it should headline *The Waste Land*.[178] Eliot also proposed a headlining citation to *The Waste Land* from the ambivalent ending to Joseph Conrad's *Heart of Darkness* (1899).[179] As in 'Gerontion', it is entirely unclear if Kurtz's closing discovery of horror in *Heart of Darkness* serves as a recognition of the depravity of civilisation or of his complicity within it.

If we accept both the poem's central position in the genealogy and this reading – the biographical overlap, the parody of Masters's poetry, the interjection into the Jepson fracas, the allusions to Osborn, the alternative poetries of war of Pound, Ford, Yeats and Whitman – then Eliot's theory of 1919 becomes unstable. Eliot ended the first part of 'Tradition and the Individual Talent' in *The Egoist* of September 1919 with something of a mock literary cliff-hanger. He invited his readers to consider a suggestive analogy, the reaction of 'finely

---

[174] On this manuscript's background see Ricks and McCue, 'Textual History: "Gerontion"', p. 339 *ms Cunard*. Lois Gordon, *Nancy Cunard: Heiress, Muse, Political Idealist* (New York: Columbia University Press, 2007), pp. 35–44 concludes Eliot and Cunard were briefly lovers. Eliot's biographers are unconvinced.

[175] The manuscript changed extraordinarily little, except for lines 69–73, between ts1 and ts3. Eliot made slight changes to the poem's physical arrangement, to sentence construction and to matters of grammar, but the major structure and tone of the poem remained unchanged. For the meaningful change of 'Nature' to 'History', see Ricks and McCue, 'Textual History: "Gerontion"', p. 340 n. 34 and Longenbach, *Modernist Poetics of History*, p. 192.

[176] Ricks and McCue, 'Textual History: "Gerontion"', pp. 339–41.

[177] John Quinn, letter to T. S. Eliot (26 August 1919), in *The Letters of T. S. Eliot*, I, pp. 389–92 (p. 390).

[178] John Middleton Murry, 'The Eternal Footman', *The Athenæum*, 4686 (20 February 1920), 239. Contrast with [Anonymous], 'A New Byronism', *TLS*, 948 (18 March 1920), 184; Robert Nichols, 'An Ironist', *The Observer*, 18 April 1920, p. 7; [Leonard and Virginia Woolf], 'Is This Poetry', *The Athenæum*, 4651 (20 June 1920), 491; Marion Strobel, 'Perilous Leaping', *Poetry*, 16.3 (June 1920), 157–9; E. E. Cummings, 'T. S. Eliot', *Dial*, 68 (June 1920), 781–4; Louis Untermeyer, 'Irony de Luxe', *Freeman*, 1 (30 June 1920), 381–2.

[179] T. S. Eliot, letter to Ezra Pound ([26? January 1922]), in *The Letters of T. S. Eliot*, I, pp. 628–30 (p. 629); T. S. Eliot, '*The Waste Land*: An Editorial Composite', in *Collected and Uncollected Poems*, pp. 323–46 (p. 323).

filiated platinum' when mixed with oxygen and sulphur dioxide.[180] It was not until December that Eliot revealed that this reaction produced 'sulphurous acid'. However, oxygen and sulphur dioxide in the presence of platinum produce sulphur trioxide. It is only in reaction with that mundane and significantly less precious substance water that we obtain the acid. The process Eliot described as the means to poetic perfection, the separation of 'the man who suffers and the mind which creates', was not the transmutative process he planned.[181] Often invisible, sulphur trioxide takes the form of an odourless vapour or a transparent liquid that produces fibrous ice crystals. It is the precursor to acid rain. Eliot's process produces then the anhydride, from the Greek *anudros*, without water and not the acid. The parched dryness of 'Gerontion', the scathing dryness of Eliot's satire, indeed the gradual withdrawal and search for water in Eliot's art, suggests a poetry constitutively bound to lack, one perpetually in search of 'lifting belly' and Whitman's compassionate 'bending'. Without that reciprocity 'Gerontion' hints at the potentially unmeetable demands of 'Tradition and the Individual Talent'. There was then a psychologically mimetic quality to Eliot's dehydrated poetic world. It amounted to a perpetual waiting for rain, a self-conscious recognition of impersonality's potential vulnerabilities in the face of the problem of combat gnosticism.

---

[180] Eliot, 'Tradition and the Individual Talent', p. 108.
[181] Ibid. p. 109.

CONCLUSION

In 1929 T. S. Eliot told E. M. Forster that his analysis of *The Waste Land* had exaggerated the impact of the war.[1] Eliot's denial of that influence reflected a position the modernists nurtured from the beginning of the war in August 1914 through to the summer of 1919. There was no looking back. It was a position consolidated in *A Survey of Modernist Poetry* (1927) where 'war-poetry' became no more than 'Georgianism's second-wind'.[2] There was no place for the genre at all in *Principles of Literary Criticism* (1924), just a single index entry, 'Sentimental, and the war', where the trope is introduced by I. A. Richards as 'the pathetic and terrible change that can too often be observed in the sentiments entertained towards the War by men who suffered from it and hated it'.[3] In *New Bearings in English Poetry* (1932) F. R. Leavis's '"war-poets"' are in scare quotes.[4] W. B. Yeats's 'distaste' of 1936, whilst infamous, was then somewhat belated and it has always seemed in any case a little contorted. It is hard to untangle from Yeats's nationalism. It is also prey to both a potential misreading of the 'passive suffering'

---

[1] T. S. Eliot, letter to E. M. Forster (10 August 1929), in *The Letters of T. S. Eliot*, IV: *1928–1929*, ed. by Valerie Eliot and John Haffenden (2013), pp. 572–3 (p. 573).

[2] Laura Riding and Robert Graves, *A Survey of Modernist Poetry*, in Laura Riding and Robert Graves, *'A Survey of Modernist Poetry' and 'A Pamphlet against Anthologies'*, ed. by Charles Mundye and Patrick McGuinness (Manchester: Carcanet, 2002), pp. 1–150 (p. 58).

[3] Richards, *Principles of Literary Criticism*, pp. 375, 260–1.

[4] F. R. Leavis, *New Bearings in English Poetry: A Study of the Contemporary Situation* (London: Chatto & Windus, 1932), p. 72.

Yeats took from Matthew Arnold's *Empedocles on Etna* ([1852]) and the accusation of hypocrisy given the terms on which Yeats rejected Sean O'Casey's *The Silver Tassie* (1929).[5] Eliot's original position became for him a creed, evidenced by his Harvard lecture notes of 1933, the occasional poem 'A Note on War Poetry' (1942) and the essay 'T. S. Eliot on Poetry in Wartime' (1942). In these texts Eliot claimed that we need to distinguish between two types of poets: the real poet who finds himself thrown into war and the soldier who finds himself prone to poetry.[6] Eliot remained unpersuaded that poetry could ever be written from within the experience of war.[7]

Has *Modernist War Poetry* then followed Forster and exaggerated the importance of the war in the genealogy of modernist poetics? It has argued that the modernist long poem arose, in part, as a response to the arrival of the twentieth century's moral witness, to the combatant's absolute claim on the representation of an increasingly traumatic modernity, a claim epitomised by, but not exclusive to, the trench lyric. In this sense, we might think of the high modernist counter poetic as a last stand for the imagination, one which, when considered within a much longer history, runs back to an ideology of the aesthetic that appeared in the early nineteenth century.

'War' was never really the core of the issue for this modernism. Yeats said in *The Oxford Book of Modern Verse* that his 'distaste' was for 'poems written in the midst of the great war' and not for those 'written long after'.[8] Afterwardness, developed in 1914 in response to the poems of Laurence Binyon and others, survived the war as a ready-made critique of Wilfred Owen and Siegfried Sassoon.

---

[5] Denis Donoghue, 'The Literature of Trouble' (1978), in Denis Donoghue, *We Irish: Essays on Irish Literature and Society* (New York: Alfred A. Knopf, 1986), pp. 182–94 (p. 185); WBY [W. B. Yeats], letter to Sean O'Casey (20 April 1928), in *The Letters of W. B. Yeats*, ed. by Allan Wade (London: Rupert Hart-Davis, 1954), pp. 740–2; Sean O'Casey, *Autobiographies III: 'Rose and Crown' and 'Sunset and Evening Star'* (London: Faber and Faber, 2011), British Library ebook, para. 71.3. One reading of Arnold's poem is that it represents not a criticism of the passivity of suffering but Arnold's nervousness about the poem's conclusion, specifically that poetry was unable to save his anti-hero from the flames of modern self-consciousness, that it could not offer liberation through the stoical endurance of the everyday. O'Casey rightly exposed Yeats's critical double standards, highlighting Yeats's poetic depictions and dealings with Major Robert Gregory. Yeats's reading stands in contrast to Seamus Heaney's historicisation of the trope of passive suffering in the Anglo-Saxon tradition. For Heaney, grief is a profound effect of trauma. Seamus Heaney, 'On his Work in the English Tongue', in Seamus Heaney, *Electric Light* (London: Faber, 2001), pp. 61–3 (p. 62).

[6] See especially T. S. Eliot, letter to M. J. Tambimuttu (22 April 1941), qtd in Christopher Ricks and Jim McCue, 'Commentary: "A Note on War Poetry"', in Eliot, *Collected and Uncollected Poems*, pp. 1050–4 (p. 1051).

[7] T. S. Eliot, 'Lecture Notes for English 26: English Literature from 1890 to the Present Day', in *English Lion, 1930–1933*, pp. 758–809 (p. 783).

[8] Yeats, 'Introduction to *The Oxford Book of Modern Verse*', p. 199.

The concept barely changed in the intra-war period and Yeats redeployed it here in 1936. He gave examples of war poetries that he could celebrate: Aeschylus's *The Persians*, first performed eight years after the Battle of Salamis, *The Ballad of Chevy Chase*, whose origins lie deep in the annals of English and Scottish folk mythology, and Michael Drayton's epic poem *The Ballad of Agincourt*, published two centuries after the events it depicts. Eliot would make the same point in 1942 with the argument that there had been so little poetry of patriotism and even less written in the middle of the war.[9] The crucial issue at stake for this modernism was the poet's location in time and space. There could never be such a thing as War Poetry; 'war' and 'poetry' could not exist together.

There is an obvious inevitability in this position. What else could these modernists believe when they had committed their art to the imagination and its place in tradition? This would be unfair. We ought to credit this modernism with vision. In *Modernist War Poetry* this appears as a 'vanguard awareness', to borrow but invert Vincent Sherry's already cited phrase, which foresaw a loss of aesthetic control to the public marketplace. These modernists pinned their hostility on the combatant-poet. In Eliot's work especially we can sense this was a form of *ressentiment* in which he projected his frustration, anger and jealousy on to the poetic other. The game was already up. The mechanics of colonialism and capitalism had already pulled apart knowledge and experience leaving the fleshwitness as the witness to genocide. Despite all its limitations the trench lyric, and war writing more generally, has, unlike the modernist long poem which now lives only within the academy, remained a powerful language for understanding historical experience and speaking truth to power. This is then suggestive of the modernism described by Peter Howarth in *British Poetry in the Age of Modernism*. Howarth shows that precepts derived from Friedrich Schiller were always central to modernist classicism. It was a poetry which, by demanding resistance to the sentimental Taylorising effects of the market-based economy, could only come into being with and through a conceptualised understanding of an opposite.[10] Howarth's concept of supplementarity, the need for an aesthetic piñata, takes its place in *Modernist War Poetry* as the necessary Other of the trench lyric.

Supplementarity was not however inevitable. *Modernist War Poetry* has also described the emergence of the counter modernism of combat agnosticism. This war poetry sensed that there may well be an inexpressible and unrepresentable quality to the affective life of the Other. It is a forgotten narrative. It is though the most interesting of all the intra-war poetic modernisms. Despite a

---

[9] T. S. Eliot, 'T. S. Eliot on Poetry in Wartime' (1942), in *The Complete Prose of T. S. Eliot*, VI: *The War Years, 1940–1946*, ed. by David E. Chinitz and Ronald Schuchard (2017), pp. 326–8 (p. 326).

[10] Howarth, *British Poetry in the Age of Modernism*, pp. 41–5.

tone of resignation, an acceptance of the diminished or particular, it is also the most radical of all the positions to appear in response to the moral witness. Its reluctance to cast the imagination too far, its focus on ambiguity and its sense for the complex nature of alterity are suggestive of a cultural posthumanism to set against modernist anti-humanism. This suggests the concept of radical otherness as it developed through Emmanuel Levinas's *Altérité et Transcendence* (1995), Jean Baudrillard's *Figures de l'altérité* (1994) and Gayatri Chakravorty Spivak's 'Who Claims Alterity?' (1989).[11] In particular it suggests the idea that the self and the Other are so inherently complex that ethics must always sensitively negotiate with different identities and refuse the inclination to totalise the Other. If we are to read Eliot's formalism as the fruit of Fredric Jameson's 'singular modernity' marked by the colonialist homogenisation of culture and its intolerance for and fear of radical alterity, then the work of H.D., Gertrude Stein and Edward Thomas might be considered a very early intuition of the challenges that lay ahead in the twentieth century, especially the relationship between the real, its clones and copies.

We have not then exaggerated the importance of the war quite enough it would seem. 'The War crippled me as it did everyone else; but me chiefly because it was something I was neither honestly in nor honestly out of, but the *Waste Land* might have been just the same without the War,' Eliot told Forster.[12] It is wonderfully rhetorical. It appears as humble acceptance but the joint denial and that 'me chiefly' point to the unique position Eliot had assigned himself. The war neither crippled him in the way it crippled the committed combatant and committed conscientious objector, neither crippled him literally (*mutilé de guerre*) nor metaphorically (cripple from *crēopel*, to creep). Some unnamed external force kept Eliot out of the war. From this purgatorial plight Eliot created a third way. It was neither *p* nor *q*. He was neither the Tommy nor the conchie. It was *p* NOR *q*, a superior poetic vantage point arising out of the very conflicted nature of the position betwixt and between.[13]

Here then lies one of the most significant problems of all. Despite theoretical and ethical opposition to Eliot's project there is a very strange similarity between modernist non-combat gnosticism and James Campbell's critique of combat gnosticism. That similarity finds itself embedded in the shift to see modernist form in general as a putative trauma aesthetic. The modernist long poem aimed to be about the war. *Aboute, abutan*: on the outside of, around the

---

[11] For a useful overview see Lisa Isherwood and David Harris, *Radical Otherness: Sociological and Theoretical Approaches* (Abingdon: Routledge, 2013), p. 9.

[12] Eliot, letter to E. M. Forster (10 August 1929), p. 573.

[13] For similar issues in Eliot's work see T. S. Eliot, 'A Note of Introduction', in David Jones, *In Parenthesis* (London: Faber and Faber, 1963), pp. vii–xv (pp. vii–viii). Eliot notes that the lives of all the modernist poets were altered by the war although Jones was the only one to have fought in it.

circumference, in the vicinity of, near in time, number or degree, rotating and spinning around an object. Hither and thither, neither in nor out. To link the cover illustration of this narrative with Eliot's phraseology in 'Gerontion', we might say the modernist long poem was always only ever knee deep in things. It got its feet wet without ever being up to the neck in it all. This is not a valorisation of being up to the neck in things. It is to suggest that being 'about' something is always a risky business. As Eliot's response to Forster suggested there has to be something inherently magical about the poetry of this *magus* and his fellow *magi*. Eliot said to Forster it was a gnosticism capable of a poem about the war that would have been just the same without the war. Really?

In the last two decades aboutness has become a positively valenced term in literary studies. In Dominick LaCapra's *Writing History, Writing Trauma* (2001) aboutness connotes a specific stylistic method which relies on metaphor to serve a referential function to deal with the inaccessibility of trauma.[14] As Joshua Pederson (2018) usefully illustrates, this form of traumatic realism functions in relation to the unsaid in much the same way that medieval allegory functioned in relation to the ineffable experience of the sacred.[15] It is a poetics of suggestion. We can see the shape of this in Allyson Booth's astute observation in *Reading 'The Waste Land'* that we now think about the war as 'everywhere and nowhere' in Eliot's long poem. It is neither quite foreground nor background but yet fully absorbed into it.[16] That is right, and it is how we read and often teach it. The cover of Lawrence Rainey's (2006) annotated edition of *The Waste Land* with its deserted landscape of broken trees, taken in fact from the tailings of a uranium mine, redeploys Eliot's method to hint at the link between the war, scientific catastrophe and ecological disaster.[17] This technique of hinting from fragments is key. The dead of *The Waste Land*, its haunted memories, the soldiers found in hell in *Hugh Selwyn Mauberley* and the repetitive beat of combatants sent to their death in *A Draft of XVI Cantos*: these punctuated, hallucinatory and luminous moments are held by Longenbach in *Stone Cottage* (1988) as the moments in which the modernist non-combatants found a visionary sensibility close to those poets who actually saw action.[18]

The problem with aboutness though is that it is difficult to see just whereabouts it begins and where it ends. Like non-combat gnosticism it is a last stand of sorts. It arose from the rubble of deconstruction's critique of referentiality

---

[14] Dominick LaCapra, *Writing History, Writing Trauma* (Baltimore: Johns Hopkins University Press, 2001), p. 188.

[15] Joshua Pederson, 'Trauma and Narrative', in Kurtz, ed., pp. 97–109 (p. 103).

[16] Booth, *Reading 'The Waste Land'*, p. 15.

[17] *The Annotated 'Waste Land' with Eliot's Contemporary Prose*, ed. by Lawrence Rainey, 2nd edn (New Haven: Yale University Press, 2006).

[18] Eliot, '*The Waste Land*', pp. 57, 59; Pound, *Hugh Selwyn Mauberley*, p. 551; Longenbach, *Stone Cottage*, p. 130.

which left behind it a dead end and the death of *écriture*. It emerged in order to reinvest the word with a figurative and highly aestheticised communication toolkit through which we could acknowledge and yet reapproach the incommunicability of trauma.[19] In Geoffrey Hartman's 'On Traumatic Knowledge and Literary Studies' (1995), for example, much rests on the relationship between trauma and the Saussurean model of language.[20] Its core assumption is that the figurative succeeds at the very moment words begin to break down. As things fragment and fall apart, as the centre fails to hold, as the signifier and signified part, language survives. It gains some brief evanescent access to traumatic horror.[21] This is not of course the only account of trauma and in Ian Hacking's *Mad Travelers* (1998) and Ruth Leys's *Trauma: A Genealogy* (2000) the model is subject to persuasive challenge.[22] We could, for example, read aboutness's desire to re-inject ethics into the dead end of textuality as no more than the recovery of a much-mutated notion of the sublime.[23]

Modernist War Poetry suggests we should treat these as complex issues. Questions related to whether we can imagine the Other's mind and whether figurative language can read wounds are very problematical. Our responses must be hypotheses. The question is whether we have recursively adopted the practices of those writers we study; whether we have elevated the imagination to a pedestal from which it can only fall.

There are then two issues to consider in closing. First, if we accept aboutness, and it seems reasonable that one would want to, then it must surely move in many directions. We have seen some modernists turn repeatedly to a language of abjection in their encounter with war verse. They turn also to heavily gendered metaphors of containerisation with a masculinist emphasis on control. Does this not appear in aggregate as a deep-seated disgust, an anxious defence mechanism in the face of the need to reclaim cultural power?[24] In this sense, if *The Waste Land* is about the war, then *The Sacred Wood* is very much about it too. The war is then everywhere.

If, however, we reject aboutness, we might read those luminescent glimpses of the war in some modernist poetries as a copy or a clone, an approximation,

---

[19] Tom Toremans, 'Deconstruction: Trauma Inscribed in Language', in Kurtz, ed., pp. 51–65 (pp. 53–5).

[20] Geoffrey Hartman, 'On Traumatic Knowledge and Literary Studies', *New Literary History*, 26.3 (1995), 537–63.

[21] Leys, p. 268.

[22] Ian Hacking, *Mad Travelers: Reflections on the Reality of Transient Mental Illness* (Cambridge, MA: Harvard University Press, 1998).

[23] In response see Dominick LaCapra, *History in Transit: Experience, Identity, Critical Theory* (Ithaca, NY: Cornell University Press, 2004), pp. 120–2.

[24] Amanda Burlingham, Chad McDaniel and David O. Wilson, 'A Historical Review of Disgust', *Modern Psychological Studies*, 5.2 (Fall 1997), 39–42.

something about somewhere. They risk the same fate as Romantic expressivity, simulacra of indistinct originals rather than the recovery of mourning from melancholia. This might be less problematic if the modernist long poem satisfied itself with being a home-front war poetry or a poetry of aftermath. It flatly rejected both. It could not accept the sensitive limits of the agnostics. It craved the death of the trench lyric. It laid claim to, it was about, the entirety of the war as a historical, social, political, cultural and personal experience. How much did it really know? Who is it who says that it feels like this? To those in pain specificity really matters. How much do the metaphors of these magnificos result in a crude mimesis, a simulation of the traumatised mind? How much does the violent effort to salvage the imagination, to bridge the gap between experience and knowledge and reclaim what capitalistic modernity has broken asunder, become a colonisation, an appalling ethical voiding?

BIBLIOGRAPHY

Ackroyd, Peter, *T. S. Eliot* (London: Penguin, 1993)

Adams, Nicholas, and others, eds, *The Oxford Handbook of Theology and Modern European Thought* (Oxford: Oxford University Press, 2013)

A. F., 'Youth at War', *Poetry*, 10.1 (April 1917), 38–41

Aiken, Conrad, 'The Ivory Tower – I', *New Republic*, 19.236 (10 May 1919), 58–60

——, *Scepticisms: Notes on Contemporary Poetry* (New York: Alfred A. Knopf, 1919)

Aldington, Richard, 'French Authors and the War', *The Egoist*, 2.2 (February 1915), 28

——, 'Penultimate Poetry: Xenophilometropolitania', *The Egoist*, 1.2 (January 1914), 36

——, 'The Poetry of Ezra Pound', *The Egoist*, 2.5 (1 May 1915), 71–2

——, 'The Poetry of the Future', *Poetry*, 14.5 (August 1919), 266–9

——, 'Remy de Gourmont, After the Interim', *Little Review*, 5.10–11 (February–March 1919), 32–4

——, 'Reviews: Recent French Poetry', *Poetry*, 15.1 (October 1919), 42–8

——, *Richard Aldington: An Autobiography in Letters*, ed. by Norman T. Gates (University Park: Pennsylvania State University Press, 1992)

——, 'Thanatos', *Little Review*, 3.9 (March 1917), 10

——, *War and Love (1915–1918)* (Boston: Four Seas, 1919)

——, 'War Poems and Others', *The Egoist*, 1.24 (15 December 1914), 458–9

Alighieri, Dante, *The Divine Comedy*, trans. by C. H. Sisson (Oxford: Oxford University Press, 1993; repr. 2008)

Allison, Jonathan, 'War, Passive Suffering, and the Poet', *Sewanee Review*, 114.2 (Spring 2006), 207–19

Anderson, Margaret C., 'The War', *Little Review*, 3.10 (April 1917), 4

——, '"The World's Immense Wound"', *Little Review*, 4.3 (July 1917), 27–8

Ansari, Humayun, *'The Infidel Within': Muslims in Britain since 1800* (London: Hurst & Company, 2004)

Ardis, Ann L., and Leslie W. Lewis, eds, *Women's Experience of Modernity, 1875–1945* (Baltimore: Johns Hopkins University Press, 2003)

Aristotle, *On the Art of Poetry*, trans. by Ingram Bywater (Oxford: Clarendon Press, 1920; repr. 1988)

Armstrong, Tim, *Modernism: A Cultural History* (Cambridge: Polity Press, 2005)

——, 'Two Types of Shock in Modernity', *Critical Quarterly*, 42.1 (2000), 60–73

Arnold, Matthew, *'Empedocles on Etna' and Other Poems* (London: B. Fellowes, 1852)

——, *Poems*, new edn (Boston: Ticknor and Fields, 1856)

A Soldier of France to his Mother: Letters from the Trenches on the Western Front, trans. by Theodore Stanton (Chicago: A. C. McClurg, 1917)

Authors Take Sides on the Spanish War (London: Left Review, 1937)

Avramides, Anita, *Other Minds* (London: Routledge, 2001)

Bainbridge, Simon, *British Poetry and the Revolutionary and Napoleonic Wars: Visions of Conflict* (Oxford: Oxford University Press, 2003)

Baker, Ernest A., 'English in War-Time', *The Athenæum*, 4647 (23 May 1919), 359–60

——, 'Slang in War-Time', *The Athenæum*, 4654 (11 July 1919), 582–3

Banfield, Ann, *The Phantom Table: Woolf, Fry, Russell and the Epistemology of Modernism* (Cambridge: Cambridge University Press, 2000)

Barbusse, Henri, *Under Fire*, trans. by Robin Buss (London: Penguin, 2003)

——, *Under Fire: The Story of a Squad (Le Feu)*, trans. by Fitzwater Wray (New York: E. P. Dutton, 1917)

Baudrillard, Jean, and Marc Guillaume, *Radical Alterity* (Los Angeles: Semiotext(e), 2008)

Beasley, Rebecca, *Theorists of Modern Poetry: T. S. Eliot, T. E. Hulme, Ezra Pound* (Abingdon: Routledge, 2007)

Bell, Michael, *Sentimentalism, Ethics and the Culture of Feeling* (Basingstoke: Palgrave, 2000)

Benjamin, Walter, *Illuminations*, ed. by Hannah Arendt, trans. by Harry Zorn (New York: Harcourt, Brace & World, 1968; repr. London: Pimlico, 1999)

Bergson, Henri, *An Introduction to Metaphysics*, trans. by T. E. Hulme, rev. edn (New York: G. P. Putnam, 1912; repr. Indianapolis: Hackett Publishing, 1999)

——, *Time and Free Will: An Essay on the Immediate Data of Consciousness*, trans. by F. L. Pogson (London: George Allen & Unwin, 1910; repr. Abingdon: Routledge, 2013)

Bick, Esther, 'Further Considerations on the Function of the Skin in Early Object Relations. Findings from Infant Observation Integrated into Child and Adult Analysis', *British Journal of Psychotherapy*, 2.4 (June 1986), 292–9

Binyon, Laurence, *The Four Years: War Poems* (London: Elkin Matthews, 1919)

Bion, Wilfred R., *Learning from Experience* (Lanham, MD: Rowman & Littlefield, 1962; repr. 2004)

Bloom, Paul, *Against Empathy: The Case for Rational Compassion* (New York: Ecco, 2016)

Boll, Theophilus E. M., *Miss May Sinclair: Novelist, A Biographical and Critical Introduction* (Cranbury, NJ: Associated University Presses, 1973)

Bonikowski, Wyatt, *Shell Shock and the Modernist Imagination: The Death Drive in Post-World War I British Fiction* (Farnham: Routledge, 2013)

Booth, Allyson, *Postcards from the Trenches: Negotiating the Space between Modernism and the First World War* (Oxford: Oxford University Press, 1996)

——, *Reading 'The Waste Land' from the Bottom Up* (New York: Palgrave Macmillan, 2015)

Bornstein, George, ed., *Ezra Pound among the Poets* (Chicago: University of Chicago Press, 1985)

Boughn, Michael, *H.D.: A Bibliography 1905–1990* (Charlottesville: University Press of Virginia, 1993)

Bourdieu, Pierre, *Practical Reason: On the Theory of Action* (Stanford: Stanford University Press, 1998)

Bourke, Joanna, *Dismembering the Male: Men's Bodies, Britain and the Great War* (London: Reaktion, 1996)

Bowie, Malcolm, *Lacan* (Cambridge, MA: Harvard University Press, 1991)

Boyd, Ernest A., 'The Imperviousness of Literature to War', *New Age*, 18.10 (6 January 1916), 227–8

Bradbury, Malcolm, and James McFarlane, eds, *Modernism: A Guide to European Literature 1890–1930*, rev. edn (London: Penguin, 1991)

Bradley, F. H., *Appearance and Reality: A Metaphysical Essay* (London: Swan Sonnenschein, 1893)

——, *The Presuppositions of Critical History* (Oxford: James Parker, 1874)

Brann, Eva T. H., *The World of the Imagination: Sum and Substance* (Lanham, MD: Rowman & Littlefield, 1991)

'British wire defences in front of sandbags at St. Eloi, May 1915', Imperial War Museum, Q 52028 Mrs Morris Alfred Collection, <https://www.iwm.org.uk/collections/item/object/205285665> [accessed 24 March 2022]

Brittain, Vera, *Because You Died: Poetry and Prose of the First World War and After*, ed. and intro. by Mark Bostridge (London: Hachette Digital, 2010), ebook

Brooke, Rupert, *The Collected Poems of Rupert Brooke* (London: John Lane, 1915)

——, *The Collected Poems of Rupert Brooke* (New York: Dodd, Mead, 1931)

——, *The Collected Poems of Rupert Brooke: With a Memoir* (London: Sidgwick & Jackson, 1918)

——, *Letters of Rupert Brooke*, ed. by Geoffrey Keynes (London: Faber and Faber, 1968)

——, The Papers of Rupert Chawner Brooke (RCB/Xb/2/2), King's College Cambridge

——, *The Poetical Works*, ed. by Geoffrey Keynes (London: Faber and Faber, 1970)

Brooker, Jewel Spears, 'The Great War at Home and Abroad: Violence and Sexuality in Eliot's "Sweeney Erect"', *Modernism/modernity*, 9.3 (September 2002), 423–38

——, *Mastery and Escape: T. S. Eliot and the Dialectic of Modernism* (Amherst: University of Massachusetts Press, 1994)

——, ed., *T. S. Eliot: The Contemporary Reviews* (Cambridge: Cambridge University Press, 2004)

Brooker, Peter, and Andrew Thacker, eds, *The Oxford Critical and Cultural History of Modernist Magazines*, 3 vols (Oxford: Oxford University Press, 2009–13), I: *Britain and Ireland 1880–1955* (2009)

Brown, Catherine, 'Anglo-German Relations and D. H. Lawrence's "All of Us"', <http://catherinebrown.org/anglo-german-relations-and-d-h-lawrences-all-of-us/> [accessed 30 March 2022]

Browning, Robert, *Sordello* (London: Edward Moxon, 1840)

Buchanan, David A., *Going Scapegoat: Post-9/11 War Literature, Language and Culture* (Jefferson, NC: McFarland, 2016)

Buelens, Gert, and others, eds, *The Future of Trauma Theory: Contemporary Literary and Cultural Criticism* (New York: Routledge, 2014)

Burke, Carolyn, *Becoming Modern: The Life of Mina Loy* (New York: Farrar, Straus and Giroux, 1996)

Burlingham, Amanda, Chad McDaniel and David O. Wilson, 'A Historical Review of Disgust', *Modern Psychological Studies*, 5.2 (Fall 1997), 39–42

Burne, Glenn S., 'Remy de Gourmont and the Aesthetics of Symbolism', *Comparative Literature Studies*, 4.1/2 (1967), 161–75

Bush, Ronald L., *The Genesis of Ezra Pound's Cantos* (Princeton: Princeton University Press, 1976)

Buttel, Robert, *Wallace Stevens: The Making of 'Harmonium'* (Princeton: Princeton University Press, 1967)

Caesar, Adrian, *Taking It Like a Man: Suffering, Sexuality and the War Poets, Brooke, Sassoon, Owen, Graves* (Manchester: Manchester University Press, 1993)

Campbell, James, 'Combat Gnosticism: The Ideology of First World War Poetry Criticism', *New Literary History*, 30.1 (1999), 203–15

Capozzola, Christopher, *Uncle Sam Wants You: World War I and the Making of the Modern American Citizen* (Oxford: Oxford University Press, 2008)

Carden-Coyne, Ana, *Reconstructing the Body: Classicism, Modernism, and the First World War* (Oxford: Oxford University Press, 2009)

Caroll, Robert, and Stephen Prickett, *The Bible: Authorized King James Version* (New York: Oxford University Press, 1997)

Carr, Helen, *The Verse Revolutionaries: Ezra Pound, H.D. and the Imagists* (London: Jonathan Cape, 2009)

Caruth, Cathy, *Unclaimed Experience: Trauma, Narrative and History* (Baltimore: Johns Hopkins University Press, 1996)

——, ed., *Trauma: Explorations in Memory* (Baltimore: Johns Hopkins University Press, 1995)

Caruth, Cathy, and Geoffrey Hartman, 'An Interview with Geoffrey Hartman', *Studies in Romanticism*, 35.4 (1996), 630–52

Castle, Gregory, ed., *A History of the Modernist Novel* (Cambridge: Cambridge University Press, 2015)

Cendrars, Blaise, *Complete Poems*, trans. by Ron Padgett (Berkeley: University of California Press, 1992)

Cesarani, David, and Tony Kushner, eds, *The Internment of Aliens in Twentieth Century Britain* (Abingdon: Routledge, 1993)

C.F., 'Montmartre at War', *The Athenæum*, 4704 (25 June 1920), 844

Chalmers, David J., 'Facing up to the Problem of Consciousness', *Journal of Consciousness Studies*, 2.3 (1995), 200–19

Chambers, Ross, *Untimely Interventions: AIDS Writing, Testimonial, and the Rhetoric of Haunting* (Ann Arbor: University of Michigan Press, 2004)

Chasseaud, Peter, *Rats Alley: Trench Names of the Western Front, 1914–1918*, 2nd edn (Stroud: History Press, 2017), British Library ebook

Chesterton, G. K., 'At the Sign of the World's End: The Jew and the Journalist', *New Witness* (11 October 1917), 562–3

Chickering, Roger, and Stig Förster, eds, *Great War, Total War: Combat and Mobilization on the Western Front, 1914–1918* (Cambridge: Cambridge University Press, 2000)

Childs, Daniel J., *Modernism and Eugenics: Woolf, Eliot, Yeats, and the Culture of Degeneration* (Cambridge: Cambridge University Press, 2001)

Chinitz, David E., ed., *A Companion to T. S. Eliot* (Chichester: Wiley-Blackwell, 2009)

Chong-Gossard, J. H. Kim On, *Gender and Communication in Euripides' Plays: Between Song and Silence* (Leiden: Brill, 2008)

Christodoulides, Nephie J., and Polina Mackay, eds, *The Cambridge Companion to H.D.* (Cambridge: Cambridge University Press, 2012)

Ciolkowska, Muriel, '"Le Feu". Goncourt Prize for 1916', *The Egoist*, 4.4 (May 1917), 55–7

——, 'The French Word in Modern Prose. II. – Henry Barbusse, *L'Enfer*', *The Egoist*, 3.2 (1 February 1916), 27–8

——, 'Passing Paris', *The Egoist*, 4.7 (August 1917), 105–6

——, 'Passing Paris', *The Egoist*, 4.11 (December 1917), 168–9

——, 'Passing Paris', *The Egoist*, 5.2 (February 1918), 23–4

Clapham, Marcus, ed., *The Wordsworth Book of First World War Poetry* (Ware: Wordsworth Editions, 1995)

Clark, Ian, *Waging War: A Philosophical Introduction*, reissued edn (Oxford: Clarendon Press, 1990)

Clayson, Hollis, *Painted Love: Prostitution in French Art of the Impressionist Era* (Los Angeles: Getty, 2003)

Coetzee, J. M., *Disgrace* (New York: Penguin, 2000)

——, *Elizabeth Costello: Eight Lessons* (London: Vintage, 2004)

Cohen, Joseph, 'Isaac Rosenberg: From Romantic to Classic', *Tulane Studies in English*, 10 (1960), 129–42

Cohn, Dorrit, *Transparent Minds: Narrative Minds for Presenting Consciousness in Fiction* (Princeton: Princeton University Press, 1978)

Cole, Margaret Postgate, *Margaret Postgate's Poems* (London: George Allen & Unwin, 1918)

Cole, Sarah, *At the Violet Hour: Modernism and Violence in England and Ireland* (Oxford: Oxford University Press, 2012)

——, *Modernism, Male Friendship, and the First World War* (Cambridge: Cambridge University Press, 2003)

——, 'Modernism, Male Intimacy, and the Great War', *ELH*, 68 (2001), 469–500

Coleridge, Samuel Taylor, and William Wordsworth, *Lyrical Ballads 1798 and 1800*, ed. by Michael Gamer and Dahlia Porter (Peterborough, Ontario: Broadview Editions, 2008)

Collecott, Diana, *H.D. and Sapphic Modernism* (Cambridge: Cambridge University Press, 1999)

Collingwood, R. G., *The Idea of History*, ed. by Jan van der Dussen, rev. edn (Oxford: Oxford University Press, 1994)

Colls, Robert, and Philip Dodd, eds, *Englishness: Politics and Culture 1880–1920*, 2nd edn (London: Bloomsbury, 2014)

Colum, Padraic, 'Rilke's Poems', *Poetry*, 14.3 (June 1919), 168–70

Comentale, Edward P., and Andrzej Gasiorek, eds, *T. E. Hulme and the Question of Modernism* (Farnham: Ashgate Publishing, 2006; repr. Abingdon: Routledge, 2016)

Commonwealth War Graves Commission, 'Lieutenant Hulme, Thomas Ernest', <https://www.cwgc.org/find-war-dead/casualty/89831/hulme,-thomas-ernest/> [accessed 24 March 2022]

Connor, Steven, 'A love letter to an unloved place', *Nightwaves*, BBC Radio 3, 22 June 2004, <http://www.stevenconnor.com/corridors/> [accessed 24 March 2022]

Conrad, Joseph, *The Nigger of the Narcissus* (London: William Heinemann, [1897]; repr. Garden City, NY: Doubleday, 1914)

Coplan, Amy, and Peter Goldie, eds, *Empathy: Philosophical and Psychological Perspectives* (Oxford: Oxford University Press, 2011)

Cork, Richard, *A Bitter Truth: Avant-Garde Art and the Great War* (New Haven: Yale University Press, 1994)

Cournos, John, 'Discussion: The Death of Vorticism', *Little Review*, 6.2 (June 1919), 46–8

Crawford, Nelson Antrim, 'New War Poets', *Poetry*, 16.6 (September 1920), 336–40

Crawford, Robert, *Young Eliot: From St Louis to 'The Waste Land'* (London: Vintage, 2015)

Culler, Jonathan, *Structuralist Poetics: Structuralism, Linguistics and the Study of Literature*, rev. edn (London: Routledge, 2002)

——, *Theory of the Lyric* (Cambridge, MA: Harvard University Press, 2015)

Cummings, E. E., 'T. S. Eliot', *Dial*, 68 (June 1920), 781–4

Das, Santanu, '"Kiss me, Hardy": Intimacy, Gender, and Gesture in World War I Trench Literature', *Modernism/modernity*, 9.1 (2002), 51–74

——, *Touch and Intimacy in First World War Literature* (Cambridge: Cambridge University Press, 2005)

——, ed., *The Cambridge Companion to the Poetry of the First World War* (Cambridge: Cambridge University Press, 2013)

Davis, Alex, and Lee M. Jenkins, eds, *The Cambridge Companion to Modernist Poetry* (Cambridge: Cambridge University Press, 2007)

'"The Day"', *The Times*, 18 February 1915, p. 11

Dean, Carolyn J., *The Moral Witness: Trials and Testimony after Genocide* (Ithaca, NY: Cornell University Press, 2019)

DeCoste, Damon Marcel, '"A Frank Expression of Personality"? Sentimentality, Silence and Early Modernist Aesthetics in *The Good Soldier*', *Journal
of Modern Literature*, 31.1 (Fall 2007), 102–23

De Gourmont, Remy, 'French Poets and the War, translated by Richard
Aldington', *Poetry*, 5.4 (January 1915), 184–8

——, *Selected Writings*, ed. and trans. by Glenn S. Burne (Ann Arbor: University of Michigan Press, 1966)

De la Selva, Salomón, 'Strains of Yesterday', *Poetry*, 11.5 (February 1918),
281–2

DeMeester, Karen, 'Trauma and Recovery in Virginia Woolf's *Mrs Dalloway*',
Modern Fiction Studies, 44.3 (1998), 649–73

Dennett, Daniel C., *Consciousness Explained* (Boston: Little, Brown, 1991)

——, *From Bacteria to Bach and Back: The Evolution of Minds* (New York:
W. W. Norton, 2017)

Derrida, Jacques, *Of Grammatology*, trans. by Gayatri Chakravorty Spivak,
corrected edn (Baltimore: Johns Hopkins University Press, 1997)

Deutsch, Babette, 'Out of the Den', *Poetry*, 16.3 (June 1920), 159–62

Dickie, Margaret, *Stein, Bishop, and Rich: Lyrics of Love, War, and Place*
(Chapel Hill: University of North Carolina Press, 1997)

Dilthey, Wilhelm, *Descriptive Psychology and Historical Understanding*, trans.
by Richard M. Zaner and Kenneth L. Heiges (The Hague: Martinus
Nijhoff, 1977)

Dodman, Trevor, *Shell Shock, Memory, and the Novel in the Wake of World
War I* (Cambridge: Cambridge University Press, 2015)

Donoghue, Denis, *We Irish: Essays on Irish Literature and Society* (New York:
Alfred A. Knopf, 1986)

Doolittle, Hilda, *Between History and Poetry: The Letters of H.D. and
Norman Holmes Pearson*, ed. by Donna Krolik Hollenberg (Iowa
City: University of Iowa Press, 1997)

——, *Bid Me to Live: A Madrigal* (Redding Ridge, CT: Black Swan Books,
1983)

——, *Collected Poems 1912–1944*, ed. by Louis L. Martz (New York: New
Directions, 1983)

——, H.D. Papers (YCAL MSS 24), Beinecke Library

——, *Heliodora and Other Poems* (Boston: Houghton Mifflin, [1924])

——, *Hymen* (London: Egoist Press, 1921)

——, 'Marianne Moore', *The Egoist*, 3.8 (August 1916), 118–19

——, *'Notes on Thought and Vision' and 'The Wise Sappho'* (San Francisco:
City Lights Books, 1982)

——, *Sea Garden* (London: Constable, 1916)

Douglas, J. D., Merrill C. Tenney and Moisés Silva, *Zondervan Illustrated
Bible Dictionary* (Grand Rapids, MI: Zondervan, 2011)

Douglass, Paul, ed., *T. S. Eliot, Dante, and the Idea of Europe* (Newcastle upon Tyne: Cambridge Scholars, 2011)

Doyle, Charles, *Richard Aldington: A Biography* (Basingstoke: Macmillan, 1989)

——, ed., *Wallace Stevens: The Critical Heritage* (London: Routledge, 1985)

Duddington, Nathalie A., 'Our Knowledge of Other Minds', *Proceedings of the Aristotelian Society*, 19 (1918–19), 147–78

Eagleton, Terry, *The Ideology of the Aesthetic* (Oxford: Blackwell, 1990)

Eagleton, Terry, Frederic Jameson and Edward W. Said, *Nationalism, Colonialism, and Literature* (Minneapolis: University of Minnesota Press, 2001)

Edwards, Justin D., and Rune Graulund, *Grotesque: New Critical Idiom* (Abingdon: Routledge, 2013)

'*The Egoist*: An Individualist Review', *Poetry*, 5.5 (February 1915), [258]

Eksteins, Modris, *Rites of Spring: The Great War and the Birth of the Modern Age* (Boston: Houghton Mifflin, 1989)

Eliot, T. S., *Ara Vos Prec* (London: Ovid Press, 1920)

——, *The Complete Prose of T. S. Eliot*, ed. by Ronald Schuchard and others, The Critical Edition, 8 vols (Baltimore and London: Johns Hopkins University Press and Faber and Faber, 2014–19), I: *Apprentice Years, 1905–1918*, ed. by Jewel Spears Brooker and Ronald Schuchard (2014)

——, *The Complete Prose of T. S. Eliot*, II: *The Perfect Critic, 1919–1926*, ed. by Anthony Cuda and Ronald Schuchard (2014)

——, *The Complete Prose of T. S. Eliot*, III: *Literature, Politics, Belief, 1927–1929*, ed. by Frances Dickey and others (2015)

——, *The Complete Prose of T. S. Eliot*, IV: *English Lion, 1930–1933*, ed. by Jason Harding and Ronald Schuchard (2015)

——, *The Complete Prose of T. S. Eliot*, V: *Tradition and Orthodoxy, 1934–1939*, ed. by Imran Javadi and others (2017)

——, *The Complete Prose of T. S. Eliot*, VI: *The War Years, 1940–1946*, ed. by David E. Chinitz and Ronald Schuchard (2017)

——, *Inventions of the March Hare, Poems 1909–1917*, ed. by Christopher Ricks (London: Faber and Faber, 1996)

——, *The Letters of T. S. Eliot*, ed. by Valerie Eliot, John Haffenden and Hugh Haughton, 9 vols to date (London: Faber and Faber, 1988–), I: *1898–1922*, ed. by Valerie Eliot and Hugh Haughton, rev. edn (2009)

——, *The Letters of T. S. Eliot*, IV: *1928–1929*, ed. by Valerie Eliot and John Haffenden (2013)

——, *The Letters of T. S. Eliot*, V: *1930–1931*, ed. by Valerie Eliot and John Haffenden (2014)

——, *Poems* (London: Hogarth Press, 1919)

——, *Poems* (New York: Alfred A. Knopf, 1920)

——, *Poems 1909–1925* (London: Faber and Gwyer, 1925)

——, *The Poems of T. S. Eliot*, ed. by Christopher Ricks and Jim McCue, 2 vols (London: Faber and Faber, 2015), I: *Collected and Uncollected Poems*

——, *The Poems of T. S. Eliot*, II: *Practical Cats and Further Verses*

——, *Prufrock and Other Observations* (London: Egoist, 1917)

——, *The Sacred Wood: Essays on Poetry and Criticism* (London: Methuen, 1920)

——, *'The Waste Land': A Facsimile and Transcript of the Original Drafts Including the Annotations of Ezra Pound*, ed. by Valerie Eliot (Orlando: Harcourt, 1971)

Engberg-Pedersen, Anders, *Empire of Chance: The Napoleonic Wars and the Disorder of Things* (Cambridge, MA: Harvard University Press, 2015)

Euripides, *Bacchae, Iphigenia at Aulis, Rhesus*, ed. and trans. by David Kovacs, Loeb Classical Library, 495 (Cambridge, MA: Harvard University Press, 2002)

——, *The Plays of Euripides, Translated into English Prose from the Text of Paley*, trans. by Edward P. Coleridge, 2 vols (London: George Bell, 1891), II

Evans, Donald, *Nine Poems from a Valetudinarium* (Philadelphia: Nicholas L. Brown, 1916)

Faber, Geoffrey, *In the Valley of Vision: Poems Written in Time of War* (Oxford: Blackwell, 1918)

F.D., 'English Youth', *Masses*, 8.11 (September 1916), 34–5

Felman, Shoshana, and Dori Laub, eds, *Testimony: Crises of Witnessing in Literature, Psychoanalysis, and History* (New York: Routledge, 1992)

Ferguson, Rex, *Criminal Law and the Modernist Novel* (Cambridge: Cambridge University Press, 2013)

Ferguson, Robert, *The Short Sharp Life of T. E. Hulme* (London: Allen Lane, 2002; repr. London: Faber and Faber, 2012)

Ficke, Arthur Davison, 'Of Rupert Brooke and Other Matters', *Little Review*, 1.5 (July 1914), 17–21

——, 'To Rupert Brooke I–V', *Poetry*, 6.3 (June 1915), 113–16

Fletcher, John Gould, *Life Is My Song* (New York: Farrar & Rinehart, 1937)

——, 'More War Poetry', *The Egoist*, 1.22 (16 November 1914), 424–6

——, 'On Subject-Matter and War Poetry', *The Egoist*, 3.12 (December 1916), 188–9

——, 'War Poetry', *The Egoist*, 1.21 (2 November 1914), 410–11

Flint, F. S., *The Fourth Imagist: Selected Poems of F. S. Flint*, ed. by Michael Copp (Madison, NJ: Fairleigh Dickinson University Press, 2007), Google ebook

——, 'The History of Imagism', *The Egoist*, 2.5 (1 May 1915), 70–1

——, 'Soldiers', *The Egoist*, 3.9 (September 1916), 134

——, 'Some Modern French Poets (A Commentary with Specimens)', *Monthly Chapbook*, 4.1 (October 1919)

——, 'War-time', *Poetry*, 7.5 (February 1916), 231–2

Ford, Ford Madox, *Antwerp* (London: Poetry Bookshop, [1915])

——, *Critical Writings of Ford Madox Ford*, ed. by Frank MacShane (Lincoln: University of Nebraska Press, 1964)

——, 'From China to Peru', *Outlook*, 35 (19 June 1915), 800–1

——, *The Good Soldier: A Tale of Passion*, ed. by Kenneth Womack and William Baker (Peterborough: Broadview, 2003)

——, 'Henri Gaudier, The Story of a Low Tea-shop', *English Review*, 26 (October 1919), 297–304

——, *'On Heaven' and Poems Written on Active Service* (London: John Lane, 1918)

——, *War Prose*, ed. by Max Saunders (Manchester: Carcanet, 1999)

——, 'W. H. Hudson: Some Reminiscences', *Little Review*, 7.1 (May–June 1920), 3–12

Forter, Greg, 'Freud, Faulkner, Caruth: Trauma and the Politics of Literary Form', *Narrative*, 15.3 (October 2007), 259–85

Foster, A. E. Manning, ed., *Lord God of Battles: A War Anthology* (London: Cope and Fenwick, 1914)

Fox, James, *British Art and the First World War 1914–1924* (Cambridge: Cambridge University Press, 2015)

Freedman, Ariela, 'Zeppelin Fictions and the British Home Front', *Journal of Modern Literature*, 27.3 (Winter 2004), 47–63

Freud, Sigmund, *The Standard Edition of the Complete Psychological Works of Sigmund Freud*, ed. and trans. by James Strachey, 24 vols (London: Hogarth Press, 1957–74; repr. London: Vintage, 2001), XIV: *1914–1916: 'On the History of the Psycho-Analytic Movement'*, *'Papers on Metapsychology'*, *and Other Works* (1957; repr. 2001)

Freytag-Loringhoven, Else von, 'Poems', *Little Review*, 6.10 (March 1920), 10–12

Friedman, Susan Stanford, *Penelope's Web: Gender, Modernity, H.D.'s Fiction* (Cambridge: Cambridge University Press, 1990)

Frost, Robert, *Collected Poems, Prose, and Plays*, ed. by Richard Poirier and Mark Richardson (New York: Library of America, 1995)

Froula, Christine, *To Write Paradise: Style and Error in Pound's 'Cantos'* (New Haven: Yale University Press, 1984)

Fuller, Henry B., 'The Brooke Letters', *Poetry*, 8.3 (June 1916), 155–7

Fussell, Paul, *The Great War and Modern Memory*, 25th anniversary edn (Oxford: Oxford University Press, 2000)

Gadamer, Hans-Georg, *Truth and Method*, trans. by Joel Weinsheimer and Donald G. Marshall (London: Bloomsbury, 2013)

Gaudier-Brzeska, Henri, 'Vortex', *Blast*, 2 (July 1915), 33–4

Georgian Poetry 1913–1915 (London: Poetry Bookshop, [1915])

Georgian Poetry 1916–1917 (London: Poetry Bookshop, 1917)

Gibbs, Philip, *From Bapaume to Passchendaele, 1917* (Toronto: William Briggs, 1918)

Gibson, Wilfrid Wilson, *Battle* (New York: Macmillan, 1915)

Gilbert, Sandra M., '"Rats' Alley": The Great War, Modernism, and the (Anti) Pastoral Elegy', *New Literary History*, 30.1 (Winter 1999), 179–201

Gilbert, Sandra M., and Susan Gubar, *No Man's Land: The Place of the Woman Writer in the Twentieth Century*, 3 vols (New Haven: Yale University Press, 1988–94), III: *Letters from the Front* (1994)

Giles, Herbert A., *A History of Chinese Literature* (New York: D. Appleton, 1901; repr. 1927)

Gluck, Mary, 'Interpreting Primitivism, Mass Culture and Modernism: The Making of Wilhelm Worringer's *Abstraction and Empathy*', *New German Critique*, 80 (Spring–Summer 2000), 149–69

Goldie, David, *A Critical Difference: T. S. Eliot and John Middleton Murry in English Literary Criticism, 1919–1928* (Oxford: Clarendon Press, 1998)

Goldring, Douglas, 'An Appreciation of D. H. Lawrence', *Art and Letters*, 2.2 (Spring 1919), 89–99

——, 'Modern Critical Prose', *Chapbook*, 2.8 (February 1920), 7–14

Goodway, David, ed., *Herbert Read Reassessed* (Liverpool: Liverpool University Press, 1998)

Gordon, Avery F., *Ghostly Matters: Haunting and the Sociological Imagination* (Minneapolis: University of Minnesota Press, 1997)

Gordon, Lois, *Nancy Cunard: Heiress, Muse, Political Idealist* (New York: Columbia University Press, 2007)

Gordon, Lyndall, *The Imperfect Life of T. S. Eliot*, rev. edn (London: Virago, 2012)

Gray, Piers, *T. S. Eliot's Intellectual and Poetic Development 1909–1922* (Brighton: Harvester Press, 1982)

The Great War Fourth Year by C. R. W. Nevinson, with an Introductory Essay by J. E. Crawford Flitch (London: Grant Richards, 1918)

Green, Russell, 'Editorial', *Coterie*, 6–7 (Winter 1920–21), 3–5

Gregory, Eileen, *H.D. and Hellenism: Classic Lines* (Cambridge: Cambridge University Press, 1997)

Gregory, Joshua C., 'Some Tendencies of Opinion on our Knowledge of Other Minds', *Philosophical Review*, 31.2 (March 1922), 148–63

Grenfell, Julian, 'Into Battle', *The Times*, 28 May 1915, p. 9

Gurney, Ivor, *Severn and Somme* (London: Sidgwick & Jackson, 1919)

——, *War's Embers and Other Verses* (London: Sidgwick & Jackson, 1919)

Hacking, Ian, *Mad Travelers: Reflections on the Reality of Transient Mental Illness* (Cambridge, MA: Harvard University Press, 1998)

——, *Rewriting the Soul: Multiple Personality and the Sciences of Memory* (Princeton: Princeton University Press, 1995)

Hadjiyiannis, Christos, *Conservative Modernists: Literature and Tory Politics in Britain, 1900–1920* (Cambridge: Cambridge University Press, 2018)

Hamburger, Käte, *The Logic of Literature*, trans. by Marilynn J. Rose (Bloomington: Indiana University Press, 1973)

Hamington, Maurice, ed., *Feminist Interpretations of Jane Addams* (University Park: Pennsylvania University Press, 2010)

Hammond, Meghan Marie, *Empathy and the Psychology of Literary Modernism* (Edinburgh: Edinburgh University Press, 2014)

Harari, Yuval Noah, 'Scholars, Eyewitnesses, and Flesh-Witnesses of War: A Tense Relationship', *Partial Answers: Journal of Literature and Ideas*, 7.2 (June 2009), 213–28

Harding, Jason, ed., *The New Cambridge Companion to T. S. Eliot* (Cambridge: Cambridge University Press, 2017)

——, *T. S. Eliot in Context* (Cambridge: Cambridge University Press, 2011)

Hardy, Thomas, *Moments of Vision and Miscellaneous Verses* (London: Macmillan, 1917)

Harrison, Jane Ellen, *Prolegomena to the Study of Greek Religion*, 2nd edn (Cambridge: Cambridge University Press, 1908)

——, *Themis: A Study of the Social Origins of Greek Religion* (Cambridge: Cambridge University Press, 1912)

Hartley, Marsden, 'Breakfast Resume', *Little Review*, 5.7 (November 1918), 46–50

——, 'The Business of Poetry', *Poetry*, 15.3 (December 1919), 152–8

——, 'Tribute to Joyce Kilmer', *Poetry*, 13.3 (December 1918), 149–54

Hartman, Geoffrey, 'On Traumatic Knowledge and Literary Studies', *New Literary History*, 26.3 (1995), 537–63

H.D., *see* Doolittle, Hilda

Heaney, Seamus, *Electric Light* (London: Faber, 2001)

Heap, Jane, 'Push-Face', *Little Review*, 4.2 (June 1917), 4–7

Hecht, Ben, 'Pounding Ezra (*A Conversation . . . .*)', *Little Review*, 5.7 (November 1918), 37–41

Henderson, Alice Corbin, 'The Great Adventure', *Poetry*, 10.6 (September 1917), 316–19

——, 'Poetry and War', *Poetry*, 5.2 (November 1914), 82–4

——, 'Reviews: *The Collected Poems of Rupert Brooke*', *Poetry*, 7.5 (February 1916), 262–4

——, 'War Poetry Again', *Poetry*, 12.5 (August 1918), 284–5

Hibberd, Dominic, *Harold Monro and Wilfrid Gibson: The Pioneers* (London: Cecil Woolf, 2006)

Hibberd, Dominic, and John Onions, eds, *The Winter of the World: Poems of the Great War* (London: Constable & Robinson, 2007)

Higonnet, Margaret R., 'Authenticity and Art in Trauma Narratives of World War I', *Modernism/modernity*, 9.1 (2002), 91–107

Hollis, Matthew, *Now All Roads Lead to France: The Last Years of Edward Thomas* (London: Faber and Faber, 2011)

Holroyd, Michael, *Lytton Strachey: The New Biography* (New York: Farrar, Straus, and Giroux, 1994; repr. New York: W. W. Norton, 2005)

Howarth, Peter, *British Poetry in the Age of Modernism* (Cambridge: Cambridge University Press, 2005)

Hueffer, Ford Madox, *see* Ford, Ford Madox

Hulme, T. E., *The Collected Writings of T. E. Hulme*, ed. by Karen Csengeri (Oxford: Clarendon Press, 1994)

——, 'Fragments', *New Age*, 29.23 (6 October 1921), 275–6

——, *Further Speculations by T. E. Hulme*, ed. by Samuel Hynes (Minneapolis: University of Minnesota Press, 1955)

——, The Papers of Thomas Ernest Hulme 1907–1974, Hull History Centre (U DHU)

——, *Selected Writings*, ed. by Patrick McGuinness (Manchester: Carcanet, 1998)

——, *Speculations: Essays on Humanism and the Philosophy of Art*, ed. by Herbert Read (London: Routledge & Kegan Paul, 1960)

——, T. E. Hulme Ferguson Papers (GB 172 HULF), Special Collections and Archives, Keele University Library

——, T. E. Hulme Papers (GB 172 HUL), Special Collections and Archives, Keele University Library

Hutchinson, Mary, 'War', *The Egoist*, 4.11 (December 1917), 169–72

Huxley, Aldous, 'The Subject-Matter of Poetry', *Chapbook*, 2.9 (March 1920), 11–16

Hynes, Samuel, *The Soldier's Tale: Bearing Witness to Modern War* (New York: Penguin, 1997)

——, *A War Imagined: The First World War and English Culture* (London: Bodley Head, 1990; repr. London: Pimlico, 1992)

Inge, William Ralph, *Christian Mysticism: Considered in Eight Lectures Delivered before the University of Oxford* (New York: Charles Scribner's Sons, 1899)

——, *Studies of English Mystics, St Margaret's Lectures 1905* (London: John Murray, 1906)

Isherwood, Lisa, and David Harris, *Radical Otherness: Sociological and Theoretical Approaches* (Abingdon: Routledge, 2013)

Jackson, Ashley, ed., *The British Empire and the First World War* (Abingdon: Routledge, 2016)

Jackson, Frank, 'Epiphenomenal Qualia', *Philosophical Quarterly*, 32.127 (April 1982), 127–36

Jaffe, Aaron, *Modernism and the Culture of Celebrity* (Cambridge: Cambridge University Press, 2005)

Jain, Manju, *T. S. Eliot and American Philosophy: The Harvard Years* (Cambridge: Cambridge University Press, 1992)

James, Henry, *The Letters of Henry James*, ed. by Percy Lubbock, 2 vols (London: Macmillan, 1920), II

James, William, *The Principles of Psychology*, 2 vols (New York: Henry Holt, 1890; repr. New York: Dover, 1950), I

——, *Writings 1878–1899*, ed. by Gerald E. Myers (New York: Library of America, 1992)

Jameson, Fredric, *The Modernist Papers* (London: Verso, 2007)

——, *The Political Unconscious: Narrative as a Socially Symbolic Act* (London: Methuen, 1981; repr. Abingdon: Routledge Classics, 2002)

——, *A Singular Modernity: Essay on the Ontology of the Present* (London: Verso, 2002)

——, 'War and Representation', *PMLA*, 124.5 (October 2009), 1532–47

Jay, Martin, *Songs of Experience: Modern American and European Variations on a Universal Theme* (Berkeley: University of California Press, 2005)

Jenkinson, Jacqueline, *Black 1919: Riots, Racism and Resistance in Imperial Britain* (Liverpool: Liverpool University Press, 2009)

Jepson, Edgar, 'Recent U.S. Poetry', *English Review*, 26 (May 1918), 419–28

——, 'That International Episode', *Little Review*, 5.10–11 (February–March 1919), 62–[5]

——, 'The Western School', *Little Review*, 5.5 (September 1918), 4–9

Jones, Alun R., *The Life and Opinions of T. E. Hulme* (London: Victor Gollancz, 1960)

Jones, David, *In Parenthesis* (London: Faber and Faber, 1963)

Jones, Paul Fortier, 'Correspondence: About Mr. Underwood's Prize', *Poetry*, 13.4 (January 1919), 228–30

——, *With Serbia into Exile: An American's Adventures with the Army that Cannot Die* (New York: Grosset & Dunlap, 1916)

Joyce, James, *Ulysses* (Paris: Shakespeare and Company, 1922)

——, 'Ulysses: Episode I', *Little Review*, 5.11 [4.11] (March 1918), 3–22

——, 'Ulysses: Episode II', *The Egoist*, 6.1 (January–February 1919), 11–14

——, 'Ulysses: Episode III', *Little Review*, 6.1 [5.1] (May 1918), 31–45

——, 'Ulysses: Episode VI', *Little Review*, 5.5 (September 1918), 15–37

——, 'Ulysses: Episode IX [part I]', *Little Review*, 5.11 [5.12] (April 1919), 30–43

——, 'Ulysses: (Episode XIII concluded)', *Little Review*, 7.2 (July–August 1920), 42–58

Joyce, James, and Clive Driver, *'Ulysses': The Manuscripts and First Printings Compared, Annotated by Clive Driver* (London and Philadelphia: Faber and Faber and Philip H. & A. S. W. Rosenbach Foundation, 1975)

Julius, Anthony, *T. S. Eliot, Anti-Semitism, and Literary Form*, new edn (London: Thames & Hudson, 2003)

Kamenetz, Rodger, 'The Lower Case Jew', *Jewish in America (Part Two)*, 42.1 (Winter 2003), <http://hdl.handle.net/2027/spo.act2080.0042.120> [accessed 24 March 2022]

Kaplan, Sydney Janet, *Circulating Genius: John Middleton Murry, Katherine Mansfield and D. H. Lawrence* (Edinburgh: Edinburgh University Press, 2010)

Kearney, Richard, *The Wake of Imagination: Towards a Postmodern Culture* (New York: Routledge, 2003)

Keen, Suzanne, *Empathy and the Novel* (Oxford: Oxford University Press, 2007)

Kendall, Tim, ed., *The Oxford Handbook of British and Irish War Poetry* (Oxford: Oxford University Press, 2007)

——, *Poetry of the First World War: An Anthology* (Oxford: Oxford University Press, 2013)

Kenner, Hugh, *The Pound Era* (Berkeley: University of California Press, 1971)

Kern, Robert T., *Orientalism, Modernism, and the American Poem* (Cambridge: Cambridge University Press, 1996)

Kind, Amy, ed., *The Routledge Handbook of Philosophy of Imagination* (London: Routledge, 2016)

King, R. W., 'Correspondence: Slang in War-Time', *The Athenæum*, 4658 (8 August 1919), 729

Kinkead-Weekes, Mark, *D. H. Lawrence: Triumph to Exile 1912–1922*, The Cambridge Biography, II (Cambridge: Cambridge University Press, 1996)

Kirkham, Michael, *The Imagination of Edward Thomas* (Cambridge: Cambridge University Press, 1986)

Kitchen, James E., *The British Imperial Army in the Middle East: Morale and Military Identity in the Sinai and Palestine Campaigns, 1916–18* (London: Bloomsbury, 2014)

Kolocotroni, Vassiliki, and Olga Taxidou, eds, *The Edinburgh Dictionary of Modernism* (Edinburgh: Edinburgh University Press, 2018)

Koss, Juliet, 'On the Limits of Empathy', *Art Bulletin*, 88.1 (March 2006), 139–57

Kreymborg, Alfred, *Others: An Anthology of the New Verse* (New York: Alfred A. Knopf, 1917)

Krockel, Carl, *War Trauma and English Modernism: T. S. Eliot and D. H. Lawrence* (Basingstoke: Palgrave Macmillan, 2011)

Kruger, Barbara, and Phil Mariani, eds, *Remaking History*, Discussions in Contemporary Culture, IV (Seattle: Bay Press, 1989)

Kurtz, J. Roger, ed., *Trauma and Literature* (Cambridge: Cambridge University Press, 2018)

Kushner, Tony, *The Persistence of Prejudice: Antisemitism in British Society during the Second World War* (Manchester: Manchester University Press, 1989)

Lacan, Jacques, *Écrits*, trans. by Bruce Fink (New York: W. W. Norton, 2006)

LaCapra, Dominick, *History in Transit: Experience, Identity, Critical Theory* (Ithaca, NY: Cornell University Press, 2004)

——, *Writing History, Writing Trauma* (Baltimore: Johns Hopkins University Press, 2001)

Laforgue, Jules, *Oeuvres complètes de Jules Laforgue*, 3 vols (Paris: Mercure de France, 1902), I: *Poésies*

Laing, R. D., *'The Politics of Experience' and 'The Bird of Paradise'* (Harmondsworth: Penguin, 1967)

Lanier, Sidney, *Poems of Sidney Lanier*, ed. by Mary D. Lanier (New York: Charles Scribner's Sons, 1920)

Lawrence, D. H., *Bay* (London: Cyril W. Beaumont, 1919)

——, *England, My England and Other Stories*, ed. by Bruce Steele, The Cambridge Edition (Cambridge: Cambridge University Press, 1990)

——, *The First 'Women in Love'*, ed. by John Worthen and Lindeth Vasey, The Cambridge Edition (Cambridge: Cambridge University Press, 1998)

——, *Kangaroo*, ed. by Bruce Steele, The Cambridge Edition (Cambridge: Cambridge University Press, 1994; repr. 2002)

——, *The Letters of D. H. Lawrence*, ed. by James T. Boulton and others, The Cambridge Edition, 8 vols (Cambridge: Cambridge University Press, 1979–2000), I: *September 1901–May 1913*, ed. by James T. Boulton (1979)

——, *The Letters of D. H. Lawrence*, II: *June 1913–October 1916*, ed. by George J. Zytaruk and James T. Boulton (1981)

——, *The Letters of D. H. Lawrence*, III: *October 1916–June 1921*, ed. by James T. Boulton and Andrew Robertson (1984)

——, *Look! We Have Come Through!* (London: Chatto & Windus, 1917)

——, *New Poems* (London: Martin Secker, 1918)

——, *New Poems* (New York: Huebsch, 1920)

——, *The Poems*, ed. by Christopher Pollnitz, The Cambridge Edition, 3 vols (Cambridge: Cambridge University Press, 2013–18), I: *Poems* (2013)

——, *The Poems*, II: *Notes and Apparatus* (2013)

——, *The Poems*, III: *Uncollected Poems and Early Versions* (2018)

——, *Studies in Classic American Literature*, ed. by Ezra Greenspan, Lindeth Vasey and John Worthen, The Cambridge Edition (Cambridge: Cambridge University Press, 2003)

——, 'Verse Free and Unfree', *Voices*, 2.4 (October 1919), 129–34

Lawrence, Jon, 'Forging a Peaceable Kingdom: War, Violence, and Fear of Brutalization in Post-First World War Britain', *Journal of Modern History*, 75.3 (September 2003), 557–89

Leavis, F. R., *New Bearings in English Poetry: A Study of the Contemporary Situation* (London: Chatto & Windus, 1932)

Leed, Eric J., *No Man's Land: Combat and Identity in World War I* (Cambridge: Cambridge University Press, 1979)

Lehman, Robert S., 'Eliot's Last Laugh: The Dissolution of Satire in *The Waste Land*', *Journal of Modern Literature*, 32.2 (2009), 65–79

Leiris, Michael, *Manhood: The Journey from Childhood into the Fierce Order of Virility*, trans. by Richard Howard (Chicago: University of Chicago Press, 1992)

Lemercier, Eugène, *Lettres d'un soldat (août 1914–avril 1915)* (Paris: M. Imhaus & R. Chapelot, 1916)

Levenson, Michael H., *A Genealogy of Modernism: A Study of English Literary Doctrine 1908–1922* (Cambridge: Cambridge University Press, 1984)

Levinas, Emmanuel, *Alterity and Transcendence*, trans. by Michael B. Smith (New York: Columbia University Press, 1999)

Lewis, Wyndham, *Blasting and Bombardiering* (London: Eyre & Spottiswoode, 1937)

——, 'Cantelman's Spring-Mate', *Little Review*, 4.6 (October 1917), 8–14

——, 'The Exploitation of Blood', *Blast*, 2 (July 1915), 24

——, 'Inferior Religions', *Little Review*, 4.5 (September 1917), 3–8

——, 'A Super-Krupp—or War's End', *Blast*, 2 (July 1915), 13–14

——, 'A Young Soldier', *The Egoist*, 3.3 (March 1916), 46

Leys, Ruth, *Trauma: A Genealogy* (Chicago: University of Chicago Press, 2000)

Lindsay, Vachel, 'A Doughboy Anthology', *Poetry*, 13.6 (March 1919), 329–35

Linett, Maren Tova, ed., *The Cambridge Companion to Modernist Women Writers* (Cambridge: Cambridge University Press, 2010)

'List of New Books', *The Athenæum*, 4641 (11 April 1919), 188

Litz, Walton, *Introspective Voyager: The Poetic Development of Wallace Stevens* (New York: Oxford University Press, 1972)

Longenbach, James, *Modernist Poetics of History: Pound, Eliot, and the Sense of the Past* (Princeton: Princeton University Press, 1987)

——, *Stone Cottage: Pound, Yeats, and Modernism* (Oxford: Oxford University Press, 1988)

——, *Wallace Stevens: The Plain Sense of Things* (New York: Oxford University Press, 1991)

Lotz, Rainer, and Ian Pegg, eds, *Under the Imperial Carpet: Essays in Black History 1780–1950* (Crawley: Rabbit Press, 1986)

Loughran, Tracey, *Shell-Shock and Medical Culture in First World War Britain* (Cambridge: Cambridge University Press, 2016)

——, 'Shell-Shock and Psychological Medicine in First World War Britain', *Social History of Medicine*, 22.1 (2009), 79–95

——, 'Shell Shock, Trauma, and the First World War: The Making of a Diagnosis and its Histories', *History of Medicine and Allied Sciences*, 67.1 (January 2012), 94–119

Lowell, Amy, *Tendencies in Modern American Poetry* (New York: Macmillan, 1917)

Loy, Mina, *The Lost Lunar Baedeker: Poems of Mina Loy*, ed. by Roger L. Conover (Manchester: Carcanet, 1996)

——, 'Love Songs', *Others*, 1.1 (July 1915), 6–5 [8]

——, 'Songs to Joannes', *Others*, 3.6 (April 1917), 3–20

Luckhurst, Roger, 'Beyond Trauma: Torturous Times', *European Journal of English Studies*, 14.1 (2010), 11–21

——, *The Trauma Question* (Abingdon: Routledge, 2008)

McCue, Jim, 'T. S. Eliot, Edgar Lee Masters and Glorious France', *Essays in Criticism*, 64.1 (January 2014), 45–73

McDonald, Peter, *Serious Poetry: Form and Authority from Yeats to Hill* (Oxford: Clarendon Press, 2002)

McGuinness, Patrick, 'From Mud and Cinders: T. E. Hulme, "A Certain Kind of Tory at War"', *TLS*, 19 November 2014, 14–15

McKible, Adam, *The Space and Place of Modernism: The Russian Revolution, Little Magazines, and New York* (New York: Routledge, 2002)

McKirahan Jr, Richard D., *Principles and Proofs: Aristotle's Theory of Demonstrative Science* (Princeton: Princeton University Press, 1992)

McLoughlin, Kate, *Authoring War: The Literary Representations of War from the 'Iliad' to Iraq* (Cambridge: Cambridge University Press, 2011)

——, *Martha Gellhorn: The War Writer in the Field and in the Text* (Manchester: Manchester University Press, 2007)

——, *Veteran Poetics: British Literature in the Age of Mass Warfare, 1790–2015* (Cambridge: Cambridge University Press, 2018)

——, ed., *The Cambridge Companion to War Writing* (Cambridge: Cambridge University Press, 2009)

Mansfield, Katherine, 'Portrait of a Little Lady', *The Athenæum*, 4643 (25 April 1919), 238

Marcus, Laura, and Peter Nicholls, eds, *The Cambridge History of Twentieth-Century Literature* (Cambridge: Cambridge University Press, 2004)

Margalit, Avishai, *The Ethics of Memory* (Cambridge, MA: Harvard University Press, 2002)

Mariani, Paul, *The Whole Harmonium: The Life of Wallace Stevens* (New York: Simon & Schuster, 2016)

Marrs, Cody, *Nineteenth-Century American Literature and the Long Civil War* (Cambridge: Cambridge University Press, 2015)

Martiny, Erik, ed., *A Companion to Poetic Genre* (Chichester: John Wiley, 2012)

Marven, Lyn, *Body and Narrative in Contemporary Literatures in German: Herta Müller, Libuše Moníková, and Kerstin Hensel* (Oxford: Clarendon Press, 2005)

Masters, Edgar Lee, 'All Life in a Life', *Poetry*, 7.6 (March 1916), 292–300

——, *Songs and Satires* (New York: Macmillan, 1916)

——, *The Spoon River Anthology* (New York: Macmillan, 1915)

Matz, Jesse, *Literary Impressionism and Modernist Aesthetics* (Cambridge: Cambridge University Press, 2001)

Mead, Henry, *T. E. Hulme and the Ideological Politics of Early Modernism* (London: Bloomsbury, 2015)

'Mentions in Dispatches', *The Times*, 18 February 1915, pp. 4–6

Mildenberg, Ariane, *Modernism and Phenomenology: Literature, Philosophy, Art* (London: Springer Nature, 2017)

Mill, John Stuart, *An Examination of Sir William Hamilton's Philosophy*, 2nd edn (London: Longmans, Green, 1865)

Miller, Alisa, *Rupert Brooke in the First World War* (Clemson, SC: Clemson University Press, 2017)

Miller Jr, James E., *T. S. Eliot: The Making of an American Poet, 1888–1922* (University Park: Pennsylvania State University Press, 2005)

'Miss Alice M. Pattinson', *First World War Volunteers*, <https://vad.redcross.org.uk/Card?fname=alice&sname=pattinson&id=168248&first=true&last=true> [accessed 24 March 2022]

'Miss Kate Elizabeth Lechmere', *First World War Volunteers*, <https://vad.red-cross.org.uk/Card?fname=Kate&sname=Lechmere&id=131644&first=true&last=true> [accessed 24 March 2022]

Mitchell, Robert, *Sympathy and the State in the Romantic Era: Systems, State Finance, and the Shadows of Futurity* (New York: Routledge, 2007)

Modern War Paintings by C. R. W. Nevinson with an Essay by P. G. Konody (London: Grant Richards, 1917)

Modlinger, Martin, and Philipp Sonntag, eds, *Other People's Pain: Narratives of Trauma and the Question of Ethics* (Oxford: Peter Lang, 2011)

Moeyes, Paul, *Siegfried Sassoon, Scorched Glory: A Critical Study* (Basingstoke: Macmillan, 1997)

Moi, Toril, *Henrik Ibsen and the Birth of Modernism: Art, Theater, Philosophy* (Oxford: Oxford University Press, 2006)

Monaco, C. S., *The Rise of Modern Jewish Politics: Extraordinary Movement* (New York: Routledge, 2013)

Monro, Harold, *Children of Love* (London: Poetry Bookshop, 1914)

——, 'Varia Notes News: War Poetry', *Poetry and Drama*, 2.3 (September 1914), 250

Monroe, Harriet, '$100 for a War Poem', *Poetry*, 4.6 (September 1914), 251

——, 'Announcement of Awards [1915]', *Poetry*, 7.2 (November 1915), 102–6

——, 'Announcement of Awards [1918]', *Poetry*, 13.2 (November 1918), 108–14

——, 'Comment: Joyce Kilmer', *Poetry*, 13.1 (October 1918), 31–4

——, 'The Death of Rupert Brooke', *Poetry*, 6.3 (June 1915), 136–8

——, 'A Decade of Gibson', *Poetry*, 9.2 (November 1916), 93–5

——, 'A Gold Star for Gladys Cromwell', *Poetry*, 13.6 (March 1919), 326–8

——, 'Great Poetry', *Poetry*, 13.4 (January 1919), 219–24

——, 'An International Episode', *Poetry*, 13.2 (November 1918), 94–5

——, 'Note by the Editor', *Poetry*, 13.4 (January 1919), 230

——, 'Notes', *Poetry*, 2.6 (September 1913), 228–9

——, 'Notes', *Poetry*, 5.2 (November 1914), 96–7

——, 'Notes', *Poetry*, 12.2 (May 1918), 115–16

——, 'Poetry: A Magazine of Verse edited by Harriet Monroe. May 1918', *Poetry*, 12.2 (May 1918), [cover]

——, 'Poetry for May, 1918', *Poetry*, 12.2 (May 1918), [contents page]

——, 'The Poetry of War', *Poetry*, 4.6 (September 1914), 237–9

——, 'A Radical-Conservative', *Poetry*, 13.6 (March 1919), 322–6

——, 'Walt Whitman', *Poetry*, 14.2 (May 1919), 89–94

——, 'The War and the Artist', *Poetry*, 11.6 (March 1918), 320–2

——, 'War Poems', *Poetry*, 10.5 (August 1917), 271–8

——, 'Will Art Happen?', *Poetry*, 10.4 (July 1917), 203–5

——, 'A Year After', *Poetry*, 14.4 (July 1919), 209–11

Monroe, Harriet, and Alice Corbin Henderson, eds, *The New Poetry: An Anthology* (New York: Macmillan, 1917; repr. 1918)

Monteiro, George, 'Robert Frost's "On Talk of Peace at This Time": A Third Version of an Uncollected Manuscript Poem', *ANQ*, 7.1 (1994), 26–8

Monthly Weather Report of the Meteorological Office, 36.5 (May 1919)

Montin, Sarah, '"What is burned in the fire of this?" In Search of the Lost Subject of Isaac Rosenberg's War Poetry', *temporal*, 13 (April 2012), <http://temporel.fr/What-is-burned-in-the-fire-of-this> [accessed 24 March 2022]

Moody, A. David, *Ezra Pound: Poet, A Portrait of the Man and his Work*, 3 vols (Oxford: Oxford University Press, 2007–15), I: *The Young Genius 1885–1920* (2007)

——, *Ezra Pound: Poet, A Portrait of the Man and his Work*, II: *The Epic Years 1921–1939* (2014)

——, *Ezra Pound: Poet, A Portrait of the Man and his Work*, III: *The Tragic Years 1939–1972* (2015)

Moore, Marianne, 'Reinforcements', *The Egoist*, 5.6 (June–July 1918), 83

Moore, Thomas Sturge, 'Tocsin to Men at Arms', *The Times*, 18 February 1915, p. 11

Moorehead, Alan, *Gallipoli*, new edn (London: Hamish Hamilton, 1967)

Morgan, David, 'The Enchantment of Art: Abstraction and Empathy from German Romanticism to Expressionism', *Journal of the History of Ideas*, 57.2 (April 1996), 317–41

Morris Jr, Roy, *The Better Angel: Walt Whitman in the Civil War* (New York: Oxford University Press, 2000)

Mosse, George L., *Fallen Soldiers: Reshaping the Memory of the World Wars* (New York: Oxford University Press, 1990)

Moult, Thomas, 'The Old Men', *Voices*, 1.2 (February 1919), 93–5

——, 'The Poetic Futility of Flanders', *English Review*, 30 (January 1920), 68–71

Muir, Edwin, 'Recent Verse', *New Age*, 27.12 (22 July 1920), 186–7

Murry, John Middleton, 'The Condition of English Literature', *The Athenæum*, 4697 (7 May 1920), 597–8

——, 'The Eternal Footman', *The Athenæum*, 4686 (20 February 1920), 239

——, *The Evolution of an Intellectual* (New York: Alfred A. Knopf)

——, 'Le Feu', *TLS*, 794 (5 April 1917), 164

——, 'The French Poetry of the Franco-German War', *TLS*, 660 (10 September 1914), 416

——, 'The Gospel of M. Duhamel', *The Athenæum*, 4641 (11 April 1919), 184

——, 'Intimations of Mortality', *The Athenæum*, 4683 (30 January 1920), 133–4

——, 'The Lost Legions', *The Athenæum*, 4683 (30 January 1920), 136–8

——, 'M. De Régnier's War Poetry', *TLS*, 890 (6 February 1919), 66

——, 'Modern Poetry and Modern Society', *The Athenæum*, 4646 (16 May 1919), 325–6

——, 'The Poet of the War', *The Athenæum*, 4647 (23 May 1919), 376–7

——, 'La Troisième France', *TLS*, 801 (24 May 1917), 246

Nagel, Thomas, *The View from Nowhere* (New York: Oxford University Press, 1986)

——, 'What Is It Like to Be a Bat?', *Philosophical Review*, 83.4 (October 1974), 435–50

Nelson, C., and L. Grossberg, eds, *Marxism and the Interpretation of Culture* (Basingstoke: Macmillan, 1988)

Nevinson, Margaret Wynne, 'Some of our Young War Poets', *English Review*, 29 (September 1919), 224

'A New Byronism', *TLS*, 948 (18 March 1920), 184

Newman, John Henry, *The Dream of Gerontius* (London: Heath Cranton, 1865)

Nicholls, Peter, *Modernisms: A Literary Guide* (Berkeley: University of California Press, 1995)

Nichols, Robert, 'An Ironist', *The Observer*, 18 April 1920, p. 7

Nievergelt, Yves, *Logic, Mathematics, and Computer Science: Modern Foundations with Practical Applications*, 2nd edn (New York: Springer, 2015)

Niland, Richard, *Conrad and History* (Oxford: Oxford University Press, 2009)

Norris, Margot, *Writing War in the Twentieth Century* (Charlottesville: University Press of Virginia, 2000)

North, Michael, *The Political Aesthetic of Yeats, Eliot, and Pound* (Cambridge: Cambridge University Press, 1991)

——, *Reading 1922: A Return to the Scene of the Modern* (New York: Oxford University Press, 1999)

Obata, Shigeyoshi, ed. and trans., *The Works of Li-Po: The Chinese Poet* (New York: E. P. Dutton, 1922)

O'Casey, Sean, *Autobiographies III: 'Rose and Crown' and 'Sunset and Evening Star'* (London: Faber and Faber, 2011), British Library ebook

——, *The Silver Tassie: A Tragi-Comedy in Four Acts* (London: Macmillan, 1929)

Ogden, Thomas H., *The Primitive Edge of Experience* (Lanham, MD: Rowman & Littlefield, 1989; repr. 2004)

Orage, A. R., 'Readers and Writers', *New Age*, 17.14 (5 August 1915), 332–3

——, 'Readers and Writers', *New Age*, 19.24 (12 October 1916), 565

——, 'Readers and Writers', *New Age*, 27.17 (26 August 1920), 259–60

Osborn, E. B., *The New Elizabethans: A First Selection of the Lives of Young Men Who Have Fallen in the Great War* (London: John Lane, 1919)

——, 'The Soldier Patriot', *TLS*, 798 (3 May 1917), 205–6

——, 'To the Editor: A Soldier's Song-Book', *TLS*, 850 (2 May 1918), 208–9

——, ed., *The Muse in Arms: A Collection of War Poems, for the Most Part Written in the Field of Action, by Seamen, Soldiers, and Flying Men Who Are Serving, or Have Served, in the Great War* (London: John Murray, 1917)

Owen, Wilfred, *The Complete Poems and Fragments*, ed. by Jon Stallworthy, 2 vols (London: Chatto & Windus, 2013), I: *The Poems*

——, *The Complete Poems and Fragments*, II: *The Manuscripts and Fragments*

Owens, David M., 'Gertrude Stein's "Lifting Belly" and the Great War', *Modern Fiction Studies*, 44.3 (Fall 1998), 608–18

Ozick, Cynthia, 'T. S. Eliot at 101', *The New Yorker*, 20 November 1989, pp. 119–54

Palmer, Jerry, *Memories from the Frontline: Memoirs and Meanings of the Great War from Britain, France and Germany* (London: Palgrave Macmillan, 2018)

Pater, Walter, *Plato and Platonism: A Series of Lectures* (London: Macmillan, 1893)

——, *The Renaissance: Studies in Art and Poetry*, rev. edn (London: Macmillan, 1888)

Pender, R. Herdman, 'John Gould Fletcher', *The Egoist*, 3.11 (November 1916), 173–4

Peppis, Paul, *Literature, Politics, and the English Avant-Garde: Nation and Empire, 1901–1918* (Cambridge: Cambridge University Press, 2000)

——, '"Surrounded by a Multitude of Other Blasts": Vorticism and the Great War', *Modernism/modernity*, 4.2 (1997), 39–66

Perkins, David, *A History of Modern Poetry: From the 1890s to the High Modernist Mode* (Cambridge, MA: Belknap Press, 1976)

Perloff, Marjorie, *Differentials: Poetry, Poetics, Pedagogy* (Tuscaloosa: University of Alabama Press, 2004)

——, *The Futurist Moment: Avant-Garde, Avant Guerre, and the Language of Rupture*, rev. edn (Chicago: University of Chicago Press, 2003)

Peterson, Harold L., *The American Sword 1775–1945* (Philadelphia: Ray Riling Arms Books, 1965; repr. Mineola, NY: Dover, 2003)

'"Pirate Day"', *The Times*, 18 February 1915, p. 10

'"*The Poems of Anyte of Tegea*". Translated by Richard Aldington. *Choruses from Iphigeneia in Aulis*. Translated by H.D.', *New Age*, 18.1229 (30 March 1916), 524

Poems of the Great War: Published on Behalf of the Prince of Wales's National Relief Fund (London: Chatto & Windus, 1914)

'The Poets' Translation Series', *The Egoist*, 2.9 (September 1915), 148

'The Poets' Translation Series (Second Prospectus)', *The Egoist*, 3.1 (January 1916), 15

Pound, Ezra, 'Affirmations—I. Arnold Dolmetsch', *New Age*, 16.10 (7 January 1915), 246–7

——, 'Affirmations IV. As for Imagisme', *New Age*, 16.13 (28 January 1915), 349–50

——, 'Affirmations: Edgar Lee Masters', *Reedy's Mirror*, 24.13 (21 May 1915), 10–12

——, 'American Chaos I', *New Age*, 17.19 (9 September 1915), 449

——, 'American Chaos II', *New Age*, 17.20 (16 September 1915), 471

——, 'An Anachronism at Chinon', *Little Review*, 4.2 (June 1917), 14–21

——, 'Breviora', *Little Review*, 5.6 (October 1918), 23–4

——, *The Cantos of Ezra Pound*, 4th edn (London: Faber and Faber, 1987)

——, *Canzoni and Ripostes of Ezra Pound, Whereto Are Appended the Complete Poetical Works of T. E. Hulme* (London: Elkin Mathews, 1913)

——, *Cathay: For the Most Part from the Chinese of Rihaku, from the Notes of the Late Ernest Fenollosa, and the Decipherings of the Professors Mori and Ariga* (London: Elkin Mathews, 1915)

——, *Collected Early Poems* (New York: New Directions, 1976)

——, 'The Coming of War: Actaeon', *Poetry*, 5.6 (March 1915), 255–6

——, 'Durability and De Bosschère's Presentation', *Art and Letters*, 2.3 (Summer 1919), 125–6

——, 'Editorial on Solicitous Doubt', *Little Review*, 4.6 (October 1917), 20–2

——, *Ezra Pound and the Visual Arts*, ed. by Harriet Zinnes (New York: New Directions, 1980)

——, *Ezra Pound to his Parents–Letters 1895–1929*, ed. by Mary de Rachewiltz, A. David Moody and Joanna Moody (Oxford: Oxford University Press, 2011)

——, 'A Few Don'ts by an Imagiste', *Poetry*, 1.6 (March 1913), 200–6

——, *The Fourth Canto* (London: Ovid Press, 1919)

——, 'Fratres Minores', *Blast*, 1 (June 1914), 48

——, 'H.D[.]'s Choruses from Euripides', *Little Review*, 5.7 (November 1918), 16–20

——, *Hugh Selwyn Mauberley* (London: Ovid Press, 1920)

——, 'Images from the Second Canto of a Long Poem', *Future*, 2.4 (March 1918), 96

——, 'An Interpolation Taken from the Third Canto of a Long Poem', *Future*, 2.5 (April 1918), 121

——, *The Letters of Ezra Pound 1907–1941*, ed. by D. D. Paige (London: Faber and Faber, 1951)

——, 'A List of Books', *Little Review*, 5.11 [4.11] (March 1918), 54–8

——, *Literary Essays of Ezra Pound*, ed. by T. S. Eliot (New York: New Directions, 1968)

——, *Lustra of Ezra Pound with Earlier Poems* (New York: privately printed, 1917)

——, *A Memoir of Gaudier-Brzeska*, rev. edn (New York: New Directions, 1970)

——, 'Music', *New Age*, 24.7 (19 December 1918), 107–8

——, 'Near Perigord', *Poetry*, 7.3 (December 1915), 111–19

——, 'On America and World War I (presented by Timothy Materer)', *Paideuma*, 18.1–2 (Spring and Fall 1989), 205–14

——, 'Passages from the Opening Address in a Long Poem', *Future*, 2.3 (February 1918), 63

——, 'Pastiche. Regional. XVI', *New Age*, 26.1 (6 November 1919), 16

——, *Personae: The Collected Poems of Ezra Pound*, new edn ([New York]: New Directions, [1949])

——, *Poems 1918–21, including Three Portraits and Four Cantos* (New York: Boni and Liveright, 1921)

——, *Poems and Translations*, ed. by Richard Sieburth (New York: Library of America, 2003)

——, *Pound/Lewis: The Letters of Ezra Pound and Wyndham Lewis*, ed. by Timothy Materer, The Correspondence of Ezra Pound (New York: New Directions, 1985)

——, *Profile: An Anthology Collected in MCMXXXI* (Milan: John Scheiwiller, 1932)

——, 'Provincia Deserta', *Poetry*, 5.6 (March 1915), 251–4

——, *Ripostes of Ezra Pound* (London: Stephen Swift, 1912)

——, *Selected Prose 1909–1965*, ed. by William Cookson (New York: New Directions, 1973)

——, 'The Seventh Canto', *Dial*, 71.2 (August 1921), 178–81

——, *The Spirit of Romance*, new edn (New York: New Directions, 1952; repr. 2005)

——, 'Three Cantos I', *Poetry*, 10.3 (June 1917), 113–21

——, 'Three Cantos II', *Poetry*, 10.4 (July 1917), 180–8

——, 'Three Cantos III', *Poetry*, 10.5 (August 1917), 248–54

——, *Umbra: The Early Poems of Ezra Pound* (London: Elkin Mathews, 1920)

——, *A Walking Tour in Southern France: Ezra Pound among the Troubadours*, ed. by Richard Sieburth (New York: New Directions, 1992)

——, 'Webster Ford', *The Egoist*, 2.1 (1 January 1915), 11–12

——, 'Wyndham Lewis', *The Egoist*, 1.12 (15 June 1914), 233–4

——, ed., *Catholic Anthology 1914–1915* (London: Elkin Mathews, 1915)

'Present-Day Criticism', *New Age*, 12.5 (5 December 1912), 109–10

Price, Evadne, *Not So Quiet. . .* (London: Albert E. Marriott, 1930; repr. London: Virago, 1988)

Qian, Zhaoming, *Orientalism and Modernism: The Legacy of China in Pound and Williams* (Durham, NC: Duke University Press, 1995)

Rabaté, Jean-Michel, *1913: The Cradle of Modernism* (Malden, MA: Blackwell, 2007)

——, ed., *A Handbook of Modernism Studies* (Chichester: John Wiley, 2013)

Rainey, Lawrence, *Institutions of Modernism: Literary Elites and Public Culture* (New Haven: Yale University Press, 1998)

——, *Revisiting 'The Waste Land'* (New Haven: Yale University Press, 2005)

——, ed., *The Annotated 'Waste Land' with Eliot's Contemporary Prose*, 2nd edn (New Haven: Yale University Press, 2006)

Rathbone, Irene, *We That Were Young* (London: Chatto & Windus, 1932; repr. London: Virago, 1989)

Rau, Patricia, ed., *Conflict, Nationhood and Corporeality in Modern Literature: Bodies-at-War* (Basingstoke: Palgrave Macmillan, 2010)

Rea, Patricia, ed., *Modernism and Mourning* (Lewisburg, PN: Bucknell University Press, 2007)

Read, Henry, *Naked Warriors* (London: Art and Letters, 1919)

Reid, Fiona, *Shell Shock, Treatment and Recovery in Britain 1914–30* (London: Bloomsbury, 2010)

Reilly, Catherine W., ed., *Scars upon my Heart: Women's Poetry and Verse of the First World War* (London: Virago, 1981; repr. 2006)

Remember Louvain! A Little Book of Liberty and War (London: Methuen, 1914)

'Reviews: Under Fire', *New Age*, 21.21 (20 September 1917), 453

Richards, I. A., *Practical Criticism: A Study of Literary Judgement* (London: Harcourt Brace, 1929)

——, *Principles of Literary Criticism*, rev. edn (London: Kegan Paul, Trench, Trübner, 1934)

Richards, Jack, and Adrian Searle, *The Quintinshill Conspiracy: The Shocking True Story behind Britain's Worst Rail Disaster* (Barnsley: Pen and Sword Transport, 2013)

Ricks, Christopher, 'A l'envers ou à Anvers? A Source for Eliot's Estaminet', *TLS*, 4902 (14 March 1997), 14

——, *Reviewery* (New York: Handsel Books, 2002)

——, *T. S. Eliot and Prejudice* (Berkeley: University of California Press, 1988)

Riding, Laura, and Robert Graves, *'A Survey of Modernist Poetry' and 'A Pamphlet against Anthologies'*, ed. by Charles Mundye and Patrick McGuinness (Manchester: Carcanet, 2002)

Roberts, Michael, *T. E. Hulme* (London: Faber and Faber, 1938)

Roberts, Warren, and Paul Poplawski, *A Bibliography of D. H. Lawrence*, 3rd edn (Cambridge: Cambridge University Press, 2001)

Rodker, John, 'List of Books', *Little Review*, 5.7 (November 1918), 31–3

Rolland, Romain, *Au-dessus de la mêlée* (Paris: Paul Ollendorff, 1915)

'Roll of Honour', *The Times*, 18 February 1915, p. 8

Romains, Jules, *Europe* (Paris: Nouvelle Revue Française, 1916)

Roper, Michael, *The Secret Battle: Emotional Survival in the Great War* (Manchester: Manchester University Press, 2009)

Rosenberg, Isaac, 'Break of Day in the Trenches', *Poetry*, 9.3 (December 1916), 128–9

——, *The Collected Works of Isaac Rosenberg*, ed. by Ian Parsons (London: Chatto & Windus, 1979)

Rosenfeld, Paul, 'The Seven Arts Chronicle for August. "Le Feu"', *Seven Arts*, 1.8 (August 1917), 518–20

Rumens, Carol, 'Poem of the Week: Trenches: St Eloi by TE [T. E.] Hulme', *The Guardian*, 10 October 2011, <https://www.theguardian.com/books/2011/oct/10/poem-of-the-week-t-e-hulme> [accessed 24 March 2022]

Russell, Bertrand, *Pacifism and Revolution, 1916–18*, ed. by Richard A. Rempel and others (London: Routledge, 1995)

——, *The Problems of Philosophy*, 2nd edn (Oxford: Oxford University Press, 1998; repr. 2001)

——, *The Selected Letters of Bertrand Russell*, ed. by Nicholas Griffin, 2 vols (Harmondsworth and London: Penguin and Routledge, 1992–2001), II: *The Public Years, 1914–1970* (London: Routledge, 2001)

Ryan, Judith, *The Vanishing Subject: Early Psychology and Literary Modernism* (Chicago: University of Chicago Press, 1991)

Sacks, Peter, *The English Elegy: Studies in the Genre from Spender to Yeats* (Baltimore: Johns Hopkins University Press, 1985)

Salmon, André, *Le Calumet* (Paris: Henri Falque, 1910)

Sandburg, Carl, 'Graves', *Little Review*, 3.2 (April 1916), 2

Sartre, Jean Paul, *Being and Nothingness: An Essay on Phenomenological Ontology*, trans. by Hazel E. Barnes (London: Methuen, 1958; repr. Abingdon: Routledge, 2003)

Sassoon, Siegfried, *Counter-Attack and Other Poems* (London: William Heinemann, 1918)

——, *Counter-Attack and Other Poems* (New York: E. P. Dutton, 1918)

——, *The Old Huntsman and Other Poems* (London: William Heinemann, 1917)

——, *The War Poems of Siegfried Sassoon* (London: William Heinemann, 1919)

Saunders, Helen, 'A Vision of Mud', *Blast*, 2 (July 1915), 73–4

Saunders, Max, *Ford Madox Ford: A Dual Life*, 2 vols (Oxford: Oxford University Press, 1996–2012), II: *The After-War World*, rev. edn (2012)

Scarry, Elaine, *The Body in Pain: The Making and Unmaking of the World* (New York: Oxford University Press, 1985)

Schiffman, Lawrence H., *From Text to Tradition: A History of Second Temple and Rabbinic Judaism* (Hoboken, NJ: Ktav Publishing House, 1991)

Schleiermacher, Friedrich, *'Hermeneutics and Criticism' and Other Writings*, ed. and trans. by Andrew Bowie (Cambridge: Cambridge University Press, 1998)

Schuchard, Ronald, 'Did Eliot Know Hulme? Final Answer', *Journal of Modern Literature*, 27.1/2 (Autumn 2003), 63–9

——, *Eliot's Dark Angel: Intersections of Life and Art* (New York: Oxford University Press, 1999)

Schwartz, Sanford, *The Matrix of Modernism: Pound, Eliot, and Early Twentieth-Century Thought* (Princeton: Princeton University Press, 1985)

Scott, Bonnie Kime, ed., *Gender in Modernism: New Geographies, Complex Intersections* (Urbana: University of Chicago Press, 2007)

Scott, Joan W., 'The Evidence of Experience', *Critical Inquiry*, 17.4 (Summer 1991), 773–97

Searle, John R., *The Mystery of Consciousness* (New York: New York Review of Books, 1997)

Seiffert, Marjorie Allen, 'Soldier and Lover', *Poetry*, 14.6 (September 1919), 338–41

Seltzer, Mark, 'Wound Culture: Trauma in the Pathological Public Sphere', *October*, 80 (Spring 1997), 3–26

Seymour-Jones, Carole, *Painted Shadow: A Life of Vivienne Eliot* (London: Constable, 2001)

Shakespeare, William, *Hamlet*, ed. by Harold Jenkins, The Arden Shakespeare (London: Methuen, 1982; repr. London: Routledge, 1989)

Shanks, E. Buxton, 'London Letter', *Little Review*, 1.9 (December 1914), 55–7

Sheehan, Paul, *Modernism and the Aesthetics of Violence* (Cambridge: Cambridge University Press, 2013)

Sherry, Vincent, *The Great War and the Language of Modernism* (New York: Oxford University Press, 2003)

——, *Modernism and the Reinvention of Decadence* (New York: Cambridge University Press, 2015)

——, ed., *The Cambridge Companion to the Literature of the Great War* (Cambridge: Cambridge University Press, 2005)

Silkin, Jon, *The Life of Metrical and Free Verse in Twentieth-Century Poetry* (Basingstoke: Macmillan, 1997)

Silverstein, Louis, 'H.D. Chronology, Part Two (1915–March 1919)', <https://www.imagists.org/hd/hdchron2.html> [accessed 25 March 2022]

Simmers, George, 'T. S. Eliot's Letter to "The Nation"', *Great War Fiction*, <https://greatwarfiction.wordpress.com/tseliots-letter-to-the-nation/> [accessed 22 March 2022]

Sinclair, May, 'After the Retreat', *The Egoist*, 2.5 (1 May 1915), 77

——, *A Journal of Impressions in Belgium* (New York: Macmillan, 1915)

Slatin, Myles, 'A History of Pound's Cantos I–XVI, 1915–1925', *American Literature*, 35.2 (May 1963), 183–95

Smith, Angela K., *The Second Battlefield: Women, Modernism and the First World War* (Manchester: Manchester University Press, 2003)

Smith, Barry, and David Woodruff Smith, eds, *The Cambridge Companion to Husserl* (Cambridge: Cambridge University Press, 1995)

Smith, Charlotte, *The Poems of Charlotte Smith*, ed. by Stuart Curran (New York: Oxford University Press, 2003)

Smith, Helen Zenna, *see* Price, Evadne

Some Imagist Poets 1916: An Annual Anthology (Boston: Houghton Mifflin, 1916)

Some Imagist Poets 1917: An Annual Anthology (Boston: Houghton Mifflin, 1917)

Some Imagist Poets: An Anthology (Boston: Houghton Mifflin, 1915)

Songs and Sonnets for England in War Time (London: John Lane, 1914)

Sorley, Charles, *Marlborough and Other Poems*, 2nd edn (Cambridge: Cambridge University Press, 1916)

Sorum, Eve C., *Modernist Empathy: Geography, Elegy, and the Uncanny* (Cambridge: Cambridge University Press, 2019)

Speake, Jennifer, ed., *The Oxford Dictionary of Proverbs*, 6th edn (Oxford: Oxford University Press, 2015)

Spiegelberg, Herbert, *The Phenomenological Movement: A Historical Introduction*, 3rd edn (Dordrecht: Kluwer Academic, 1994)

Spurr, David, 'Myths of Anthropology: Eliot, Joyce, Lévy-Bruhl', *PMLA*, 109.2 (March 1994), 266–80

Squire, J. C., 'Georgian Poetry', *New Statesman*, 14.346 (22 November 1919), 224, 226

——, 'Recent Verse', *New Age*, 10.12 (18 January 1912), 281–2

Stallworthy, Jon, *Between the Lines: Yeats's Poetry in the Making* (Oxford: Clarendon Press, 1963)

——, *Wilfred Owen*, rev. edn (London: Pimlico, 2013)

Stein, Gertrude, *The Autobiography of Alice B. Toklas* (New York: Harcourt Brace, 1933; repr. New York: Vintage, 1990)

——, *Lifting Belly*, ed. by Rebecca Mark ([Tallahassee]: Naiad Press, 1989)

——, *Lifting Belly: An Erotic Poem*, Counterpoints 5 (Berkeley: Counterpoint, 2020)

——, *The Previously Uncollected Writings of Gertrude Stein*, ed. by Robert Bartlett Haas, 2 vols (Los Angeles: Black Sparrow Press, 1973), I: *Reflection on the Atomic Bomb*

——, *The Unpublished Writings of Gertrude Stein*, ed. by Carl Van Vechten and others, The Yale Edition, 8 vols (New Haven: Yale University Press, 1951–8), III: *Bee Time Vine and Other Pieces [1913–1927]* (1953)

——, *Wars I Have Seen* (London: B. T. Batsford, 1945)

Stevens, Wallace, *Collected Poetry and Prose*, ed. by Frank Kermode and Joan Richardson (New York: Library of America, 1997)

——, *Harmonium* (New York: Alfred A. Knopf, 1923)

——, *Harmonium* (New York: Alfred A. Knopf, 1931)

——, *The Letters of Wallace Stevens*, ed. by Holly Stevens (Berkeley: University of California Press, 1996)

——, '"Lettres d'un Soldat" I–IX', *Poetry*, 12.2 (May 1918), 59–65

——, 'Metaphors of a Magnifico', *Little Review*, 6.2 [5.2] (June 1918), 4

——, *Opus Posthumous*, ed. by Milton J. Bates, rev. edn (New York: Knopf, 1989; repr. New York: Vintage, 1990)

——, 'Phases', *Poetry*, 5.2 (November 1914), 70–1

Stevenson, Randall, *Literature and the Great War 1914–1918* (Oxford: Oxford University Press, 2013)

Stock, Noel, *Poet in Exile: Ezra Pound* (Manchester: Manchester University Press, 1964)

Stone, Constantia, 'Letters to the Editor: Imagisme', *New Age*, 16.14 (4 February 1915), 390

——, 'Letters to the Editor: What Is a Nation?', *New Age*, 16.15 (11 February 1915), 413–14

Stout, G. F., *A Manual of Psychology* (London: University Correspondence College, 1899)

Strachey, Lytton, *Eminent Victorians* (London: Chatto & Windus, 1918)

Strobel, Marion, 'Perilous Leaping', *Poetry*, 16.3 (June 1920), 157–9

Stueber, Karsten R., *Rediscovering Empathy: Agency, Folk Psychology, and the Human Sciences* (Cambridge, MA: MIT Press, 2006)

Sugano, Marian Zwerling, *The Poetics of the Occasion: Mallarmé and the Poetry of Circumstance* (Stanford: Stanford University Press, 1992)

Sullivan, J. W. N., 'The Dreamer Awakes', *The Athenæum*, 4677 (19 December 1919), 1364–5

Surette, Leon, *The Birth of Modernism: Ezra Pound, T. S. Eliot, W. B. Yeats, and the Occult* (Montreal: McGill-Queen's University Press, 1993)

——, *The Modern Dilemma: Wallace Stevens, T. S. Eliot, and Humanism* (Montreal: McGill-Queen's University Press, 2008)

Swenarton, Mark, *Homes Fit for Heroes: The Politics and Architecture of Early State Housing in Britain*, reissue (Abingdon: Routledge, 2018)

Tate, Trudi, *Modernism, History and the First World War* (Manchester: Manchester University Press, 1998)

Taylor, Julie, ed., *Modernism and Affect* (Edinburgh: Edinburgh University Press, 2015), British Library ebook

Tearle, Oliver, *The Great War, 'The Waste Land' and the Modernist Long Poem* (London: Bloomsbury, 2019)

——, *T. E. Hulme and Modernism* (London: Bloomsbury, 2013)

Tennyson, Alfred, *Poems*, 2 vols (London: Edward Moxon, 1842)

Terraine, John, *White Heat: The New Warfare* (London: Sidgwick & Jackson, 1982)

Thacker, Toby, *British Culture and the First World War: Experience, Representation and Memory* (London: Bloomsbury, 2014)

Thomas, Edward, *The Annotated Collected Poems*, ed. by Edna Longley (Tarset: Bloodaxe Books, 2008)

——, *Collected Poems*, ed. by R. George Thomas (London: Faber and Faber, 2004)

——, *A Language Not to Be Betrayed: Selected Prose of Edward Thomas*, ed. by Edna Longley (Manchester: Carcanet, 1981)

Tietjens, Eunice, 'The Spiritual Dangers of Writing Vers Libre', *Little Review*, 1.8 (November 1914), 25–9

Tiffany, Daniel, *Radio Corpse: Imagism and the Cryptaesthetic of Ezra Pound* (Cambridge, MA: Harvard University Press, 1995)

Timayenis, Telemachus Thomas, *The American Jew: An Exposé of his Career* (New York: Minerva, 1888)

The Times, 18 February 1915

Tomlinson, Henry Major, 'On Leave', *The Nation*, 21.9 (2 June 1917), 220

Tryphonopoulos, Demetres P., and Stephen J. Adams, eds, *The Ezra Pound Encyclopedia* (Westport, CT: Greenwood Press, 2005)

Underhill, Hugh, *The Problem of Consciousness in Modern Poetry* (Cambridge: Cambridge University Press, 1992)

Underwood, John Curtis, 'The Song of the Cheechas', *Poetry*, 11.3 (June 1918), 117–18

——, *War Flames* (New York: Macmillan, 1917)

United States War Department, *Conventional Signs and Abbreviations in Use on French and German Maps* (Washington, DC: Central Map Reproduction Plan Engineer School, 1918)

Untermeyer, Louis, 'Irony de Luxe', *Freeman*, 1 (30 June 1920), 381–2

——, 'The Ivory Tower – II', *New Republic*, 19.236 (10 May 1919), 60–1

Upward, Allen, *The Divine Mystery: A Reading of the History of Christianity Down to the Time of Christ* (Boston: Houghton Mifflin, 1915)

Vance, Jonathan F., *Death So Noble: Memory, Meaning, and the First World War* (Vancouver: UBC Press, 1997)

Vincent, Timothy C., 'From Sympathy to Empathy: Baudelaire, Vischer, and Early Modernism', *Mosaic: A Journal for the Interdisciplinary Study of Literature*, 45.1 (2012), 1–15

Virgil, *Aeneid Book VI*, trans. by Seamus Heaney (London: Faber and Faber, 2016)

Walsh, Michael J. K., ed., *London, Modernism, and 1914* (Cambridge: Cambridge University Press, 2010)

Walter, George, ed., *The Penguin Book of First World War Poetry*, rev. edn (London: Penguin, 2006)

Watts, A. E., 'Pastiche: Echoes of Croce', *New Age*, 18.2 (11 November 1915), 45

Waugh, Alec, 'A Bibliography of Modern Poetry with Notes on Some Contemporary Poets (Compiled and Edited by Recorder)', *Chapbook*, 2.12 (June 1920)

Waugh, Patricia, ed., *Literary Theory and Criticism* (Oxford: Oxford University Press, 2006)

Weil, Simone, '*The Iliad*, or the Poem of Force', *Chicago Review*, 18.2 (1965), 5–30

Weiner, Eugene, ed., *The Handbook of Interethnic Coexistence* (New York: Abraham Fund, 1998)

Weinstein, Samuel, 'Notes on Present-Day Art: Painting', *Voices*, 3.2 (March 1920), 81–2

'We Jews', *New Age*, 24.18 (6 March 1919), 292–4

West, Rebecca, *The Return of the Soldier* (New York: Century, 1918)

Wharton, Edith, ed., *The Book of the Homeless (Le livre des Sans-Foyer)* (New York: Charles Scribner, 1916)

Wheels: Fourth Cycle, ed. by Edith Sitwell and others (Oxford: B. H. Blackwell, 1919)

Whitman, Walt, *Complete Poetry and Collected Prose*, ed. by Justin Kaplan (New York: Library of America, 1982)

Whitworth, Michael H., 'Pièces d'identité: T. S. Eliot, J. W. N. Sullivan and Poetic Impersonality', *English Literature in Transition, 1880–1920*, 39.2 (1996), 149–70

——, *Reading Modernist Poetry* (Chichester: Wiley-Blackwell, 2010)

——, ed., *Modernism* (Malden, MA: Blackwell, 2007)

Wiesel, Elie, 'Art and the Holocaust: Trivializing Memory', *New York Times*, 11 June 1989, section 2, p. 1

——, 'TV View: The Trivializing of the Holocaust: Semi-Fact and Semi-Fiction', *New York Times*, 16 April 1978, section 2, p. 29

Williams, Raymond, *Culture and Society 1780–1950*, rev. edn (New York: Columbia University Press, 1983)

——, *Keywords: A Vocabulary of Culture and Society*, rev. edn (London: Fontana Press, 1983)

Williams, William Carlos, 'Four Foreigners', *Little Review*, 6.5 (September 1919), 36–9

——, *Kora in Hell: Improvisations* (Boston: Four Seas, 1920)

Wilson, Jean Moorcroft, *Isaac Rosenberg: The Making of a Great War Poet, A New Life* (Evanston, IL: Northwestern University Press, 2008)

Wilson, Peter, *A Preface to Ezra Pound* (Abingdon: Routledge, 2014)

Winant, Johanna, 'Empathy and Other Minds in *Ulysses*', *James Joyce Quarterly*, 55.3–4 (2018), 371–89

Winter, Jay, 'The "Moral Witness" and the Two World Wars', *Ethnologie française*, 37.3 (March 2007), 467–74

——, *Sites of Memory, Sites of Mourning: The Great War in European Cultural History* (Cambridge: Cambridge University Press, 1995)

——, ed., *The Cambridge History of the First World War*, 3 vols (Cambridge: Cambridge University Press, 2013), I: *Global War*

Wolff, Janet, *AngloModern: Painting and Modernity in Britain and the United States* (Ithaca, NY: Cornell University Press, 2003)

Wood, Jamie, '"Here I Am": Eliot, "Gerontion", and the Great War', *Biography*, 41.1 (2018), 116–42

Woolf, Leonard, and Virginia Woolf, 'Is This Poetry?', *The Athenæum*, 4651 (20 June 1920), 491

Woolf, Virginia, *The Diary of Virginia Woolf*, ed. by Anne Olivier Bell and Andrew McNeillie, 5 vols (Orlando: Harcourt Brace, 1977–84), I: *1915–1919*, ed. by Anne Olivier Bell (1977)

——, *The Essays of Virginia Woolf*, ed. by Andrew McNeillie and Stuart N. Clarke, 6 vols (London: Hogarth Press, 1986–2011), II: *1912–1918*, ed. by Andrew McNeillie (London: Hogarth Press, 1987; repr. Orlando: Harcourt Brace Jovanovich, 1990)

——, *The Essays of Virginia Woolf*, III: *1919–1924*, ed. by Andrew McNeillie (London: Hogarth Press, 1988; repr. Orlando: Harcourt Brace Jovanovich, [undated])

Worringer, Wilhelm, *Abstraction and Empathy: A Contribution to the Psychology of Style*, trans. by Michael Bullock (London: Routledge & Kegan Paul, 1953; repr. Chicago: Elephant Paperbacks, 1997)

'WW1 Age at Enlistment', <https://mq.edu.au/on_campus/museums_and_collections/australian_history_museum/online_exhibitions/oua_anzac_unit/wwi_age_at_enlistment/> [accessed 25 March 2022]

Yanks: A.E.F. Verse (New York: G. P. Putnam's Sons, 1919)

Yeats, W. B., *The Collected Poems of W. B. Yeats* (New York: Macmillan, 1933)

——, *The Collected Works of W. B. Yeats*, ed. by Richard J. Finneran and George Mills Harper, 14 vols (New York: Scribner and others, 1989–2015), I: *The Poems*, ed. by Richard J. Finneran, 2nd edn (New York: Scribner, 1997)

——, *The Collected Works of W. B. Yeats*, V: *Later Essays*, ed. by William H. O'Donnell (New York: Charles Scribner's Sons, 1994)

——, *The Letters of W. B. Yeats*, ed. by Allan Wade (London: Rupert Hart-Davis, 1954)

——, *Letters on Poetry from W. B. Yeats to Dorothy Wellesley* (Oxford: Oxford University Press, 1940)

——, *Responsibilities and Other Poems* (New York: Macmillan, 1916)

——, *Responsibilities: Poems and a Play* (Dundrum: Cuala Press, 1916)

——, *The Wild Swans at Coole, Other Verses and a Play in Verse* (Dundrum: Cuala Press, 1917)

Young, Allan, *The Harmony of Illusions: Inventing Post-Traumatic Stress Disorder* (Princeton: Princeton University Press, 1995)

Young, Francis Brett, *Poems, 1916–1918* (London: Collins, 1919)

Zahavi, Dan, 'Empathy, Embodiment and Interpersonal Understanding: From Lipps to Schutz', *Inquiry*, 53.3 (2010), 285–306

Zeepvat, Charlotte, *Before Action: William Noel Hodgson and the 9th Devons* (Barnsley: Pen and Sword Books, 2015)

Zilboorg, Caroline, ed., *Richard Aldington and H.D.: Their Lives in Letters 1918–61*, new collected edn (Manchester: Manchester University Press, 2003)

Zunshine, Lisa, *Why We Read Fiction: Theory of Mind and the Novel* (Columbus: Ohio State University Press, 2006)

INDEX

aboutness, 217–9
Ackroyd, Peter, 139
Action française, 164
Adams, Henry, 168
Addams, Jane, 88
Aeschylus, 84, 216
afterwardness *see* impersonality
Agamemnon, 43, 88, 163, 164, 208
agnosticism *see* gnosticisms
Aiken, Conrad, 32, 138, 186
alchemy *see* chemistry
Aldington, Richard, 33, 37, 38, 41,
   61–2, 64, 69n, 83, 91, 92, 103,
   104, 105–6, 109, 137, 155
Aliens Order 1920, 189
alley *see* corridor
Aliens Restriction (Amendment) Bill
   1919, 189
Alighieri, Dante, 131n, 148–51,
   175, 207
Allison, Jonathan, 15n
analogical inference, 17, 27, 29,
   140–1
Anderson, Margaret C., 92, 175

Andrewes, Lancelot, 203
anti-Semitism *see* prejudice
Apperzeptionsmass, 183, 184–5, 192–3,
   196, 197
Aquinas, Thomas, 45, 143, 187
Aristotle, 36, 197
   Aristotelian, 36, 170, 187
Armstrong, Martin, 138
Armstrong, Paul, 25–6
Armstrong, Tim, 12n, 13, 104
Arnold, Matthew, 215
Art and Letters, 33, 186
Arts League, The, 174, 193, 196–7
Asquith, Cynthia, 107
Asquith, Violet, 59
Atheling, William *see* Pound, Ezra
The Athenæum, 34, 154, 164, 167, 168,
   172, 173, 174n, 206n, 210n
Authors Take Sides on the Spanish War,
   133n
Avramides, Anita, 3n

Bainbridge, Simon, 7n
Baker, Ernest A., 210n

Baker, Guy, 129
The Ballad of Chevy Chase, 216
Banfield, Ann, 25n
Barbusse, Henri, 91–2, 94–5, 129, 160
Baudrillard, Jean, 217
  Baudrillardian, 74
Beasley, Rebecca, 9n
Beaumont, Cyril, 108
Bell, Michael, 18n
Benjamin, Walter, 3–4, 8, 65, 76
Bennett, Andrew, 6n
Bergson, Henri, 17, 68
  Bergsonism, 142, 29
Bhagavad Gita, 133
bias, 6, 39, 140, 141; *see also* prejudice
Bick, Esther, 195
Binyon, Laurence, 30, 34, 207, 215
Bion, Wilfred R., 194–5
Blanton, C. D., 71
Blast, 22, 34, 47, 50n, 79–80, 95, 111, 112, 155, 163
Bloom, Paul, 6n
Bodenheim, Maxwell, 33
body in pieces, the, 4, 7–8, 12, 43, 44, 49, 52, 54, 58, 92, 95, 102, 109, 117, 119, 143, 157–9, 181, 184, 193–5
Boll, Theophilus E. M., 62
Bomberg, David, 79
Bonikowski, Wyatt, 12
Booth, Allyson, 4n, 12, 151, 218
Borden, Mary, 21, 58, 97–8
Bourdieu, Pierre, 133
Bourke, Joanna, 4n
Boyd, Ernest A., 119–20
Bradbury, Malcolm, 9
Bradley, F. H., 19, 36, 139–42, 148, 150, 151, 192
Bridges, Robert, 30
British Nationality and Status of Aliens Act 1918, 189
Brittain, Vera, 7

Brooke, Rupert, 21, 34, 54–6, 103, 108, 134, 137, 148, 152, 155n, 160, 165–6, 169–73, 175–7, 180, 181
  '1914', 30, 53–6, 58–60, 64, 76, 108, 134
Brooker, Jewel Spears, 12n, 203n
Brooker, Peter, 164n
Brown, Catherine, 108
Browning, Robert, 77
Brunner, Edward, 211
Bryher, 122
Buchanan, David A., 7n
Buck, Claire, 83
Bush, Ronald, 9, 48, 49n, 78
Butt, Clara, 207

Cabanes, Bruno, 65
Caesar, Adrian, 172
Campbell, James, 2–3, 5–6, 9, 13, 14–15, 71, 154, 193, 217
Campbell, Joseph, 33
Canadian War Memorials Fund, 163
Cannan, Gilbert, 30
Carden-Coyne, Ana, 9
Carr, Helen, 28, 61–2, 81
Catholic Anthology 1914–1915 see Pound, Ezra
Cendrars, Blaise, 74
Century Magazine, 152
Cesarani, David, 189
Chalmers, David J., 6n–7n
Chambers, Ross, 16, 99
The Chapbook, 33, 34, 155
Chapman, George, 184
Chasseaud, Peter, 66
Chatto & Windus, 30, 32
chemistry, 59, 95, 137, 144n, 157, 193–4
Chesterton, G. K., 30
Chevrillon, André, 133
Childs, Daniel J., 139
Chong-Gossard, J. H. Kim On, 84
Churchill, William, 54
Ciolkowska, Muriel, 91–2
Clark, Ian, 5n

class, 30, 32, 39, 91–2, 139, 143, 172, 199n, 209; *see also* prejudice
classicism, 11, 68, 84, 216
Coetzee, J. M., 6n
Cohen, Joseph, 96n
Cohn, Dorrit, 23
Cole, Margaret Postgate, 112, 115
Coleman's Hatch, 50–1
Coleridge, E. P., 85, 86, 87
Cole, Sarah, 4, 8, 15n, 172
Collecott, Diana, 81
Collingwood, R. G., 139–40
colonialism, 6, 20–1, 188, 216, 217, 220
Colum, Padraic, 193n
combat agnosticism *see* gnosticisms
combat gnosticism *see* gnosticisms
Connor, Steven, 67
Conrad, Joseph, 25, 212
Constable, 81
Coplan, Amy, 18n
corridor, 10, 66–7, 143–4, 147–51, 175
Coterie, 34, 182
Cournos, John, 137
Craiglockhart Hospital, 153
Crawford Flitch, J. E., 96
Crawford, Nelson Antrim, 37n
Crawford, Robert, 139, 143
Creekmore, Hubert, 45
Cromwell, Gladys, 177
Crump, Jeremy, 207
Csengeri, Karen, 69
Cuala Press, 40
Culler, Jonathan, 7, 74
Cunard, Nancy, 11, 211–12

'"Daddy, what did YOU do in the Great War?"', 199n
The Daily Chronicle, 30
The Daily Herald, 34
Daily News, 144
Daniel, Arnaut, 126
Das, Santanu, 4, 184
De Born, Bertran, 126
DeCoste, Damon Marcel, 25–6

De Gourmont, Remy, 38–9, 46, 61, 63, 67, 141n, 142–3, 157
De la Mare, Walter, 54
De la Selva, Salomón, 177
DeMeester, Karen, 12
Dennett, Daniel C., 7n
Derrida, Jacques, 14; *see also écriture, parole*
Deutsch, Babette, 55
De Villiers, Rick, 204
Dickie, Margaret, 101–2
Dilthey, Wilhelm, 17, 29
disgust, 16, 33–5, 41, 121, 156, 219
disinterested action, 133, 134
disinterestedness, 3n, 105, 139, 176
distaste, 16, 21, 32, 171, 194, 214–15
Dodman, Trevor, 10
Doolittle, Hilda, 3, 21, 82n, 104, 119, 120–1, 122–3, 131, 134, 217
  'Circe', 109n, 112–13
  'From the *Iphigeneia in Aulis* of Euripides', 83–9
  The Islands and 'The God' series, 109–13
  Sea Garden, 81–4, 86, 110–11
Drayton, Michael, 216
Drinkwater, John, 30
Driscoll, Louise, 33
Drummond, Guy, 200
Duchamp, Marcel, 74
Duddington, Nathalie A., 27n
Duhamel, Georges, 160, 173

écriture, 13, 14, 38, 41, 63, 65, 159, 184, 219
The Egoist, 30, 32–3, 42, 61–2, 64, 65, 68, 71, 84n, 91, 103, 110, 165, 168
Einfühlung, 26–9, 32, 35
elegy, 8, 11, 15, 26
Eliot, Charlotte, 138, 143, 174, 186, 191, 196n, 206
Eliot, Henry Ware, 144–5, 168, 206
Eliot Jr, Henry Ware, 144–5, 183

Eliot, T. S., 3, 9, 10, 13, 14, 15, 18–19, 19n–20n, 21, 22, 27, 32, 34–5, 36, 42, 45, 49, 55–6, 69n, 79, 87–8, 89, 90–1, 95, 96, 103, 105n, 122, 133, 137–9, 140, 141–3, 144n, 146n, 152, 155, 156, 157, 158, 163n, 164–5, 166–8, 171n, 174–5, 176, 177, 179, 180, 181–2, 182–4, 184–5, 186, 193–4, 197, 205–6, 207n, 210n, 212n, 214, 215, 216, 217–18, 219
  'A Cooking Egg', 182, 190n
  'Gerontion', 21, 22, 23, 86, 88, 117, 139, 140, 144n, 150, 172, 182, 184, 185, 186, 187–8, 190, 198–213, 218
  'In silent corridors of death', 143–4, 146–9, 150, 151, 152, 166, 175, 203–4, 210n
  'Modern Tendencies in Poetry', 193, 196–8
  'The New Elizabethans and the Old', 167–8, 169–71, 172–3, 174–5, 177, 181, 182, 191, 199, 200
  'Sweeney Among the Nightingales', 163–4, 185
  'Tradition and the Individual Talent', 21, 133, 182, 185, 190–6, 198, 201, 207, 212–13
  The Waste Land, 9, 11, 13, 22, 71, 78, 149–51, 156, 204, 212, 214, 217, 218, 219
Eliot, Vivien, 139, 148–9, 171n, 205n, 206
Elkin Matthews, 60
embodiment, 6, 36, 56, 63, 80, 97, 112, 116, 121, 123, 126, 148, 170, 180
empathy, 3n, 5, 18, 19–20, 26–9, 103, 194–5; *see also Einfühlung*
empire *see* colonialism
Engberg-Pedersen, Anders, 4–5
Erfahrung, 5n
Erlebnis, 5, 20
esotericism, 12, 56
Euripides, 83–8, 92
Evans, Donald, 69

experience past, 182
experience present, 182
expressivity, 6, 71, 149, 159, 220
eyewitness *see* witnessing practices

Faber, Geoffrey, 167, 172–3
Fenollosa, Ernest, 49
Ferguson, Rex, 5n
Ferguson, Robert, 70
Festival Gerontius, 207
Ficke, Arthur Davison, 155, 175n
First World War
  age of combatants, 191
  American Expeditionary Force, 180–1
  Antwerp, 41–3, 58, 60, 187, 209, 210n
  Aubers Ridge, 53, 65
  British Expeditionary Force, 53, 91
  Charleroi, 39
  East African front, 1
  Festubart, 201
  Gallipoli, 54, 175n
  gas weaponry, 144
  injury statistics, 4n
  Kut Al Amara, 107
  Messines Ridge, 128–9
  Oostduinkerke, 200n
  Passchendaele, 1, 163
  Saint Eloi, 65n, 66, 71, 76
  Selective Service Act 1917, 122
  Somme, 37, 91, 97–8, 110, 119, 170
  United States Navy, the, 200n
  Verdun, 100–2, 207
  Wareham Camp, 109–10
  Wytschaete, 66n
  Ypres, 61, 65, 66, 119
  Zeppelin attacks, 8, 50, 106–7, 148, 207
flesh *see* embodiment
fleshwitness *see* witnessing practices
Fletcher, John Gould, 32, 42, 68n, 103–4, 156n
Flint, F. S., 34, 61, 68, 105n, 107n, 109
  'Soldiers', 105–6
  'War-time', 105
  'Zeppelins', 106–7

Ford, Ford Madox, 25–6, 29, 37, 38,
    48–9, 91, 137, 152, 212
    Antwerp, 41–3, 44, 60, 79, 134, 163,
    164, 165, 202
    'Arms and the Mind/War and the
    Mind', 119–20, 121, 158, 193
    'Footsloggers', 202
Ford, Webster *see* Masters, Edgar Lee
Forster, E. M., 214, 215, 217, 218
French Foreign Legion, the, 122
French impressionism, 209–10; *see also*
    literary impressionism
French, Sir John, 53
Freud, Sigmund, 3, 39, 48
Freytag-Loringhoven, Else von, 176
Friedman, Susan Stanford, 81
Frost, Robert, 114
Froula, Christine, 10, 76–7, 127, 138n
Fussell, Paul, 9, 11, 13, 76

Gadamer, Hans-Georg, 5, 65
Gardner, Isabella, 138
Gaudier-Brzeska, Henri, 46–8, 53, 65,
    72, 73, 79, 91, 121, 129, 137, 149
gender, 2, 6, 8, 27, 29, 41, 60, 79, 81, 97,
    103, 104, 191, 219; *see also* prejudice
genre, 2, 9, 11, 16, 21, 23, 30, 33–5, 55,
    113, 137, 179, 214
Georgianism, 10, 11, 58, 74, 137, 167,
    171, 174, 196n, 214
Georgian Poetry, 137, 152, 165, 167, 197
Gertler, Mark, 96n, 188
Gibbs, Philip, 94
Gibson, Wilfrid Wilson, 152, 165
    Battle, 74–6, 165
Gilbert, Sandra, 2n, 11–12
Giles, Herbert A., 45–6, 48
gnosticisms
    combat agnosticism, 3, 21,
    109–119, 162
    combat gnosticism, 2–3, 5, 6–8,
    13–16, 20–2, 23, 29, 46, 56, 62–4,
    69, 73, 86, 91–2, 94–103, 109,
    119–21, 128–9, 147, 152, 157, 185,
    191, 200, 204, 211, 213

critique of combat gnosticism, the, 3,
    5–6, 11–12, 71, 154, 217
    non-combat gnosticism, 3, 123–4,
    126–8, 130–4, 147–51, 157,
    154–60, 163–4, 183–5, 190–8,
    217–18
Goldie, David, 160, 166, 191
Goldie, Peter, 18n
Goldring, Douglas, 33
Gongorism, 80
Gordon, Avery F., 99–100
Gordon, Lois, 212n
Gordon, Lyndall, 138
Granville-Barker, Harley, 88
Graves, Robert, 152, 166
Gray, Piers, 139
The Great War Fourth Year, 96
Gregory, Eileen, 84
Gregory, William Robert, 202
Grenfell, Julian, 30, 53, 168, 200–1
grotesque, the, 1, 11, 16, 43, 74, 78, 97,
    98, 147, 173n; *see also* unheimlich
Gurney, Ivor, 152, 166

Hacking, Ian, 219
Haigh-Wood, Maurice, 143–4, 146–9,
    150–1, 166, 167, 181, 199, 204,
    210n
Hamburger, Käte, 23
Hammond, Meghan Marie, 18
Hankey, Donald, 201
Harari, Yuval Noah, 4–5, 15
Hardy, Thomas, 30, 107n
Harrison, Jane Ellen, 17, 44
Hartley, Marsden, 177, 186, 193n
Hartman, Geoffrey, 219
haunted, 11, 16, 55, 71, 85, 99–102,
    150, 208; *see also* grotesque
H. D. *see* Doolittle, Hilda
Heaney, Seamus, 215n
Heap, Jane, 208n
Hecht, Ben, 68n
Hegelian, 35
    neo-Hegelian, 140
Helle, Anita, 175

Henderson, Alice Corbin, 176, 179
Herbart, Johann Friedrich, 183
Hibberd, Dominic, 75
Hickman, Miranda B., 82, 83
high modernism, 8, 9, 215
Higonnet, Margaret R., 12
Hinkley, Eleanor, 138, 143, 147
Hodgson, William, 201
home front elegy, the, 8
Homer, 84; see also The Iliad
Howarth, Peter, 12–13, 79, 118, 216
Hudson, W. H., 29
Hueffer, Ford Madox see Ford, Ford
    Madox
Hulme, T. E., 19n–20n, 21, 26–9,
    55, 61, 64n, 65–72, 91, 96n,
    147n–148n, 156n, 180, 196, 200n
Husserl, Edmund, 19, 19n–20n, 27
Hutchinson, Mary, 149, 190n, 192, 200
Huxley, Aldous, 34
Hynes, Samuel, 9, 69

The Iliad, 4, 84, 208
Image see Imagism
imagination, 1, 3, 5–7, 11–19, 26, 38–9,
    92, 131, 153, 215–20
  and Doolittle, Hilda, 86, 109, 112–13
  and Eliot, T. S., 18–19, 140, 141–2
  and Flint, F. S., 105–7
  and Lawrence, D. H., 107
  and Murry, John Middleton, 158–60,
    163
  and Pound, Ezra, 18, 44–6, 48, 123,
    127–9, 141–3
  and Sinclair, May, 64
  and Stein, Gertrude, 102, 109
  and Stevens, Wallace, 104–5, 132
  and Thomas, Edward, 115–17
Imagism, 21, 26, 29, 33, 50–1, 60–2, 65,
    68, 103–9, 110, 155–6
impersonality, 21, 81, 117, 133,
    159, 186, 198, 199, 204, 207,
    211, 213
  afterwardness, 35–9, 45, 63, 98, 193
  remote imaginativeness, 193n

tranquillity, 37, 38, 56, 63–4, 158–9,
    170, 180, 196
  see also looker-on
impression see literary impressionism
inference see analogical inference
Inge, William Ralph, 54, 56, 58–60
irony, 11–12, 56, 59–60, 132, 133, 186,
    200, 204–5, 211

Jackson, Frank, 6n
Jaffe, Aaron, 54
Jain, Manju, 25n
James, Henry, 23, 25, 40, 55, 91
Jameson, Fredric, 2, 20–1, 24, 217
James, William, 15n, 183, 192–3, 196;
    see also Apperzeptionsmass
Jay, Martin, 5
Jepson, Edgar, 156, 168, 185–7,
    199, 212
John Lane, 30, 56n, 207
Johnson, Donald, 172
joint denial, 199, 200, 201–2, 217
Jones, Alun R., 69
Jones, David, 217n
Jones, Paul Fortier, 135–6
Joyce, James, 151
  Ulysses, 120n, 149–50, 208–9

Kamenetz, Rodger, 208n
Kantianism, 6; see also disinterestedness
Kaplan, Sydney Janet, 153
kennen, 15n
Kenner, Hugh, 9, 44n, 126n
Kern, Robert T., 45
Kilmer, Joyce, 137, 177
Kind, Amy, 6n
Kinkead-Weekes, Mark, 120
Kipling, Rudyard, 30, 168
Kirkham, Michael, 115
Knopf, Alfred, 174, 175n, 181, 186, 212
knowledge-about, 15n
knowledge by acquaintance, 15n
knowledge-by-acquaintance of
    suffering, 15
knowledge of acquaintance, 15n

knowledge of things by description, 15n
Konody, P. G., 95–6
Koteliansky, S. S., 41
Kovacs, David, 85, 86, 87
Krenkow, Fritz, 108
Krockel, Carl, 143

Lacan, Jacques, 195
LaCapra, Dominick, 218, 219n
Laforgue, Jules, 210n
  Laforguian, 137
Laing, R. D., 6n
The Lancet, 147
Langdale, Stella, 207
Lanier, Sidney, 200
Lawrence, D. H., 21, 23, 35, 49,
    82, 89, 90, 120–1, 155, 180n,
    206
  'All of Us', 107–9, 113, 116, 131,
    210n
  'Eloi, Eloi, Lama Sabachthani?', 33,
    41, 43–4, 51, 61
  'Preface to *New Poems*', 179–80,
    181, 194
Lawrence, Jon, 188–9
Leavis, F. R., 214
Lebensphilosophie, 5, 17, 44, 141
Lechmere, Kate, 64n, 70, 71–2
Lehman, Robert S., 204
Leibniz, Gottfried, 91
Leiris, Michael, 211
Lemercier, Eugène, 130–4
Levenson, Michael, 10, 25–6
Levinas, Emmanuel, 217
Lewis, Pericles, 12
Lewis, Wyndham, 21, 26, 34, 42, 47,
    66, 80–1, 87, 91, 111, 128–9, 151,
    155, 163, 164, 165, 171, 176,
    190n, 200n, 206, 208, 209
Leys, Ruth, 4n, 219
limbo patrum, 150–1
Lincoln, Bishop of, 30
Lindsay, Vachel, 180–1
Li Po [Li Bai], 45–6, 48, 49, 72, 74
Lipps, Theodor, 27n

literary impressionism, 21, 25–6, 29, 37,
    62–4, 73, 119
The Little Review, 30, 37, 80, 81, 88,
    89, 91, 92, 155, 163n, 175–6
Lloyd George, David, 209
L'Œuvre, 91
Longenbach, James, 7, 9n, 11n, 25,
    47n, 50n, 121, 130n, 132, 141n,
    212n, 218
looker-on, the, 120–1, 134, 158, 193
*Lord God of Battles: A War
    Anthology,* 30
Lowell, Amy, 61, 82, 104, 110, 181
Loy, Mina, 8, 80–1, 109
Luckhurst, Roger, 13, 16n

McCue, Jim, 133n, 143–4, 148, 164n,
    175n, 190n, 199, 212n, 215n
McDonald, Peter, 40n
McGuinness, Patrick, 70
McKible, Adam, 208
Mackintosh, Ewart, 168
McLoughlin, Kate, 2n, 3n, 5
magus, the, 105, 112, 128, 134, 136,
    142, 193, 199, 218
Mallarmé, Stéphane, 35
Mansfield, Katherine, 196n, 210n
Margalit, Avishai, 15, 95, 129
Mariani, Paul, 132
Mark, Rebecca, 98–9
Marsh, Edward, 55, 152, 167
Marven, Lyn, 16n
Masefield, John, 103
The Masses, 54
Massingham, Henry, 153
Masters, Edgar Lee, 48, 72, 181, 185,
    187–8, 189, 212
Mather, Loris-Emerson, 71n
Matz, Jesse, 26
Mencken, H. L., 50n, 51
Mercure de France, 61
meteorology, 46, 97, 107, 116–17, 164,
    184, 187, 205
Mew, Charlotte, 53–4, 62
Mildenberg, Ariane, 20

Mill, John Stuart, 17, 140–1
Miller, James E., 141n, 196n
Mirrlees, Hope, 11
Modernism *see* high modernism
modernisms, 2, 29, 30, 97, 216
  and war, 9–13
modernist long poem, the, 8, 9, 79, 215,
    216, 217–18, 220
modernist studies, 2, 9–13, 19
Modern War Paintings, 95
Moi, Toril, 24
Monaco, C. S., 190n
Monroe, Harriet, 32n, 33, 34, 40, 41,
    49, 50n, 51–2, 62, 83, 96n, 108,
    121, 127, 130, 131, 132, 133,
    135–6, 164–5, 176–7, 181, 186,
    186, 202
Monro, Harold, 33, 35, 196
  'Youth in Arms', 75–6, 165
Montagu, Lily, 210n
Monteiro, George, 114n
The Monthly Chapbook see The
  Chapbook
Moody, A. David, 70, 122
Moore, Marianne, 35n, 111
Moore, Thomas Sturge, 50, 52, 152
moral witness *see* witnessing practices
morcellation *see* body in pieces
Morgenthau, Henry, 190
Morrell, Ottoline, 153–4
Morrell, Philip, 153
Moult, Thomas, 38, 154, 206n
Muir, Edwin, 69n
Murray, Gilbert, 88
Murry, John Middleton, 32, 34, 38, 91,
    160, 162–3, 164, 166, 168, 173,
    181, 193, 196n, 206n, 212
  'Mr. Sassoon's War Verses', 21, 152–9,
    167, 170, 171, 177, 182, 186, 192,
    194, 197–8
mysticism, 40, 56, 141–2, 203

Nagel, Thomas, 6n–7n
Nash, Paul, 172
The Nation, 143–4, 147, 152, 210n

The Nation's War Paintings, 38
Nevinson, C. R. W., 95–6, 103
Nevinson, Margaret Wynne, 169
The New Age, 30, 55, 68, 73, 88n, 92,
    119, 155, 156
Newbolt, Henry, 30, 42
New Criticism, 9, 198, 214
New Directions, 70
Newman, John Henry, 206–7
New Numbers, 54, 55
The New Statesman, 41
The New York Sun, 170
Nicholls, Peter, 10
Nichols, Robert, 152, 166
Nietzscheanism, 10
Niland, Richard, 139–40
nishpala karma see disinterested action
non-combat gnosticism *see* gnosticisms
North, Michael, 10
Noyes, Alfred, 30

O'Casey, Sean, 215
Ogden, Thomas H., 195
Orage, A. R., 48n, 55, 68
Osborn, E. B., 212
  The Muse in Arms, 165–6, 201
  The New Elizabethans, 168–73, 180,
    181, 184, 200–1
O'Sheel, Shaemas, 33n
other minds, 3, 6, 6n–7n, 18,
    24–5, 27
Others, 80, 155
Owens, David. A., 102
Owen, Wilfred, 2, 11, 14–15, 58, 137,
    152, 154, 215
Ozick, Cynthia, 204

parole, 14, 34, 41, 159, 164
passivity, 12, 15, 19, 32, 196, 214–15
pastoral, 11, 115, 167
Pater, Walter, 24, 25
Pattinson, Alice M., 72n
Peppis, Paul, 10n, 79
Perloff, Marjorie, 10, 203, 211
Pender, R. Herdman, 156n

The Penguin Book of First World War Poetry, 70

Perkins, David, 24–5

phenomenology, 1, 3n, 7–8, 12, 18, 19–20, 26, 107, 129, 142

phonocentrism *see parole*

physics, 156–7, 194

Peirce, Charles Sanders, 200

Piette, Adam, 13

Pinker, J. B., 107, 108

Playboy: A Portfolio of Art and Satire, 179

'Poem: Abbreviated from the Conversation of Mr. T.E.H.' *see* Pound, Ezra

Poems of the Great War, 30

Poetry, 37n, 50n, 55, 81, 92, 96, 97, 108, 127, 130–1, 135–7, 175n, 176–7, 179, 180–1, 185, 202

'$100 for a War Poem', 32–3, 38n, 40n, 41, 176

Sheep's Wool correspondence, the, 185–6

Poetry and Drama, 33, 35, 50n

Poets' Translation Series, the, 82, 83, 84, 87

Pound, Ezra, 3, 9, 11n, 18, 20n, 21, 22, 26, 27, 30, 32, 33, 34, 37, 40, 41, 42, 45, 48, 50n, 53, 56, 68, 69, 76–7, 79, 80, 81, 87, 88, 89, 90–1, 96n, 104, 105, 109, 121–3, 127n, 128–9, 136n, 137, 139, 141–3, 146n, 149–51, 155–7, 171, 175, 176, 180, 185–6, 187, 190n, 192, 194, 197, 207, 208, 209, 212

'1915: February', 49–50, 51–2, 67, 126

Cathay, 44, 45–9, 50, 72, 78, 109, 115, 116, 126n, 129, 149, 196, 201

Catholic Anthology 1914–1915, 60–2, 64, 65–6, 68, 72n, 147

'The Coming of War: Actaeon', 50–1, 69, 165

'Homage to Sextus Propertius', 88, 201

Hugh Selwyn Mauberley, 22, 49, 218

'Near Perigord', 72–3, 88, 126–7

'Poem: Abbreviated from the Conversation of Mr. T.E.H.', 64–74, 76, 78, 79, 95, 115, 126, 133, 134, 136, 147–8, 149

'Provincia Deserta', 50n, 88, 126, 151, 195

'Three Cantos', 127–8

A Walking Tour in Southern France, 123–4, 184

Pound, Homer, 104, 122

prejudice, 140, 187–90, 198, 204, 206n, 208–11

Price, Evadne, 8

Punch, 30

purgatory, 175, 206–7, 217

Qian, Zhaoming, 46

Quest Society, The, 26, 28–9, 66

Quinn, John, 37, 143, 156, 174–5, 177, 186, 190n, 212

Quintinshill rail disaster, 53–4

Rabaté, Jean-Michel, 10

race, 6, 189–90, 204, 211; *see also* prejudice

racism *see* prejudice

Rainey, Lawrence, 10, 144n, 164n, 218

Raleigh, Walter, 170

Rathbone, Irene, 8

Rau, Patricia, 4n

Read, Henry, 173, 183–4

reification, 20–1

religiosity, 11, 44, 45, 54, 56, 59, 86, 98, 109, 111, 113, 127, 133–4, 139–40, 150, 159, 176, 180, 187, 188, 194, 199, 203, 206

Remember Louvain! A Little Book of Liberty and War, 30

ressentiment, 216

Richards, I. A., 6n, 214

Ricks, Christopher, 133n, 143–4, 144, 147n, 148, 151, 164n, 175n, 190n, 210n, 212n

Roberts, Michael, 69
Rockwell, Kiffin, 122
Rodker, John, 80, 96n, 182n
Rolland, Romain, 160, 164
Romains, Jules, 160
romanticism, 11, 55
Romanticism, 6, 29, 37, 68, 180
Roper, Michael, 194
Rosenberg, Isaac, 21, 96–7, 152, 177
Rosenfeld, Paul, 92
Rowntree, Arnold, 168
Rumens, Carol, 70–1
Russell, Bertrand, 15n, 24–5, 141n,
    153–4, 158, 206, 207
Ryan, Judith, 18n

Sacks, Peter, 15
Salmon, André, 210n
Sandburg, Carl, 33, 175
Sartre, Jean Paul, 180n
Sassoon, Siegfried, 2, 15n, 21, 94–5,
    152–9, 166, 172, 192, 198
satire, 55, 56, 164, 198, 213
Saunders, Helen, 79, 82, 109
Scarry, Elaine, 4, 7n, 8
Schäfer, Heinrich, 108
Scheler, Max, 19n–20n
Schiller, Friedrich, 216
Schlegel, Friedrich, 79
Schleiermacher, Friedrich, 18
Schuchard, Ronald, 27n, 204, 207n
Schwartz, Sanford, 9, 142–3
Scott, Bonnie Kime, 18n
Seeger, Alan, 122, 137, 168, 170,
    177, 181
Seiffert, Marjorie Allen, 167n
Seltzer, Mark, 12
sentimentality, 8, 15, 18, 30, 32, 47, 52,
    55, 59, 60, 81, 96, 103, 165, 166,
    168, 171, 172, 184, 191, 214, 216
The Seven Arts, 92
Shanks, E. Buxton, 30, 32, 33–4
Shakespear, Dorothy, 129
Shakespeare, William, 150, 198, 199
Shakespear, Olivia, 47

Sheehan, Paul, 10, 13, 70n
Sheep's Wool correspondence, the,
    see Poetry
shellshock, 12, 13, 17, 71–9
Sherry, Vincent, 11–12, 26, 58, 200, 216
shock, 13; see also shellshock
simile, 14–15, 51, 112, 115
Simmers, George, 143
simulacrum, 17, 48–9, 74, 220
Sinclair, May, 21, 61–2, 68, 74
    A Journal of Impressions in Belgium,
        62–4, 65, 73, 95, 135, 136
Sitwell, Edith, 137
Sitwell, Osbert, 166
Smith, Adam, 17
Smith, Helen Zenna see Price, Evadne
solipsism, 18, 148, 151, 202, 211
Some Imagist Poets, 81, 103, 156
Songs and Sonnets for England in
    War Time, 30
Sophocles, 84
Sorel, Georges, 148n
Sorley, Charles, 34, 91n, 166, 168, 172
Sorum, Eve C., 18
Spivak, Gayatri Chakravorty, 6, 217
Spurr, David, 249
Squire, J. C., 41, 55, 152
Stars and Stripes, 180
Stein, Edith, 19n–20n
Stein, Gertrude, 3, 21, 100n, 101, 109, 217
    The Autobiography of Alice B. Toklas,
        98, 100, 119
    'Lifting Belly', 98–103, 171, 213
Stephens, James, 197–8
Stevenson, Randall, 9, 70n
Stevens, Wallace, 3, 11n, 21, 33
    '"Lettres d'un Soldat"', 39, 130–4,
        135, 142, 148, 159, 181
    'Metaphors of a Magnifico', 104–5,
        109, 220; see also magus
    'Phases', 32–3, 43, 44, 49, 75, 112,
        132, 133, 163, 165
Stone, Constantia, 155–6
Stone Cottage see Coleman's Hatch
Storer, Edward, 61

Stout, G. F., 24n
Strachey, Lytton, 171–2
Stueber, Karsten R., 6n, 18n, 19n
Sullivan, J. W. N., 154
Surette, Leon, 25, 132
sympathy, 5, 17–20, 44, 56, 96, 103,
 113, 114, 117, 151, 154, 205
sympathetic imagination, 1, 5, 6, 16,
 19–20, 23, 27, 29, 44, 46, 102, 113,
 116, 119, 121, 123, 127, 140, 143

taste, 16, 43, 55, 92, 134, 142, 165,
 171, 183
Tate, Trudi, 4
Taylorism, 20–1
Tearle, Oliver, 11, 13
Tennyson, Alfred, 200
testimony *see* witnessing practices
Thacker, Toby, 206n
theory of relativity, 205n
Thomas, Edward, 3, 21, 109, 114,
 134, 217
 'March', 114–15
 'In Memoriam [Easter 1915]', 115–16
 'The Owl', 116
 'Rain', 117
 'The sun used to shine', 116–17
 'As the team's head-brass', 117–19
 'War Poetry', 35–7, 64, 113, 193, 196
Tietjens, Eunice, 155
Tiffany, Daniel, 26, 104n
The Times, 42, 50, 51, 52, 53, 54, 59, 144
The TLS, 30, 32, 54, 56, 59, 91, 153,
 160, 166, 172
Toklas, Alice B., 98–101
Tomlinson, Henry Major, 144, 147, 210n
tranquillity *see* impersonality
Traubel, Horace, 37n
trauma, 1, 3–4, 11–13, 16, 64, 73, 78–9,
 86–7, 99, 110, 159, 215–20
 post-traumatic stress disorder, 13
 see also shellshock
trench lyric, 2, 5, 8, 9, 13–16, 20, 22,
 30, 32, 71, 86, 97, 112, 157, 172,
 199–203, 209, 215, 216, 220

troubadours, 123–4, 126, 127, 141,
 184

Underhill, Evelyn, 30
Underhill, Hugh, 23
Underwood, John Curtis, 135–6
Unheimlich, 11, 30, 63, 74, 107, 128;
 see also grotesque
Untermeyer, Louis, 186
Upanishads, 151
Upward, Allen, 44, 122

Vance, Jonathan F., 210
Vandiver, Elizabeth, 30, 91n
Vechten, Carl Van, 8
Verdenal, Jean, 53, 137, 138,
 175
Verstehen, 21, 141
Virgil, 148n, 149, 151
virtù, 45, 73, 141
Vischer, Robert, 27n
Voices, 154, 206n
Vorticism, 64, 66, 79, 80, 81, 82, 111,
 147, 155

war
 and poetry, 7–8
 and relationship to body, 3–5
 see also First World War
wars
 Acre, 117
 American Civil, 37, 202
 Antioch, 117
 Bibracte, 117
 Chalus, 72
 English Civil, 109
 Franco-Prussian, 32, 120
 Lacedæmonian, 202
 Napoleonic, 202
 Punic, 201
 Spanish Civil, 133n
 Thermopylae, 117, 200, 202
 Troy, 58, 84, 86, 88
 Vosges, 117
 see also First World War

war poetry *see* war writing
war writing, 2, 22, 30, 89, 99, 108, 109,
    172, 216
  imagined war poem, the, 45, 76, 130,
    137, 144, 147, 163, 199
  patriotic war verse, 21, 30, 35n,
    52, 59
  war poetries, 2, 16, 21, 22, 33, 52,
    131, 137, 152, 154, 165, 174, 181,
    212, 216, 219
  War Poetry, 2, 22
  war verse, 22, 30, 33–4, 37, 40, 42,
    89, 103, 152, 159, 165, 171, 176,
    179, 191, 194, 198, 219
Watt, Basil, 75
Watts, A. E., 32
Waugh, Alec, 154–5
Weil, Simone, 4, 8
Weinstein, Samuel, 38
Wellesley, Dorothy, 14
West, Rebecca, 23, 152
Wharton, Edith, 40
Whitman, Walt, 37, 179, 181, 183, 184,
    202–3, 212, 213
Whitworth, Michael H., 205n
Wiesel, Elie, 16
Wilde, Oscar, 148
Williams, Raymond, 182, 186, 193
Williams, William Carlos, 37–8, 155
Wilson Jr, Edmund, 156
Wilson, Peter, 121n
Wilson, Stephen, 36n
Winant, Johanna, 18
Winter, Jay, 9, 11, 15, 91
The Winter of the World: Poems of the
    Great War, 70
Wissen, 15n, 19n, 27n, 65, 95

witnessing practices, 8, 12, 15–16, 29,
    37, 51, 75, 85, 107, 119, 131, 135,
    140–3, 151, 196
  eyewitness, 123, 133, 150
  fleshwitness, 5, 15, 20, 45, 95, 117,
    133, 191, 199, 216
  moral witness, 15–16, 20, 91, 95,
    129, 142, 143, 148–9, 152, 154,
    157, 159, 160, 194, 196, 198,
    215, 217
  uncorrupted witness, 96
Wolff, Janet, 188n
Woodberry, George, 55
Woolf, Virginia, 37, 54–5, 56, 153, 155,
    171n, 172, 188
The Wordsworth Book of First World
    War Poetry, 70
Wordsworth, William, 37, 196
Worringer, Wilhelm, 26–9
Wray, W. Fitzwater, 91

Yanks: A.E.F. Verse, 180
Yeats, W. B., 14, 25, 26, 43, 49–50, 52,
    61, 82, 86, 111, 112, 128, 191, 197
  'An Irish Airman Foresees his Death',
    202, 212
  'A Meditation in Time of War', 40
  The Oxford Book of Modern Verse,
    15, 32, 214–15, 215–16
  'A Reason for Keeping Silent', 40–1, 42
Young, Allan, 13n
Young, Francis Brett, 1–2

Zahavi, Dan, 3n
Zeepvat, Charlotte, 201n
Zola, Émile, 209
Zunshine, Lisa, 23n